1981

THE MODERN SUPREME COURT

THE MODERN SUPREME COURT

ROBERT G. McCLOSKEY

HARVARD UNIVERSITY PRESS

CAMBRIDGE, MASSACHUSETTS
LONDON, ENGLAND

FOREWORD BY MARTIN SHAPIRO

IT SOMETIMES SEEMS AS IF THE SUPREME COURT suddenly sprang upon the American scene full grown from the head of Chief Justice Earl Warren. It is not only that the Court nas done so much and inspired such opposition, but that it, rather than the congress or the presidency, has been the principal agent of domestic reform in post-World War II American politics. Even those of us with more than a passing knowledge of the Court are wont to think of it as at most a great nay-sayer, as the most famous of the "checks" in our system of "checks and balances." Now we find a Court that issues momentous positive commands: Desegregate! Reapportion! Provide Counsel for the Accused and warn him of his rights! And we find that even the Court's negatives—as in its intervention against literary and pictorial censorship—can create massive changes in the quality of American life. If we review the major areas of the Warren Court's concerns, a strikingly similar pattern emerges in each: sluggishness in the state governments; the inability of both state and federal legislatures to serve interests that do not fall into focused and powerful constituencies; the preoccupation of political executives with cold war problems; the resort of men with small voices that have been unheeded elsewhere to the adversary proceedings of the courts, where all voices are at least treated formally as equally entitled to a hearing; the intervention of the Supreme Court; opposition, resistance, and change.

The Supreme Court gives us one more glimpse of the terrible mysteries of political evolution. For who could have consciously designed an institution that would be forced by its weaknesses to concentrate on the domestic scene while the presidency, the strongest political institution in the free world, perforce turned its eyes to the international security of American life rather than the quality of what was being secured. Or one so bound by the procedural format of conflict and so lacking in the fiscal resources needed to grease the squeakiest wheel that it could not hope to compete with the marvelous machine of compromise and mutual adjustment that Congress had become. Or one sufficiently em-

bedded in the central government to see that it had some super
visory responsibility for the states, but not so embedded in the
mountainous treasures of that government as to instinctively
believe that the best thing to do with the states would be to bypass
or buy them. And because of all these things, one that could
attack political and social wrongs that would otherwise have gone
unattended.

In the last analysis there is something compelling about an
institution that can say with authority that the south may not
preserve slavery any longer, that one man's vote is not to be
worth seventeen times that of another, that the police too must
obey the law, that the poor and ignorant are entitled to the same
legal protection as the rich and educated, that one man may not
tell another man what he may not read or what he must pray.
The ability of the Court to say these things, not on the basis that
they would help us achieve more than the Russians or soothe
powerful and demanding social interests, but because they were
somehow right, returns us to the mysterious. In 1950 who would
have believed that anyone in American politics would ever again
speak of right and wrong rather than security and plenty. Right
and wrong also bring us to the resistance, conflict, and change
that are the legacy of the new Court.

We know perfectly well of course that the Court is not new in
the institutional sense, that it has existed from the beginning of
the republic. But it is not always so obvious that the contemporary
achievements (or if you are of a different persuasion, escapades)
of the Court are the product of a painful period of readjustment
that began after its encounter with the New Deal, and that even
the early years of the Warren Court were more closely linked to
the tentativeness of its predecessors than the boldness that we
retrospectively read into the record. Much of the black and white,
or should we say White Knight, image of the Warren Court
evaporates when the record is seen in fuller historical perspective
and when the wanderings through the valley are charted as well
as the ascents to the summit. At the very least it becomes clear
that the contemporary Supreme Court can be more fully under-

stood as the latest phase in the life of a unique institution than as a unique or fortuitous episode in American politics.

At the time of his death the author of this book was, as he had been for the preceding twenty-five years, deeply involved in these problems of continuity and change. He was by training a political scientist and by scholarly instinct a historian concerned with contemporary events; the modern Court created a challenge that filled the major portion of his intellectual life. For it was particularly difficult to bring a historically based critical intelligence to bear on a Court that after 1937 appeared to have closed its historical career—to have reached its twilight, as one famous authority expressed it. Throughout the nineteen-forties and even fifties, the judicial philosophies of Felix Frankfurter and Learned Hand held center stage. These great judges, constantly warning of the inherent and enormous risks to the Court of engaging in constitutional politics—risks dramatically illustrated in the preceding years—counseled a Court that had just freed itself from the dangers of defending economic freedoms to avoid becoming involved in any new constitutional adventure, even in such a worthwhile cause as the individual liberties guaranteed by the Bill of Rights.

Much of this philosophy of judicial self-restraint and judicial modesty in the light of the Court's very limited competence and resources appealed to Robert McCloskey at least in part because it struck a dominant chord in his own character. He himself distrusted the flamboyant and dramatic. He preferred sound interpretation, that had a chance of survival, to startling originality; the right word to the flashing one; the tempered evaluation to the scintillating criticism. He was by nature judicious, and by persuasion an adherent of the measured democracy that the "sense of the meeting" produces. And he was suspicious of a Court that too precipitously proclaimed eternal verities.

On the other hand he was pretty well persuaded that there were some verities, basically involving the dignity and the autonomy of the individual. And so throughout the forties and the fifties, as the momentum of demands on the Supreme Court to acknowledge the claims of individual liberties increased, the student of the Court and the justices went through a strikingly similar process. Much of what McCloskey writes about the Stone and Vinson and even the Warren Court is curiously autobiographical. The wisdom of his analysis derives largely from his distrust of easy formulas and his concern for the ethical and political com-plexities of the real world; but the sympathetic, almost empathic quality of what he writes is surely the product of a fellow sufferer

The analysis of the Stone and Vinson Courts presented as Chapters II and III of this book, clearly show the value of an approach that is fundamentally historical but also acutely sensi tive to the situation of the decision-makers at the time they had to make their decisions. As McCloskey indicated in his own intro- duction and in the evaluation of the Warren Court that concludes this volume, a careful historical analysis also suggests that the Warren Court passed through two relatively distinct phases. Ac-cordingly, Chapter IV is devoted to its earlier and Chapter V to its later periods.

To be sure, the great activist event of the entire Warren Court was, as Professor McCloskey points out, the Desegregation decisions that were delivered in the first terms after the Chief Justice's appointment. Even these decisions, however, with their proviso of "all deliberate speed," seemed to move slowly in the early years. Meanwhile the justices' own views on subversion, combined with the great weight of our anti-Communist crusade, led the Court to make haste very slowly indeed down the civil liberties road. The Warren Court's careful and marginal contri-butions, its tentative advances and cautious screening maneuvers are suggested by the titles in Chapter IV—useful toil, stepping stones, deeds without doctrines. Such a jurisprudence does not yield to broad-stroke analysis. Its tone and tactics can be ap-preciated best by following the details of the play, and this chapter provides close analysis of four of the early terms of the Warren Court.

It probably would be fruitless to argue over an exact starting point for the second stage of the Warren Court when what we actually observe is a curve of acceleration. By the 1961 Term, with the salience of the internal subversion issue somewhat reduced, Professor McCloskey felt that the Warren Court had entered a new phase characterized more by "paths of glory" than "stepping stones." His assessment is based as much on the rising tempo and changing tone of the Court's civil liberties opinions as on any single event. Nevertheless the 1961 Term is also the point at which the Court dropped the other shoe, so to speak, adding *Baker* v. *Carr*—the Reapportionment decision—to its school desegregation holdings. Chapter V begins with an extended analysis of that decision; and McCloskey's proposals for what tactics the Court might have employed following *Baker* serve as a good critique of its subsequent adoption of the full one-man one-vote standard.

Compared to its race and reapportionment decisions, the Warren Court's excursion into the area of school religious exercises seems a minor matter in terms of its actual impact on social practices. But it raises dramatically the crucial political problems of congressional opposition and public reception that were acute during the Warren Court's second phase and indeed are central to the whole modern role of the Supreme Court. Professor McCloskey chose to use these cases as the vehicle for presenting a method of evaluating the work of the justices that has particular relevance for a Court as deeply embroiled in public policy as was the Warren Court at phase two.

The analysis then proceeds to a perspective of the Warren Court, placing its most activist period in the context of its earlier and more tentative steps. The Warren Court still had four years left to go after the four years of superenergetic action which served as the final base for McCloskey's reflections; but by the time he wrote the Court had already pulled the neat anatomical trick of dropping its third shoe in *Gideon, Mapp,* and *Escobedo.* Its final years were largely devoted to elaborating this major incursion into the rights-of-accused and police-practices areas in the style that McCloskey so cogently describes in his general overview.

The editorial chores for this book have been very light. Each essay is complete and each was designed both to stand by itself and build toward a completed picture of the modern Supreme

Court. It was only necessary to provide two paragraphs of continuity (p. 9) to the Introduction, the substance of which was clearly adumbrated by the surrounding text.

The modern Supreme Court surely vies with the Marshall Court in political importance. Many books will be written about it aided by hindsight. But most historians have surely found that the greatest treasure is that rare record of an acute and dispassionate but deeply concerned contemporary observer written from the firing line. Professor McCloskey was there, and the record of his own struggle to make sense of and objectively evaluate the most chaotic and exciting period in the life of an institution to which he was devoted, and to do so in the context of an American intellectual tradition to which he was unreservedly dedicated, must enrich the lives of his contemporaries and of future generations.

June 1971

CONTENTS

I INTRODUCTION

THE YEAR 1941, SO AGONIZING AND DECISIVE for America and the world, was no such climacteric in the history of the Supreme Court of the United States. The Court's great modern crisis had arrived several years earlier when Franklin Roosevelt and his New Deal were pitted against the judges and their "laissez-faire" version of the Constitution. In this contest of wills the Court had finally wavered, and since 1937 it had been fairly manifest that the welfare state no longer was to be thwarted by constitutional barriers. Nor was there much evidence, in 1941, that the judges were deeply tormented by their problems in a spacious, newer area of judicial responsibility: the field of "civil liberties." The easy generalities of depression-decade liberalism still seemed to most of them tolerably adequate. Economic rights ought to be subject to such governmental control as the community desires; civil rights ought to be cherished and constitutionally protected. Sustained by those two simple verities, the judges' special universe seemed orderly and predictable.

The latter-day problems were just around the corner. The comparative tidiness and tranquillity of 1941 contrast sharply with the disorder and tension of the judicial decades that followed. The extent of the modern Court's inner conflicts and uncertainties should not be exaggerated. The virtual consensus of 1941, that the liberties of the individual indispensable to an open society merited greater judicial protection than liberties which derive from shifting economic arrangements, established a modern concord for the Court that is at least as noteworthy as its discords about how the outlook should be applied in specific areas. The secular trend of judicial doctrine since 1941 has been toward an enlargement of civil rights, and this salient fact should not be lost to view.

But when all this has been stipulated, it must also be said that within the general consensus the discordancies have been numerous and often strident; that the tendency of the modern Court to enlarge civil liberties has been cross-threaded by many doubts and pauses and vacillations. The symptoms of this judicial disagreement and perplexity are several, but perhaps the most obvious is the high proportion of nonunanimous opinions. In the early 1930's, usually thought of as a contentious period in the history of constitutional doctrine, less than twenty percent of the Court's opinions were nonunanimous. In the first four years after the "revolution" of 1937 the proportion rose to about thirty percent, but in the twenty-one terms from 1948 until the end of the Warren Court, the annual proportion dipped *below* sixty percent only four times and was almost as often in the seventies as the sixties.

An explanation for the inner conflicts and hesitations of the modern Court is not hard to find. It rests primarily on two special circumstances and the relations between them. In the first place the Court has undertaken in these years the task of creating a vast and almost wholly new body of constitutional jurisprudence in the field of civil rights. And in the second place, it has been compelled to build this new structure during an historical era that was peculiarly unfavorable to such an enterprise.

The relative newness of civil rights as a constitutional issue is one of those obvious facts whose significance is easy to overlook. America has regarded itself as the land of the free since at least 1776, and the Constitution has been revered as the palladium of freedom since its inception. But although the literature of American democracy is rich in libertarian generalities, this rhetoric of individual rights had rarely been translated into concrete legislative prescriptions and judicial doctrines in the nineteenth or even in the early twentieth century. The political and religious rights associated with the First Amendment had not become a matter of active judicial concern until the 1920's. Equal protection and due process rights had been almost entirely associated with economic activities until the very eve of the Stone Court. Thus the modern Supreme Court inherited only a few scattered and incomplete theoretical and doctrinal tools to handle the problems of civil and political rights with which the justices were now confronted.

By 1941 the Court had spent seventy-five years learning to trace the complex consequences of its economic decisions for the quality of American life. The Stone Court, faced with the depression and the international failure of democracy, which had emphasized the explosive and sometimes self-defeating quality of individual liberty and the fragility of domestic tranquillity, was aware that the translation of liberal rhetoric into constitutional commands might entail serious consequences beyond its powers to anticipate.

The Court also brought to this confrontation with demands for new judicial action in support of individual rights the experience of fifty years of liberal struggle against judicial interventions in public policy. Judicial self-restraint was the credo of both judges and laymen who identified themselves with advanced social policies. Their arguments had quite naturally broadened from objections concerned with the specific things judges had been doing to general queries about judicial capacity to do anything in the policy sphere. The doubts spawned in an era when the Court had intervened in behalf of the economic rights of some necessarily remained to trouble justices who were asked to intervene in behalf of the civil and political rights of others.

All of these considerations—the comparative newness of civil rights as a constitutional subject, the primitive state of theory and doctrine with respect to that subject, the vastness and complexity of the implications it generated, and the tradition of liberal distaste for judicial power—might alone be quite sufficient to explain the modern Court's disagreements and self-doubts. But the difficulties did not end there. Internal, conceptual problems have been compounded by a dynamic, unpredictable, and bewildering external environment. It would have been hard enough to deal with the unfolding complexities of the civil liberties issue in an era of relative calm. It has been much harder to do so in the decades that history with its usual perversity has chosen for this constitutional reconstruction. The modern era began, we need hardly be reminded, with the greatest war in human experience; and this massive event muddied the constitutional waters. America was committed to a "total" war against "totalitarian" enemies. Both aspects of the experience were largely novel. Indeed, the very idea of mobilizing the whole resources of the nation against a deadly threat was one America had hardly thought about before, or had thought about with the innocence of superpatriotism on the one hand or facile liberalism on the other. Nor did the Supreme Court seem to have moved very far ahead of the country in its thinking about such matters. In 1940 an eight-judge majority upheld a state's power to compel schoolchildren to salute the flag against their religious scruples, and Justices Black, Douglas, and Murphy joined an opinion by Justice Frankfurter, an anointed liberal, that solemnly discussed the question in terms of Lincoln's classic dilemma: "Must a government of necessity be too *strong* for the liberties of its people, or too *weak* to maintain its own existence?" It is easy enough with hindsight to say that the refusal of a few moppets to salute the flag hardly imperilled the republic; and Justice Stone, to his credit, made the point at the time. But he was the only one who then saw the problem in such sensible terms, and the attitude of his brethren suggests the difficulty of maintaining balance in unique and distorting historical circumstances.

Nor did the arrival of victory simplify matters much. To be sure, some of the wartime bugaboos were seen in retrospect as less formidable than they had once appeared. The Court managed to retrieve part of the ground that had been conceded to military necessity, and the early postwar years witnessed some noteworthy constitutional advances in such fields as Negro rights and religious freedom. But the pace of progress was slow, and it is hard to doubt that the continuing unsettled character of politics, both international and domestic, helped account for some of the judicial hesitancy. The war had been not merely a profoundly unsettling experience in itself; it had also marked for America the beginning of unaccustomed and vexing entanglements in international affairs. Moreover, these entanglements were complicated by the fact that Communism was no longer the "vague terror" of other days, but a palpable, hostile, and well-armored rival. A series of specific shocks—the fall of China under Communist control, the revelation that Russia had detonated an atomic bomb, the Hiss and Fuchs cases involving charges of Soviet espionage, the outbreak of the Korean War—created a national climate peculiarly receptive to political appeals based on denunciation of scapegoats and dreams of a simpler, unspoiled American past. The mood found its spokesman in a heretofore little-known Republican Senator, and the "McCarthy movement" gave liberalism the worst scare it had encountered for more than twenty years. Contemplating a world which seemed more complex and fraught with dangers than ever before, some of the judges grew diffident about their capacity to answer that world's hard questions. Contemplating a popular temper that looked more reactionary than progressive, some of them developed renewed doubts that the nation would tolerate judicial control of its impatient spirit.

In succeeding years, though McCarthyism faded to less menacing dimensions, the environment never really reverted to the calm, settled state that would seem most appropriate for the operation of judicial review. And, by an ironic twist, the Court's own decisions were helping to compound the uncertainties. It is one of the dilemmas of a progressive Court that new problems are forever unfolding and that their very novelty makes it difficult to foresee the consequences of proposed solutions. Each time the Supreme Court of the 1950's pushed the frontier of constitutional liberty another step forward, it stirred up forces in the environment that compounded the problem of prediction. The Desegregation decision of 1954, for example, produced the Southern reaction of "massive resistance" and earned the judiciary the antagonism of most of the south's reigning political satraps. But the decision also played a part in stimulating the Negro's demand for a redress of grievances, and perhaps it helped engender an alteration of Northern white attitudes toward racial discrimination. How these multiple developments would ultimately balance out remained questionable throughout the 1950's and the early 1960's. And the same thing can be said, *mutatis mutandis,* about still other decisions in other areas of public policy. The social and political organism was dynamic enough in its own right to tax the wisdom and authority of the judges. When it was galvanized even further by the judiciary itself, the implications for judicial review became surpassingly hard to calculate.

These then were the problems—or some of them—that lay in wait for the modern Supreme Court. Amidst this jungle of internal and external difficulties the judges have toiled since 1941 to fashion, almost out of whole cloth, a constitutional jurisprudence in the field of civil rights. And somehow, in spite of the difficulties, two products of profound importance to American governmental history have emerged from their labors. The first is a vast new body of constitutional rules and understandings. The acorns of 1941 have matured into oaks. Judicial review now extends to dozens of personal liberty questions that lay almost untouched only a few years before. In purely legal terms America has become a significantly different polity than the one the judges of 1941 contemplated, and that development in itself is profoundly important to trace and assess. But at least as interesting to the student of political science is the concept of the judicial function that seems to have evolved in this era of doctrinal creativity.

Historical events seldom arrange themselves as tidily as we would like them to, and the historian must beware of creating, rather than finding, comprehensible order in his materials. But the story of the modern Supreme Court does seem to fall naturally (I do not say inevitably) into rough but readily discernible patterns, and the delineation of them is helpful to an understanding of the course of judicial government in contemporary America.

For some purposes the years 1941–1968 can be thought of as subdivided into four fairly separable periods. There is, to begin with, the period of the Stone Court, comprising the 1940–1945 terms.[1] This was of course the time during which all humanity, including the Court, was much preoccupied with the problems of the second world war, a circumstance which alone makes these six terms distinctive. But there are other reasons for treating them as a piece. Second is the seven-term span of the Vinson Court, 1946–1952. Again the justifications for separate treatment are several, but perhaps the most patent is the fact that the novel problems of the cold war were now tormenting the world and the nation. The use of the names of the Chief Justices to identify these phases in judicial history is not meant to suggest that they were decisive in giving each phase its character. Indeed, in the cases of

1. A term of the Supreme Court runs from October to July and is designated by the year in which it begins.

Stone and Vinson that would be a most dubious proposition; and in any event the role of individual judges is a matter to be appraised carefully, not assumed in advance. But whatever the truth about this, the fact is that the Court of the 1940–1945 terms behaved differently from the Court of the 1946–1952 terms, and the difference is great enough to provide a basis for subdivision.

The third period embraces the 1953–1960 terms. These were in national politics the years of Eisenhower, and once more it may be only a convenient coincidence that the beginning of this constitutional period coincides with the advent of a new Chief Justice, Earl Warren. But the break with the past seems plain enough in retrospect, whatever may have accounted for it. It is signalized, though not summarized, by the Desegregation decision of 1954 and the reverberations set going by that seismic event. [Chapter IV presents Professor McCloskey's detailed analyses of four representative terms of the early Warren Court.] The fourth period runs from the 1961 Term through Warren's resignation at the close of the 1968 Term. [Chapter V presents Professor McCloskey's treatment of the Reapportionment case, the key case of the crucial 1961 Term; a critical review of the religion cases, one of the most dramatic aspects of the later Warren Court's work; and a general review of the achievements of the Warren Court.]

Such a four-fold division of modern constitutional history is useful, but it should not cause one to overlook the fact that from another viewpoint the division might be regarded as two-fold. The Stone-Vinson years offer enough similarities and continuities so that they constitute in some sense a unit in their own right; this is also true of the Warren years. On the whole the Stone-Vinson era was a creative one: it produced a substantial amount of significant new constitutional law. But it was also, as has been intimated, an era of groping readjustment, of ambivalence and uncertainty about the judicial role. Doctrinal growth, though perceptible, was irregular and relatively slow. The analogy that comes to mind is the era from *Munn* v. *Illinois* in 1876 to about 1888. Like most analogies, this one is imperfect. But the eras are comparable in that each is marked by a strong trend which is however cross-threaded by retarding doubts and hesitations.

In the fifteen years of the Warren Court on the other hand, the judicial self-doubts are pushed farther and farther into the background and the creative impulse becomes unmistakably dominant. The jurisprudence of civil liberties becomes more symmetrical. The anomalies—judicial activism in some areas and judicial restraint in others—are progressively ironed out. In spite of misgivings persistently expressed by such judges as Frankfurter and Harlan, one senses almost from the beginning of the era a distinctly higher level of confidence among the Court majority, a greater willingness to intervene in any major policy question that affects personal freedom. This quality, though varying from time to time, is nevertheless constant enough to give the Warren years a unitary character. They are, we might say, the Court's intrepid era, contrasting with the irresolution of the Stone-Vinson years.

The Court of the modern period has altered not only the constitutional rules but the constitutional arrangement. It has cast itself not merely in the negative, restraining role of judicial tradition, but also as a major initiative-producing agency of modern government. It has claimed a part in the governing process more imposing and more daring than any court of the past has ever claimed. And it has played that part with enough success to suggest that our traditional ideas about the range of judicial capacity may require reappraisal. The story of the modern Court is, in short, one of the classic chapters in the history of one of America's most peculiar institutions: government by judiciary. In order to understand that institution we must consider both the rules it has enunciated and the status it has attained. But beyond that we must trace the process by which those rules and that status came into being.

II   THE STONE COURT

IF CONSIDERATION OF THE 1940-1945 TERMS
were confined to certain classes of civil liberties adjudication, there
would be few signs of the hesitant, tentative spirit I have imputed
to the Stone Court. Freedom of expression, for example, was
granted a measure of protection far greater than had ever been
accorded before. And the striking thing is not merely that individual claims were more often favored, but that the constitutional
principles supporting the claims were stated in peculiarly uncompromising terms, and that the judges seemed willing to recognize
such claims in areas of governmental power that had theretofore
been comparatively free from the Court's surveillance. For purposes of analysis, it is convenient to distinguish between decisions
involving what might be called "secular" freedom of expression
and those involving religious freedom. The distinction was not
always scrupulously drawn by the Court itself. But the two kinds
of liberty do present somewhat different constitutional problems
and, broadly speaking, the Court's decisions reflect this difference.

Bridges v. *California*[1] was the first really important case involving secular freedom of expression decided in the years covered by
this study. For that reason alone it would merit special attention.
It is the Stone Court's initial full-dress performance in this vital
constitutional area, and one need not press far to see it epitomizing
much of the history of the next few years.

The case illustrates, for one thing, the zeal of the present majority to defend freedom of expression, its willingness to erect
formidable new constitutional barriers in order to provide that
protection. The issue was "trial by newspaper." The *Los Angeles
Times* and Harry Bridges, a militant west-coast labor leader, had
both been found in contempt by a state court for publicly criticizing pending judicial proceedings. The newspaper had editorially
urged a judge, while sentence was pending, to commit two convicted members of a labor "goon squad" to the state prison. Bridges
had sent and released to the newspapers a telegram in which he

1. 314 U.S. 252 (1941).

warned the Secretary of Labor that a strike would ensue if the state court enforced a recent "outrageous" decision in a labor dispute. Now these two improbable bedfellows argued before the Supreme Court that the contempt citations unconstitutionally abridged their freedom of expression.

The principal justification for the citations was the contention that such public comment would "directly tend to prevent the proper discharge of judicial function," that is, that free speech in this context might impair the fairness of a trial. "Tendency" is a loose concept which can range in meaning from a little to a lot, and in the past the Court had made small effort to explain how great a tendency to pervert justice is constitutionally necessary in order to warrant abridgment of expression. In the *Bridges* case, however, the Court seized upon the "clear and present danger" formula, as developed by Justices Holmes and Brandeis in two famous opinions,[2] and applied it to the trial by newspaper issue.

The state cannot inhibit freedom of expression, said Justice Black for the Court, except perhaps to avert an extremely serious evil which is also extremely imminent. Speech that threatens only minor public inconvenience or annoyance is immune from state control; and even if the evil is grave, a mere "inherent" or "reasonable" tendency to bring it about will not justify restriction. But in any event, he went on, the speech involved in this case falls well short of fulfilling these conditions. A genuine threat to the fair administration of justice would indeed be a serious evil, but the danger of it from the editorial and telegram is remote. Far from creating the requisite clear and present danger, it cannot even be fairly said that they tend to interfere with justice.

This majority opinion must be read carefully in order to understand the agitation of Justice Frankfurter, who spoke for himself and three other dissenters. Frankfurter eschewed the clear and present danger terminology, but he argued that the editorials and telegram did constitute a "real and substantial threat" to impartial

2. Schenck v. United States, 249 U.S. 47 (1919); Abrams v. United States, 250 U.S. 616, 624 (1919) (dissenting). The rule was further elaborated in an opinion by Justice Brandeis in Whitney v. California, 274 U.S. 357, 372 (1927) (concurring).

decision. At first glance it might seem that Black was merely disputing this point; that he thought the publicity was unlikely to influence the judge, while Frankfurter thought it might. The difference between them would then be comparatively small— analogous, say, to the difference between one juror in a criminal case who thinks that the state has not quite proved guilt beyond a reasonable doubt, and another who thinks that the proof, though not perhaps airtight, is sufficient. But when Black's opinion is examined, it becomes apparent that the distance between him and Frankfurter is much greater than that. Black was not merely saying that the expression held contemptuous here failed to meet the requisite standard; he was saying that it did not even come close to that level. If Black sees this publicity as not even *tending* to obstruct justice, it follows that more admonitory expression would be necessary in order for him to recognize such a tendency. Yet even that would still fall well below the constitutional benchmark of clear and present danger. If forceful exhortation from a powerful newspaper and a palpable threat to tie up the port facilities of the Pacific coast, both addressed to elective judges, do not create at least a tendency to influence the course of justice, one might well ask how flagrant and inflammatory the commentary can be before it will be held to create a clear and present danger. Must a speaker successfully urge a mob to stone the courthouse? Moreover, Black hinted strongly that he would prefer to push the requirement still further, remarking that the clear and present danger standard itself did not "mark the furthest constitutional boundaries of protected expression," but only the "minimum compulsion of the Bill of Rights."

In short, the majority opinion in the *Bridges* case came close to saying, though somewhat obliquely, that speech is absolutely immune from government interference. This in itself suggests a striking alteration in the judicial attitude toward freedom of expression. But equally remarkable is the almost casual assumption, apparently shared by the whole Court, that the free speech guaranties of the Constitution restrict the judicial power to punish contemptuous utterances summarily. Such a restriction had never been plainly recognized before, and a powerful argument could be made that neither the First nor the Fourteenth Amendment contemplate it. Yet the dissenters explicitly agreed with the majority that "the Due Process Clause of the Fourteenth Amendment protects the right to comment on a judicial proceeding." Evidently the petty constraints of history and precedent will not prevent this new Court from finding new applications for its belief that the "channels of inquiry and thought must be kept open to new conquests of reason."

If *Bridges* nicely illustrates the modern Court's "core of agreement" about the value of free expression, it also illustrates the discord that had already begun to appear about enforcing such a value in practice. It provides the dress rehearsal of a dialogue that extended over the next two decades. And it is particularly fitting that the opposing spokesmen in this case should have been the two judges who most persistently represented this conflict of viewpoint in the years to come, Black and Frankfurter.

As Justice Frankfurter saw it, the vice of the majority opinion was its "absolute" and "doctrinaire" preference for free speech over all other claims, either of society or of the individual. Whether or not one subscribes to the pejorative spirit in which the quoted words were used, it must be conceded that they come close to describing the attitude of a bloc that was then taking shape on the Stone Court. Justice Black was perhaps its leading exemplar. Both in character and intellect he surely merits a place among the great judges in our history, and his influence on the growth of modern constitutional law was to be profound. But he viewed the constitutional problems the Court faced with a grandly simple outlook. Civil liberties like freedom of expression were sacrosanct, and that was that. There was no need, or even justification, for nice qualifications about the circumstances or nature of the utterances in question. He had a taste for sweeping, categorical doctrines and was prepared to reach them in seven-league strides with few preliminary pauses for agonized reflection.

In *Bridges* his strong libertarian pronouncements were concurred in by four others: Douglas, Murphy, Reed, and Jackson. The first two were in the future, like Black himself, very commonly on the side of civil liberties claimants. Douglas had sound legal training and a fine mind, but a somewhat more devious one than Black's. Nevertheless he seldom wavered in his opposition to government inroads on personal freedom. Murphy seems to have suffered some early uncertainties about such matters, but few hints of irresolution were ever recorded in his votes or opinions, and he became the most dependably libertarian judge on the Stone Court. When Black, Douglas, and Murphy were joined by Rutledge in 1943, the bloc was complete. Rutledge was second only to Murphy in his predictability; the upshot was that a civil liberties claimant could usually count on four Supreme Court votes. This meant that he needed the support of only one other judge to win his case.

But the remaining members of the Court were less reliable. Reed, who helped make up the libertarian majority in *Bridges,* turned out to be a temporary ally. In subsequent terms he was more often than not with the opposition in civil liberties cases. Jackson, the fifth majority judge in *Bridges,* was a brilliant eccentric. In 1943 he made one of the most stirring and uncompromising statements about freedom in our constitutional annals: "If there is any fixed star in our constitutional constellation, it is that no official, high or petty, can prescribe what shall be orthodox in politics, nationalism, religion, or other matters of opinion . . . If there are any circumstances that permit an exception, they do not now occur to us."[3] And from time to time, as in *Bridges,* he did support some of the more extreme positions of the libertarian bloc. But in other cases he lined up, with equal self-certainty, on the other side. At least in the period of the Stone Court, his vote on any given civil liberties question was hard to foretell. With all his splendid rhetorical and intellectual gifts, he seemed less concerned than any of his colleagues about the supposed virtues of consistency.

As for the minority in *Bridges,* Byrnes graced the Court for only one term and had no significant impact on constitutional law. Chief Justice Stone assumed some notably libertarian positions in the early years, but later apparently developed second

3. West Virginia State Board of Education v. Barnette, 319 U.S. 624, 642 (1943).

thoughts and could seldom be enlisted by the Black-Douglas-Murphy-Rutledge contingent in close decisions. Roberts was already famous among Court-watchers for his bewildering shifts of attitude during the 1930's. In the period of the Stone Court he occasionally appeared unexpectedly on the libertarian side, especially in war-related cases; but on the whole he leaned the other way.

Justice Frankfurter became the self-elected spokesman of that other way. His *Bridges* dissent was his second major state paper on behalf of a go-slower judicial policy in the civil liberties field; his majority opinion in the first Flag Salute case[4] had been the first. It must be re-emphasized that he was not in general opposed to the trend toward enlargement of judicially guaranteed civil rights. But he was less single-minded than his colleagues on the other wing of the Court, more inclined to take into account competing claims such as state autonomy, community need, or, as in *Bridges,* the right to impartial trial. Moreover, he was troubled more than they by a sense of judicial modesty. In a lifetime devoted to progressive causes he had developed the conviction that the people, rather than the courts, should decide most questions of public policy; and he was more apprehensive than some of his brethren about the nation's willingness to wear any collar the judiciary might fashion. Finally, the basic disposition of his mind was very different from theirs, and the contrast is plainest when we set him beside Black. Frankfurter was prone, as Black was not, to look for distinctions of degree, to acknowledge subtleties. This is not to say that his mind was necessarily the better one: subtleties may obscure wisdom as often as they enlighten it. But the quality did cause him to react more tentatively when a new constitutional frontier was approached, and in *Bridges* he thought the majority was moving too far too fast. He detected and was dismayed by Black's implication that all other values are submerged when a free speech claim is presented.

Frankfurter's fear that this attitude and others like it would be translated into explicit ruling dogmas of the Court may account

4. Minersville School District v. Gobitis, 310 U.S. 586 (1940).

for much of his judicial behavior in the 1940's. He often voted against personal liberty claims, much to the disappointment of those who had admired the militant liberalism of his pre-judicial career. The question of his judicial motives is a complex one, and no single factor can explain him. But it seems possible that in the 1940's he was influenced by the danger (as he saw it) that the Court would embrace an "uncritically libertarian" policy, and that in reaction to that threat he took a less libertarian line than his initial instincts might have dictated. In *Bridges,* Black seemed to him to be marking out a range of constitutionally protected freedom far beyond what was either desirable or expedient for the Court to provide. If the position of Black and his cohorts in that case and others had been less extreme, if it had merely favored individual claims without insisting on such sweeping principles, Frankfurter might have been more often on their side. His fine talents might have been devoted more to the articulation of a temperate and viable civil liberties jurisprudence and less to lengthy warnings about judicial "conceptualism" and other sins. The failure of the Court to develop such a jurisprudence more fully in the 1940's may be attributable to the polarization revealing itself in the *Bridges* case.

That decision also illustrates and in fact inaugurates a disagreement over the clear and present danger formula in particular between the libertarian bloc who would erect it into a nearly universal rule for protecting free expression in a wide variety of circumstances, and Frankfurter who dismissed it as a "literary phrase" inappropriate as a rule of law outside the special context in which Holmes and Brandeis had fashioned it, that is, the sedition cases in the years after World War I. The truth is that the rule surely expressed a principle of constitutional common sense in some situations. If the evil apprehended from speech is not immediate, then free discussion may generate countervailing opinion to prevent the evil, and there is no need for government to provide therapy by repression. Yet this rationale is hardly applicable to such forms of speech as newspaper comment on judicial proceedings: the "discussion" that affects the outcome of a trial is supposed to take place in the courtroom, not in the marketplace. Between the majority's misuse of the formula and Justice Frankfurter's indignation over that misuse, a doctrine of limited but real value as a tool of decision was ultimately lost. But meantime the controversy over it consumed a good deal of judicial time during the 1940's.

For another thing, the *Bridges* case suggests the place occupied by Justice Holmes in the minds of his successors in these early years of the modern Court. The opinions of both Black and Frankfurter invoke his authority in support of their very different views, reminding one of the way the shade of Marshall hung over the Taney Court at its beginning. It is easy to see why the justices of the Stone Court leaned so heavily on Holmes. Civil liberty was a comparatively youthful constitutional problem; no American jurist had said much about it, but Holmes had said more than most and often said it vividly. It is natural that those who tread unfamiliar terrain should seek guidance from those who have been there before. Beyond that, Holmes had become by 1941 the chief saint in America's legal-liberal hagiography, though whether he would have appreciated this compliment is another matter. As time goes on and the modern justices begin to feel more at home with their subject matter—and perhaps as they begin to be aware that not even the wisest precepts or most glittering epigrams will resolve new issues in unprecedented circumstances—we hear less of Holmes; but in these first years he seems to turn up everywhere in support of both sides in every argument.

Bridges v. *California* is to a considerable extent a prototypal case. It anticipates and exemplifies not only the personal and doctrinal clashes between the judges, but the broad tendency of the Stone Court to favor the speaker, to endow speech with a "preferred position" among our constitutional guaranties.[5]

This is not to say that free speech claimants won quite all of their battles. The new Court was often accused of unreflecting partiality to organized labor. Perhaps it was natural for judges with New Deal origins to see a relationship between labor's cause and

5. See Robert McKay, "The Preference For Freedom," *New York University Law Review*, 34:1182 (1959).

the cause of civil liberties; at any rate, in 1940 the Court had held eight to one that picketers in a labor dispute were protected by the free speech guaranties of the Constitution.[6] However, though this premise was never wholly repudiated, some of the judges were inclined to qualify it as time went on. Evidently they became impressed by the criticisms that picketing, though partly a form of communication, was also in large part an economic weapon and in that guise subject to reasonable public restraint. Eventually the majority upheld injunctions against picketers under certain circumstances, recognizing at least by implication that different forms of expression might require different applications of constitutional rules.[7]

Otherwise the Stone Court's record with respect to "secular" freedom of expression was steadily libertarian. The Court protected a motley collection of alleged subversives against various governmentally imposed pains and penalties.[8] It took the first step toward the conclusion, ultimately reached in the 1950's, that congressional power over the mails is subject to the First Amendment—holding that Congress had not granted to the Postmaster General the power to deny *Esquire* second-class mailing privileges and stating that "grave constitutional questions" would be raised if the law were construed otherwise.[9] In 1946 it actually invalidated a federal statute designed to punish certain federal employees for their leftish views by denying them their paychecks.[10] This was a noteworthy constitutional event, not merely because it was rare for this Court to overthrow a federal law (only one other had been overthrown since 1936) but because the traditional interpretation of the bill of attainder clause had to be stretched to reach the result.

6. Thornhill v. Alabama, 310 U.S. 88 (1940).
7. Milk Wagon Drivers v. Meadowmoor Dairies, 312 U.S. 287 (1941); Carpenters and Joiners Union v. Ritter's Cafe, 315 U.S. 722 (1942).
8. See Viereck v. United States, 318 U.S. 236 (1943); Schneiderman v. United States, 320 U.S. 115 (1943); Baumgartner v. United States, 322 U.S. 665 (1944); Hartzel v. United States, 322 U.S. 680 (1944); Keegan and Kunze v. United States, 325 U.S. 478 (1945); Cramer v. United States, 322 U.S. 773 (1944).
9. Hannegan v. Esquire, 327 U.S. 146 (1946).
10. United States v. Lovett, 328 U.S. 303 (1946).

What is probably the high point of the Stone Court's enthusiasm for freedom of expression was reached in *Thomas* v. *Collins*.[11] The case involved a Texas statute requiring union organizers to identify themselves and obtain a card from the state before soliciting for union members. R. J. Thomas, vice president of the C.I.O., had gone to Texas for the publicly announced purpose of challenging the law. In the face of an injunction issued by a state court he had refused to apply for a card but had nevertheless addressed a public meeting, praising unionism in general, urging the workers present to join the union, and specifically soliciting one Pat O'Sullivan to become a member. His subsequent conviction for contempt was reversed by the Supreme Court in a five to four decision. The libertarian bloc was joined, as in *Bridges,* by Justice Jackson.

What made the case sticky was the fact that the Court had repeatedly upheld the power of the state to regulate economic activity, and the solicitation of union members might well be regarded as falling precisely in that category. But Mr. Justice Rutledge speaking for the Court saw it otherwise. The law, he said, struck at freedom of expression, for as construed in the injunction it forbade Thomas not only to solicit individually without getting a card, but also to make a general speech on the subject of unionism. Perhaps a man can be required to register before engaging in individual solicitation; but he cannot be required to do so before speaking to an audience about a matter of public concern like labor relations. Such a speech by a union official almost inevitably at least implies an invitation to join the union; and the injunction, by forbidding the invitation, forbids the speech.

This was one way of looking at the issue, but not necessarily the only way. Neither the state court nor Thomas seem to have thought that his general right to discuss unionism was being enjoined. He was not restrained from implied solicitation but from solicitation itself. In fact, Thomas was explicitly contending that solicitation as such was protected speech. The majority were unwilling to concede so much, but they were willing to strain

11. 323 U.S. 516 (1945).

rather hard in order to convert an economic activities issue into a free expression issue. It is hard to escape the feeling that at least for some of them this alchemy was made easier by the reflection that organized labor was a party to the dispute.

Two or three other points about the *Thomas* case deserve mention. One is the majority's invocation of the clear and present danger standard in a somewhat extreme form. *Any* restriction on free expression, said the Court, can only be justified by clear and present danger of "the gravest abuses, endangering paramount interests." This idea—that the evil anticipated must be "serious" as well as imminent—was not new. Although Holmes' original formulation in *Schenck* had carried no such suggestion, Brandeis had propounded the idea in *Whitney* v. *California* (1927) ; Black had reiterated it in *Bridges*. But *Thomas* underscored it once again, and added something further. The state had argued that the mere registration requirement was hardly a restriction at all. Nevertheless, said the Court, even such a thistledown burden on expression can be justified only by a present danger to paramount public interests.

Moreover, when freedom of expression is involved, the law will not be given the benefit of the doubt. "The rational connection between the remedy provided and the evil to be curbed, which in other contexts might support legislation against attack on due process grounds, will not suffice." This language appears to reverse the traditional "presumption of constitutionality"—that is, the understanding that laws will be presumed valid in the absence of a clear case against them. The only previous explicit challenge to the presumption had been in the cases involving "freedom of contract" beginning with *Lochner* v. *New York*[12] in 1905; and those precedents had been repudiated in 1937. Now the challenge was renewed; but with respect not to liberty of contract, an economic right, but to liberty of expression. No case better illustrates how different yet similar this modern Court was to its predecessors.

Turning to a second category of free expression cases—those involving not secular claims but religious beliefs and practices—

12. 198 U.S. 45.

the libertarian fervor of the majority is seen to burn no less brightly. To be sure, the objective record looks more uneven. In any accounting of individual-against-government claims for the Stone period, a number of decisions against religious dissenters would be listed, and it might appear from them that the Court was providing only grudging support for freedom in this field. But that appearance alters in closer examination of the record. In the first place, in several of the cases presenting religious claims the individual was asking for more elbowroom than even the most libertarian tribunal could be expected to concede. Most of them involved the sect called Jehovah's Witnesses, whose members simply refused as a matter of principle to acknowledge the authority of the state and asserted a religious justification for some rather extraordinary kinds of secular conduct. A Witness arrested for calling a policeman a "God-damned racketeer" lost his appeal. The Court refused to take seriously his claim that freedom of worship was being infringed when such "fighting words" were punished.[13] Nor, said Justice Murphy, does the prohibition of such language infringe the free speech guaranties. In other Witness cases, the Court upheld the power of a municipality to forbid a parade down crowded city streets on a busy Saturday night,[14] and the power of a state to apply its child labor laws to a nine-year-old girl peddling the sect's literature.[15] The first two of these decisions were unanimous, and only Justice Murphy dissented in the third. As the concurrence of even such staunch libertarians as Rutledge, Douglas, and Black suggests, these were "easy" cases, in which the argument for state control seemed very strong and the burden on freedom of religion almost negligible. Such judgments hardly suggest any significant flagging of the Court's libertarian resolve.

Certain of the other negative decisions that would appear in a simple listing of religious freedom cases in the 1940–1945 terms must be discounted when we examine the balance sheet more closely. Some early decisions denying Witnesses' claims were

13. Chaplinsky v. New Hampshire, 315 U.S. 568 (1942).
14. Cox v. New Hampshire, 312 U.S. 569 (1941).
15. Prince v. Massachusetts, 321 U.S. 158 (1944).

later reversed,[16] so that the net doctrinal result was clearly libertarian. Other decisions "against" religious claimants rest on procedural grounds and do not reflect a parsimonious judicial attitude toward the substantive rights in question. In fact the only net and unambiguous aberration in the Court's otherwise libertarian record in this field is *In re Summers*,[17] which upheld the power of Illinois to refuse bar admission to a conscientious objector. Perhaps the explanation of this anomaly is the lingering persuasiveness of the old doctrine that professional standing is a "privilege" which government may withhold or grant as a matter of grace. Perhaps the explanation is that *raison de guerre* seemed marginally involved. The Stone Court's determination to defend freedom often lost its edge when war-related government actions were in question.

Disappointing as this deviation was to the four dissenting libertarians, standing alone it does not seriously undermine the impression that this was a Court remarkably receptive to the claims of religious conscience. The first Flag Salute case had been decided in 1940 at a time when the prospect of war and the call for a new patriotism were obscuring the judicial vision even more than they did later. The state's power to establish a compulsory flag salute in school classrooms was upheld. Justice Frankfurter, speaking for an eight-man majority, composed an elaborate theoretical rationale for a policy of self-restraint even in the free expression field. For him the argument never lost its force: he continued to vote against religious dissenters who came before the Court.

As the years provided opportunity for further reflection and new appointments, Frankfurter's majority in the religious field attenuated. In June 1942, Justices Black, Douglas, and Murphy announced, in a note appended to a dissenting opinion,[18] that they repented their stand on the flag salute issue; and when Rutledge

16. See West Virginia State Board of Education v. Barnette; Minersville School District v. Gobitis; Jones v. Opelika, 316 U.S. 584 (1941) vacated on rehearing 319 U.S. 98 (1943).

17. 325 U.S. 561 (1945).

18. Jones v. Opelika, 316 U.S. 584, 623 (1942).

was appointed in 1943, the basis was established for an extraordinary series of libertarian decisions during that year. The second flag salute decision[19] is notable, not only because it explicitly overturned the earlier holding, but because Justice Jackson's opinion for the new six-man majority eloquently joined issue with Justice Frankfurter's dissertation on judicial self-restraint. Interesting though their debate was in its own right, the flag salute issue appears in retrospect a fairly simple one. If the courts are ever to protect freedom of conscience this would seem to be an occasion for it, where the public need supposedly justifying the requirement was all but invisible. It was in a way unfortunate that Frankfurter made his classic plea for self-restraint in cases like these: they forced him to imply that judicial intervention was almost never warranted, even though he probably intended no such oversimplification, and this impaired the chances that the majority of his colleagues would listen.

The decision that most dramatically illustrates the extent of this Court's commitment to religious liberty is not the second Flag Salute case, but *Murdock* v. *Pennsylvania*,[20] also decided in 1943, which can fairly be called the Jehovah's Witnesses' Year. The case was one of several that involved municipal peddler taxes as applied to the Witnesses' door-to-door selling of religious literature. Of course it would be conceded by all members of the Court that the city could impose such a tax on salesmen of ordinary merchandise such as furniture brushes. Is the exaction rendered invalid when it falls on one who is selling religious pamphlets in furtherance of his faith? Five members of the Court, speaking through Justice Douglas, thought it was: "the mere fact that the literature is 'sold' by itinerant preachers . . . does not transform evangelism into a commercial enterprise . . . . The way of the religious dissenter has long been hard. But if the formula of this type of ordinance is approved, a new device for the suppression of minorities will have been found."[21]

One can sympathize with Douglas' feeling that there is a

19. West Virginia State Board of Education v. Barnette.
20. 319 U.S. 105.
21. *Ibid.* at 111, 115.

difference between what the Witnesses were doing and a primarily commercial activity, yet agree with his statement that drawing the line "will at times be difficult." Certainly his own attempts to draw the line are not notable for their lucidity. His problem would have been more tractable if he could have held that the taxes were so high as to constitute a practical restriction on the Witnesses' religious proselyting activities. But no such claim had been made: the Witnesses were asserting an absolute privilege against any tax, however small. He could hardly hold that all dispensers of the printed word are immune from taxation. As Frankfurter says in dissent, a tax on newspaper publishing falls upon the exercise of the constitutional right to freedom of press; yet no one can suppose that newspapers are exempted from contributing their fair share of tax revenue. An alternative might be to hold that hawkers of *religious* literature enjoy a special immunity. But one difficulty with this is that it implies a constitutional difference between religious and secular expression and a priority of the former over the latter. The textual or historical basis for such a discrimination would be hard to locate. And another difficulty is that to grant to religious expression constitutional exemption from the tax burdens others pay is to require the state to subsidize religion. Such a claim, as Frankfurter said, would seem to offend against the principle of separation of church and state.

Burdened by such encumbrances yet determined to strike down the tax, Justice Douglas produced an opinion that is not easy to interpret. What he seems to have said is that there are certain kinds of privileged literature-salesmen whose essential purpose is persuasion rather than profit, and that the most obvious and likely example is the itinerant religious zealot. This enabled him to intimate that a secular colporteur might enjoy a similar exemption, but to avoid the ticklish question of how such a claimant would be identified (the only illustration he offers is the sale of the pamphlets of Thomas Paine). And it enabled him without quite admitting it to assign religious activity de facto superiority over other forms of expression, since it seems to be the only form that naturally and typically qualifies for the immunity.

The unanswered questions and ambiguities in the *Murdock*

opinion should not obscure our realization that the decision elevated religious liberty to an exalted plane—at least for some purposes arguably superior to secular expression. It had become, so to speak, the most preferred of the "preferred freedoms." And an extreme solicitude for religious claimants was carried forward in other decisions of the era. Not only did the Court frequently hinder the efforts of municipal authorities to hinder Jehovah's Witnesses. It also struck a glancing blow at those who would penalize conscientious objectors to military services, reinterpreting federal law so that an applicant for naturalization need not agree to bear arms. Nor should the indignation of the dissenters in *Murdock* nor the closeness of the vote cause us to overlook the fact that libertarianism was in this field firmly established. In 1944 one of the dissenters, Justice Reed, joined in overthrowing a similar license tax requirement;[22] in 1944, Justice Frankfurter went along with extensions of the *Murdock* principle.[23] Both of them justified their votes on the ground that *Murdock* was now the law of the land to which they were reluctantly submitting; but surely this ground would not have been compelling if their objections had been very strong. The Court had written a solid new chapter in the history of religious freedom.

The main drift of doctrine during the 1940–1945 terms was strongly libertarian in the areas of both secular and religious expression. In a third area—cases involving the issue of race discrimination—the bias in favor of the individual claimant was in some ways even more pronounced. This is not to say that the Stone Court conjured into being a golden age of constitutional privilege for the Negro. The achievements of the period do not look very spectacular when compared with the advances, much less the demands, of the civil rights movement in the 1950's and 1960's. There are some curious gaps in the story. For example, not one case involving school segregation was decided by the

22. Follet v. McCormick, 321 U.S. 573 (1944).
23. Marsh v. Alabama, 326 U.S. 501 (1944).

Stone Court; apparently no such case was even presented for consideration. But the plain fact is that Negroes claiming discrimination won almost all the cases they did bring before the Court in these years, and that most of the decisions were unanimous, or nearly so. The dissension that was so common in other cases was hardly evident at all in this field.

The Court's increasing alertness to race discrimination is illustrated in a handful of decisions affecting the behavior of businesses and labor unions. Interstate travel had been subject to state segregation laws in the south since the heyday of the Jim Crow movement in the early twentieth century. Passenger accommodations provided under these laws were supposed to be "separate but equal"; however, although the separation requirement was uniformly enforced, the equality requirement was not. In 1941, the Court held that the Interstate Commerce Act compelled a railroad to supply equal, though still separate, Pullman accommodations to Negroes.[24] Five years later it went a substantial step farther, ruling that enforced segregation of interstate bus passengers was flatly forbidden:[25] forcing the traveller to move from one seat to another as the bus proceeded from north to south imposed an "undue burden" on interstate commerce. As for labor unions, they had been blithely discriminating against Negroes for years. As "private associations" they were uninhibited by the Fourteenth Amendment, which applied only to state action. But now the Court interpreted the Railway Labor Act to prohibit union discrimination in that industry[26] and upheld a state antidiscrimination law against constitutional attack.[27]

These decisions affecting travel and employment were small beginnings against Jim Crow; they whittled away at some of the symptoms of a national malady. But meanwhile the Court was also starting to unlock new forces that might, in the fullness of time, palliate the disease itself.

24. Mitchell v. United States, 313 U.S. 80.
25. Morgan v. Virginia, 328 U.S. 373 (1946).
26. Steele v. Louisville and Nashville Railroad Co., 323 U.S. 192 (1944).
27. Railway Mail Ass'n. v. Corsi, 326 U.S. 88 (1945).

One such development is illustrated by decisions involving the power of Congress to protect individual rights. To appropriate a metaphor once employed by Justice Jackson, rights can be protected by "both a shield and a sword," that is, by self-executing constitutional prohibitions or by positive congressional legislation. For example, the first clause of the Fourteenth Amendment prohibits state acts that deny "equal protection of the laws," and a person affected by such an act may ask the courts to hold it invalid. But the fifth clause gives Congress authority to enforce the amendment "by appropriate legislation"; this empowers Congress to add something to the protection automatically available under the first clause—to make it, let us say, a federal crime for a state official to enforce a discriminatory statute. The "shield" will always be important, but from the viewpoint of a civil rights advocate there are obvious advantages in exploiting the legislative sword as well. Federal enforcement agents and prosecutors can on their own incentive seek out invasions of civil rights, while the courts must wait for a case to be presented. Legislative acts can be tailored and altered to fit arising problems, while constitutional provisions, though subject to growth by interpretation, set some constraints on the range of judicial choice. Most significant of all, the courts are in a stronger position politically when they apply a federal law based on the Constitution than when they apply the Constitution directly. For in the former case their pronouncement is backed, not only by the prestige of the judiciary, but by the will and the power resources of the political branches of government.

In the years just after the Civil War the partisans of the newly emancipated Negroes were well aware of the role federal legislation could play in forwarding their cause, and they pushed through Congress a number of so-called Civil Rights Acts. But as the nation grew weary of or indifferent to the Negroes' plight these statutes were almost forgotten, partly because court decisions had curtailed some of their provisions and partly because no one seemed concerned enough to enforce the remnants that survived. At last, in 1939, Attorney General Frank Murphy established a Civil Rights Section in the Department of Justice, and this event set going a re-examination of both the statutes and the constitutional questions that underlay them.

United States v. *Classic*[28] did not involve Negro rights directly but concerned issues indirectly vital to that problem. Patrick Classic and his fellow defendants were white election officials accused of falsely counting votes in a congressional Democratic primary in New Orleans. They were indicted under two federal laws that had originated in the reconstruction era Civil Rights Act: Section 241, Title 18, of the *United States Code,* which punished conspiracy to interfere with a right secured by the federal Constitution or laws; and Section 242, Title 18, which punished anyone who "under color of law" willfully deprived an inhabitant of such a right. The contention was that Classic had violated Section 241 by conspiring to deny the constitutional right to vote and have one's vote counted and 242 by using his public office (in other words, color of law) to deny that right. This raised some interesting questions both of constitutional power and of statutory construction. Does Congress have the constitutional authority to protect the right to vote in congressional elections? If so, can it protect that right against deprivation by private individuals? (The rights of the Fourteenth and Fifteenth Amendments, it should be remembered, are secured only against "state action"; yet 241 punishes "persons" in general.) Can the protective law apply to *primary* elections, which were unknown when the Constitution was framed and thus may not be embraced in the constitutional clauses relating to the electoral process? And, whatever may be the answer to these questions of constitutional power, were the laws *intended* to reach Mr. Classic? Is the right to vote in congressional elections, including primaries: one "secured by the Constitution" in the meaning of the statute? Does "under color of law" refer to officials who are violating state laws—as Classic of course was—rather than only to those who are acting in conformity with it?

The Court said yes to all these pregnant questions. The right to vote in congressional elections is secured by Article I of the

Constitution, and Congress has power under the same article to protect the right against impairment by anyone. Both the right and the power extend to primaries. The first part of this declaration was well grounded in precedent. But the ruling on primaries was a new departure, and Justice Stone hedged it a little. The primary is, constitutionally speaking, a part of the election process at least where state law has made it an integral part of the procedure of choice, or where it normally determines the ultimate election to office (as was the case with the Democratic primary in Louisiana). It follows that Section 241 also applies because the phrase "under color of law" includes "misuse of power, possessed by virtue of state law and made possible only because the wrongdoer is clothed with the authority of state law."

The implications of all this were considerable for those who advocated use of the sword to ensure civil rights. The old statutes had been revitalized by the broad interpretation of the rights they protected and by the holding that under color of law applies to state officials who act in violation of state law. All states forbid murder, but this is small help to a Georgia Negro who may be killed by a brutal sheriff if it is understood in advance that the state will not prosecute the killer. Now it appeared that federal punishment under Section 242 could be invoked in such a case. The breadth of these statutory interpretations troubled three justices who dissented, arguing that the "rights" mentioned in 241 should not be construed to cover voting in primary elections. Specific crimes should not be read into such vague and general language unless Congress has spoken unmistakably.

But it is important to note that the dissenters did not challenge Congress' power to reach primaries if it explicitly chose to do so. Nor did they in this case question either the application of 242 to lawless officials, or the constitutionality of that application. Thus, quite apart from issues of statutory construction, the *Classic* decision seemed to recognize, unanimously, that Congress could legislate on a broad front to protect the rights of individuals. And thereby it added—if its implications were accepted—another significant dimension to the jurisprudence of civil rights being constructed for the modern Court.

Screws v. *United States*[29] tested some of these implications and at the same time underlined their relevance to the issue of Negro rights. Sheriff Claude Screws had been convicted, under Section 242, of an offense like the one mentioned above: he had beaten to death a Negro whom he had held in custody. According to the indictment, this meant that he had "under color of law" deprived the prisoner of his Fourteenth Amendment right to due process of law. The majority of the Court reaffirmed the *Classic* holding, that under color of law refers to those officials who break the state law as well as those who abide by it. On this issue of statutory interpretation there was a sharp dissent from three justices. Although two of the three (Frankfurter and Roberts) had joined the majority in *Classic*, they now argued that the focus of that decision had been on the primary election problem, that the interpretation of the color of law provision had not there been fully considered, and that Congress in 1870 intended the provision to apply only to officials who act in accordance with state law. But whatever the merits of their appeal to remote history, it was too much to expect that a libertarian-inclined Court, having committed itself to libertarian policy in *Classic*, would retract that policy three years later because of a plea that it had been adopted absentmindedly.

And on the important constitutional issue—whether unlawful official acts are "state action" reachable by Congress under the enforcement clause of the Fourteenth Amendment—the Court position was even stronger. Six members of the Court were unequivocally in the affirmative; even the dissenters, though somewhat grudging, conceded that "it may well be" that Congress has such authority. Many questions remained about the further scope of constitutional possibilities, and even about other applications of Sections 241 and 242. But *Classic* and *Screws* had made it clear that the sword now had an edge.

A quite different but equally important implication of the *Classic* decision was realized in the White Primary case, *Smith* v. *Allwright*,[30] and the platitude about making a bed that one must

29. 325 U.S. 91 (1945).
30. 321 U.S. 649 (1944).

lie in comes to mind. In 1935 the Court had held that a Texas Democratic party convention could deny Negroes party membership and thus the right to vote in the Democratic primary.[31] This was private, rather than state, action and outside the reach of the Fourteenth and Fifteenth Amendments. Neither Negroes nor these two amendments had been directly involved in *Classic*. But if the primary can be, as that decision recognized, a part of the election process, then it would seem anomalous indeed that the Negro could be barred from participation despite the Fifteenth Amendment's plain concern to protect voting against racial discrimination. This anomaly led the Court, when the convention's action was again challenged after *Classic*, to reconsider the matter and to hold that Negroes could not be barred. Texas regulates primaries in various ways and, most decisive of all, "limits the choice of the electorate in general elections . . . practically speaking" to those who are chosen in the primary. Such relationships between state law and the primary stamp the primary with the mark of state action, and the 1935 decision was overruled. Justice Roberts, who had written the decision in that case, was outraged to find that *Classic*, in which he had joined, led to the present result; he filed a lonely dissent, chiding the majority for its departure from precedent. But the precedent itself had been a strangely unrealistic one, and the overruling seems in retrospect almost inevitable once *Classic* had precipitated reconsideration. It is perhaps some indication of the difference between the 1935 and 1944 judicial spirits that a nine to nothing vote one way should become an eight to one vote the other way, on identical facts.

More specifically, the reversal and the vote well illustrate the mood of the Court in this period toward the subject of racial discrimination. The justices were more receptive to individual claims, and more united in their receptivity, than in any other civil rights area. All of the major decisions concerning Negro rights were decided in favor of the Negro claimant, and only in one (*Screws*) was there more than a single dissenting vote.

But arithmetic tells only part of the story, or rather the part it

31. Grovey v. Townsend, 295 U.S. 45 (1935).

tells is corroborated when the substance of the decisions is considered. Several would be landmarks in any view of the history of public law. The Court not only took steps to dilute Jim Crow directly through the reinterpretation of statutes and constitutional doctrine. It also, particularly in the *Classic-Screws-Allwright* line of decisions, started opening the way for more fundamental developments. If the pattern of racial discrimination were ever to be basically altered, it would require an ample range of governmental authority spurred by the political demands of the victims of discrimination. In *Classic* and *Screws* the justices began the process of unyoking the constitutional potential of the national government, which was the only one that could hope to deal effectively with this national problem. In *Classic* and *Allwright* they began the process of releasing Negro political power from the ties that had retarded its maturation. Evidently the comfortable world of white supremacy was at last being disturbed; and with these developments and the temper of the modern Court in view, it was easy to foretell that further disturbances were in the offing.

On the basis of the developments chronicled so far, the net tendency of the Stone Court appears almost unreservedly libertarian. Freedom of expression, both secular and religious, was dramatically enlarged; the right against racial discrimination was revitalized. Here, it would seem, is a Court enthusiastically dedicated to a new birth of constitutional freedom and confident that its own wisdom and authority are sufficient to bring the infant into being. But a constitutional period, like a book or a life, must be judged as a whole; and in other aspects the libertarian ardor was more qualified, the self-confidence less secure.

One field in which judicial trends were a good deal more equivocal was that of criminal procedures. Among the main categories of civil liberties issues, this was the only one that rested on a fairly substantial history of prior adjudication. Especially with respect to problems arising in federal criminal law, the justices could feel a moderate sense of familiarity. As for state procedures challenged under the due process clause, the pre-established guidelines were, to be sure, newer and vaguer. But criminals are criminals, courts have been dealing with them for centuries; and it might be thought that even here the justices would be prepared to implement their libertarian prepossessions more confidently than in almost chart-less areas like freedom of expression and Negro rights.

On the contrary, the Court was less decisively libertarian about criminal procedures than about the other personal rights categories just discussed. And although the hesitation was greater when state procedures were being challenged, it was also evident in cases involving federal arrest and trial. In both categories there were, it is true, some notable advances; but there were also notable re-fusals to advance. Individual claims, whether arising from state or federal proceedings, were rejected in substantial numbers. More-over the majority seemed reluctant to pronounce the kind of sweeping, unqualified doctrines that were tossed off so boldly in some of the other areas.

It was common knowledge that American police sometimes used the "third degree" to wring confessions from suspected crimi-nals, and in 1931 the famous Wickersham Commission had re-emphasized this fact in its report on "lawlessness in law enforce-ment." As the report conceded, the practice was doubtless less frequent in federal police stations than state, but it was far from unknown despite a well-established federal rule that confessions are inadmissible as evidence if they are involuntary or obtained by threats or inducements. One of the perennial problems in enforc-ing such a rule is to prove that the accused was coerced: the inter-rogation takes place in private, and a reviewing court is often confronted only by the bare statement of the suspect that he felt compulsion and the flat denial of the police that they did anything to justify the feeling. An obvious solution would be to adopt the English rule that rejects any confession produced by police interro-gation alone. But even Zechariah Chafee, co-author of the report to the Wickersham Commission and a zealous libertarian, feared that the third degree was too deeply rooted for such a drastic im-mediate remedy. He proposed a more gradual attack on the evil, beginning with a shortening of the "danger period" during which the police hold a prisoner until they take him before a magistrate.

This was the approach chosen by the Supreme Court in *McNabb*

v. *United States.*[32] Three members of a clan of Tennessee moun-
taineers had been convicted of murdering a federal revenue agent,
on the basis of incriminating statements obtained after long questioning. The Court was urged by the petitioners to hold that the
use of evidence so obtained was constitutionally forbidden; and by
the government to hold that confessions were admissible, despite
protracted questioning, unless shown to be "involuntary." Mr.
Justice Frankfurter, speaking for the majority, rejected both suggestions. The convictions were thrown out without reaching the
question of whether the statements were involuntary. But the
reason for excluding them seemed to be not a constitututional requirement, but that the statements had been made while the accused were unlawfully detained. Federal statutes prescribe that
arrested persons must be promptly taken before a committing
authority; the officers in this case flagrantly disregarded that command of Congress. The Supreme Court has supervisory authority
over federal courts; it has the duty of maintaining "civilized standards of procedure and evidence." It is simply exercising that authority and performing that duty when it excludes evidence obtained by flouting the congressional command.

Thus, although the *McNabb* decision certainly made it harder
for federal police to employ the third degree, this was accomplished without adding anew to the temple of constitutional law
and with the help of the idea that congressional policy had ordained the result. This at least left open the possibility that the
rule could be modified if Congress preferred to give its police more
leeway. The *McNabb* rule was a significant advance, but the terms
of its statement hardly suggested a headlong rush toward a libertarian millennium.

The third degree issue was even more difficult for the Supreme
Court to handle in cases arising in state courts. Since the only basis
for challenging state criminal procedures was the Fourteenth
Amendment, the halfway house of *McNabb* was not available; any
rule must rest on constitutional grounds. Furthermore, review of
state action was always complicated, for some justices at least, by

32. 318 U.S. 332 (1943).

considerations of federalism. The Supreme Court cannot claim the broad supervisory authority over state law enforcement proceedings that it enjoys over the police and courts of the national government. And it had long been assumed that the Fourteenth Amendment left the states a large area of autonomy in devising criminal procedures. In comparatively recent years, however, the Court had made it plain that the area was not limitless. The leading case was *Palko* v. *Connecticut*,[33] in which the states were forbidden to adopt procedures inconsistent with the "essence of a scheme of ordered liberty." But the very distinction made by this so-called "Palko rule" between fundamental and nonfundamental rights reflected the persisting idea that local option is still entitled to a special measure of weight when constitutional balances are struck.

The Court had found no difficulty in holding, in *Brown* v. *Mississippi*,[34] that such fundamental rights were denied by a state trial in which the only evidence was brutally extorted confessions. Under the common law rule coerced confessions are inadmissible because they may be false, and a trial based on them is clearly incompatible with a scheme of ordered liberty. This was simple enough if the coercion was manifest and undisputed, as in *Brown*. But the familiar problem observed earlier in connection with the federal cases at once arises: unless the actual fact of coercion is provable, and it seldom will be, the third degree can flourish almost undisturbed in the sanctum of the police station despite the *Brown* precedent. Again, an obvious root-and-branch remedy would be to exclude all police-obtained confessions. But if such a drastic rule were deemed excessive when federal procedures were in question, it would be all the more unlikely that the Court, considering the claims of federalism, would forthwith impose it on the states.

The judicial perplexities over this quandary are reflected in the tangled course of doctrine and rationale. Several cases were enough like *Brown* so that the Court had no difficulty in holding the confessions involuntary and therefore inadmissible. But in *Lisenba* v.

33. 302 U.S. 319 (1937).
34. 297 U.S. 278 (1936).

California[35] the Court confronted a different situation. Law enforcement officers had kept a prisoner incommunicado for a long period and committed various illegal acts in the course of questioning him. Yet there remained substantial doubt that the defendant, who seems to have been a cool customer, was actually broken in will by this official misbehavior; and the Court upheld a state finding that his confession had been voluntary. This accorded with the common law idea that coerced confessions are excluded only because they may be unreliable: it is not the business of the Supreme Court to censor police conduct before the trial except insofar as that conduct may have made the trial itself unfair.

This traditional way of looking at the matter did not satisfy Justices Black and Douglas because it left a loophole for arbitrary police conduct. By 1944 they managed to assemble a majority to hold that a confession was inadmissible if the product of an "inherently coercive" interrogation, without regard to the specific question of whether the defendant's will had been overborne by the questioning.[36] This subtly shifted the focus and purpose of review. The Court might now throw out a confession if the procedures used in obtaining it "offend those canons of decency and fairness which express the notions of justice of English-speaking peoples,"[37] even if it could not be shown that the defendant had actually broken because of the pressure. In short, the justices were now not merely trying to ensure the reliability of a specific confession; they were also—and this is a separable matter—trying to discipline the police. Yet they carefully refrained from admitting this, and from defining the official misconduct that was "inherently coercive" and thus forbidden. Long interrogation was evidently one factor, but the Court did not explain how to draw the line between too-long and not-too-long. Other aspects of police behavior were also to be taken into account; and in sum, the injunction to the police was that they must not offend "accepted notions of justice." This was hardly a precise recipe, but it was one that

35. 314 U.S. 219 (1941).
36. Ashcraft v. Tennessee, 322 U.S. 143.
37. Malinski v. New York, 324 U.S. 401, 416 (1945).

enabled the Court to edge into the state third degree problem step by step. Such a gradual and half-camouflaged incursion was the best the Court could offer at this stage of its doctrinal development.

In other procedural areas the pace of constitutional progress was similarly fitful and hesitant. The question of unreasonable or illegal search and seizure, which bulked so large in later years, consumed little judicial time during the Stone period. To be sure, some of the standards in this field for federal officers and courts were already fairly well established. Since 1914 it had been clear that illegally seized evidence could not be introduced in a federal court,[38] and in 1939 the Supreme Court had held that evidence based on wire-tapping was also barred because the Federal Communications Act made the interception and divulgence of telephone conversations illegal.[39] But the Stone Court refused to enlarge these protections of the right to privacy, even in federal courts. As for state practices, the record of the 1940–1945 terms is entirely silent. The law stood as it had before.

But perhaps the best example of this Court's relatively frugal approach to the problem of procedural rights is its treatment of the right to counsel. The issue presented few immediate difficulties in federal criminal proceedings, for it had been clearly held in 1938 that the Sixth Amendment secured not only the right to employ a lawyer but the right of a defendant who lacked funds to have one provided for his trial.[40] However, the rule for indigent defendants in state courts was a good deal more primitive, and the 1941–1946 justices were curiously obstinate about renovating it. As long before as 1932 the Court had held that the Fourteenth Amendment required appointment of counsel in a capital case when the defendant was too poor to hire his own lawyer and too ignorant to conduct his own defense.[41] This decision and a couple of later ones had nourished the hope that the Court would impose on the states the federal rule requiring appointment of counsel in

38. Weeks v. United States, 232 U.S. 383.
39. United States v. Nardone, 308 U.S. 338.
40. Johnson v. Zerbst, 304 U.S. 458.
41. Powell v. Alabama, 287 U.S. 45.

all criminal cases. But in *Betts* v. *Brady*,[42] a majority dug in its heels and declared that counsel need not be provided in state courts if an appraisal of "the totality of facts in a given case" reveals that the trial is fundamentally fair. Hence there was no denial of due process when Smith Betts, a farmhand of little education but "ordinary intelligence" and, because of a previous larceny conviction, "not wholly unfamiliar with criminal procedure" was obliged to conduct his own defense against a burglary charge.

Three dissenters speaking through Justice Black sharply challenged this holding, and the disagreement between majority and minority is complex enough to merit a few words of explanation. The Court had long since agreed to the doctrine, recently reiterated in the Palko case, that state procedures violated the Fourteenth Amendment if they denied a "fundamental" principle of justice. But this doctrine was itself oper to at least three implementing interpretations. A fundamental right might be simply defined as one listed in the Bill of Rights; this is the idea that the Fourteenth Amendment "incorporates" the Bill of Rights, that it is a "shorthand summary" of the first eight amendments. Justice Black advanced the idea in his *Betts* dissent but did not rest his case on this point alone. Second, it might be held that a certain right, like the right to counsel, is always fundamental in a trial for a serious crime, quite apart from anything the Bill of Rights has to say on the subject. This alternative point is also urged in Black's dissent, though he evidently prefers the incorporation principle. Finally, it might be held that certain rights are always fundamental (like the right against tortured confessions), while others are sometimes fundamental (like the right to provision of counsel); and that whether a right in the latter category is or is not fundamental in a particular trial depends on the overall fairness of that proceeding. This formula, which came to be called the "fair trial rule," was the one adopted by the majority in *Betts* over Black's protest.

Obviously the disagreement between the majority and Justice Black goes beyond a difference of opinion over the right to counsel: it concerns the nature of the judicial process itself. Black was

42. 316 U.S. 455 (1942).

urging not only a bold libertarian advance; he was also urging that the advance be pegged to a precise standard that would channel and confine the Court's discretion to decide cases in this field. He purported to derive that confining standard from an explicit mandate in the Constitution. On the other hand, Justice Roberts (with Justice Frankfurter at his elbow, we can be sure) prescribed a more cautious libertarianism, a more flexible and subjective standard that would preserve the Court's freedom of choice; and a view that the constitutional text provides only the most general guidelines for decision. These conflicting attitudes toward the very essence of the judicial assignment run through the history of the modern Court.

In the meantime, the fair trial rule was the order of the day. Due process did not require appointment of counsel in all criminal trials; but the results in the immediate future were not as harsh for accused persons as a bare reading of *Betts* might suggest. In fact, of six right-to-counsel cases in the four Court terms after *Betts*, all but one were decided in favor of the defendant;[43] in that one even Justices Black and Douglas agreed. In spite of the distaste for rigid formulas that was reflected in the fair trial doctrine, the Court did adopt the flat rule that counsel must *always* be supplied in trials for a capital crime.[44] This adoption was achieved by a curious process of assumption rather than explicit reasoning, for it involved a simplified reading of *Powell* v. *Alabama*, which had rested not only on the capital nature of the offense, but on the intellectual inadequacies of the defendants. There was certainly nothing in the language of the Constitution to warrant a distinction between capital and non-capital offenses. But the distinction did mean that the Court had hedged a little on the open-ended doctrine of *Betts*. Nevertheless, that decision stood as a salient example of the judicial disposition to make haste slowly in the procedural field.

The reaction of the 1941–1946 Court to the problem of pro-

43. Hawk v. Olson, 326 U.S. 271 (1945); House v. Mayo, 324 U.S. 42 (1945); Williams v. Kaiser, 323 U.S. 471 (1945); Tomkins v. Missouri, 323 U.S. 485 (1945); Rice v. Olson, 324 U.S. 786 (1945); White v. Ragen, 324 U.S. 760 (1945) (decided against defendant).
44. Williams v. Kaiser.

cedural rights modifies somewhat the initial impression that the Court of this period was dauntless in its pursuit of libertarian ideals. That impression is clouded further when we turn to a final area of judicial policy-making: the relation of civil rights to the war effort. It must be conceded that the category itself is a bit shadowy at the edges. Surely so engrossing an event as the great war could never have been far from the justices' minds no matter what specific cause they were considering. No doubt there is a sense in which most of the matters already discussed can be called war-related. The almost complete abandonment of old doctrines like "economic due process" and "dual federalism" may have been accelerated by a judicial conviction that a government at war must be freed from such nagging restraints. The impulse to enlarge the constitutional rights of minority groups was surely traceable in part to a feeling that America should be not only the "arsenal of democracy" but its exemplar as well. But one body of cases raised rather more directly a set of war-power problems, and it is of interest to see how the then most libertarian Court in American history responded to them.

In 1943 Robert Cushman declared that in spite of the war civil liberty was enjoying "a vitality which even the optimist had hardly dared hope for" before Pearl Harbor.[45] Up to a point he was certainly correct, and he was probably also correct in crediting the Supreme Court with some responsibility for generating an atmosphere in which personal rights would be respected. In addition to the libertarian drift of decisions in certain fields that has already been chronicled, the Court found for the individual in several cases bearing more directly on the war effort. Convictions under the Espionage Act and the Selective Service Act were overturned by narrow readings of the statutes;[46] a similarly strict standard was applied to denaturalization proceedings[47] and to a prosecution

45. Robert E. Cushman, "The American Government in War Time: The First Year: Civil Liberties," *American Political Science Review*, 37:49 (1943).

46. Hartzel v. United States, 322 U.S. 680 (1944); Keegan and Kunze v. United States, 325 U.S. 478 (1945).

47. Schneiderman v. United States, 320 U.S. 118 (1943); Baumgartner v. United States, 322 U.S. 665 (1944).

for treason.[48] It seems likely that all these rulings, taken together, helped curb excesses of the martial spirit. The effect of court decisions is not limited to the immediate litigation; they can have a secondary influence on popular and official attitudes, and surely the national climate was tempered by the Court's reminders that personal rights and legal proprieties exist even in time of war.

But it is worth observing that few if any of the decisions so far touched upon imposed serious limits on government's actual power to harry individuals in the name of patriotism or national defense. The ringing pronouncements of the Court in cases like *Bridges, Thomas,* and the religious freedom decisions related to that power only by implication—and implications may or may not be carried out. In most of the war-related cases just mentioned the holdings rested on statutory interpretations; and such interpretations are, by definition, subject to legislative correction.

Moreover, we must weigh against these mild rebuffs to official zeal a number of more acquiescent decisions. Though it is true that the nation as a whole was less hysterical in this war than in World War I, it is also true that we had been fighting the Kaiser for over a year before Congress passed legislation in any way similar to Section 2 of the Alien Registration Act of 1940, the section embodying the first national peacetime sedition law since the Alien and Sedition Acts of 1798. In 1941 the government indicted under the provisions of Section 2 eighteen members of the Socialist Workers party (Trotskyist). Recent decisions of the Supreme Court had suggested that the validity of such an indictment would be measured by the clear and present danger standard, and it would have been hard indeed to find that this puny gaggle of revolutionaries represented an imminent insurrectionist threat. But their convictions were upheld in the Court of Appeals, which relied not on the clear and present danger precedents, but on the less stringent standard of the *Gitlow* case (1925). The Supreme Court denied the writ of certiorari and the convictions stood.[49]

Another group of cases involved a painful and curious question:

48. Cramer v. United States, 325 U.S. 1 (1945).
49. Dunne v. United States, 138 F.2d 137, cert. denied 320 U.S. 790 (1943).

what enforceable constitutional rights do enemy belligerents enjoy? The question first arose when seven saboteurs who had been landed by German submarines on the American east coast were apprehended, tried by a military tribunal, and sentenced to death.[50] It arose again in 1946 when "the Tiger of Malaya," General Yamashita, was sentenced by a military commission to hang for atrocities committed by his troops during the Japanese occupations of the Philippines.[51] In both cases the Court denied permission to file for a writ of habeas corpus. That much is clear; but the opinions by Chief Justice Stone explaining the denials are otherwise almost inscrutable. Perhaps the most unfortunate thing about the cases is that the Court, while seeking to ensure the petitioners a hearing and thus vindicate the rule of law, was forced to appear to ratify procedures that did violence to that ideal. It might have been wiser to deny jurisdiction and say nothing. Sometimes a little explanation is as undesirable as a little knowledge.

It would be expecting a lot to ask a civil tribunal to intervene effectively in such circumstances. But a far more disturbing failure of both administrative and judicial mettle is revealed in the story of the Japanese-Americans on the Pacific coast after Pearl Harbor. In the days following that disaster there were fears that our military security was threatened by 112,000 "potential enemies" in the western states. On February 19, 1942, President Roosevelt issued an order authorizing the Secretary of War and designated military commanders to prescribe "military areas," and at their discretion to exclude "any or all persons" from such areas or to impose restrictions on their right to remain. A month later a congressional resolution made it a misdemeanor to disobey orders issued under this authority. In response to these executive and legislative invitations, the military commander on the west coast eventually moved out of that area substantially all persons of Japanese descent, including about 70,000 native-born American citizens, and incarcerated them in "relocation centers" elsewhere in the United States. This has been justly called the most drastic

50. Ex Parte Quirin, 317 U.S. 1 (1942).
51. In Re Yamashita, 327 U.S. 1 (1946).

invasion of the rights of citizens of this country that has occurred in its history. The scope of power given to the military by the presidential order was almost breathtaking. Congress calmly and almost offhandedly ratified this extraordinary carte blanche. The evacuation meant financial ruin for most of the victims, besides the loss of liberty and dignity; and it was based on no concrete evidence of espionage or sabotage. Racist overtones made the whole affair particularly repellent: the orders applied to those who had as little as one-sixteenth Japanese ancestry whether or not they were aware of it.

Obviously this was a hot potato for the judiciary to handle: it involved old ethnic prejudices now backed by claims of military necessity and the high authority of Franklin Roosevelt and Henry Stimson, as well as the Congress of the United States. But the issue could hardly be evaded, for the congressional act had enlisted the civil courts in enforcement of the policy. Despite this, the justices did what they could to postpone the questions of greatest difficulty. In the first case to reach them[52] the appellant, Kiyoshi Hirabayashi, had been sentenced to two three-month prison terms for violating a curfew order and for failing to report to a "Civil Control Station" as a preliminary to exclusion from the area. Since the terms were concurrent the conviction could be sustained on the basis of either offense, and the Court chose to consider only the curfew issue. The conviction was unanimously upheld.

But the vital question was not whether the curfew order would be sustained, but how the Court would formulate the standards for reviewing it; Chief Justice Stone's opinion makes that a hard question to answer. On the one hand, he suggests that such a discriminatory curtailment of private rights can be permitted only in time of war and then only if there is "substantial basis" for the conclusion that the curfew is a military necessity. On the other hand he grants the executive and Congress such wide discretion in judging necessity as to render judicial review nearly meaningless. He finds a sufficiently substantial basis in the "facts" that residents having ethnic affiliations with the enemy may be more dangerous than others, and that it might be difficult in a critical

52. Hirabayashi v. United States, 320 U.S. 81 (1943).

hour to identify the disloyal as individuals and deal with them separately. Conceding that military judgment must be allowed some latitude in such circumstances, we might nevertheless ask that the generals make out a better case than this before abridging the rights of American citizens.

But the curfew was, after all, a rather mild restraint, and perhaps even a weak case was enough to justify it. The exclusion policy was another matter, as the Court's reluctance to confront it implied. It could not be deferred indefinitely, and the petition of Fred Toyasaburo Korematsu, convicted of remaining in a military area in violation of the exclusion order, brought the problem squarely before the Court.[53] Conceding that it is a "far greater deprivation" to uproot a man from his home than to confine him there, the majority opinion by Justice Black was nevertheless even more cursory than the *Hirabayashi* opinion had been in finding a "substantial basis" for the policy and upholding the conviction. Indeed, the Court here simply applied the justifications relied on in the earlier case, although the deprivation was admittedly greater and although a different measure might be expected to require a separate showing of military need. The foot-in-the-door doctrine of *Hirabayashi*—that the Court will at least demand *some* factual grounds on which a judgment of need might reasonably be based—was all but ignored.

In *Hirabayashi* the Court refused to reach the hard question of exclusion; in *Korematsu* it refused to reach the even harder question of detention. In fact, the validity of the detention program as carried out in the War Relocation Centers was never determined by the Supreme Court. In the case of Miss Mitsuye Endo, decided on the same day as *Korematsu,* the Court ruled that the appellant, whose loyalty was conceded, was entitled to unconditional release from a Center. But no question was raised of the government's power to hold her until her loyalty was positively established, even though she was an American citizen and "disloyalty" (or perhaps "unloyalty") is not an offense recognized in American law.

Such an outline narrative of the Japanese-American measures

53. Korematsu v. United States, 323 U.S. 214 (1945).

and the judicial decisions that substantially upheld them may leave the impression that the narrator views the whole affair in simple terms as an unextenuable triumph of despotism over justice. There was of course nothing simple about the situation, and one should not beat the Court too hard with the heavy stick of hindsight. We know that the fears of invasion were groundless; that Hawaii survived without sequestering its citizens of Japanese blood; that Great Britain, though in constant and deadly hazard, managed to check aliens individually and thus avoid such wholesale action. We know that not a single case of sabotage or espionage was ever proved against a Japanese-American citizen. The military authorities at the time were less knowledgeable than we, and the Court in hearing a case had to take account of this circumstance. The judges *did* have some benefit of perspective; they *could* confidently feel that the threat had been exaggerated and the remedy excessive. But they were also aware that the judicial process is ill-adapted to the kind of fast judgments—pro or con—required here, a point emphasized by the very fact that they reached the problems so long after the crisis had waned. We can see why they might hesitate to second-guess the generals on a Monday morning three thousand miles and three years removed from the hot spot. What they perhaps failed to recognize was that the handicap of distance might also be an opportunity. They might have taken the occasion of *Korematsu,* when the fever had passed, to enforce the *Hirabayashi* principle that there must be some plausible factual basis for a military decision of this kind. This would not have helped the Japanese-Americans, but it might cause future generals to be a little more diligent and objective about collecting evidence. The *Milligan* decision[54] following the Civil War, which had invalidated the court martial conviction of civilians in a region where civil courts were still operating, has been criticized because it seemed simply to substitute judicial for military judgment. *Korematsu* went to the other extreme by abdicating in favor of the military. There is a middle ground: to ask that a substantial or rational basis be shown. Such a rule of reason could preserve the principle of limit without crippling the

54. Ex Parte Milligan, 4 Wall. 2 (1866).

nation's defense, and it would be comforting if such a principle stood solidly on our constitutional books. Because of *Korematsu* it stands precariously, if at all.

But it is not necessary to agree that the Court should have done more in order to recognize that it did very little to dampen the martial spirit in this instance. Among nine judges who were as a group more alert to claims of individual rights than any Court in our history until then, only three dissented against ratifying the most extreme invasion of rights in our history. One of them, Jackson, can be discounted: whatever his mysterious opinion meant, he certainly was not proposing a judicial check on military policy, but absolute forbearance. Another was Justice Roberts, who on other personal liberties issues was usually the most conservative judge on the Court. Those three ordinarily relentless libertarians Black, Douglas, and Rutledge were all on the side of the government; Murphy was the lone member of the bloc who stood firm.

However the Court's record on "wartime freedoms" is assessed with *Korematsu* excluded, when that decision is taken into account the reckoning is plain. The judicial acquiescence there counterbalances with a vengeance any other, moderately libertarian decisions in this category.

What generalizations are warranted about the eventful years of the Stone Court? To begin with, it is worth underlining the fact that civil liberties questions were moving into an increasingly significant position on the judicial agenda. In the 1935 Term the Court had handed down only two decisions with opinion involving civil liberties. In the 1940 Term there were seventeen such decisions, and by the 1945 Term the total was twenty-seven. Plainly the secular trend was upward. It was easy to foretell that such cases would thence forward claim a considerable share of the judges' attention.

By any reckoning, the Court was more devoted to the protection of "the helpless and the oppressed," to "the values of free thought, free utterance, and fair play," than ever before in our history. Figures may give this generality concreteness. In these six terms as a whole, the Court decided about two-thirds of all civil liberties cases in favor of the individual claimant. There was some cyclical variation from term to term, but in no term did the pro-individual decisions drop below fifty percent, and in three terms they exceeded seventy percent. If the proportion of decisions against government can be taken as a rough measure of "judicial activism," then the Stone Court's overall record was impressively activist in the civil liberties area; and though some of the libertarian holdings were routine or comparatively trivial, a number of them blazed new and important trails. The definitions of constitutional rights and liberties had been significantly extended.

In light of these trends it might well have been expected that the activism and the extensions would continue unabated in the years that followed. Many implications of the new constitutional libertarianism remained undeveloped, and the natural course of litigation would surely press them into judicial attention. The bold language in some of the Stone Court's opinions—in *Bridges, Thomas,* and the Second Flag Salute case, for example—seemed to invite claimants and to promise them a generous reception. At the time, it might have been anticipated that, as these promises were redeemed, the boundaries of legal liberty would be pushed rapidly forward.

But a closer look might have engendered some doubts. For one thing, signs of discord among the judges were more and more marked through these years. Not only were nonunanimous opinions multiplying; there was also an increase in five-to-four votes. Moreover, when the opinions are analyzed a strong undertone of disagreement about doctrine becomes apparent. "Clear and present danger" was the official incantatory phrase for free speech cases, but its tenure of office was precarious, resting as it did on closely divided decisions. Even the doctrine that civil liberties are "preferred freedoms" had been challenged by formidable minority spokesmen. The prospect that civil liberties frontiers would move ahead to some degree seemed assured by the general commitment of all the judges to some minimal libertarian premises. But the balance in favor of boldly creative advances was at best a delicate one.

Equally important is the related fact—evident from both the judges' votes and their opinions—that no solid conception of the Court's role had been established. Frankfurter's blueprint for extreme self-restraint had certainly not been subscribed to by the Court as a whole: it was not even clear that he himself consistently followed it. But neither had the Court unmistakably embraced a program of resolute activism. It oscillated in an area between these poles, sometimes approaching one, sometimes the other, but in general stopping short of both. The judges were still in the process of adjusting their minds to the new constitutional law they were forging. They had not achieved a stable majority understanding, much less a consensus, about either the propriety or the expediency of judicial supervision in the civil liberties field.

These uncertainties were reflected in the variable patterns of behavior observed above. With respect to both secular and religious expression, the objective record is decidedly libertarian. At least for a majority of the judges, the merits here seemed easy enough to weigh: open discussion of public issues and the expression of deeply held spiritual beliefs against a governmental desire to harass the unorthodox and to maintain minor housekeeping requirements. In the cases involving racial discrimination the trend in favor of individual claimants is even plainer. Of all the imperfections of American democracy, legalized discrimination against Negroes had been the crudest and the most gratuitous; of all the "helpless and oppressed" in our society, Negroes had been the most numerous and most neglected. It is not surprising that a Court concerned with personal rights found the case for judicial intervention here easy to endorse.

But the decisions involving the rights of the accused were harder: the merits seemed less obvious. Here there was a weighty societal claim to place in the balance. Government does after all have a legitimate interest in convicting criminals. In this field many of the easy questions had already been answered. The American legal tradition had defined some standards of fair play for the criminal accused, as it had not for the Negro. And finally, the judges' relative sophistication about this matter was an impediment to quick and sweeping judgments. They had thought about the subject before and were alive to some of its complexities. They had thought about speech, if at all, only in the simplistic terms of the anthologies. In the field of criminal procedure it seemed harder to be sure what the Court-imposed standards ought to be, and the judicial course was accordingly more irregular and hesitant.

The hesitancy is even more apparent in our final category of judicial concerns, war-related freedoms. And here there is perhaps reason to suspect that considerations of expediency as well as propriety may have been clouding the hue of judicial resolution. Judges seldom tell us explicitly that their refusal to intervene is influenced by the feeling that a subject is too high or too critical for court control. Technical-sounding phrases like "the police power" or "the political question doctrine" are often employed as surrogates for a candor that might undermine the myth of judicial imperturbability. But most Supreme Court judges have been aware at some level of consciousness that judicial review is subject to practical limitations. No such awareness is evident in the bold rhetoric of the Stone Court's free expression cases, to be sure. But those cases involved, despite the rhetorical fireworks, rather minor exertions of governmental power. No great wave of public indignation was likely to be provoked by a holding that Texas could not enforce a largely meaningless labor-baiting measure. The Jehovah's Witnesses were a nuisance to some municipal officials and householders, but the sect was too small and the problems it raised too singular to matter much in a national perspective. We must consider, side by side with the apostrophes to freedom in those cases, the Court's refusal even to review the constitutionality of the Smith Act. This law was a genuine, not trivial, menace to freedom of expression and association. But it was a national statute, and the judges left it severely alone.

Indeed, no national statute abridging expression had ever been held unconstitutional, and the Stone Court did not break this record. In cases arising under the immigration laws, the postal laws, and the Espionage Act of 1917 the Court reached its libertarian results by statutory interpretation and avoided the constitutional issues. Such a policy of avoidance by interpretation is of course perfectly proper. But it suggests some consciousness that to challenge the legislative power of the United States is a grave thing.

Most of all must be considered, in contrast to the libertarian pronouncements in other fields, the decisions concerning military action itself. The issues of those cases, so saturated with the passions of a nation at war, were approached by the Stone Court with truly Frankfurterian modesty. A tribunal that could hand down the *Korematsu* decision is not wholly insensitive to the practical case for self-restraint. It is not unaware that people and powers outside the courtroom may set some limits on the judicial will.

In the Stone Court years there were from time to time audible rumblings from such external constituencies. The mere fact that eight of the judges owed their appointments to Franklin Roosevelt was enough to generate unfriendliness in some quarters. Nor did those quarters fail to notice the further fact that the Court had written an abrupt end to the long judicial love affair with the businessman. A powerful element of American society, which had traditionally defended the judiciary in time of need, was now at best indifferent and at worst in hostile array. Journalists and statesmen who had fervently championed the Court against Rooseveltian menaces in 1937 now welcomed occasions for assailing it.

The Court, it must be said, did its part to provide occasions. The trend toward decisions on behalf of "the helpless and oppressed" was itself of course a grievance for some: such litigants are not always popular with the forces of respectability. But beyond that, these judges were an unsettling and unsettled lot. In six terms the Stone Court handed down fifteen decisions reversing precedents; there had been only sixty such reversals in the entire previous history of the republic. This cavalier attitude toward *stare decisis* troubled observers who set a high value on continuity and predictability in the law, and not all such critics were merely disgruntled Roosevelt-haters. In 1944 Justice Roberts filed a dissent, in which Justice Frankfurter joined, bitterly castigating the majority for converting the law into a "game of chance." This evidence of intramural disagreement was eagerly seized upon as suggesting an unseemly feud among the judges. Justice Jackson supplied further supportive evidence: in 1946 he issued a public statement from Nuremberg, where he was chief American prosecutor in the war-crime trials, attacking Justice Black as a "stealthy assassin" whose disregard of judicial proprieties threatened to bring the Court into disrepute. There had been personal animosities on the Court at times in the past, but they had seldom if ever been thus exposed to the popular view.

It is not possible to assert flatly that this combination of circumstances seriously eroded the Court's prestige. Prestige is a difficult commodity to measure accurately. But we do know, as Justice Frankfurter said many years later, that "the Court's authority—possessed neither of the purse nor the sword—ultimately rests on sustained public confidence in its moral sanction." We know that most judges know this. And we know that, if we cannot be certain how the judicial bank account stood in 1946, neither could the judges. For six years the Stone Court groped in a forest of problems largely new to American jurisprudence. It had begun the adventure with an air of engaging but perhaps ingenuous self-assurance. But during the years the problems began to look more difficult, not simpler; and although significant progress was made, the signs of uneasiness were perceptible. No stable agreement was reached about the judicial role, about what the Court ought to do, or could do, in this largely novel terrain. The course of further progress was not then predetermined. It would depend on developments, still unforeseeable, in the inner life of the Court and in its environment.

III THE VINSON COURT

CHIEF JUSTICE HARLAN F. STONE DIED SUD-
denly on April 22, 1946, and President Truman nominated Fred
M. Vinson as his successor. The new Chief had been a congress-
man, then a Federal Court of Appeals judge, then wartime Direc-
tor of Economic Stabilization; he was Secretary of the Treasury
at the time of his appointment to the Court. In the course of
acquiring his richly varied background in governmental affairs,
he had also acquired repute as a smoother of ruffles, a manager
of men. It was widely believed that Stone's lack of administrative
ability was partly responsible for the judicial factionalism of recent
years, and it was hoped that Vinson's conciliatory talents would
bring a new order to the courtroom.

A new order began to be apparent soon enough, but not in the
sense intended. The percentage of nonunanimous decisions did
not decrease; it rose to new heights, reaching 64 percent in the
1946 term; 74 percent in the 1948 term; and a record 81 percent
in the 1952 term, the last under Vinson's leadership. And although
nothing comparable to the Jackson Nuremberg statement captured
headlines during the Vinson years, there is no reason to imagine
that the judicial conference became a feast of love. Stone had
called his Court a "team of wild horses." It is doubtful that Vinson's team was any more domesticated.

On the other hand, there was a clear difference between the
Vinson Court and the Stone Court, and the differentiation began
to manifest itself almost at once. The Vinson Court would be on
the whole much less hospitable to civil liberties claims, distinctly
more inclined to approach problems in this field in a spirit of
"judicial modesty." Arithmetic reckonings alone illustrate the
contrast. The proportion of decisions favorable to the individual
never in any term of the Stone Court dropped below 50 percent;
there was only one term of the Vinson Court (1947) in which the
percentage of favorable decisions rose *above* fifty. As for totals,
in the six terms of the Stone Court, 65 percent of the decisions in
the field favored the individual; for the Vinson Court's seven

terms the figure is 42 percent. And turning from quantitative to qualitative assessments, the impression of a new judicial temper seems confirmed. Writing in 1952 near the close of the Vinson period, the editors of a comprehensive tome on "political and civil rights" reported gloomily that the trend toward expansion of such rights had been reversed.[1] Another contemporaneous observer called this a noncreative, passive phase in the Court's history. Plainly something had dampened the libertarian ardor of the recent past; plainly the spirit of judicial activism had diminished.

The intriguing thing is that the Court's alteration in mood became evident immediately, in the 1946 term, the first of the Vinson period. Again arithmetic is suggestive. Among twenty-four cases that can be described as involving civil liberty issues, only five were decided in favor of the individual claimant. This proportion—21 percent—was by far the lowest to date; in the preceding term, 1945, the claimant had won in some 63 percent of the cases.

Among the five decisions favoring the individual, moreover, only one was moderately important: *Craig* v. *Harney*,[2] which overturned a contempt judgment for newspaper comments on pending judicial proceedings. The decision made more obvious what had been implied in *Bridges* v. *California*—that only the most flagrant and unmistakable threat to the administration of justice would warrant the use of the summary contempt power. This invoked another indignant dissent from Justice Frankfurter, but not even he could complain that the holding was a surprise after Black's opinion in *Bridges*.[3] The *Craig* case was merely a refusal to go back; it was not really another step forward.

Evidence of an increased reluctance to take such steps is shown through the "negative" decisions of the term. The question of whether government employees have legally protectable rights was coming to attention at this time. Dark suspicions that sub-

1. Thomas I. Emerson and Thomas Haber, *Political and Civil Rights in the United States* (1952).
2. 331 U.S. 367 (1947).
3. Bridges v. California, 314 U.S. 252 (1941).

versives infested the councils of government had produced such measures as Executive Order 9835 (promulgated March 21, 1947), providing for a Loyalty Program in the executive branch of the federal government. In the Hatch Act cases,[4] the Court considered earlier legislation forbidding political activity by government workers. Despite the impact of such a law on the freedom of expression of some three million civil servants, Mr. Justice Reed for the majority upheld it against constitutional attack. Previous decisions had declared that the Court would ask in free expression cases whether the law was "narrowly drawn to define and punish specific conduct as constituting a clear and present danger to a substantial interest" of government. But Justice Reed now seemed to confirm validity of the statute if Congress might reasonably have thought that enforced political neutrality would produce an improved merit system, and if provisions for accomplishing that result do not pass beyond "the general existing conception of governmental power." Whatever that phrase may mean, it was evidently intended to be more tolerant of government's claims than the clear and present danger formula. The Court's hesitation about intruding in this now ticklish area was further illustrated in the 1946 term when it denied certiorari in the first case challenging a dismissal under the Loyalty Program.

In the field of procedural rights a similar attitude is at once observable. Out of ten cases decided with opinions in this category, the Court upheld the claimant in only two. Among the eight negative cases, the most famous one is perhaps *Adamson* v. *California*,[5] because Justices Frankfurter and Black there joined issue in major opinions over the question of whether the Fourteenth Amendment incorporates the Bill of Rights. Adamson had argued that the Sixth Amendment's prohibition against compulsory self-incrimination was applicable to the states via the Fourteenth. The claim was denied. Justice Black, in a dissent elaborating the point he had set forth in *Betts*, was sure that the framers in 1868 had intended to make Amendments One through Eight binding on the states in all particulars and that such an interpretation was

4. United Public Workers v. Mitchell, 330 U.S. 75 (1947).
5. 332 U.S. 46 (1947).

just and desirable. Justice Frankfurter, concurring with the Court, was equally sure that the framers had intended nothing of the kind and that the incorporation principle would unduly constrict the states' leeway to adopt their criminal procedures to changing times. The opinions are an important chapter in the continuing debate between these two champions—a debate begun in *Bridges* v. *California*—and they present a tantalizing paradox, or rather two of them. Frankfurter, the supposed proponent of judicial self-restraint, would grant the Court license to contract or expand due process in accord with the judge's reckonings about accepted notions of justice; but he did not think that immunity from compulsory self-incrimination was such a notion. Thus, though claiming very broad discretionary power for the judiciary, he reached a modest result. Black, the supposed activist, would hold the Court to the specific provisions of the Bill of Rights, nominally reducing its "sovereign prerogative of choice" but asserting by the same stroke of the pen a breathtaking new nay-saying power over state law. Evidently judicial activism and judicial restraint are not simple conceptions.

Another disagreement between these chronic adversaries was given a further airing in *Foster* v. *Illinois*.[6] Several decisions since 1942 had upheld claims that the right to counsel had been improperly denied in state courts,[7] and this had generated the hope among libertarian that the *Betts* doctrine was being silently whittled away. But now Justice Frankfurter for a five-man majority explicitly reaffirmed it over Justice Black's vigorous objections.

While *Adamson* and *Foster* can be thought of as merely illustrating the judges' reluctance in the 1946 term to chart new libertarian advances, *Harris* v. *United States*[8] sounds very much like a retreat. This was a rare event in the history of the modern Court: most of the not infrequent breaks with precedents since 1941 have enlarged, not narrowed, the scope of individual rights. It had been generally held in the past that officers making a lawful

6. 332 U.S. 134 (1946).
7. See *ibid.* at 137.
8. 331 U.S. 145 (1947).

arrest could search only the part of a house where the arrest was made and could seize only items in plain view or easily found. Now the Court sustained as incident to a valid arrest a five-hour ransacking of a four-room apartment and seizure of papers not related to the crime that occasioned the arrest. Since a search warrant could not have been issued for the items found (officers ignorant of their existence could not have described them in applying for the warrant) the decision had, in Frankfurter's words, "the novel and startling result of making the scope of search without warrant broader than an authorized search." The case also revealed a curious variation in the usual lineup of the Court in cases involving personal rights. Black and Douglas helped make up the five-man majority upholding the search and seizure; Frankfurter and Jackson joined Rutledge and Murphy in protesting. It would seem that the distinction between the "libertarians" and their opponents, like the one between "activism" and "restraint," conceals some interesting cross-threads.

Among other cases of the time bearing on civil liberties, the most important was *Everson* v. *Board of Education*,[9] which provides one of those instances—not uncommon in the history of the Court—in which a decision denying a claimed right offers warm encouragement to future claimants. A citizen of New Jersey had challenged in a taxpayer's suit an application of a state law authorizing the Board to reimburse parents for bus fares paid to transport pupils to school. His contention, among others, was that such reimbursement to parents of Catholic school children violated the "establishment of religion" clause of the First Amendment as embodied in the Fourteenth. The Court had clearly stated in 1940 that the Fourteenth Amendment embraced the "no establishment" principle,[10] but it had not had much occasion until now to determine what the principle implied. Now Justice Black announced a singularly uncompromising interpretation: the Amendment, he said, "means at least this: Neither a state nor the federal government can pass laws which . . . aid all religions . . . No tax in any amount, large or small can be levied to support any religious

9. 330 U.S. 1 (1947).
10. Cantwell v. Connecticut, 310 U.S. 296 (1940).

activities or institutions, whatever they may be called, or whatever form they may adopt to teach or practice religion."[11]

It would be hard to compose a more unqualified statement of the inhibition. No state aid to religion is permissible. However, Black continued, executing a 180-degree turnabout, this payment for bus fares is *not* aid to religion; it is a public welfare measure. Thus New Jersey has not breached the wall between church and state.

The opinion is a beautiful example of Justice Black's jurisprudence: the taste for absolutist pronouncements of constitutional doctrine; the tendency to think in labeled categories ("aid to religion," "public welfare legislation"); the assumption that the distinction between the categories is self-evident and needs no reasoned explication. And it took no great perception to see that government attempts to support religious education would thenceforth be on thin constitutional ice, that justiciable challenges to such attempts would be sympathetically met. Despite Everson's failure to win his case, the announced principle was so sweeping that religious schools could take small comfort from the decision.

Nevertheless, setting aside its pledges to the future, *Everson* did reject the claim of personal right, and it therefore leaves intact the impression that the Court in the 1946 term was generally less hospitable to such claims than the Stone Court had been. It is tempting to speculate about the reasons for this development, but confident answers are hard to come by. The most obvious possible explanation is simply change of personnel. Jackson had returned from his year in Nuremberg and Vinson had replaced Stone. These two did vote against the claimant in all but a few cases, and Vinson's tendency does contrast with Stone's, who had stood near the middle in his Court's alignments. The new Chief did at once help tip the balance toward the "right," and this is itself noteworthy, for appointees usually take a more centrist position in their first years.

The trouble with personnel changes as an explanation of the 1946 term is that the Court in the following term produced a

11. 330 U.S. 1, 15–16.

quite impressively libertarian record with no changes in personnel. Jackson and Vinson continued to stand, with Reed and Burton, among those most often opposing civil liberties claims; but all members of the Court, including Jackson and Vinson, voted for the claimants far more often than in the term before. Why? Perhaps external factors were affecting the judicial outlook. In the 1946 term the criticism that came to a head after the Jackson-Black dispute was still reverberating, and this may have brought on a temporary access of modesty among those who were sensitive to such stimuli. Perhaps the fortuities of litigation account for some of the contrast. The Court decided no race relations cases in the 1946 term; in the 1947 term there were seven, all decided for the claimant. If those seven had come up in the term before, they would probably have been similarly decided; for this is the one field in which the Vinson Court seldom wavered from its predecessor's path.

Whatever the explanation, the fact remains that the 1946 term Court did shift perceptibly toward a less libertarian and more modest position, and the further fact is that this 1946 term fairly well foreshadowed the general record of the Vinson Court in the personal rights field. After the brief renascence of the 1947 term, it became apparent that the journey toward a new jurisprudence of civil liberties had slowed down.

But the journey had not come to a halt. Just as the libertarian, activist tendency of the Stone Court had been qualified by lingering doubts and hesitations, so the Vinson Court's passive tendency was qualified by contrary impulses. There had been periods in the past when the Supreme Court seemed to recoil from a previously assumed task of judicial supervision. From 1906 to 1934, for example, the Court at intervals bowed to regulatory legislation, generating periodic hopes—or fears—that the judicial commitment to constitutional laissez-faire had wasted away. But the judges, as the event showed, had never really abandoned the commitment on their own claim to enforce it in ripe instances. Neither did the judges of the Vinson Court surrender the commitment to build from the Bill of Rights and the Fourteenth Amendment a judicially enforceable "modern creed of political morals." Their dedication to that task was moderated in these years, but it never fully broke down.

This subtle and complex fabric of Court attitudes in the Vinson period is illustrated even in the cases involving freedom of expression and related rights like freedom of association. In these decisions, of course, the shadow of the Red Menace bulked largest; and they are chiefly responsible for allegations that the Court of these years failed to defend democratic ideals.

The Court did in this area fall short of fulfilling the brave implied promises of the early 1940's; it did water down the clear and present danger doctrine; it did display an extreme deference to the other branches of government when words like "communism," "disloyalty," or "subversion," words that were being used with increasing frequency, were involved. Winston Churchill delivered his historic iron curtain speech at Fulton, Missouri, in March 1946; it was, if not an announcement of, at least a summons to the "cold war." America, somewhat grudgingly but unmistakably, shouldered this new assignment. But the external cold war was expensive, irritating, and indefinite in duration. Many who on the whole supported it also deplored the train of events that had led to it; and the setbacks that occurred as the contest ran its course shocked them deeply. They were tempted to seek explanations and fix blame, and the most beguiling explanation was that America had been misled and was still being misled by subversives in or out of government.

The idea was attractive partly because it was simple and offered a domestic escape from the frustrating complexities of foreign affairs. Eugene Dennis or Alger Hiss could be jailed; Joseph Stalin and Mao Tse-tung could not be reached at all. It was also attractive because it contained a modicum of plausibility. There *were* Communists in America, albeit not many; and a few had found their way into labor unions and the public service. No nation in a shooting war had ever knowingly tolerated active enemies within. A cold war was something new in American experience. Should a nation involved in such a conflict be governed by the conventions of peacetime, or those of wartime? For some, including Supreme Court judges like Black and Douglas, the answer was "peacetime."

But for many others, including a solid majority of Congress, it seemed more logical, and safer, to assume that a war is a war. We need not agree with such an artless tautology in order to recognize its appeal in the novel and perplexing circumstances the country then faced.

The Supreme Court was not much better prepared than America to grapple with these circumstances. The opinions of Holmes and Brandeis in cases of the 1920's had been elevated to the status of scriptural authority by certain free expression decisions of the Stone Court. But the Holmes-Brandeis doctrines had been composed at a time when the Red Menace was a purely imaginary bugaboo. The decisions of the early 1940's had applied them to comparatively trivial exertions of state authority. Now the bugaboo was given a color of reality by its linkage with the second greatest military power on earth, and nuclear weapons raised the idea of national danger to a new dimension. The measures and policies now presented for judicial scrutiny had been adopted in the name of the nation's security and were sometimes backed, not merely by random state officials, but by the majesty of the federal government and—or so it seemed—a great preponderance of public opinion. We have seen that the Stone Court never decisively settled the question of the modern judicial role. We have seen that Court falter when it confronted the hazardous issue of war-related inroads on freedom. It is not surprising that the Vinson Court faltered, too, before its own most daunting problem.

The natural difficulties of coping with that problem in the context of the period were great enough. But in many instances they were further complicated by the fact that the measures in question struck at subversion obliquely, rather than head-on. The Holmes-Brandeis opinions and the precedents laid down by the Hughes Court had chiefly concerned direct prohibition and criminal punishment of expression and association. The red-hunters of the post-war years had discovered other, more sophisticated, ways of harassing their quarry, and established doctrine provided little support for judicial review of such devices.

The Federal Loyalty Program, for example, surely impinged on freedom of expression and association; yet the old precedents weighed against any holding that would limit governmental power to set conditions for public employment. They suggested that a public job was not a right, but a privilege which the sovereign could grant or take away at will. It would seem to follow that no effective constitutional claim could be lodged by a man dismissed for his expressed opinions or his associations.

With only this doctrinal heritage to draw on, the Court was in a weak position to stand firm against the excesses of public service loyalty measures in the cold war period. And it did not stand firm. The Loyalty Program survived the Vinson years virtually unscathed by judicial hands. Although an employee could be fired if it was found that there were "reasonable grounds for belief in (his) disloyalty" and, shifting the burden of proof, after April 1951 if there were merely "reasonable doubt" of his loyalty, these vague standards were never challenged by the Court. To aid the loyalty boards in their inquiries the Attorney General maintained a list of allegedly subversive organizations; certain issues presented by this listing did reach the Court in 1951, and the complaint of a listed organization was sustained.[12] But the majority were so divided in their reasons for the judgment that there was no official opinion of the Court, and the decisive vote of Justice Burton rested on an extremely narrow and technical ground that enabled him to evade all constitutional issues. This case, coming some four years after the Loyalty Program had been established, was the only one the Court actually decided on this controversial matter.

It is one of the many attributes of our celebrated federal system that popular causes need not always be surrendered to the monopoly of the federal establishment; that fifty state governments—not to mention innumerable local units—can often join in a game that promises personal satisfaction, notoriety, and votes. As might be expected, then, many of the states zestfully enlisted in the "cold civil war" against disloyalty. A favorite device of the state-level warriors was a loyalty oath, prescribed as a condition for public employment. The Vinson Court duly upheld a municipal ordinance requiring city employees to swear that they had never advocated violent overthrow of government nor belonged to an or-

12. Joint Anti-Fascist Refugee Com. v. McGrath, 341 U.S. 123 (1951).

ganization that advocated it or, specifically, to the Communist party.[13] It also sustained unanimously a Maryland law requiring candidates for public office to make affidavit that they were not subversive persons.[14]

Perhaps the most elaborate state program for banishing subversives from the public payroll was New York's Feinberg Law, authorizing the Board of Regents to compile a list of organizations advocating violent overthrow and making membership in a listed group prima facie evidence for disqualifying public school employees. The law thus raised the grave issue of academic freedom and compounded the gravity by ratifying the principle of "guilt by association." This law, too, passed the Vinson Court's mild scrutiny. In *Adler* v. *Board of Education*,[15] Mr. Justice Minton for the majority brushed aside counsel's sophisticated objections to guilt by association with his own version of bluff, layman's common sense: "One's associates, past and present . . . may properly be considered in determining fitness and loyalty. From time immemorial, one's reputation has been determined in part by the company he keeps."[16] His opinion is pervaded with the idea that since public employment is a "privilege," no denial of right can be claimed when conditions are imposed on it. If teachers do not like the conditions, he says, "they are at liberty to retain their beliefs and associations and go elsewhere . . . [a teacher's] freedom of choice between membership in the organization and employment in the school system might be limited, but not his freedom of speech and assembly except in the remote sense that limitation is inherent in any choice."[17] Analysis of the last sentence would be a nice problem to set for a logician.

Another promising subject for the red-hunters' attentions was the alien or, more generally, the foreign-born. Measures aimed at the subversive immigrant were likely to be popular, for they appealed not only to current fears of communism but also to chronic American xenophobia. Moreover, like laws relating to public em-

13. Garner v. Board of Public Works, 341 U.S. 716 (1951).
14. Gerende v. Board of Supervisors, 341 U.S. 56 (1951).
15. 342 U.S. 485 (1952).
16. *Ibid.* at 493.
17. *Ibid.* at 492–493.

ployees, they enjoyed the further advantage that their precedents left roomy openings for action. Congressional authority to exclude aliens had been regarded as plenary, and it had been held without much ambiguity that the power to expel them was equally "absolute and unqualified." Although, as Justice Brandeis later said, deportation may result in the loss of "all that makes life worth living," it was not technically a punishment and did not raise a due process issue. It presented, the Court had sometimes intimated, a political question; and the judiciary could not properly express an opinion about the "wisdom, the policy, or the justice" of exclusionary measures. As for "denaturalization" (which might of course be followed by deportation), the background was more equivocal. Naturalized citizens stood on equal footing with citizens so long as the title to citizenship was not questioned. But it had been held that a certificate of citizenship once granted could be taken away if later found to be fraudulently or illegally obtained. And although the Stone Court had ruled that the evidence in such a proceeding must be "clear, unequivocal and convincing," it had not expressly said that this was a *constitutional* requirement.

The vulnerability of the alien-born radical made him, therefore, an inviting target in periods of stress. In the red scare after World War I a large number of aliens were deported (four hundred forty-six in 1921, the peak year) and a great many more were arrested or otherwise harassed (about ten thousand were arrested in the Palmer raids on January 2 and 6, 1920). In the years of the Vinson Court the figures were not remotely comparable. During the year ending June 30, 1949, only four were deported for "subversive or anarchistic causes," and even though the total crept up as time went on it reached only thirty-seven by 1953. Nevertheless, congressmen and other enthusiasts throughout this period were urging sterner action, and some of the cases that were brought forced to the Court's attention the constitutional issues raised.

The judges handled them warily. In a couple of deportation cases they held that the Immigration Service had been too arbitrary;[18] but no allegation of subversion was involved, and in any

18. Kwong Hai Chew v. Colding, 344 U.S. 590 (1952); Wong Yang Sung v. McGrath, 339 U.S. 33 (1950).

event the decisions were based on statutory construction. There was no suggestion of a limit on Congress' power to deport whom it may please for whatever reason it may choose. Nor was there any suggestion by a majority of the Court in any of the cases that did involve a subversion charge. Deportation was upheld for three aliens who had once been Communists but were so no longer, the Court declaring that "in the present state of the world, it would be rash and irresponsible to reinterpret our fundamental law to deny or qualify the Government's power of deportation."[19] In another case, a five-judge majority ratified administrative detention without bail of aliens accused of communism, although it was conceded that the proceedings to prove the charge might drag on for years.[20] As Justice Jackson said, the practice of deporting aliens after long residence "bristles with severities." But he spoke for the Vinson Court when he also said, in *Harisiades,* that as far as Congress' substantive power is concerned, "we leave the law on the subject as we found it."[21]

The cases involving public employees and the alien-born underline a fact referred to more than once already in this study: the new constitutional jurisprudence of civil liberties was still at this stage relatively primitive and incomplete. A government armed with untrammeled powers to fire public servants and deport aliens could accomplish an impressive amount of suppression by such authority alone. Yet no accepted constitutional doctrines seemed to bar, or even qualify the exercise of those powers.

The Congress was not slow to recognize that such gaps in the constitutional barricades offered a legislative opportunity. The Smith Act, passed in 1940, provided criminal penalties for advocating or affiliating with an organization that advocated forceful overthrow of the government. But there was some apprehension that this kind of direct attack on expression and association might run afoul of judicial doctrines like the clear and present danger rule. As early as 1948, hearings were held on new legislation. The "Mundt-Nixon" bill gradually took shape in the next two years,

19. Harisiades v. Shaughnessy, 342 U.S. 580, 591 (1952).
20. Carlson v. Landon, 342 U.S. 524 (1952).
21. 342 U.S. 580, 587–588.

and it was ingeniously drafted so as to exploit constitutional openings and bypass likely roadblocks. Finally enacted as part of the McCarran bill in 1950, it singled out the areas where judicial doctrine was most rudimentary and permissive. The law imposed certain registration requirements on "Communist organizations" and their officers and members.

In 1928 the Court had squarely and unanimously upheld as reasonable a state law requiring members of oath-bound organizations (in this case the Ku Klux Klan) to register.[22] The constitutionality of various federal registration statutes had never been questioned seriously. Justice Black himself had offered the following defense of the Foreign Agents Registration Act of 1938:

As the House and Senate Committees considering the Bill said, it "does not in any way impair the right of freedom of speech, or of a free press, or other constitutional rights." Resting on the fundamental constitutional principle that our people, adequately informed, may be trusted to distinguish between the true and the false, the bill is intended to label information of a foreign origin so that hearers and readers may not be deceived by the belief that the information comes from a disinterested source. Such legislation implements rather than detracts from the prized freedoms guaranteed by the First Amendment.[23]

After registration under the McCarran Act, registrants were subjected to various burdens. Their mail had to carry identification showing that it was disseminated by a Communist organization. This provision rested on the idea, never so far explicitly repudiated by the Court, that the congressional postal power was plenary, Congress having the same virtually unlimited control over the flow of mail as it did over the flow of goods in interstate commerce. The related doctrine about public employment was reflected in a clause prohibiting a registrant from holding, or even seeking, a nonelective federal job. The vulnerability of the alien-born was not overlooked. Existing laws providing for exclusion and deportation of subversives were tightened and extended. Membership in a Communist organization or advocacy of "the ideas of

22. New York ex rel. Bryant v. Zimmerman, 278 U.S. 63 (1928).
23. Viereck v. United States, 318 U.S. 236, 251 (1943) (dissenting).

world communism" within five years after naturalization was made prima facie evidence to support denaturalization. Various other dusty corners were swept in search of governmental authority that might be exempt from judicial control. Registrants were forbidden to apply for passports; certain classes of registrants were barred from employment in defense plants. The whole law was grounded on the premise that precedent recognized few limits on arbitrary power in these areas. The premise was sound.

A similar situation existed with respect to still another form of governmental activity that began to expand and capture headlines in these years: the legislative investigation. Since the early days of the republic, Congress had employed its investigatory power to probe various matters and had claimed the right to compel testimony in pursuance of its inquiries. During the heyday of the New Deal such explorations, most of them aimed at businessmen, had multiplied; and the resulting publicity had been gratifying. It is not surprising that the searchlights were trained on new scapegoats when the political mood changed. In 1938 the House of Representatives established a temporary committee to investigate "un-American activities," and in 1945 this body achieved such immortality as Congress can bestow: it became a standing committee. As the cold war developed, the House investigators attracted increasing attention, and the Senate, as might be expected, contested their monopoly. A permanent Senate subcommittee to scrutinize the Executive Department sprang into being in 1946; and in 1950 a Subcommittee on Internal Security was created. Senator Joseph McCarthy did not attain chairmanship of one of these bodies until 1953, but long before that he had become the symbol of the whole movement—its sometimes punitive and ruthless methods, its success in catching the ear of the nation.

These inquiries inevitably raised issues of personal rights and public powers. "Unfriendly" witnesses were grilled about their activities, their associations, and their political convictions. "Friendly" witnesses were offered the forum of the committee room and the shield of legislative immunity for their accusations against groups and individuals. No one doubted that Congress had the right to such knowledge as an aid to lawmaking, but there was some question whether the Constitution empowered it to use the inquiry merely as a medium of public information or as a device to punish individuals by compulsory interrogation and exposure.

The judiciary was ill-armed to cope with these issues. To be sure, the leading decision of the nineteenth century had held that the investigatory power and its compulsory process could only be invoked for a "valid legislative purpose" and not to inflict punishment or inquire into private affairs.[24] But this doctrine provided small aid to those who hoped for a judicial check on committee excesses. In 1927 the Court ruled that a legislative purpose would be presumed if the subject investigated was "one on which legislation could be had."[25] This presumption rendered the limitation virtually meaningless, for under post-1937 interpretations of the necessary and proper clause the subjects about which Congress could not legislate at all were very few. There was surely no doubt that subversive activities could be reached by the legislative power. Nor did it seem possible to invoke doctrines like clear and present danger when the investigation impinged on speech and association, for the ostensible purpose of the inquiry was to determine whether such a danger existed. Congress could not be asked to prove before the investigation what the investigators were trying to find out.

Other potential judicial checks on inquisitorial zeal were also illusory or marginal. In theory it had been recognized that a witness was bound to answer only questions pertinent to the matter under inquiry; in practice the Court had never ruled that a question was impertinent. Indeed, it would be hard to contend that a query about subversive beliefs or associations was not relevant to the subject of subversion, whatever else might be thought about the propriety or necessity of the investigation. As for the Fifth Amendment's right against self-incrimination, though the Supreme Court had never squarely held it available to congressional witnesses, weighty opinion suggested that it might be successfully claimed. But this was at best a last-ditch defense, for in the public mind the harried victim incurred infamy merely by asserting it.

24. Kilbourn v. Thompson, 103 U.S. 168 (1881).
25. McGrain v. Daugherty, 273 U.S. 135 (1927).

Hence the term contemptuously popularized by Senator McCarthy: "Fifth-Amendment Communist."

Legal precedents were not very encouraging to judicial review in this field. But there was another reason for the Court to set its feet down with special care. The power of inquiry is an institutional prerogative that cuts across party lines and conflicting policy views. It is one thing for the judiciary to invalidate a law; the legislators who voted against or had small interest in it might well view such judicial action equably. It is another thing for a Court to challenge the investigating power in which all congressmen have at least a latent corporate interest. Congress is usually the Court's most dangerous potential critic. There is a strong case for avoiding the nerve endings that are most likely to exacerbate its critical spirit.

The Vinson Court did avoid this particular tender spot almost completely. In only one case involving congressional investigations and the subversion issue did the Court rule for the defendant.[26] And that decision was, in spite of the result, a rather pathetic illustration of the impotence of judicial review in this emotionally charged area. It rested on the almost frivolous ground that a man who had denied Communist affiliations during an inquiry could be convicted of perjury only if a quorum of the committee had been present at the time of the testimony. Even this gentle and largely meaningless restraint was qualified in a later decision, after the deaths of Murphy and Rutledge.[27]

Apart from that, the congressional red-hunters went their way unmolested. The Supreme Court simply denied certiorari in the cases presenting the most fundamental, substantive challenges to the investigatory power. Since those challenges—based primarily on the issue of a valid legislative purpose, on the First Amendment, and on due process—had been rejected by the lower courts, the effect of the refusal to review was to leave all convictions standing. The cases that were reviewed raised procedural points, but they led to the same result. Eugene Dennis, general secretary

26. Christoffel v. United States, 338 U.S. 84 (1949).
27. United States v. Bryan, 339 U.S. 323 (1950).

of the Communist party, attempted to challenge for cause in his contempt trial all prospective jurors who were federal employees. He advanced the rather persuasive argument that such jurors could not, in the present climate, render an impartial verdict in his case; but the Court upheld the conviction.[28] It also sustained against various procedural objections the contempt convictions of two officials of the Joint Anti-Fascist Refugee Committee.[29] And it held that a woman who had initially admitted being a Communist party officer had thus waived her privilege against self-incrimination and could not invoke it when she was later asked to name the person to whom she had given the party records.[30]

One might think that the investigators would have been satisfied with the near carte blanche conceded them by the Court in these cases. But in 1950 the Committee on Un-American Activities, irked by increasingly frequent claims of the privilege against self-incrimination, decided to challenge that single light inhibition on investigatory powers. The House, at the Committee's request, voted contempt proceedings against several silent witnesses. It can probably be assumed even in a case involving legislative investigation of subversion that the privilege would have been upheld, even during these tense years. But as it happened, no case presenting the flat issue reached the Court in the Vinson period, and the judicial record of tolerance in these matters remained, for the time being, unsullied.

While the red-hunting measures so far discussed unquestionably impinged on expression and association, they were not direct efforts to stop speaking or publication as such.[31] Their indirection was one reason for the Court's seeming helplessness in dealing with them. An unsettled question was how far the authorities could push this technique of "associating the speaking with some other factor which the state may regulate so as to bring the whole within official control."[32]

28. Dennis v. United States, 339 U.S. 162 (1950).
29. United States v. Bryan; United States v. Fleishman, 339 U.S. 349 (1950).
30. Rogers v. United States, 340 U.S. 367 (1951).
31. See Cox v. New Hampshire, 312 U.S. 569 (1947).
32. See Giboney v. Empire Storage and Ice Co., 336 U.S. 490 (1949).

The question was presented by the non-Communist affidavit provision of the Taft-Hartley Act (1947). This law restricted most of the privileges of the National Labor Relations Act to unions whose officers had sworn that they neither belonged to the Communist party nor believed in illegal overthrow of government. The natural effect was to require union officials to take the oath or lose their positions, for few unions could afford to dispense with the privileges. The constitutional justification offered was the congressional power to protect interstate commerce by preventing obstructions to its flow. In this instance the obstruction that concerned the lawmakers was the "political strike," a work stoppage fostered not for conventional union objectives but for extraneous political purposes. Communist union leaders were thought likely to promote such strikes, therefore pressure on unions to deny leadership to Communists would reduce the probability of these obstructions.

The conceptual difficulties presented by such oblique attacks on association and belief were no doubt partly responsible for the tortuosities of Chief Justice Vinson's opinion in *American Communications* v. *Douds*,[33] upholding the law. His argument seems to have been somewhat as follows. Congress could rationally find that Communist union officials were likely to foment political strikes, and the proscriptions of the statute are thus reasonably related to the end of preventing such strikes. Since there is no doubt of the power to legislate against obstructions to interstate commerce, this reasonable relation between end and means would ordinarily settle the matter. But here the problem is complicated by the fact that a measure designed to reduce obstructions also discourages the exercise of political rights protected by the First Amendment. That fact makes this in some sense a free speech case, though not the kind of free speech case to which the clear and present danger formula is applicable. In the Holmes-Brandeis decisions from which that formula derives, the statutes forbade the expression of Communist doctrine because of a concern that hearers might be persuaded to unlawful action. The concern of the present law is that men who subscribe to such doctrines will

33. 339 U.S. 382 (1950).

themselves engage in action: the fomenting of political strikes.

Diagrammatically the classic problem might be represented as follows:

Speech (including belief and association)
toward
Persuasion
toward
Action

The problem of *Douds* on the other hand is·

Speech (including belief and association)
toward
Action

In the first situation, countervailing discussion can enter at the second stage and thus avert action, unless the action is so imminent that discussion has no time to do its therapeutic work. The clear and present danger rule is directed to the question of whether that time-interval is adequate to allow for such discussion. But in the *Douds* situation there is no second stage, and a different constitutional question is presented.

The question for the Court in these circumstances is whether the "reasons advanced in support of the regulation" outweigh the dampening effect of the regulation on First Amendment rights. Has Congress deterred one evil—in this instance political strikes— at the cost of creating a greater evil, excessive curtailment of political freedoms? For the majority in *Douds* the answer is no. The reasons for the law (taking due account of judicial deference to congressional judgment) are substantial. The impact on liberty is moderate. Only a handful of persons are affected, and even they are not flatly prohibited from exercising their freedom, but only subjected to conditions. The constitutional scales thus tip in favor of the legislation.

This is, I think, a plausible interpretation of what the Chief Justice was laboring to say: laws inhibiting speech because of its supposed persuasion-potential would be judged by the clear and present danger test; laws aimed at the threat of action from those who profess certain doctrines would be judged by the more permissive "balancing test." But the opinion was so disorderly, so deficient in sequiturs, so criss-crossed with unfinished lines of analysis, that it is hard to be sure what was intended.

Whatever understandings or hopes Vinson may have had for the distinction he seemed to draw in *Douds,* it was not fated for long survival. Circumstances were already conspiring to make its life precarious; the chief of these circumstances was the fact that there now existed, at least conceptually speaking, not one clear and present danger doctrine, but two. The first might be called, without prejudice, the "elementary" formulation of the doctrine. This formulation rested upon, and was confined by, the bare language of the phrase itself. The judge confronted by a government action inhibiting speech was to inquire whether the proscribed expression created a clear and present danger of a serious evil. If the danger was remote either in likelihood or time, or if the threatened evil was trivial, the inhibition was unconstitutional. No further judicial questions were in order.

No one denied that these queries were often relevant to the task of judgment in the free speech field. But for some years powerful voices had been arguing that the criteria prescribed by the elementary formulation represented a part, not the whole, of that task. There are, it was said, other considerations that merit attention—factors not reckoned with by the explicit language of the test as ordinarily stated. Herbert Wechsler had offered a broader formulation:

Speech or assembly may be repressed or limited when it gives rise or is intended to give rise or may reasonably be thought by the legislature to give rise to a genuine danger of some substantive evil which the state has a right to prevent, unless the evil is not great enough to warrant the suppression of speech or assembly as a means to its prevention, or to say the same thing in a different way, unless the speech or assembly is justified by some end which outweighs the evil which it admittedly threatens.[34]

34. "Symposium on Civil Liberties," *American Law School Review,* 9:887 (1941).

In 1949 Paul Freund remarked:

The truth is that the clear-and-present-danger test is an oversimplified judgment unless it takes account also of a number of other factors: the relative seriousness of the danger in comparison with the value of the occasion for speech or political activity; the availability of more moderate controls than those which the state has imposed; and perhaps the specific intent with which the speech or activity was launched. No matter how rapidly we utter the phrase "clear and present danger" or how closely we hyphenate the words, they are not a substitute for the weighing of values.[35]

The most salient point about these restatements is that they add a whole new dimension to the judgment process described by the rhetoric of the elementary formulation. The judge is to ask not merely whether the danger is clear and present and the evil serious, but whether the value of the speech outweighs the threatened evil. In Freund's sentences there is the further implication that the relative repressiveness of the government control should also be entered in the balance. Meantime an even more potent spokesman, Mr. Justice Frankfurter, had been maintaining a steady drumfire of similar criticism against simplistic applications of the clear and present danger concept. "The phrase 'clear and present danger,'" he had said as early as 1941, "is merely a justification for curbing utterance where that is warranted by the substantive evil to be prevented."[36]

There is a degree of ambiguity in the way these critiques are presented. It is not altogether plain whether they are put forward as interpretations of the clear and present danger doctrine or as alternative analyses of the criteria by which free speech problems should be judged. No doubt the ambiguity was purposeful. The writers were saying: If the phraseology of the elementary clear and present danger test is thought to provide a comprehensive and sufficient definition of the judgment process in free speech cases, then it probably ought to be abandoned. So understood it leaves too many vital considerations out of account. But if the phraseology is thought of as merely shorthand for a value-weighing process which takes account of all relevant factors, *including*

35. *On Understanding the Supreme Court* 27 (1949).
36. Bridges v. California, 314 U.S. 252, 296 (1941) (dissenting).

those specifically suggested by these words—then very well. Short-hand terms are convenient so long as we understand them, and this one has a certain symbolic status in the modern liberal-judicial tradition.

Unfortunately for the Chief Justice's distinction in *Douds,* what the proponents of the broader formulation appeared to have in mind for speech problems in general was something very like the balancing process Vinson had reserved for a special category of such problems. And the clear and present danger doctrine he had set aside for application to another category was already half assimilated to the broader formulation at the time he wrote. In short, if the *Douds* "balancing process" A equals the "broader formulation" B, and the "broader formulation" B equals the "clear and present danger test" C, then A equals C. What becomes of the distinction?

There is a certain fitness in the fact that the decisive merger of clear and present danger and the balancing process was ac-complished by Judge Learned Hand—by almost universal assent the most distinguished living American judge. Hand's thinking about problems of free speech extended at least as far back as the *Masses* case in 1917.[37] Now, at the height of the "McCarthy era," he was called upon to think about them again.

In *Douds* the judiciary was still dealing with indirect and con-ditional curtailment of political rights, and the Chief Justice's special formula for such government action permitted the ma-jority to avoid the clear and present danger question. But the question could not be postponed indefinitely. The Smith Act of 1940 flatly prohibited (among other things) advocating forceful overthrow of government, organizing a group to advocate forceful overthrow, and conspiracy so to advocate or organize. In eight years only two prosecutions had been brought under this law; neither had involved the Communist party, and neither had resulted in an opinion of the Supreme Court on the validity of the act. In the climate of the late 1940's, however, it could hardly be expected that such a statutory bludgeon would be left to gather dust. In 1948 eleven top leaders of the party were convicted of

37. Masses Publishing Co. v. Patten, 244 Fed. 535 (S.D.N.Y.).

conspiracy to teach and advocate the forceful overthrow of the
national government and of conspiring to organize a group (the
party) to teach and advocate such overthrow. The language of
both law and indictment appeared to be aimed directly at the
threat of persuasion to a revolutionary attempt, not—or at least
not merely—at the threat of illegal action by the persuaders.
Here then the courts were brought face-to-face with the problem
bypassed in *Douds*: are these conspiracies to teach and advocate
punishable under the clear and present danger standard?

Judge Hand, speaking for the Court of Appeals in *United
States* v. *Dennis*,[38] answered "yes" and affirmed the conviction. His
gloss of the clear and present danger doctrine amounted to an
adoption of the broader formulation of the balancing test. The
phrase, he said, "has come to be used as a shorthand statement" for
utterances not protected by the First Amendment. "It is a way to
describe a penumbra of occasions, even the outskirts of which are
indefinable, but within which the courts . . . must find their way as
they can. In each case they must ask whether the gravity of the evil
discounted by its *improbability, justifies* such invasion of free
speech as is necessary to avoid the danger."[39]

The critical words in the last sentence are those italicized. The
requirement of a "present" danger is subordinated to the requirement of a "probable" one. Immediacy is still relevant but only
insofar as it may affect probability. Given the same probability, an
immediate danger and a danger remote in time are equally
menacing and equally preventable.

And just as presentness is reduced to an ingredient of probability
in the clear and present danger phrase, so the phrase itself is reduced to an ingredient in a broader calculus by the use of the term
"justifies." The judge estimates the probability and seriousness
("gravity") of the evil; he calculates the repression necessary to
prevent it; and he weighs the one against the other. This is the
"balancing test"; it is Freund's "weighing of values"; it is Frankfurter's "justification for curbing utterance where that is warranted"; it is, to draw from Wechsler again, "extended judicial re-

38. 183 F.2d 201 (C.C.A. 2d 1950).
39 Ibid. at 212 (italics added).

view in the fullest legislative sense of the competing values which the particular situation presents."[40]

The alchemy that was taking place here was subtle, and it seems to have left Chief Justice Vinson hopelessly baffled. In an opinion upholding the convictions for the Supreme Court (not strictly the Court opinion, for only three others joined it) he re-affirmed the *Douds* distinction between occasions for the balancing test and for the clear and present danger test; declared that *Dennis* was an occasion for the latter; then, mirabile dictu, accepted Hand's definition merging the one with the other.[41]

It does not greatly matter whether we call the alloy that emerged from all this the balancing test or the clear and present danger test, although the latter seems an infelicitous label for such a comprehensive judgment standard. Whatever name is chosen, the point is that the judicial inquiry becomes by this formulation as broad and as conjectural as the legislative process itself. The elementary clear and present danger test, whatever its faults, has some color of objectivity and definition about it. The likelihood of the danger and its imminence in time are not precise, litmus-paper questions. But it is at least arguable that they canalize the judgment process "within banks that keep it from overflowing." The judge's role conceived in these terms is not "unconfined and vagrant."

But the elaborate calculation of probabilities and weighing of values implied by Judge Hand's pregnant sentence is not so canalized. It suggests a roving commission to make judicial guesses on a wholesale basis. The absorption of "presentness" into "probability" eliminates one factor that might circumscribe a judge's freedom of choice. The word "justifies," with all that it imports, completes the liberation. The judge is now licensed to wander at large among the conditions and preferences that dictate public policy and to call the conclusion he reaches a judicial decision.

By one of those paradoxes not uncommon in constitutional history, however, emancipation becomes, simultaneously, abnegation: the freedom to decide becomes the compulsion to decide in

40. "Symposium on Civil Liberties," 887.
41. Dennis v. Uuited States, 341 U.S. 494 (1951).

only one way. When the full scope of the question was revealed by the broader formulation, the awesomeness of the task it implied was also revealed—at any rate when national laws related to national defense were involved. The concurring opinions of Justices Frankfurter and Jackson were pervaded with the idea that the judiciary was unqualified to second-guess Congress about such far-flung judgments and on issues of such magnitude. Justice Frankfurter went through the motions of balancing speech against "competing interests," but he gave such weight to the principle of deference to Congress that the scales could tip only one way. Justice Jackson's admirably lucid sentences accumulated into an opinion that was almost completely opaque. But one point was clear enough: he believed the Court incompetent to appraise the validity of such legislation. And on this point, at least, the two in effect spoke for the Court. The balancing test, now established as official doctrine, simply provided a metaphorical way of explaining why the judiciary felt unable to challenge, on substantive grounds, the congressional will to scotch the Red Menace.

With *Dennis* the pattern of acquiescence in the face of that issue was complete. Measures aimed at "subversion" among public employees and the alien-born had been upheld. Various conditional pains and penalties, such as registration requirements and restrictions on the use of the mails, appeared immune from judicial hindrance. Legislative red-hunting inquiries were unchecked. Now the supposed limits on governmental power to provide criminal punishments for subversive speech and association had apparently evaporated. The Vinson Court decided with opinion twenty-four cases involving in some sense the issue of red or pink activity. Seventeen ruled in favor of the government. Of the seven in which the individual claimant was upheld, several went off on such narrow or trivial grounds that they are hardly worth mentioning as judicial events. The Court of the early 1940's had raised freedom of expression to an exalted plane and nourished the impression that judicial review would defend unorthodoxy against all comers. When the pinch came in the cold war period, the defenses had crumbled. Governmental actions aimed at "subversion" or "disloyalty" surely posed the gravest constitutional problem of the Vinson years, yet judicial review seemed helpless to contribute to its solution.

Compliance was indeed the main theme of the Vinson Court's reaction to the cold civil war. But there was a subtheme as well. The judges would not—perhaps they felt they could not—strike down the repressive measures that the spirit of the times had spawned. What they could do on the other hand was some doctrinal housekeeping and remodeling that might prove useful in a later, more auspicious day. They could, that is, build into the very decisions upholding government action doctrines that looked in the other direction.

This contrapuntal tendency is most evident in some of the areas already touched and where old precedent supplied the frailest support for judicial intervention. In the cases involving public employment, for example, the Court with one exception rejected the immediate challenge to the laws. But when the opinions are examined carefully, it can be seen that the judges were simultaneously whittling away the traditional notion of public employment as a privilege to be granted or withheld on any terms whatever. This and the allied idea that loss of a government job is not punishment had made it hard to find a handle for judicial review in this field. Now the handle was brought into being by the state loyalty oath decisions wherein it gradually transpired that a state was restricted by the due process clause in dealing with its employees. While upholding the laws, the Court tucked into each opinion a few sentences pointing out that the particular oath requirement was not unreasonable.[42] The employee, said the Court, had only been asked to swear that he was not *knowingly* a member of a subversive organization. The implication was that an oath omitting this *scienter* element would be held unconstitutional as a denial of due process. It followed that a public employee had some claim to constitutional rights after all, despite the latitudinarian language of such decisions as *Adler*. Finally in *Wieman* v. *Updegraff*[43] the Court made this explicit, unanimously

42. See Garner v. Board of Public Works; Adler v. Board of Education; Gerende v. Board of Supervisors.

43. 344 U.S. 183 (1952).

invalidating a state oath that did not require *scienter* and thus offended due process. The opinion by Mr. Justice Clark referred disapprovingly to "the facile generalization that there is no constitutionally protected right to public employment . . . We need not pause to consider whether an abstract right to public employment exists. It is sufficient to say that constitutional protection does extend to the public servant whose exclusion is patently arbitrary or discriminating."[44]

The principle enunciated was an important one even though its practical application so far had been limited to the somewhat minor, procedural *scienter* issue. For if a public employee can claim one constitutional right, like due process, there is no logical basis for barring him from claiming others, like those included in the First Amendment. The "privilege doctrine" as applied to public employment was evidently dead, or at least in a late stage of terminal illness. This fact may have been obscured by the Vinson Court's generally acquiescent trends and by the clamor of the McCarthy era, but a fact it was.

A similar cross-current is detectable in the deportation field. It is true that the Court validated certain savagely harsh deportation measures, especially when charges of radical association were involved. But it is also true that a series of decisions in the Vinson period eroded the old doctrine that expulsion from the country— not being punishment—is simply immune from constitutional challenge. The Court edged up to this result with caution in a couple of decisions construing the statutes generously for aliens threatened by deportation: since deportation is a "drastic measure" and a "penalty," doubts about interpretation must be resolved in the individual's favor.[45] Then, in *Jordan* v. *De George*,[46] it moved a gingerly step farther, clearly acknowledging that the procedures imposing the penalty must meet due process standards, but holding that those standards had been met in this instance. There was no hint of a judicial disposition to challenge Congress' substantive control over the subject. For the moment only procedural pro-

44. *Ibid.* at 192.
45. Fong Haw Tan v. Phelan, 33 U.S. 6 (1948); Delgadillo v. Carmichael, 332 U.S. 388 (1947).
46. 341 U.S. 223 (1951).

tection for the deportee was suggested, and even that was rather niggardly. But the door to constitutional review had been quietly left ajar.

The "red scare" doubtless posed the most imposing constitutional problem of the Vinson period, but not all of the free expression cases that reached the Court entailed that febrile and ungovernable issue. For example, the happenstances of litigation brought before the judges a series of cases involving the relation between free expression and municipal convenience and order. In some the speech was religious in character, in others not. At all events, the Court drew no sharp distinction between the religious and the secular speaker in most of the cases; thus they can be considered together as raising the general question of unorthodox and often strident expression in public places versus local regulatory power.

Here was a subject unquestionably important in a society that took liberty for its slogan. Because of America's decentralized governmental system local officials, backed by local community sentiment, can persecute unorthodoxy almost at will unless they are themselves bound by constitutional standards. The repression achieved by these city Caesars may turn out to be substantial when their scattered efforts are added up. On the other hand, this is not a subject of such formidable dimension that the judiciary need be unduly diffident about intervening. It might well be thought that a tribunal too modest to curb the congressionally sponsored redhunt would nevertheless feel qualified to provide some guidelines. Indeed, the cases presenting the issue might have been seized upon as an opportunity to develop precepts that would help dissidents, the public, and officialdom to think straight about a hard, but not insuperable, problem.

If that opportunity did exist, the Vinson Court made very little of it. An old idea, classically expressed by the sainted Holmes, had been that "for the Legislature absolutely or conditionally to forbid public speaking in a highway or public park is no more an infringement of rights . . . than for an owner to forbid it in his house."[47] In 1897 the Supreme Court had unanimously endorsed

47. Commonwealth v. Davis, 162 Mass. 510, 511 (1895).

this view,[48] but a series of decisions beginning in 1937 undermined it badly. By the time the Vinson period dawned, it seemed fairly clear that a right did exist to use streets and parks for communicating ideas. Furthermore, although the city could enforce some regulations as to "time, place, and manner" of the communication, the fact that speech was involved would weigh heavily in determining the validity of a regulation. The city could *not* forbid the distribution of handbills in order to keep the streets clean; it could deny a parade permit in order to cope with traffic problems, but this limited authority must not be used to "deny or unwarrantedly abridge" rights of free expression.

With respect to such routine municipal housekeeping issues, the Vinson Court did nothing of much importance to alter inheritances from the recent past. Local prohibition of soundtrucks was upheld, at least when they emitted "loud and raucous" noises.[49] But it is hard in retrospect to take very seriously Justice Black's contention that this form of aural aggression should stand on the same constitutional level as ordinary speech, or his warning that the decision upholding the regulation makes a "dangerous" breach in our constitutional defenses. Justice Frankfurter chose these cases to mount an attack against the "preferred position" doctrine as applied to speech.[50] But his objection was not to the idea that speech merits special constitutional consideration, but to the implication that any law regulating it is "infected with presumptive invalidity." The distinction was important to him in defining his own understanding of the nature of jurisprudence, but it is doubtful that it mattered a great deal in determining how cases were decided. The rhetorical artillery fired off by himself and Black in these opinions may obscure the fact that there was, after all, a broad area of agreement on the Court about these housekeeping matters. This was evidenced by other decisions affirming, with little or no dissent, that an exercise of the licensing power must be based on clear standards and could not be used to discriminate against the expression of ideas. The Vinson Court did

48. Davis v. Massachusetts, 167 U.S. 43 (1897).
49. Kovacs v. Cooper, 336 U.S. 77 (1949).
50. *Ibid.* at 89.

not add anything to what had been said by earlier courts about these matters; but neither did it subtract anything of great significance.

Where the Vinson Court did fail its responsibilities was in cases presenting a far more serious form of the municipal convenience and order issue: the charge that speech threatens to create a breach of the peace. This would seem on its face to be the classic free speech situation for which such formulas as clear and present danger had been designed. But in three cases the situation was complicated by a factor that apparently puzzled the judicial will: the "hostile audience" problem. Can a speech or assembly, otherwise lawful, become unlawful because it evokes unlawful opposition? If so, then street bullies can shut off speech at a whim and enlist the law as their ally. But if not, street meetings may erupt into trials by battle.

The Court's first chance to shed light on this dilemma was badly fumbled. One Terminiello, a suspended Catholic priest, made a violently anti-Semitic speech to eight hundred enthusiastic listeners in a Chicago auditorium while an even larger crowd of angry adversaries howled outside the door and hurled stones through the windows. His conviction and fine (one hundred dollars) for disorderly conduct provided the Court with an opportunity for spelling out the criteria that should govern both participants and officials in such circumstances.[51] The conditions sounded explosive enough to warrant upholding the conviction yet drawing some guidelines for the future, just as Holmes had done in *Schenck* v. *United States* some thirty years before. Instead, Mr. Justice Douglas for a five-man majority seized upon a supposed error in the trial judge's jury instructions and voided the conviction on that ground, never reaching the issues that mattered. The case is perhaps the supreme illustration of how fixed resolve to reach an immediate "pro-libertarian" result can blind judges to more valuable long-run possibilities. Nor were the dissenters much more provident, for Frankfurter and Vinson simply castigated the majority for reaching a point that had not been advanced by the petitioner. Jackson's opinion, though decorated with phrases that

51. Terminiello v. Chicago, 337 U.S. 1 (1949).

captured newspaper headlines, offered no standards whatever for reconciling the claims of liberty and order.

What the "libertarian four" (Black, Douglas, Murphy, and Rutledge) had sacrificed in order to save Terminiello a hundred dollars became evident two years later in *Feiner* v. *New York*.[52] A college student with a taste for soapbox invective had made to a crowd of about eighty a speech berating various officials and groups, including President Truman ("a bum"), the Mayor of Syracuse ("a champagne-sipping bum") and the American Legion ("a Nazi Gestapo"). Some restiveness developed among spectators, and one man told a policeman: "If you don't get that son-of-a-bitch off, I'll go over and get him off myself." The officers then demanded that Feiner get down, and when he refused he was arrested for disorderly conduct and sentenced to jail for thirty days.

If *Terminiello* had addressed the central question, the Court in *Feiner* might have felt constrained in some degree by previously enunciated standards. Suppose, for example, that the earlier case had upheld the conviction on the ground that, owing to the size and emotions of the crowd, the police would have been hard put to forestall violence even if they had tried. In *Feiner* it might have been difficult to avoid the question whether the situation looked comparably menacing and whether the police had, or might have, made a good faith effort to restrain the crowd rather than the speaker.

But when *Feiner* was decided Murphy and Rutledge had died; the Korean War was in progress; and a new Court majority, speaking through Chief Justice Vinson, felt no compulsion to ask these questions, much less to overturn the conviction. The most regrettable thing is not that the conviction was upheld, but that it is hard to see in the Chief Justice's opinion a basis for ever curbing such suppressions. He simply accepted the judgment of the police, backed by the state courts, that a riot was imminent; and he offered no criteria for determining whether this was the case, or whether the police had done enough to quiet the crowd. The crowd's muttering and shoving sound like a far cry from the *Terminiello* im-

52. 340 U.S. 315 (1951).

broglio, and from the record it appears that the police did nothing at all to control the audience. As Justice Black said, dissenting, this decision seemed to mean that "as a practical matter, minority speakers can be silenced in any city."[53] Though in two other cases decided on the same day the Court disallowed previous restraints on unpopular orators,[54] *Feiner* suggested that the police have discretion to silence such a speaker "as soon as the customary hostility to his views develops."[55] Whether or not the Vinson Court intended to grant the police such arbitrary suppressive power, there was no stated ground for inferring anything different. In the context of the times "the problem of the hostile audience" had simply been shirked by the Court.

The Court's failure to deal fruitfully with the municipal order problem was a dereliction—less important, perhaps, but also less excusable than the failure to keep the red-hunt within bounds. It left a needless gap in our constitutional understandings about freedom of expression. But meanwhile those understandings were being amplified in another area, and this development carried vast implications for the future of civil liberties jurisprudence in the United States.

In the legal control of literary and artistic expression, as elsewhere, the state of constitutional law was surprisingly immature when the Vinson period began. The Supreme Court had never decided a case involving suppression of a book or other publication on grounds of "obscenity." Scattered dicta came close to suggesting that no constitutional objection to such a suppression could be entertained. In 1931 the Court had said that "the primary requirements of decency may be enforced against obscene publication";[56] a decade later it had listed "the lewd and obscene" among the classes of speech "punishment of which has never been thought to raise any Constitutional problem."[57] Potentially,

53. *Ibid.* at 328.
54. Kunz v. New York, 340 U.S. 290 (1951); Niemotko v. Maryland, 340 U.S. 268 (1951).
55. 340 U.S. 315, 329 (1951).
56. Near v. Minnesota, 283 U.S. 1 (1931).
57. Chaplinsky v. New Hampshire, 315 U.S. 568 (1942).

these invitations to Mrs. Grundy might be qualified by defining "the primary requirements of decency" and the words "lewd" and "obscene," but the Court had never offered such confining definitions. As for the movies, the situation was even stickier. Not only were they subject, as books were, to the charge of obscenity, but a case decided in 1915 had also strongly intimated that they were a medium of communication which inherently fell outside the constitutional guarantees of freedom of expression.[58] So far as the precedents went, films could presumably be suppressed not merely for obscenity, but for any reason that might commend itself to public authorities.

Plainly, there was a certain logical conflict between this state of affairs and the modern Court's major premise: that civil liberties, particularly freedom of expression, merit special protection. And even in the Vinson period, when the progressive impulse had in general somewhat flagged, the premise still exerted pressure to move doctrine forward, to erase incompatibilities.

The earliest hints of such movements came in 1948. For one thing, the Court casually remarked in a dictum: "We have no doubt that moving pictures, like newspapers and radio, are included in the press whose freedom is guaranteed by the First Amendment."[59] A second straw in the wind appeared when Edmund Wilson's novel *Memoirs of Hecate County* was found obscene by the New York courts. The case was appealed to the Supreme Court, which noted probable jurisdiction despite a contention by counsel for the state that an obscenity proceeding did not present a substantial constitutional issue. Though the Supreme Court ultimately affirmed the state holding by an equally divided vote,[60] some doubt had thus been cast on the idea that the obscenity label could be used by authorities without fear of constitutional review. Equally suggestive was *Winters* v. *New York*,[61] involving prosecution for possession, with intent to sell, of a lurid magazine called *Headquarters Detective*. The state court had construed the law as forbidding publications that "so massed their collection of

58. Mutual Film Corp. v. Industrial Cmm'n., 236 U.S. 230.
59. United States v. Paramount Pictures, Inc., 334 U.S. 131 (1948).
60. Doubleday & Co. v. New York, 335 U.S. 848 (1948).
61. 333 U.S. 507 (1948).

pictures and stories of bloodshed and lust as to become vehicles for inciting violent and depraved crimes against the person." The Supreme Court struck down the conviction on the ground that this standard was too vague.

At first glance it might appear that this decision merely enforced the procedural standard of definiteness that must be met by any criminal statute. But the Court approached the case as one involving rights "under procedural due process and freedom of speech or press." The idea seemed to be that vagueness was an especially serious vice in a law aimed at free expression, because unexceptionable speech may be muffled by ambiguous prohibitions. Mr. Justice Reed took occasion to answer an argument often heard and here advanced by counsel: that the constitutional safeguards of a free press extend only to exposition of ideas, not to publications designed to entertain. The distinction, he said, is "too elusive for the protection of that basic right." These vulgar magazines are "as much entitled to the protection of free speech as the best of literature."

These comparatively unspectacular judicial events suggested a portentous inference—that literature and the arts were at last to be brought within the constitutional palisades. In 1952 the inference became unmistakable. Under pressure from such forces as the Catholic War Veterans, the Holy Name Society, and the redoubtable Cardinal Spellman, New York denied an exhibitor's license to show an Italian film directed by Roberto Rossellini. Signor Rossellini had recently engaged in a much-publicized extramarital affair with actress Ingrid Bergman, and this doubtless helped to set the pressures going. But the stated ground for the denial was that the film was "sacrilegious." The Supreme Court unanimously reversed in *Burstyn Inc.* v. *Wilson.*[62] The fact that movies are produced for profit or that they may have a special influence on the young does not exclude them from the free speech guarantees, said Justice Clark. "Expression by means of motion picture is included within the free speech and free press guaranty of the First and Fourteenth Amendments."[63] Any curtailment of

62. 343 U.S. 495 (1952).
63. *Ibid.* at 502.

free expression must be justified by a societal need. When the curtailment takes the form of previous restraint by a board of censors the justification must be stronger, for this kind of control has been traditionally regarded as especially doubtful. When the standard the board employs is as broad and vague as the term "sacrilegious" the censor's range is almost unlimited, and the burden of justifying the curtailment is still greater. Society's interest in protecting the religious from distasteful views is far from sufficient to carry this cumulative burden.

It should be observed that the Court did not here condemn all previous restraint on movies. The priorness of inhibition and the breadth of the standard make the state action dubious; then, when the feebleness of the supposed justification is weighed, the scales tip against the law. Justice Clark suggested that movies might be subject to different and perhaps more stringent controls than some other forms of expression, and that a state could still prevent obscene films from being shown. The censor's job was circumscribed, not eliminated.

Nevertheless, the *Burstyn* decision, taken together with the 1948 cases mentioned earlier, did open up a spacious prospect in constitutional law. A few years earlier there had been ground for uncertainty whether entertaining or esthetic expression fell within the free speech guarantees, and also whether certain media of communication raised First Amendment questions. Those uncertainties were surely now settled. All media could claim some degree of constitutional protection; beauty, as well as truth, had become an acknowledged judicial concern. A gaping hole in civil liberties jurisprudence had been closed. To be sure, these departures produced for the judiciary, as is so often the case, more problems than they resolved. If the free speech guarantees extend to various media, then the Court is faced with the task of formulating the standards that apply to each. If artistic expression is constitutionally protected, then the judges must decide where the protection begins and ends. The Court had carved out a new task for itself. But it had carved out a new scope for constitutional freedom, too. And it is worth emphasizing that this advance was made in the face of strong localized opposition at the height of the

"McCarthyist" movement. Even in such times the logical impulsion of the major premise had overpowered judicial modesty.

Before appraising the Vinson Court's total performance in areas related to free expression, one more important doctrinal development must be taken into account: the interpretation of the constitutional prohibition against an "establishment of religion." The first significant Court pronouncement on this matter came in the 1946 term, in connection with a New Jersey plan to provide school-bus fares for children attending parochial schools. After waiting one hundred fifty-six years, the Court might have been thought ready to produce an interpretation that had been well deliberated; and the *Everson*[64] opinions were adorned with scholarly-looking footnotes that did suggest exhaustive judicial consideration. Unfortunately, few of these citations had much bearing on the critical question, which was: what *kind* of governmental connection with religion does the First Amendment (and therefore the Fourteenth) forbid? No one, on or off the Court, disputed that it forbade setting up a state church or aiding one religion in preference to another. Did it also forbid all forms of nonpreferential aid to religions in general? Justice Black in *Everson* declared that it did, resting his gloss chiefly on the assumption that James Madison and Thomas Jefferson so understood the Amendment and that the Amendment, passed by Congress in 1789, necessarily reflected their understanding. Both assumptions were at least debatable, and the footnoted sources did little to support them. Beyond that, a rigid prohibition of any state aid at all might invalidate a host of practices deeply engrained in American life—tax exemptions and police and fire protection for churches, chaplains in legislatures and in the armed forces, for example. There is no evidence that the judges had reflected about such implications when Black almost offhandedly endorsed the "no aid" principle. Nevertheless the dissenters, far from voicing reservations about the principle, castigated the majority for breaching it by permitting the bus fares to be reimbursed by the state.

Sometimes the actual holding in a Supreme Court decision may

64. Everson v. Board of Education, 330 U.S. 1 (1947).

obscure its more momentous implications. When the Supreme Court in 1925 repudiated the clear and present danger rule and ratified Benjamin Gitlow's conviction for criminal anarchy, the champions of civil liberty regarded the decision as a defeat. In retrospect it became clear that the defeat was more than offset by the statement in the majority opinion that speech and press do fall within the protections of the Fourteenth Amendment. So it was with *Everson.* Justice Black's characteristically sweeping interpretation of the "no establishment" prohibition was apparently accepted by the whole Court, and this commitment was of far more consequence than the holding that the bus fare reimbursement was permissible.

Those who either hoped or feared that *Everson* had opened the way to public support for religious education were due for an awakening; and it came quickly. Less than a year later the Court held unconstitutional a religious education program in the public schools of Champaign, Illinois.[65] Under the program, religious teachers were supplied by various denominations to conduct weekly classes in the public school buildings. This arrangement, said the Court, "falls squarely under the ban of the First Amendment (made applicable to the States by the Fourteenth) as we interpreted it in Everson v. Board of Education."[66] Because of the use of tax-supported buildings for the classes, and the use of compulsory public school machinery to provide pupils for the classes, the program doubly violates the principle of separation of church and state.

The *McCollum* decision excited a storm of denunciation from pietists, both lay and clerical, who charged the Court with hostility toward religion. It also stimulated a scholarly re-examination of the assumptions about the historical intent of the First Amendment. Mr. Justice Reed, the lone dissenter, began this round of challenges; it was carried forward by a procession of extrajudicial critics in the next four years. Though the Court position also found scholarly defenders, the critics at least raised some doubt that the

65. Illinois ex rel. McCollum v. Board of Education, 333 U.S. 203 (1948).
66. *Ibid.* at 210.

intent of the Amendment was as easy to fathom as had been initially assumed.

Because judicial opinion-writers are purposely inscrutable about their motives, it is hard to say confidently that this chorus of reproof influenced the new majority that assembled for the *Zorach* decision in 1952.[67] But the surmise is not implausible. The case involved a "released time" religious instruction program in New York. Since the instruction was offered in church-provided premises rather than public school buildings, the program avoided one of the constitutional snags that had been decisive in *McCollum*. On the other hand, students were released from school only on the condition that they attend the religious classes, and this clearly enlisted the compulsory public education laws in aid of religion. Such use of state power to provide pupils for religious instruction had been the second basis for the *McCollum* holding. Nevertheless, Justice Douglas declared for the Court that the New York arrangement was constitutionally permissible; yet he also declared, "We follow the *McCollum* case."

This singular result was accomplished by judicial sleight of hand that stirred indignation among the dissenters. Justice Douglas could find no evidence in the record that compulsion had actually taken place. But he slid adroitly over the fact that the record was barren on this point because the lower court had refused to admit evidence of coercion. Then, not content with thus dodging the *McCollum* doctrine, he proceeded to fudge it: though the separation of church and state must be "complete and unequivocal," this does not mean "that in every and all respects there shall be a separation of Church and state"; when the state "encourages" or "cooperates" in a program of religious teaching, it does not violate the Constitution.

Such a position, emphasizing distinctions of degree rather than the categorical "no aid" principle of *Everson-McCollum*, may represent, as Douglas said, "the common sense of the matter." Perhaps the Court had erred in espousing at the outset such an uncompromising standard. Indeed, it is a peculiarity of these cases

67. Zorach v. Clauson, 343 U.S. 306 (1952).

that judges like Frankfurter and Jackson, who ordinarily professed a self-restrained and relativist approach, here took a stand as absolutist as Justice Black's. But whatever might be said for the *Zorach* position in these terms, the plain fact is that it was not, as Douglas claimed, consistent with *McCollum*. The Court had veered. Two of the eight-man *McCollum* majority had died and been replaced; three (Douglas, Vinson, and Burton) had changed their minds. An eight to one decision pointing north had been succeeded by a six to three decision pointing, if not south, at least east. But since the *McCollum* doctrine had been nominally reaffirmed in *Zorach,* despite logical incompatibilities, the result was that *both* chartings could claim the stamp of constitutional authority. As often before in its history, the Court had modified a politically awkward course, not by repudiating it, but by creating an alternative. It remained to be seen which option the judges would choose when the next occasion for choice arose in this field.

Although the *Zorach* case does represent a judicial relaxation of initial rigidities, the net result of the "no establishment" cases was a substantial addition to constitutional law. The Vinson judges gave birth to more doctrine in this area than had been produced in the previous century and a half of Court history. And when other increments are taken into account, the total development of law relating to liberty of expression is not unimpressive. The Vinson Court's level of activism in such cases did fall numerically below the mark set by the Stone Court; and the failure of judicial nerve —or the revival of judicial modesty—is especially striking in decisions relating to the Red Menace. But even in those cases the libertarian impulse did not collapse altogether. Doctrinal bridge-building continued, though few of the bridges were completed and still fewer crossed. And with the move away from issues of "subversion" or "radicalism" the evidence of a still vital progressive impulse became stronger. In the municipal order cases the impulse is faltering, perhaps because these are seen as presenting the "subversion" problem in petto. But both the controversial church-state issue and the broad subject of literary and artistic expression are drawn for the first time within the judicial purview. These would be significant chapters in any constitutional history of America and they must be reckoned with in the balance sheet of the Vinson Court's civil liberties performance.

The modern Court's journey toward libertarian goals was abated but not halted in the free expression area during the Vinson period. In the cases involving criminal procedures, the tendency to apply brakes and even sometimes to reverse gears emerged more clearly; and here there were fewer of the counter-currents that complicated the free expression record. This is also the field where it seems easiest to trace the shifts and conflicts of viewpoint among individual judges, and the effect of "unexpected changes in the Court's composition and the contingencies in the appointment of successors."[68] The decisions were relatively numerous and the problems they raised relatively uniform. When a judge changed his mind—or refused to change it—the fact was tolerably evident. When Clark and Minton succeeded Murphy and Rutledge after the 1948 term, the impact on doctrine was hard to overlook.

The Vinson Court was plagued, as its predecessors had been, by the problem of coerced confessions and self-incrimination. Although the "*McNabb* rule" for federal courts—rejecting confessions obtained during unlawful detention—had provoked sharp criticisms in Congress and elsewhere, it was reconfirmed in 1948.[69] But the vote was five to four, Justice Frankfurter joining Black, Douglas, Murphy, and Rutledge to tip the balance. In 1943, when the rule was established, only Justice Reed had dissented.

In state decisions involving confessions the votes of these same five judges produced results favorable to the accused during the early Vinson years. The Stone Court had broadened the scope of judicial review in confession cases, asking not merely whether coercion had actually occurred, but also whether police procedures in obtaining a confession offended "accepted notions of justice";[70] some of the judges had been uneasy about this extension from the first, yet while Murphy and Rutledge survived, this extension

68. United States v. Rabinowitz, 339 U.S. 56, 86 (1950) (Frankfurter dissenting).
69. Upshaw v. United States, 335 U.S. 410 (1948).
70. See pages 36–40 above.

survived as the *"Ashcraft-Malinski* rationale." When they died and were replaced by Clark and Minton the Court began to hedge, and the defendants in confession cases began to meet a less hospitable reception. The Vinson Court thereafter seldom even granted certiorari in such cases from state courts. And when it did, the language of the opinions (usually rejecting the claims of the accused) suggested a tendency to turn back toward the pre-*Ashcraft* standard—that is, to concentrate on the question whether the confession was in fact voluntary even though police practices might have been questionable. The trend was not unequivocal. A physical third degree, or even the threat of one, would still automatically invalidate a confession, whatever the actual effect on the will of the defendant. But the possibility of psychological coercion was viewed more leniently than in *Ashcraft;* and the Court flatly refused to apply to the states the federal rule against confessions obtained during illegal detention.[71] The attitude of the majority after 1948 was fairly well represented by Justice Jackson, who had often voiced worries about the handicaps society already faced in enforcing the criminal law and was indisposed to augment them by tightening the standards for interrogation. Justices Black and Douglas of course usually felt otherwise. But they found support in these years only from Justice Frankfurter, who—interestingly enough—seemed to have developed an increased tenderness for the rights of the accused in confession cases since his dissent in *Ashcraft.*

These patterns of division were intriguingly altered when the Vinson Court turned to another procedural issue, search and seizure; again, the passing of Murphy and Rutledge was decisive in the net result. In the curious mood that seemed to grip the Court during the 1946 term, a five-judge majority sanctioned an extraordinarily wide-ranging warrantless search by federal officers.[72] For some reason Justices Black and Douglas, who supported the holding, were less concerned about the rights of the defendant in this field than in the confession cases. On the other hand, Justice Jackson, who filed an uncompromising dissent,

71. Gallegos v. Nebraska, 342 U.S. 55 (1951).
72. Harris v. United States, 331 U.S. 145 (1947).

seemed here less worried about increasing society's handicaps. A year later Justice Douglas (but not Black) changed his mind; and the Court in *Trupiano* v. *United States*[73] executed a virtual about-face, again by a five to four vote. Revenue agents who had been observing the operation of an illegal still for some weeks finally raided the barn where the still was maintained, arrested the operator, and seized the equipment. Although *Harris* had ratified warrantless search and seizure of objects well concealed, the Court now held that even objects in plain view could not be seized if there had been time enough to obtain a search warrant. The arrest of the operator was valid without a warrant, for he had been observed in the act of lawbreaking. But the emergency conditions that validate an arrest in such circumstances did not apply to the seizure of the still, which was in no danger of disappearing before a warrant could be obtained.

For the moment, the rule seemed to be the strict one Jackson had urged in his *Harris* dissent: a search and seizure without warrant as an incident to a valid arrest is limited to objects in immediate physical control of the arrested person. But as constitutional time is reckoned, the moment was brief. Some nineteen months after *Trupiano* the Court, now unencumbered by Murphy and Rutledge, again reversed its field, in *United States* v. *Rabinowitz*.[74] Bearing an arrest warrant but not a search warrant, officers had arrested a postage stamp forger and ransacked the one-room office where the arrest had taken place. Mr. Justice Minton, speaking for a five-man majority, upheld the admission in evidence of the forged stamps which the searchers found, even though there had been ample time to procure a search warrant. *Trupiano,* insofar as it based the warrant requirement solely upon "the practicability of procuring it rather than upon the reasonableness of the search after a lawful arrest," was specifically overruled.

This is one of the fastest reversals recorded in constitutional history, and it seems about as solid an example as one could ask of a switch traceable to personnel changes. Moreover, it promulgated some novel and dubious constitutional theory, for it

73. 334 U.S. 699 (1948).
74. 339 U.S. 56 (1950).

suggested that a warrantless search is valid if a reviewing court finds it retrospectively "reasonable." The purpose of the Fourth Amendment, argued Frankfurter in dissent, is to protect privacy by assuring that a judicial officer will decide *before* arrest whether there is probable cause for search and seizure.

The upshot of the judicial zigzag—from *Harris* to *Trupiano* and back again—was a regression in federal court standards. With respect to state court cases and the search and seizure problem the record is different, for the Court had never held that unreasonable search by state officers was constitutionally forbidden. But these cases do provide an egregious illustration of the Vinson Court's reluctance to chart new advances in the law of criminal procedure. And again enigmatic variations in the alignments of the judges were revealed.

In *Wolf* v. *Colorado*[75] the Court confronted the claim that evidence obtained in an illegal search by state officers is barred by the Fourteenth Amendment from admission at a state trial. Justice Frankfurter, rejecting the claim for a six-man majority, produced one of those opinions that suggest the judge is "riding a horse in two directions at the same time" (compare Black in *Everson*). Said Frankfurter: "The security of one's privacy against arbitrary intrusion by the police—which is at the core of the Fourth Amendment—is basic to a free society. It is therefore implicit in 'the concept of ordered liberty' and as such enforceable against the States through the Due Process Clause." A state law affirmatively sanctioning police incursions into privacy would thus be unconstitutional. One might think that this settled the matter. But Frankfurter continued: "the ways of enforcing such a right raise problems of a different order"; it does not follow that the Weeks doctrine, requiring exclusion of arbitrarily obtained evidence in federal courts, necessarily applies to the states; many civilized jurisdictions, while respecting the right to privacy, do not treat the exclusion rule as an essential ingredient of the right. The opinion went on: a majority of the states themselves reject the rule, and so do ten jurisdictions within the United Kingdom and the British Commonwealth; in view of this and in view of the

75. 338 U.S. 25 (1949).

fact that there are other ways to enforce the right (for example, private action for damages against offending officers and "the internal discipline of the police, under the eyes of an alert public opinion") we cannot say that the states are constitutionally bound to exclude evidence obtained by unreasonable search and seizure.

This was a strange opinion to come from a judge who had written so eloquently on behalf of the right to privacy in federal court cases. As the dissenters said, Frankfurter had in one breath proclaimed a new constitutional privilege against state action and in the next rejected the only means that might render the privilege effective. No doubt his commitment to the values of federalism partly explains the paradox: he sometimes expressed an almost Jeffersonian faith in the wisdom and efficacy of local democratic control. But one suspects that Frankfurter was also swayed by the knowledge that British jurisdictions had never embraced the exclusion rule; unlike Jefferson, he was an unabashed Anglophile. At any rate, he was joined here by Jackson, who had also acted grudgingly towards the right to privacy in federal cases; and by Black, whose views about search and seizure were always idiosyncratic. The Wolf rule (or nonrule—that illegally seized evidence is constitutionally admissible) was firmly established even before the death of Murphy and Rutledge as one of the Vinson Court's least edifying legacies to the future.

The Stone Court had bequeathed an equally dubious legacy of its own in cases involving the right to counsel in state courts: the doctrine of *Betts* v. *Brady*[76] that state failure to provide an indigent with a lawyer in a noncapital criminal case does not violate due process if the trial is judged fundamentally fair. After enunciating this principle, the Stone Court majority seems to have tried to forget it; but Justice Frankfurter restored it to visible life in that memorable first term of the Vinson Court.[77]

Subsequent decisions dispelled any lingering hopes that this "fair trial rule" might be moribund. Indeed, because *Betts* was never cited as authority during 1942–1946 and was frequently

76. 316 U.S. 455 (1942).
77. Foster v. Illinois, 332 U.S. 134 (1947).

so cited thereafter, the Vinson Court contribution was to endow the rule with greater vitality than it had ever enjoyed. This was reflected in the results of the cases. After *Betts,* the Stone Court never upheld a state denial of counsel. In the Vinson period the state was upheld in about half of the decided cases; that is, in half the cases denial of counsel was fair and in the remainder it was unfair. In the face of the reasonable criticism that this pattern provided ambiguous guidance to state prosecutors and judges, the Court washed its hands on the grounds that the due process clause could not be reduced to a mathematical formula.[78] Such lack of sympathy for the officials of other jurisdictions is perhaps understandable, whether or not it is justifiable.

But the Supreme Court's own oxen were not ungored. Requests for review of state criminal convictions were becoming so numerous that they greatly burdened the judicial time chart. Petitions under the *in forma pauperis* statute (which permits the poor to proceed without cost) totaled twenty-two in 1930. In the 1948 term there were four hundred fifty-five, most filed by prisoners. Almost half of all matters now coming before the Court were presented by prisoners asking for postconviction relief. There was nothing the Court could do to stem this deluge so long as the vague and unpredictable fair trial rule remained the standard of decision. Yet the majority seemed resigned to the rule.[79]

Although Justice Roberts had authored the *Betts* opinion, it was Justice Frankfurter who became in the 1940's the chief defender of the fair trial rule and of the uncertainty in the law which it exemplified. This is important, for Frankfurter's weight was often decisive in determining how the Vinson Court would turn on issues of criminal procedure. And he was, at least in that area, the most complex and least predictable of the Vinson judges. In the federal cases, to be sure, he was dependable enough. His vote swung the scales against weakening the McNabb rule, and he also consistently voted for the defendant in federal search and seizure cases. Anyone who contemplates his career, both before and after his appointment to the bench, will detect an

78. See Wolf v. Colorado, 338 U.S. 25 (1949).
79. See David Fellman, *The Defendant's Rights* (1958).

abiding repugnance toward procedural irregularity. Indeed, his pre-judicial reputation as a civil liberties zealot rested heavily on his preoccupation with such matters, notably in the Sacco-Vanzetti affair. Presumably he felt that the Supreme Court's supervisory role in relation to the federal judiciary warranted his indulging this bias when the doings of federal courts and police were called into question. It is perhaps worth remarking that some of the most brilliant opinions of his judicial life, for example, his dissents in *Harris* and *Rabinowitz,* were composed in these cases.

But when the behavior of state courts and police was being reviewed, his decisional agonies became acute, and his opinions lost much of their cogency. Here a neo-Brandeisian respect for local autonomy asserted itself; it was joined by a neo-Holmesian access of judicial "humility," a reluctance about infusing into the "vague contours" of the Constitution one's "merely personal and private notions."[80] These various impulses and restraints were perhaps further complicated by such secondary factors as his Anglophile tendency. The result was a bewildering series of votes which reveal no guiding principle unless indeterminacy can itself be called a principle.

In state confession cases of the Vinson period Frankfurter usually voted in favor of the defendant, but he never joined Douglas and Black in urging a flat rule against confessions obtained between arrest and arraignment. He preferred a case-by-case process of distinguishing between voluntary and coerced confessions through a "psychological judgment," the judges finding their way "as best they can from all the relevant evidence and light which they can bring to bear."[81] In state search and seizure cases, he seems to have adopted a clear self-denying ordinance, that is, the *Wolf* principle. But this position was clouded by his opinion for the Court in *Rochin* v. *California* (1952). At the moment of arrest the defendant had swallowed two capsules containing morphine; the police had forcibly pumped his stomach, extracted the capsules, and presented them in evidence at his

80. Rochin v. California, 342 U.S. 165, 170 (1952).
81. Haley v. Ohio, 332 U.S. 596, 603 (1948) (concurring).

trial for possession of narcotics. The evidence, said Justice Frankfurter, should have been excluded, but he had some trouble
explaining why. He implied that this was a coerced confession
case, but surely it would be regarded more appropriately as raising
a search and seizure question; and Wolf had held or seemed to
hold that the search and seizure method had no bearing on
admissibility of the evidence. But in *Rochin* Frankfurter declared
that the brutality of the police methods "shocks the conscience,"[82]
and that convictions brought about by such methods violate due
process.

The Wolf doctrine, whatever else might be said about it, had
at least the virtue of lucidity. Now it appeared that state judges
were consigned to a guessing contest, the prizes going to those
who could predict what would shock the conscience of five members of the Supreme Court. This was still another variation of the
oracular process that was represented by the fair trial rule in the
right to counsel cases and by "psychological judgment" in the
confession cases. As he cast the lots in this game of hazard, the
defendant won about fifty percent of the time. Frankfurter was,
after Murphy, Rutledge, Douglas, and Black, the most "libertarian" of the Vinson judges, even in the state criminal procedure
field. But at the same time he did more than any other judge to
give "fair ground for the belief that the Law is the expression of
chance."[83]

It was this chanciness and subjectivity of the fair trial rule and
its kindred that Justice Black so eloquently deplored. Like Frankfurter, he had come to political maturity in a period when pro-
gressives were criticizing the Court for imposing its personal
standard of "reasonableness" on legislatures in the economic
realm; like Frankfurter he had learned to deprecate such judicial
immodesty. The ghost of the Court's earlier, and in their view
fundamentally incorrect, attempt to substitute its own policies for
those of the legislatures was never far from their thoughts. Neither
wished to inherit the mantle of those turn-of-the-century judicial

82. 342 U.S. 165, 168 (1952)
83. United States *v.* Rabinowitz, 339 U.S. 56, 86 (1950) (Frankfurter
dissenting)

policy-makers whom Justice Holmes had denounced in his classic *Lochner* v. *New York* dissent.[84]

Nor were they very far apart in their belief in the importance of procedural fair play. But otherwise the cast of their minds was different. Frankfurter's was, both by instinct and by conviction, what we loosely call pragmatic. He questioned the possibility of certitude; incertitude did not trouble him. He was in a way fact-obsessed. He looked for differences between the circumstances of one case and those of another, and differences of degree were to him not incidental but decisive. Simple and universal rules were not only impossible, but distasteful.

Black, on the other hand, was a natural universalist. His mind reached out for the categorical, self-executing rule, rather than subtle distinctions of degree. And his need for such reassuring axioms was so great that he was able to find them, where others could not, in the unmistakable commands of the constitutional text. He remained unperturbed, for example, when Charles Fairman's historical research cast grave doubts on the proposition that the Fourteenth Amendment had been intended by its framers to "incorporate" the Bill of Rights—as Black had contended in his *Adamson* dissent. To accept these doubts would be to renounce the certitude his temperament required. So he continued to read the historical record in the light of his personal revelation.

This Frankfurter-Black conflict about the nature of the constitutional process was real, and it cuts across such classifications as that between libertarians and nonlibertarians. This is not to say, of course, that the two men were "value-free." Few mortals are that. It is not mere happenstance that Black's quest for certainty reached libertarian results rather more frequently than did Frankfurter's pragmatic weighing of complexities. No doubt those results were sometimes marginally warped by the instinctive sympathies of the two men. But they both belonged to that comparatively rare breed who take such matters as approach and method seriously and can be influenced by them. The quality is illustrated by the bizarre "Electric Chair case."[85] Louisiana had

84. 198 U.S. 45, 75 (1905).
85. Louisiana ex rel. Francis v. Resweber, 329 U.S. 459 (1947).

tried to electrocute a convicted murderer; but, though some elec-
trical current had apparently reached his body, the equipment had
proved defective and the prisoner survived. Now the state proposed to try again, but the defendant argued that this "second
execution" would violate due process. It is hard to doubt that
Justice Frankfurter, a lifelong opponent of capital punishment,
or Justice Black, a notorious humanitarian, would have preferred
to rule for the prisoner. Yet Frankfurter could not persuade himself that carrying out the sentence would offend a principle of
justice "rooted in the traditions and conscience of our people."
And Black could not contend that the execution would amount to
either "double jeopardy" in the sense of the Fifth Amendment or
"cruel and unusual punishment" in the sense of the Eighth. Bound
by their conceptual commitments, they reached by different routes
the same personally repugnant result. The prisoner died on the
second try.

But Frankfurter and Black were unusual. In the votes of the
remaining judges of the Vinson Court a simpler pattern of division can be detected, based more clearly on fundamental leanings toward the claims of either society or the defendant. Among
those who tended to emphasize society's claims—Jackson, Clark,
Burton, Minton, and Reed—Jackson seems at first blush the most
difficult to classify in these terms. He did favor the defendant more
often than did the other four, and he was especially solicitous when
arbitrary search and seizure was charged against federal officers.
He did inveigh against those who recommended a policy-making
role for the judiciary. But for all his protestations he was at root
an advocate, not a dispassionate judge. His views of public policy
ran through his decisions, and those views were in general opposed
to "unnecessary expansion" of defendants' rights. And for the
others on his side of the bench in these matters the case is even
plainer.

The case is equally plain for Murphy, Rutledge, and Douglas
on the other side. The first two simply favored the defendant in
practically all decisions; Douglas lagged only a pace or two
behind. Murphy classically expressed the "result-oriented" outlook
of the trio when he said: "The law knows no finer hour than when

it cuts through formal concepts and transitory emotions to protect unpopular citizens against discrimination and persecution."[86]

It seems reasonable to conclude that both these wings of the Court were primarily swayed, not by technical legal compulsions nor by convictions about the nature of the judicial process, but by the different weights they assigned to "law and order" on the one hand or "defendants' rights" on the other. The net result of this weighing process on the criminal procedures record of the Vinson Court is easy enough to describe. Before Murphy and Rutledge died, a certain balance was maintained. Progressive tendencies in one area were paralleled by static tendencies in another, with Frankfurter usually casting the determinative vote for either option. After 1948, the last term for the two trusty libertarians, the balance swung decisively toward "law and order." Frankfurter now appeared more often as a dissenter against, rather than a spokesman for, the Court's dominant trend. There were no significant procedural advances for the remaining four terms of the Vinson Court; on the other hand, there were some signs of regression. These signs did not, indeed, suggest a headlong retreat. Even in the 1949–1952 terms, the Court favored the individual in some 35 percent of its criminal procedure decisions. But this is far below the 65 percent record of the Stone years, and the message to defendants and their lawyers was clear. They would still have their day in the Supreme Court. But they could no longer expect the hospitable and expansive welcome that had sometimes served their cause in the preceding decade. Constitutional development had always been more fitful and hesitant in this area than in the other major civil liberties areas that preoccupied the modern Court. But hesitancy had now become cessation. Progress, if that is the word, had reached at least a temporary stopping point in the criminal procedures field.

The Vinson Court's tendencies to slow down in the field of free expression and to pause and ever backtrack in the field of criminal procedures—these tendencies make it all the more striking that

86. On Justice Murphy see J. Woodford Howard, *Mr. Justice Murphy: A Political Biography* (1968).

the same judges in the same period determinedly pushed ahead
to erase a third major constitutional discordancy, legalized racial
discrimination. Here was a Court that seemed in many areas increasingly cautious about overreaching its authority and increasingly reluctant about further extending constitutional liberty. The
political weathervanes indicated a growing conservative humor in
the nation at large. The Truman appointees to the bench—Burton,
Vinson, Clark, and Minton—reflected this trend. However slippery the "conservative-liberal" distinction may be, it is hard to
imagine definitions that would not place these four, as a whole,
nearer the conservative side than the foursome they replaced.

But in the race relations field this Court's libertarian progress
did not slacken from the pace set by its predecessor. On the contrary, by most reckonings the rate of advance was accelerated. The
cardinal achievements of the Stone Court had been the decision
outlawing the "white primary" and the recognition in the *Screws*
case that Congress enjoyed under the Fourteenth Amendment
broad power to protect civil rights. These were noteworthy constitutional events. The Vinson Court not only expanded some of
these earlier precedents, it ploughed new furrows in important
areas theretofore underdeveloped: housing and education. And
not a single case directly involving a Negro's rights was decided
against the claimant.

In the judicial world as elsewhere, progress carries a price tag;
a court that makes headway is likely to make problems for itself
as well. The chief problems entailed in the Vinson Court's advance
against racial discrimination were two, one logical, the other
practical. Both were difficult; both were destined to torture the
judges and their critics for many years to come.

The first was the problem of "state action." The Stone Court
had begun to view more liberally than courts of the past the language which limits the restrictions of the Fourteenth and Fifteenth Amendments to states alone. A political party, formerly
deemed a purely private association, was seen as an instrumentality
of the state and thus forbidden to practice racial discrimination
A police official who broke state law was nevertheless a state
agent, thus punishable by federal statute passed under the author-

ity of the enforcement clauses of the two amendments. The Vinson Court, in its evident determination to strike at discrimination whenever opportunity offered, continued this expansive tendency to the point where the Constitution and its own precedents had sometimes to be wrenched rather painfully.

Racial segregation in housing was and is undoubtedly one of the most pernicious and solidly established affronts to the American ideal of equality before the law. Unlike such devices as the white primary or the Jim Crow law for public accommodations, it was not exclusively, or even primarily, a southern phenomenon. In fact, the maintenance of "black ghettos" in the cities was the north's substitute for the segregation laws of the south: legal prohibitions against racial mingling in public schools, playgrounds, and restaurants were not necessary if Negro residence was confined to certain city areas; geography and convenience could effectively insure that black and white kept their distance.

The existence of the ghettos depended of course on several factors, and some of them were of a kind that the judiciary alone could do little about. The Court could not erase the income disparities that helped maintain Harlem and Watts, nor did it seem possible at the time that it could on its own authority reach the real estate dealer or owner who refused to sell suburban property to "non-Caucasians." But when a policy of housing discrimination sought the aid of state law the Fourteenth Amendment became applicable: as early as 1917 the Court held contrary to due process a zoning ordinance forbidding occupancy by one race in areas predominantly inhabited by another. Such direct state assistance to segregation went too far, even at a time when the "separate but equal" doctrine was unchallenged. There was, however, a more subtle device for accomplishing the same result. Real property owners in a given area could agree in a "restrictive covenant" that they would not sell to Negroes. Such an agreement was regarded as the action of private individuals and thus immune from constitutional control. Moreover, state courts could enforce the covenants by restraining violation or by entertaining damage suits against violations. Although the Supreme Court had not directly ratified such judicial enforcement, a 1926 decision had strongly implied ratification,[87] and it was widely assumed that no objection under the Fourteenth Amendment would be sustained. The idea was that the state judiciary was not itself discriminating, but merely giving sanction to an admittedly legal private contract. Within the comfortable shelter of this doctrine, segregation in housing flourished undisturbed. The President's Committee on Civil Rights reported in 1947 that the amount of land covered by racial restriction in Chicago was as high as 80 percent and that, according to students of the subject, "virtually all new subdivisions are blanketed by these covenants."[88]

Forces were marshalling to unsettle this state of affairs. The postwar housing shortage made a system of restrictions that had always been aggravating seem intolerable, and Negroes were more and more emboldened to fight back. After a special conference to discuss strategies, the National Association for the Advancement of Colored People announced in 1945 that a determined campaign against restrictive covenants would be launched. Scholarly criticism of the prevailing constitutional doctrines began to mount; and although appellate courts continued to tolerate those doctrines, some premonitory judicial rumblings were heard. Justices Murphy and Rutledge dissented from the Supreme Court's denial of certiorari in a 1945 covenant case in which Judge Edgerton of the District of Columbia Court of Appeals had filed a powerful and influential dissent.[89] In light of these developments and the Vinson Court's growing receptivity to complaints against racial discrimination, it was foreseeable that the restrictive covenant device would face constitutional reexamination before long.

The occasion arrived in 1947, when the Supreme Court granted certiorari in four restrictive covenant cases, two involving states and two involving the District of Columbia.[90] An elaborate effort, largely planned and coordinated by the NAACP, was mounted to

87. Corrigan v. Buckley, 271 U.S. 323.
88. *To Secure These Rights*, 67–70 (1947).
89. Mays v. Burgess, 147 F.2d 869 (D.C. Cir.), cert. denied 395 U.S. 858 (1945).
90. Consolidated and decided as Shelley v. Kraemer, 334 U.S. 1 (1948); Hurd v. Hodge, 334 U.S. 24 (1948).

argue before the Court that covenants were judicially unenforce-able. Sociological data on the subject was assembled and circulated. No less than eighteen organizations filed amicus curiae briefs urging a decision favorable to the Negroes' cause. Most important of all, perhaps, the United States Department of Justice joined the array, presenting through Solicitor General Philip B. Perlman an anticovenant brief of its own. Against this formidable lineup the white property-owners could invoke the weight of precedent, but they were outmanned and outmaneuvered. In *Shelley* v. *Kraemer* the Court held unanimously that state courts were for-bidden by the Fourteenth Amendment to enforce restrictive covenants, in the companion case of *Hurd* v. *Hodge* that federal court enforcement was likewise forbidden by the 1866 Civil Rights Act and by "the public policy of the United States."

Of course the state cases presented the gravest problem to Mr. Chief Justice Vinson, who wrote the opinion for the Court. If state court enforcement was prohibited, it had to be for con-stitutional reasons; this meant that the judicial action must be interpreted as state action within the meaning of the Fourteenth Amendment. The Chief's argument may seem straightforward enough. To be sure, he said, the restrictive agreements do not in themselves breach the amendment; constitutionally speaking, two white persons are free to contract against sale to "non-Caucasians." But when the courts, who are agents of the state, enforce the covenant, the equal protection guarantee of the Fourteenth Amendment is violated. It is no defense to say that Negroes may equally covenant against the occupancy of whites. "Equal protec-tion of the laws is not achieved through indiscriminate imposition of inequalities."[91]

But the matter was not so simple as these neat propositions made it appear. Indeed, what a state judiciary does is admittedly "state action" in a sense; but is it the kind of state action that the Fourteenth Amendment forbids? The difficulty is suggested when we try to apply the principle of the opinion to other situations. Sup-pose a private property owner, admittedly biased against Negroes, calls on the police and the courts to exclude trespassing Negroes

91. Shelley v. Kraemer at 22.

from his premises. If these law enforcement agencies respond, are they not, under the Shelley doctrine, engaging in state action in support of discrimination? Yet if they are forbidden by the amendment to respond, does this not mean that the amendment is effectively limiting private choice? In short, as a later critic put it, "why is the enforcement of the private covenant a state discrimination rather than a legal recognition of the freedom of the individual?"[92] No answer to such questions can be found in the Chief Justice's opinion. Clearly the concept of state action had been extended, but no basis had been laid for determining where and how the limits of the extension could be drawn.

These cases involved suits to restrain Negroes from owning or occupying property covered by restrictive agreements. Defenders of the "Caucasians only" principle continued for a while to nourish the glimmering hope that courts could still constitutionally entertain damage suits brought by one party to a covenant against another party who broke it. In order to avoid an explicit departure from precedent, the Chief Justice in *Shelley* had reaffirmed that covenants between white owners are legal, though unenforceable against Negroes who purchase restricted property. The white covenant-breaker sued for damages was not himself being discriminated against on racial grounds, and there was a strong tradition that a defendant cannot assert in his own behalf the rights of someone else who is not before the court. But in 1953 Justice Minton held for the Supreme Court that circumstances warranted one of the rare exceptions to this rule. The white seller was permitted to set up the rights of hypothetical Negroes as defense against a damages action; this hurdle cleared, the Court had no difficulty in finding that the damages award would amount to unconstitutional racial discrimination by the state.[93]

In the same year—the last of the Vinson Court—the judges' willingness to stretch the state action doctrine was further illustrated in an election case.[94] The Jaybird Democratic Association,

92. Herbert Wechsler, "Toward Neutral Principles of Constitutional Law," *Harvard Law Review* 73:1 (1959) 29.
93. Barrows v. Jackson, 346 U.S. 249.
94. Terry v. Adams, 345 U.S. 461

whose membership was limited to whites, had for many years conducted a "pre-primary" in Fort Bend County, Texas. Winners of this election received the Jaybird endorsement in the regular Democratic primary, a certification that normally assured their victory. The Jaybirds had, apparently, devised a way to discriminate on racial grounds in the election process; yet their "unworthy scheme," as one judge called it, seemed beyond constitutional reach, for the Jaybirds were a private group and the state played no part in their electoral arrangements. The Supreme Court held that their all-white pre-primary constituted state action forbidden by the Fifteenth Amendment. Again the judges were forced to strain hard in order to attain this result, and again the logical implications of their decision raised ticklish questions. Justice Black appeared to suggest that the Fifteenth Amendment applied if the state *permitted* racial discrimination in any election, even though the state had no part in the election itself. This interpretation would represent a startling departure from received understandings. For a state to tolerate discrimination at any stage in the electoral process may well be immoral. But there is a difference between the toleration of a result and the perpetration of a result; and the restrictions of the Amendment had theretofore been applied only to the latter. Does the decision mean that no private political association can set up conditions for membership that could not be prescribed as conditions for enjoyment of the franchise in general elections? If so, the constitutional line between private and public would seem to be nearly obliterated, at least where the electoral process is involved.

The point is not that these attenuations of the state action doctrine were indefensible, or that these questions about the implications of the decisions were unanswerable, but that no adequate defenses or answers were supplied in the opinions of the Court. It was anomalous that legalized segregation in housing should persist in the face of the Fourteenth Amendment's guarantee of "equal protection of the laws," and that racial exclusion from the electoral process should be condoned despite the Fifteenth Amendment's command against discrimination on grounds of color. Certain legal scholars later undertook to provide a rationale that would accommodate the results of these cases to the "state action" concept, and to delineate more carefully and logically the distinction between what is private and what is not.[95] These efforts were often ingenious and at least partially persuasive. But they were in the nature of opinions that the Court might have composed if its members had been more willing to shoulder the task of reasoned explanation. Justice Minton's statement in the *Barrows* case that the situation was "unique," and Justice Black's statement in the Jaybird case that the amendment "clearly" does not apply to private clubs—these were not explanations, but assertions that called for explanations. In failing to answer the call, the Court lent substance to a charge heard more and more often in subsequent years: that in its eagerness to achieve unarguably moral results, it was shirking its responsibility to fashion a craftsmanlike structure of constitutional jurisprudence. In these decisions at any rate the impeachment is hard to refute.

The second great problem raised by the Vinson Court's crusade against racial discrimination was still more troublesome: does the judiciary, viewed realistically, have the power to alter patterns so deeply entrenched in the mores of the nation? Doubts on this score had been expressed long before in W. G. Sumner's aphorism that "stateways cannot change folkways"; and though Gunnar Myrdal had powerfully challenged this excuse for governmental passivity, the stubbornness of race prejudice was a fact of American life. And ever since Georgia had defied a Court ruling in 1793 the Court had lived with another fact, seldom acknowledged but nonetheless real—that its own "supremacy" depended on the acquiescence of the other branches of government and the people. Awareness of this fact helped support the pleas for "judicial modesty" that such judges as Frankfurter so often composed. Could the Court then, in view of all this, sustain the task of progressively enlarging Negro rights? Could it impose on the republic and the constituent states a moral standard that had been honored only in the breach for some three hundred years?

95. Louis Henkin, "Shelley v. Kraemer: Notes for a Revised Opinion," *University of Pennsylvania Law Review*, 110:473 (1962); Louis Pollak, "Racial Discrimination and Judicial Integrity: A Reply to Professor Wechsler," *University of Pennsylvania Law Review*, 108:1 (1959).

The problem was posed to some degree by all of the race relations decisions examined here so far. But the mandate for integration at the voting booth, though potentially dangerous to the cause of white supremacy, seems to have provoked southern tempers only moderately. And the restrictive covenant decisions met a similar reception. Rumblings were heard, but no real tempest was generated. Presumably segregationists realized that extralegal (and even illegal) factors could still operate to forestall the menace of black political power asserting itself in the south or of urban ghetto-dwellers invading the suburbs of the north.

The threat of desegregation of the public schools was a different thing. Integrated polling places bring together adults of two races in an impersonal relationship at long intervals. Integrated schools mix black and white youth in a continuous and much more intimate situation. Moreover, public schools are at least formally run by governmental bodies (school boards); and their administration is thus subject, again at least in formal terms, to judicial control—as the distribution of real estate is not. Perhaps for these reasons, and no doubt for others, a policy of school desegregation can be seen as a very special attack on established folkways and can be calculated to stir up the spirit of resistance as almost nothing else could, presenting in the most acute form the question whether judicial fiat could prevail against the mores of a region.

The full dimensions and difficulties of that question could only be revealed as the next two decades of constitutional history ran their course. But there is ample reason to believe that it was already recognized by the Vinson judges as an issue that would gravely test judicial capacity and will.

No case involving school segregation had been decided by the Supreme Court since 1938. Although application of the separate but equal doctrine to education had never been squarely ratified by the Supreme Court (*Plessy* v. *Ferguson,* usually cited as authority for the doctrine, was concerned with transportation[96]), lawyers and lawmakers generally assumed that separate public schools were constitutionally permissible so long as the facilities

96. Cf. Gong Lum v. Rice, 275 U.S. 78 (1921).

provided for Negroes were not substantially inferior. Now Negro claimants began to press for their rights to equality in education, and to present more insistently the question whether segregation is under any circumstances compatible with the Fourteenth Amendment. This new development, encouraged and supported by the NAACP, focused to begin with on graduate schools of the southern and border states.

The Vinson Court, faced by these growing demands, adhered to and ultimately strengthened the equality requirement, but displayed no great eagerness to reconsider the separate but equal doctrine head-on. In the 1947 term it ordered Oklahoma to provide legal education to a Negro applicant "as soon as ... for applicants of any other group."[97] But it declined to decide whether the equality standard could be met by establishing a separate Negro law school and admitting the would-be student, Mrs. Ada Fisher. Only Justice Rutledge was at this point willing to confront the issue and to argue that such a school, created overnight, would be incapable of offering Mrs. Fisher a legal education equal to that provided by the well-established state university.

By 1950 the Court as a whole was ready to embrace that argument and carry it an important step further. When a Negro, Herman Sweatt, demanded admission to the University of Texas Law School, the state rejected the demand but offered the applicant admission to a separate school boasting four part-time professors but virtually no library and no accreditation. He refused this princely opportunity and continued to press his original request. Before the case of *Sweatt* v. *Painter*[98] reached the Supreme Court the state made a more serious effort to meet the need of its Negro citizens for legal education, opening at Texas State University for Negroes a law school with a library, a faculty of its own, various other facilities, and a prospect of accreditation.

Neither of these segregated educational arrangements, said the Court, meets the standard of equal protection of the laws. The Negro schools are not comparable to the University of Texas Law School in objective facilities such as size of faculty and variety of

97. Sipuel v. Board of Regents, 332 U.S. 631 (1948).
98. 339 U.S. 629 (1950).

courses, nor, "what is more important . . . [in] those qualities which are incapable of objective measurement" such as reputation, traditions, and prestige. A law school which excludes whites and which thus denies its students contact with the most numerous and influential segment of the population cannot claim that its students will have an equal chance to succeed in the "intensely practical" profession they have chosen. Sweatt must be admitted to the University of Texas Law School.

The Court's emphasis here on intangible factors in the measurement of educational equality meant, at the very least, that no segregated professional or graduate school could now pass constitutional muster. But the implications of the *Sweatt* decision could easily be traced much farther than that. The college one goes to is surely also related to the "intensely practical" business of making a living. So is the high school. In fact, it would be hard to argue that any public school which isolates its students from interaction with the dominant class in the population is providing them with an equal opportunity to make their way in the economic world. *Sweatt* can thus be seen as containing, potentially, a repudiation of the separate but equal doctrine as applied to education. But the potentiality was not developed in the Court opinion. The Chief Justice explicitly refused to re-examine the *Plessy* precedent and confined the holding to the facts of the case. The judicial expedition against the color bar was moving forward, but the judges were not yet ready to ordain its legal abolition.

They contrived to temporize for the remaining years of the Vinson Court. In *Sweatt,* one hundred eighty-eight professors of law filed a brief urging that *Plessy* be overthrown; pressure of this sort mounted in the early 1950's. The scene of litigation shifted from the halls of higher education to secondary and primary schools. Four cases from states and one from the District of Columbia made their way to the Supreme Court by various routes. In all of them Negro students were seeking entrance to segregated white schools; in all it was argued that segregation per se meant inequality. Few expected that the Court would return a flat "no" to this proposition when the time for an answer came; yet to accept the proposition might present the naked question of the Court versus the white south. In December 1952 the Court heard argument on the cases, and the world waited for the decision throughout the remainder of the term. But in June 1953 it was told that the wait would be extended: the cases would be re-argued in October. Counsel were asked to address such questions as the intent of the Fourteenth Amendment's framers concerning segregated schools, and the methods of enforcement available to the Court if segregation were held unconstitutional. It is a fair inference that such a holding was seriously considered. But it was also evident that the judges recognized the practical difficulties of implementing the new constitutional policy in a reluctant region. When Chief Justice Vinson died on September 8, 1953, these great issues were all still pending.[99]

There is of course no warrant to criticize the Vinson Court for prolonging this period of preliminary consideration. The judges were preparing, we now know, to stake out the boldest claims to judicial governance in legal history. Prudence dictated that such a momentous step should be taken only with "deliberate speed." It is worth emphasizing that the judges appear to have seen the need for prudence as clearly as we, with hindsight, can see it. They must have known—they had good reason to know—that when these five cases were decided, a new and perilous era in the history of judicial review would begin.

There is some validity in the generalization, cited earlier, that the Supreme Court was in the Vinson period an institution of "dwindling significance in American life." Comparing the record of these years to the Stone Court's performance and, even more, taking into account some of the Stone Court's promissory rhetoric, the sense of a letdown is unmistakable. The earlier judges had threatened a greater degree of judicial control, especially in the free expression area, than their successors were willing to impose. Individuals appealing to the Court for redress of grievances against an overbearing government were now losing more cases than they

99. They are of course the cases subsequently decided by the Warren Court as Brown v. Board of Education, 347 U.S. 483 (1954), and Bolling v. Sharpe, 347 U.S. 497 (1954).

won. The creative trends of 1941–1946 had slackened and in some areas even halted. America itself was experiencing the letdown that so often follows a war. The Vinson Court reflected this mood, and shared it.

The self-doubts and hesitations that had sometimes surfaced in the Stone period were now more frequent and more marked. Justice Frankfurter's entreaties for judicial humility, usually heard as the voice of a minority in the past, now came closer to representing the dominant outlook of the Court. But in fact there was no clearly dominant outlook toward the great modern question of the Court's role in relation to civil liberties. That question remained in the category of unfinished business during the Vinson years. Justice Jackson, who had once spoken bravely about acting "not by authority of our competence, but by force of our commissions," now seemed a good deal less confident that their commissions charged the judges to defend unorthodoxy against the minions of repression. But neither he nor the majority of his colleagues were very plain about what they *were* charged to do in that area and in others involving civil freedoms. Less, on the whole, than the Stone Court did is a fairly accurate but not entirely satisfying answer.

The truth is that the judges were still groping with a modern version of a paradox almost as old as the Constitution itself. At least since the time of John Marshall, the Court had been performing two functions. One was the function of supreme moral preceptor for the nation; to an important extent the judiciary had articulated the principles of political ethics to which the republic was supposed to subscribe and had claimed to be the final authority in defining those principles. The other was the function of wise and prudent governor; because judicial review could affect large issues of public policy, and because the "confidence of the people is the ultimate reliance of the Court as an institution,"[100] the judges felt bound sometimes to reckon with the problems that beset all governors—the "felt necessities of the time,"[101] the tolerance-level

100. Felix Frankfurter, "The Supreme Court in the Mirror of the Justices," *University of Pennsylvania Law Review*, 105:796 (1957).
101. Oliver Wendell Holmes, Jr., *The Common Law* 1–2 (1881).

of the governed. The difficulty was that the two functions were not always compatible. The tendency of the moralist is to follow his premises toward their natural conclusions; the practical governor is inclined to seek halfway houses, to count costs, and to husband power.

Probably no agency that wields governmental authority does or can, confine itself entirely to one of these functions or the other. The most dedicated would-be Moses will recognize some realistic constraints; the canniest political trimmer will not be wholly insensitive to the compulsions of principle. As for the judiciary, in the Stone-Vinson years the two functions, and the urges they fostered, hung in a fairly close balance. The premise—that the constitutional freedom of Americans should be enlarged—pressed steadily for realization; but it often collided with and was qualified by considerations of prudence, moderation, even expediency. Neither the Stone Court nor the Vinson Court made a distinct choice in favor of either of these concepts of judicial duty. That indecision about role is one of the measures of their similarity. But the Stone Court leaned more toward libertarian activism and the Vinson Court more toward a policy of "prudent" self-restraint. And that is a measure of their difference.

The Vinson Court's reluctance to carry the premise forward at the 1941–1946 pace has been illustrated above. The campaign against domestic subversion, stimulated and symbolized by the McCarthyist movement, encountered no significant judicial check. Federal and state red-hunters harried their suspects among public employees, among the foreign-born, and among the general citizenry, and the Court stood aside. The clear and present danger doctrine was obligingly altered to save sedition laws from serious constitutional scrutiny. With respect to freedom of political expression, the Vinson Court backed quite a distance from the standard that had been implied (though never, it is true, squarely implemented) by the opinions of its predecessor.

This retreat involved the public policy issue that excited, or was thought to excite, the angriest public sentiments of the moment; and the Vinson Court's diffidence about subversion was analogous to the Stone Court's attitude toward war-related freedoms. Memories of 1937 had not completely faded, and the burnt child can be expected to avoid the hottest part of the political fire. But this hardly suffices as explanation for the concomitant withdrawal in the area of criminal procedures. And yet the withdrawal there was more pronounced and less qualified than in any other major area. It went so far, as seen earlier, that Justice Frankfurter, the prophet of judicial self-restraint, found reason to cast his vote against too much of a good thing. Perhaps the phenomenon is best explained by a factor that of course plays some part in all these judicial trends: the sequence of deaths, retirements, and appointments. Vinson, Clark, and Minton were simply more sympathetic to "the war against crime" than Stone, Rutledge, and Murphy.

There are other scattered examples of the Vinson Court's tendency to reject or defer demands that the range of constitutional liberty be consolidated and extended. The doctrine of *Thornhill* v. *Alabama*[102]—that labor picketing is protected by the free speech guarantees—was diluted to such an extent that the precedent was rendered nearly meaningless.[103] When Judge Medina held Harry Sacher in contempt for his conduct as counsel during the *Dennis* trial, the Supreme Court first denied certiorari, then granted it on limited grounds and upheld the contempt judgment.[104] The question of a court's power to punish those who publicly comment on pending criminal cases was raised again in new circumstances, but the Court refused to review it.[105] In these last two cases Justice Frankfurter filed powerful dissents, urging his brethren to join in protecting the fair administration of justice.

One line of cases not considered in this chapter merits special attention as exemplifying the Vinson Court's unwillingness to move boldly forward in certain areas importantly related to civil liberties. These cases presented the question of whether "malapportionment" of electoral districts is constitutionally challenge-

---

102. 310 U.S. 88 (1940).
103. Giboney v. Empire Storage and Ice Co., 336 U.S. 490 (1949); Hughes v. Superior Court, 339 U.S. 460 (1950); International Brotherhood of Teamsters Unions v. Hanke, 339 U.S. 470 (1950); Local 262, Building Service Employees Union v. Gazzam, 339 U.S. 532 (1950).
104. Sacher v. United States, 343 U.S. 1 (1952).
105. Maryland v. Baltimore Radio Show, 338 U.S. 912 (1950).

able. Judicial tradition on the subject was ambiguous. On one
hand the modern Court's legacy included the doctrine of "political
questions": certain matters, mostly having to do with the structure
and organization of other branches of government, are not justiciable by the federal courts. The idea was that the judicial process
was inappropriate for devising satisfactory standards to govern
such matters; and there was also a strong implication that these
questions were often too "high" for court determination. On the
other hand, the Supreme Court of the early 1930's had assumed
jurisdiction in several cases presenting challenges to apportionment and districting arrangements.[106] Even more recently the
Stone Court had undertaken, in the *Classic* and the white primary
decisions, to protect the franchise against state denial. Now it faced
the argument that unless political districts were equal in population, the right to vote was being unconstitutionally abridged. If,
for example, there is one legislative representative for each of two
districts, and the population of the second district is twice that of
the first, then the citizen of the second is underrepresented and a
victim of arbitrary discrimination. Whatever may be the ultimate
validity of such logic, it was widely accepted at the time. The
literature of political science almost universally condemned the
injustice of malapportionment and blamed it for the rurally ori-
ented backwardness of our political system.

Here, it might be thought, was a wrong ripe for correction by a
bench that was formulating "a modern creed of political morals"
for America. Yet the Vinson Court steadily declined to shoulder
the assignment. In the interval after Stone's death but before
Vinson's appointment, it was presented with the case of *Colegrove*
v. *Green*,[107] in which qualified voters of Illinois attacked the
state's congressional districting system. In spite of the fact that
Illinois's largest district was more than eight times as populous as
its smallest, the appellants' claim was rejected. Justice Frankfurter
declared that the determination of congressional district lines was
a question "of a peculiarly political nature and therefore not meet

106. Smiley v. Holm, 285 U.S. 355 (1932); Wood v. Broom, 287 U.S. 1
(1932).
107. 328 U.S. 549 (1946).

for judicial determination." He went on: "To sustain this action would cut very deep into the very being of Congress. Courts ought not to enter this political thicket."[108]

The case was decided by a bench of only seven judges, and Frankfurter spoke only for himself and two others. Justice Rutledge concurred separately, assuming arguendo that such matters were justiciable but contending that the particular cause was so delicate that the Court ought, for discretion's sake, to dismiss for "want of equity." Because three dissenting judges (Black, Douglas, and Murphy) clearly maintained that districting questions were within the Court's power to adjudicate, Frankfurter's contrary position was supported only by a minority, and the *Colegrove* precedent hardly seemed a solid one. Nevertheless, the Vinson Court thereafter, in a series of per curiam rulings, denied claims arising from various maldistributions of electoral power[109]—including both an Illinois law making it hard for third parties to win a place on the presidential ballot and the Georgia "county-unit" system that handicapped the more populous counties in primary elections. There is room for argument whether the Court formally stamped all such claims as presenting "political questions," though Justice Frankfurter seems to have so interpreted the rulings. But there is no doubt that the judges, for one reason or another, refrained from entering the thicket Frankfurter had warned them against. The Vinson Court's record in this field is accurately summarized by a terse sentence explaining the Georgia decision: "Federal courts consistently refuse to exercise their equity powers in cases posing political issues arising from a state's geographical distribution of electoral strength among its political subdivisions."[110]

The districting cases further confirm the fact that the Vinson Court suffered from a crisis of confidence about the desirability and feasibility of steadily increased "libertarian activism." No observer of the times could overlook these signals that judicial assuredness

108. *Ibid.* at 552, 556.
109. See Martin Shapiro, *Law and Politics In the Supreme Court* 196 (1964).
110. South v. Peters, 339 U.S. 276 (1950).

had faltered. The political climate, the changes in personnel, the Frankfurterian preachments about self-restraint had combined to retard doctrinal progress. And the signals were not overlooked. Comment about the Court in the Stone period had emphasized, either with praise or with misgivings, the judicial tendency to extend constitutional guarantees. Now the emphasis of commentary fell heavily on the Court's acquiescent spirit. The Vinson period was widely regarded as a static one, a time in which the judiciary had not liberalized the freedoms guaranteed by the Constitution and had sustained drastic relaxations of procedural safeguards.

This was, and to an extent still is, the main theme of conventional wisdom about the Vinson Court's record. Like much conventional wisdom, it contains a substantial quantity of truth. But recognition of this should not cause one to overlook another, in some ways more interesting, truth: in spite of the postwar climate, in spite of the accession of new and "less libertarian" judges, in spite of the revival of judicial modesty the Vinson Court did beget a surprising amount of constitutional law. The judges had not surrendered their claim to provide moral precepts for the nation; and they were still inclined to press that claim in selected but important areas.

Even in matters related to the Red Menace there were affirmative developments that must be weighed against the general trend toward passivity. The recognition that constitutional questions can be raised by measures governing public employment, and by deportation procedures, are two such developments. Although the review conceded was, for the time being, only procedural (and very sparingly applied at that), the implications were substantial for anyone who remembered how often in the past decisions about procedure had led the way to doctrines of substantive limitation. Similar premonitory hints were detectable in *United States* v. *Rumely*,[111] which went off on a point of statutory construction, but not before the Court had declared that the congressional investigation could raise "doubts of constitutionality in view of the prohibitions of the First Amendment." Still more noteworthy were the decisions bringing artistic and literary expression within the

111. 345 U.S. 41 (1953).

reach of constitutional guarantees and those applying the "no establishment" clause limits to the states. And most impressive of all were the advances against racial discrimination.

Perhaps the most spectacular reminder that judicial review retained vitality was offered in the Steel Seizure decision,[112] involving no less an issue than the "inherent" power of the president of the United States. In order to avert a strike in the steel industry while the Korean War was in progress, President Truman had ordered his Secretary of Commerce to seize most of the nation's steel mills. The President invoked in justification of this order "the aggregate of his constitutional powers" as Chief Executive and Commander in Chief. Although the complainants against this action were not individuals but giant corporations, the claim of an executive right to act without legislative authorization raised great questions pertaining to civil liberties, and the judges doubtless saw it in those terms. Nevertheless, the temptation must have been strong to leave this awesome controversy to the potent forces already embroiled in it: the President, Congress, the steel owners, and the labor unions. Although there were ample procedural grounds for evading the issue of the order's validity, the Court went to the substantive merits and held that the order could not stand. It thus deliberately chose to pronounce on the constitutional question that had been left undetermined in one hundred sixty-three years of judicial history. A Court that plunged so boldly into the caldron of political strife to reach a constitutional question of such magnitude can hardly be thought of as a tribunal immobilized by a sense of humility.

The death of the Chief Justice on September 8, 1953, brought the Vinson Court to its official end. The seven years of his incumbency had been a hard and frustrating time for both Court and nation. During the Stone period the judiciary had sometimes floundered in the unmapped problems posed by its relatively novel civil liberties assignment. But the ill wind of the war had transmitted a certain progressive dynamism to many institutions of American life, and the Court had captured some of it. The postwar period, on the other hand, uncovered contradictions and bitter-

112. Youngstown Sheet and Tube Co. v. Sawyer, 343 U.S. 579 (1952).

ness and the threat of political reaction. Uncertainties about what the judiciary ought to do, or could do, were compounded by these circumstances. The growth of modern constitutional law slowed down.

Yet the power of a premise should not be underrated, and the Vinson Court never abandoned the premise embraced by its predecessor. Somehow the civil liberties commitment survived the vicissitudes of those years, to become one of the "givens" of judgehood —as laissez-faire had been a given for a judge who sat on the Court in the 1890's. A Frankfurter might urge judicial modesty; the new Truman appointees might listen more sympathetically than Murphy and Rutledge did to society's claims against the individual. But none of them abjured the basic idea that underlay the history of the modern Court. And, accepting that idea, they continued to be animated by it. It pressed against their misgivings about judicial capacity and their bias toward public authority. It competed with their awareness that the national mood was unreceptive to libertarian judicial ventures; and it produced, despite that awareness, such remarkable constitutional breakthroughs as the church-state cases, the censorship cases, the Negro education cases, and the Steel Seizure case. The Vinson Court disappointed those who hoped that the judiciary would singlehandedly lead America to a libertarian Promised Land. The Court did not shake off the doubts about its role that had been bequeathed to it by the Stone Court; in fact, those doubts deepened. But it maintained the essential continuity of modern constitutional law. It kept the light of freedom alive through a dark hour in the country's history; that light could now be passed on to the care of its successor.

IV THE EARLY WARREN COURT

The notes to Chapter IV, "The Early Warren Court," and Chapter V, "The Later Warren Court," remain in the same form as when they appeared as notes to articles.

THE SUPREME COURT FINDS A ROLE*

[This article first appeared in the *Virginia Law Review*, 42, no. 5 (October 1956), 735–760.]

There was a time not so very long ago when certain standard conceptions of the Supreme Court's role in the American polity seemed fairly well articulated. On the one hand could be found those who subscribed, more or less whole-heartedly, to the amiable myths of our native jurisprudence—that the Constitution which the judges guard is immutable,[1] that the judicial function "does not include the power of amendment under the guise of interpretation,"[2] and that "courts are the mere instruments of the law, and can will nothing."[3] On the other hand were those who, taking the advice of Justice Holmes, had washed legal formulae in "cynical acid"[4] and had arrived at quite different evaluations—that "the Constitution is what the judges say it is"[5] and that the Supreme Court, far from willing nothing, can only be understood "as a definite participant in the formation of public policy."[6] This conflict between what might be called respectively the innocent and the initiated viewpoints simmered through the early decades of the twentieth century and came to a boil in the 1930's when the New Deal met the Old head on.

---

* Thanks are due Professor Samuel H. Beer of Harvard for suggestions concerning the theme of this paper.

1. See, for example, Taney, C. J., in Dred Scott v. Sanford, 60 U.S. (19 How.) 393, 426 (1857): the Constitution "speaks not only in the same words, but with the same meaning and intent with which it spoke when it came from the hands of its framers, and was voted on and adopted by the people of the United States. Any other rule of construction would abrogate the judicial character of this court, and make it the mere reflex of the popular opinion or passion of the day."

2. Sutherland, J., dissenting in West Coast Hotel Co. v. Parrish, 300 U.S. 379, 404 (1937).

3. Marshall, C. J., in Osborn v. Bank of the United States, 22 U.S. (9 Wheat.) 738, 866 (1824).

4. Holmes, *The Path of the Law*, 10 HARV. L. REV. 457, 462 (1897).

5. Chief Justice Hughes when Governor of New York, quoted in I PUSEY, CHARLES EVANS HUGHES 204 (1951).

6. Lerner, *The Supreme Court and the American Capitalism*, in 2 SELECTED ESSAYS ON CONSTITUTIONAL LAW, 154, 180 (1938).

The resulting battle is now remote enough in time to be called history, and, though it deserves a more thorough accounting than it has so far received, the task of providing such an account cannot detain us here. For present purposes, it is enough to note that the upshot was to shred the "innocent" view beyond any reasonable hope of mending. The idea of judges as self-determining human beings, rather than helpless tools of constitutional logic, became a nearly universal premise of American political thinking. Modern America was little dismayed when the late Mr. Justice Jackson declared that the answer to a grave constitutional question was based, not on the words of the organic law, but on judicial "prepossessions."[7] And if any still doubt that the notion of judges as willing, purposeful creatures has passed into the common coinage, they have only to read a page on the Warren Court in a *Time* of the summer of 1956,[8] which informs its millions of readers that the present Chief Justice "views his role as 'steering the law' rather than being steered by it." One wonders how the editors of this journal always know with such infallible assurance how presidents, senators, and chief justices view their roles; but that interesting question must be by-passed. The point is the almost matter-of-course acceptance of an evaluation that would have profoundly shocked an earlier generation.

When this percept—that the Court has will and purpose—is pressed to the uses of scholarly analysis it must be employed with due care. No sophisticated observer imagines that the Court is simply a free-wheeling superlegislature; he recognizes the half-truth in the description Brooks Adams and others once offered,[9] but he acknowledges that the "courtly" attributes of the institution seriously modify the analogy's validity.[10] Moreover, it must be conceded, as it always has been by students who know what they are talking about, that the Court's interests are never singular. In any period of the Supreme Court's history, in fact in any single

7. Illinois *ex rel.* McCollum v. Board of Educ., 333 U.S. 203, 238 (1948) (concurring opinion).
8. June 25, p. 15.
9. ADAMS, THE THEORY OF SOCIAL REVOLUTIONS 80 (1913); see Brandeis, J., dissenting in Burns Baking Co. v. Bryan, 264 U.S. 504, 534 (1924).
10. See CURTIS, LIONS UNDER THE THRONE c. 7 (1947).

term, it is possible to discern cross-currents that are incompatible with any uncompromising single-factor analysis, and the observer must be content to find a "trend," rather than an unvarying line of purpose. Finally, great caution is advisable in imputing wilfulness to an institution like the Supreme Court, partly because intent is an elusive concept when applied to judges as well as to litigants, and partly because the members of the Court are notoriously individuals, each of whom may well have his own inner reasons for doing what he does. The Court is not to be thought of as a sort of collective knight-errant who decides each day what maidens he will rescue, what wrongs he will right. The development of judicial purpose is a subtle process, and a simplistic interpretation would be not only unsubtle, but wrong.

Nevertheless, when these caveats have been duly entered, it is still useful to seek for the dominant factors, or "interests," that help determine the course of Supreme Court doctrine. Admitting that such a quest cannot explain all, it may explain much. For though the Court consists of individuals, they are individuals bound together by a broadly similar heritage; their training, both professional and general, is a common link; and most important of all they have shared the experience of living in America in the twentieth century. It would be strange indeed if a thread of common purpose could not be descried.

It is the suggestion of this paper that such a broad common purpose can be detected in the civil liberty decisions of the modern Supreme Court and is particularly well-illustrated by certain key decisions of the 1955 Term. But before proceeding to explore that suggestion more fully, it is necessary to establish a perspective on the basis of which the inquiry can begin.

One result of the increasingly realistic view of judicial power has been a widespread conviction that the Court in the early twentieth century marshalled to defend a particular economic dogma. In its soberer forms, this conviction fell short of the charge that the Court was composed of "representatives of a class—a tool of the money power."[11] But by the middle 1930's there were prob-

---

11. The words are those of Mr. Justice Holmes, quoted in LERNER, THE MIND AND FAITH OF JUSTICE HOLMES 388 (1954).

ably few informed observers who would have denied that the Court was heavily concerned with protecting the economic order which was popularly though inaccurately called laissez-faire. That order was, as A. M. Kales said in 1917, the "inarticulate major premise" which underlay the decisions of the modern Court, and he offered an impressive and on the whole friendly description of its outlines.[12] Max Lerner put it somewhat differently when he said that the Supreme Court "effects a nexus between our fundamental law and our fundamental economic institutions."[13] This formula was offered as a description of the Court throughout our history, and within the broad assignment there was room, the author felt, for "the humanistic individualism of Justice Holmes, and the social constructivism of Justice Brandeis" as well as "the absolute individualism of Justice Sutherland."[14] However, he left no doubt that he regarded the modern Court as predominantly concerned with protection of the property owner, and without pausing to argue the proprieties of this concern, we can probably agree that it existed. No account of the Supreme Court from 1890 to 1937 could be complete if it failed to take notice of the judicial "interest" in protecting the business community.[15]

But if the behavior of the Supreme Court in the 1890–1937 period can be partly explained on the basis of this interest, the explanation abruptly falters in the latter year. The Court's abdication of its function of economic supervision, announced in such decisions as *West Coast Hotel Co.* v. *Parrish*,[16] *NLRB* v. *Jones & Laughlin Steel Corp.*,[17] and *Steward Machine Co.* v. *Davis*,[18] left dangling not only a series of recent constitutional judgments, but also the interpretation of the Court as the defender of laissez-faire. In fact it is hard, when we view the Court since that time, to sustain

12. Kales, *"Due Process," the Inarticulate Major Premise and the Adamson Act,* 26 YALE L. J. 519 (1917).
13. Lerner, *The Supreme Court and American Capitalism,* in 2 SELECTED ESSAYS ON CONSTITUTIONAL LAW 154, 184 (1938).
14. *Ibid.*
15. The dates correspond to Chicago M. & St. P. Ry. v Minnesota, 134 U.S. 418 (1890), and West Coast Hotel Co. v. Parrish, 300 U.S. 379 (1937).
16. 300 U.S. 379 (1973).
17. 301 U.S. 1 (1937).
18. 301 U.S. 548 (1937).

even the broad Lerner thesis that the Court "effects a nexus between our fundamental law and our fundamental economic institutions," unless indeed a nexus is effected with a subject by leaving that subject alone. The student who searches for a dominant interest (or "purpose," or "inarticulate major premise") in the post-1937 Supreme Court is confronted by the fact that the old "pro-business" explanation will no longer do, and, even further, that the economic order, once in the center of the Court's purview, has been shifted to a point very near the periphery. Plainly he must look ahead of the comfortable vistas of yesteryear in order to understand what the modern Court has been up to.

But if he does look, he will find that history, which displaced the Court's old ideal of free enterprise and its old fear of social control, was quick to fill the gaps. A new ideal of humane democracy was already gaining judicial currency in the late 1930's, and a new danger, which was soon popularly known as totalitarianism, was rising up to menace that ideal. And just as the earlier period is illuminated when we understand what the judges cherished and what they feared, so the post-1937 march of doctrine is clarified when it is seen as a reflex of the libertarian democratic ideal and the totalitarian challenge. Differing though they may in their specific responses, the members of the modern Court have, like the Western world itself, shared the common problem of adjusting democratic postulates to the hard fact of totalitarianism.

Bearing in mind the reservations and qualifications already noted, it is possible to identify three fairly distinct phases in this general development. The first might be called, for the sake of convenience, the phase of judicial New Dealism, during which the Court's concern with totalitarianism was diluted by attitudes inherited from the early Roosevelt era. In the second phase, the totalitarian menace plainly weighs heavily on the judges' minds, but the Court reaction is uncertain and inchoate, almost suggesting that the judicial processes are incapable of dealing with a problem of such formidable dimensions. In the third phase, which may be hopefully called the phase of maturity, the development of a judicial outlook is seen that is mindful of totalitarianism as a major social fact, yet unwilling to surrender judicial review before it. It is no accident that the premises which seem to underlie the march of judicial doctrine in each of these phases reflect in a broad way the corresponding climate of opinion in the educated community as a whole; for the history of the Supreme Court since 1937 is, *mutatis mutandis,* an intellectual history of America as well.

In the first phase of judicial doctrine after 1937, the decisions involving civil liberties suggest judicial commitment to a congeries of ideals and attitudes that characterized, if not the New Deal itself, at any rate what might be described as the New Deal mentality. By way of example, organized labor, which had flourished so vigorously under the sympathetic auspices of the national administration, became equally the darling of the Supreme Court, so that Corwin remarked in 1941: "Constitutional law has always a central interest to guard. Today it appears to be that of organized labor."[19] The steady line of judicial acquiescence in cases involving business regulation is, of course, too well known to merit emphasis. Racial equality, once a minor element in the Court's value hierarchy, moved to the forefront of judicial concerns: the "separate but equal" doctrine was applied with new rigor in the field of education;[20] racial discrimination on interstate carriers was disapproved;[21] the right of Negroes to vote was given new constitutional protection.[22] Meanwhile, in cases involving freedom of expression, the Court was venturing far on the basis of what Mr. Justice Frankfurter has stigmatized as "uncritical libertarian generalities."[23] The "clear and present danger" rubric, revitalized in *Herndon v. Lowry,*[24] was given a strong libertarian thrust by the Court's application of it in such decisions as *Thornhill* v. *Alabama,*[25] *Bridges* v. *California,*[26] and *Thomas* v. *Collins,*[27] as well

19. CORWIN, THE CONSTITUTION AND WHAT IT MEANS TODAY vi (1948).
20. Missouri *ex rel.* Gaines v. Canada, 305 U.S. 337 (1938).
21. Morgan v. Virginia, 328 U.S. 373 (1946); Mitchell v. United States, 313 U.S. 80 (1941).
22. Smith v. Allwright, 321 U.S. 649 (1944); Lane v. Wilson, 307 U.S. 268 (1939).
23. Concurring in Dennis v. United States, 341 U.S. 494, 527 (1951).
24. 301 U.S. 242 (1937).
25. 310 U.S. 88 (1940).
26. 314 U.S. 252 (1941).
27. 323 U.S. 516 (1945).

as cases raising the direct issue of domestic subsersion, like *Taylor* v. *Mississippi*[28] and *Hartzel* v. *United States*.[29]

What emerges from all this is an inference that is hardly surprising: the Court, having renounced its old concern for the protection of the business community, was now concerned to protect the values that had been enshrined by more recent political history. But the point to note is that this judicial outlook, like the intellectual climate from whence it sprang, was pregnant with unforeseen difficulties. The New Deal mentality, with all its verve and its virtues, was more disposed to reach conclusions than to think its problems through, and the doctrines of the Court in these years echoed these New Deal qualities. The Court's position, especially with respect to civil liberty, rested on an engaging but unreflecting enthusiasm for certain assumed values, and it left out of account the fact that the world of the New Deal was already changing.

For one thing, of course, an alteration was taking place in the traditional status of organized labor. The wealthy and powerful unions of the 1940's no longer looked good in the underdog garments that became them so well a decade before, and the Supreme Court decisions based on the underdog assumption often seemed correspondingly incongruous. But this is secondary, almost a footnote. The great development of the era was the rise of the totalitarian threat to its modern proportions.

It seems clear enough now that the nature of that threat was ill-understood by most Americans in the 1930's and even during most of the 1940's, no less on the Court than elsewhere. Nazism and Stalinism caught American political thought by surprise, and for an unconscionably long time our response to them was more instinctive than analytical. There was a wishful effort to distinguish between them, if not on the ground that they varied in the degree of their immorality, then on the ground that Stalinism, unlike its German counterpart, was not a threat to other countries. Later, reacting against this comfortable view, the nation permitted itself one of those outbursts of indiscriminate malignancy that have from time to time attended the course of American history.

28. 319 U.S. 583 (1943).
29. 322 U.S. 680 (1944).

The Supreme Court, like the American nation, faced the problem of developing a mature response to totalitarianism, and constitutional doctrine, like political thought, was largely unprepared for the job. Especially it was unprepared to cope with laws that purported to combat totalitarianism by punishing freedom of expression, for on the one hand such laws seemed to attack the humane democratic ideal which the Court had chosen to defend, and on the other hand they were aimed, ostensibly at least, against the very force that threatened that ideal most. In the earlier period after 1937 the Court's tendency had been flatly hostile to legislation of this sort, but as the 1940's continued, signs of judicial second thoughts began to appear, and a second doctrinal phase dawned. Without arguing the individual merits of the free speech cases cited above, it must be conceded that they simplified an intricate problem and assumed, without arguing, that the Court could properly sit in judgment on the substantive power of the legislature to cope with the subversive issue. In any event, the wholesale libertarian temper of these decisions was more than the Court of the late 1940's was prepared to sustain. The judges were now more aware than they had seemed before that the totalitarian threat was neither temporary nor ordinary, and the growth of this awareness should no doubt be recorded as an advance.[30] But the problem of hammering out a viable constitutional doctrine in terms of these facts was still unsolved, and such decisions as *American Communications Ass'n* v. *Douds*,[31] *Dennis* v. *United States*,[32] and *Adler* v. *Board of Educ.*[33] contributed little to its solution. Their tendency was, in fact, so tolerant of substantive governmental restrictions on free expression as to give the impression that the Court was abdicating the field.

The difficulty arose partly from the inadequacy of received doctrine and partly from uncertainty about the function of the Court in a democratic system of government. Whatever the theoretical

30. See, for example, the opinion of Judge Hand in United States v. Dennis, 183 F.2d 201 (1950), and Mr. Justice Jackson's analysis of the nature of Stalinism in Dennis v. United States, 341 U.S. 494, 563, 563–567 (1951).

31. 339 U.S. 382 (1950).

32. 341 U.S. 494 (1951).

33. 342 U.S. 485 (1952).

potentiality of the clear and present danger rule might have been, for example, in practice it proved nearly unusable, and the *Douds* and *Dennis* decisions left serious doubt that it any longer meant very much as a constitutional doctrine. As for the doctrine of *Adler* v. *Board of Educ.*—that public employment is a privilege and that deprivation of it is not punishment—this had so little to do with the realities of the situation that it seemed almost cynically irrelevant.[34] Moreover, plainly there were members of the Court who entertained grave doubts about judicial competence to evaluate the actual substance of anti-subversive legislation.[35] The result was a stage of apparent submission to the legislative drive against political unorthodoxy.

But it now seems that the pattern of still another phase in this history of judicial responses was taking shape at the very time these spectacularly acquiescent decisions were being handed down. For one thing, it was easy to overlook the fact that the Court had not ceased widening the area of freedom in cases involving what might be called "non-seditious" rights. In *Winters* v. *New York*[36] and in the "Miracle" case,[37] for example, constitutional protection

34. See Frankfurter, J., concurring in part and dissenting in part, Garner v. Los Angeles Bd., 341 U.S. 716, 725 (1951): "To describe public employment as a privilege does not meet the problem."

35. Justice Jackson has said: "The question that the present times put into the minds of thoughtful people is to what extent Supreme Court interpretations of the Constitution will or can preserve the free government of which the Court is a part. A cult of libertarian judicial activists now assails the Court almost as bitterly for renouncing power as the earlier "liberals" once did for assuming too much power. This cult appears to believe that the Court can find in a 4,000-word eighteenth-century document or its nineteenth-century Amendments, or can plausibly supply, some clear bulwark against all dangers and evils that today beset us internally. This assumes that the Court will be the dominant factor in shaping the constitutional practice of the future and can and will maintain, not only equality with the elective branches, but a large measure of supremacy and control over them. I may be biased against this attitude because it is so contrary to the doctrines of the critics of the Court of whom I was one, at the time of the Roosevelt proposal to reorganize the judiciary. But it seems to me a doctrine wholly incompatible with faith in democracy, and in so far as it encourages a belief that the judges may be left to correct the result of public indifference to issues of liberty in choosing Presidents, Senators, and Representatives, it is a vicious teaching." JACKSON, THE SUPREME COURT IN THE AMERICAN SYSTEM OF GOVERNMENT 57–58 (1955).

36. 333 U.S. 507 (1948).

37. Joseph Burstyn, Inc. v. Wilson, 343 U.S. 495 (1952).

was extended to magazines and motion pictures. The scope of constitutional religious freedom had been enlarged in cases involving both the "free exercise" and "no establishment" clauses of the first amendment.[38] State criminal procedures were from time to time disapproved as lacking "due process."[39] The Court's hostility to race discrimination was sharply emphasized by such decisions as *Shelley* v. *Kraemer*,[40] *Sweatt* v. *Painter*,[41] and *McLaurin* v. *Oklahoma State Regents*.[42] It could hardly be contended that the Court responsible for these judgments had become insensible to the values of humane democracy.

For another thing, the judicial record even in cases involving "sedition" or "disloyalty" was not after all a simple story of surrender and abdication. Though yielding to the legislature on the issue of substantive power, the Court had begun to adumbrate a judicial warning that the zest to belabor subversives must be tempered by some respect for procedural regularity. Perhaps the most familiar of the cases making this point was *Blau* v. *United States*,[43] which recognized that the right against self-incrimination could be claimed by a witness asked to admit membership in the Communist party. The Court also held in *Anti-Fascist Refugee Committee* v. *McGrath*[44] that an organization could not be stigmatized as "subversive" without a hearing; in *Stack* v. *Boyle*[45] it found $50,000 bail excessive even for persons indicted under the Smith Act; and in *Bridges* v. *United States*,[46] a majority of the participating justices found that this perennial petitioner's conviction for falsely denying Communist party membership was barred by the three-year statute of limitations. Finally, in *Peters* v.

38. See 14 LAW & CONTEMP. PROB. *passim* (Winter 1949).

39. WOOD, DUE PROCESS OF LAW (1951); Fraenkel, *The Supreme Court as Protector of Civil Rights: Criminal Justice*, 275 ANNALS 86 (1951); Whalen, *Punishment for Crime: The Supreme Court and the Constitution*, 35 MINN. L. REV. 109 (1951).

40. 334 U.S. 1 (1948).

41. 339 U.S. 629 (1950).

42. 339 U.S. 637 (1950).

43. 340 U.S. 159 (1950).

44. 341 U.S. 123 (1951).

45. 342 U.S. 1 (1951).

46. 346 U.S. 209 (1953).

Hobby,[47] the Court held that a Loyalty Review Board had exceeded its statutory powers, and it is worth emphasizing that this narrowly restricted decision anticipated the judicial spirit of the 1955 Term. As for state law, *Wieman* v. *Updegraff*[48] struck down an Oklahoma loyalty oath for public employees on the ground that such a requirement could constitutionally apply only to those who knowingly join proscribed organizations, a procedural reservation which had been foreshadowed in previous decisions.[49]

In retrospect it now appears that the Court, in these cases, was feeling its way toward a mature definition of its position in the field of private rights, a position that finally emerges with a good deal of clarity in the decisions of the 1955 Term. That position can be described as follows: the Court, as always since the 1930's, shapes its decisions in this area by the light of an ideal, which has here been called "humane democracy," and a threat to that ideal, modern totalitarianism. But it also works with a lively awareness of both the limitations and the capacities of the judicial power. In some fields, like that of non-seditious rights, totalitarianism is not a direct factor but only a bad example, and the Court is inclined to press the frontiers of constitutional liberty ahead fairly steadily, even to the extent of laying substantive limitations on governmental power. Especially in the field of race relations, the Court has been bold, spurred, we may conjecture, by both the democratic ideal and the realization that the totalitarian world has made invaluable propaganda out of American discriminatory practices.

When, however, the judiciary is presented with the question of laws that circumscribe liberty for the very purpose of combatting liberty's most menacing enemy, the judicial response is less venturesome. Perhaps for the reasons already suggested, the Court is unwilling to curtail government's substantive power to pass measures of this kind. But it does apparently feel warranted to moderate the virulence of such laws in ways that do *not* challenge the sub-

47. 349 U.S. 331 (1955).
48. 344 U.S. 183 (1952).
49. Adler v. Board of Educ., 342 U.S. 485 (1952); Garner v. Board of Pub. Works, 341 U.S. 716 (1951); Gerende v. Board of Supervisors, 341 U.S. 56 (1951).

stantive power; and the principal device for accomplishing that result has so far been the concept of due procedure sometimes supplemented by the strict reading of statutes so as to avoid constitutional problems, if at all possible. Government, the Court seems to be saying, may harry "subversives" if it chooses to. The judicial responsibility in this connection will be to hold the incidence and operation of the law to what the Court feels are reasonably narrow limits. It is an appropriately modest role, but no one who has grasped the significance of procedure in a system of ordered liberties will doubt its importance. By the time of the 1955 Term at any rate, the role seemed to be taking fairly definite shape, and the major civil liberty cases of the term can be understood within this context of modern judicial purposes.

The course of development in a series of 1955 Term cases that did not involve the issue of subversion can be dealt with rather quickly. No major decisions on the subject of race relations were announced, but per curiam judgments and denials of certiorari suggest that the Court will push the *School Segregation* cases[50] doctrine to its logical extreme by holding educational authorities to a strict compliance standard,[51] and sometimes by striking at other state-sanctioned discriminations.[52] In the field of state criminal procedure, the record was as usual somewhat mixed, but the holding of *Griffin* v. *Illinois*[53]—that the State, if it grants a right of appeal at all, must not discriminate against some criminal defendants on the ground of their poverty by denying them an appeal if they cannot afford to purchase a transcript of the trial

50. Brown v. Board of Educ., 347 U.S. 483 (1954), *subsequent opinion rendered,* 349 U.S. 294 (1955); Bolling v. Sharpe, 347 U.S. 497 (1954), *subsequent opinion rendered,* 349 U.S. 294 (1955).

51. Board of Educ. v. Clemons, 350 U.S. 1006 (1956); Florida *ex rel.* Hawkins v. Board of Control, 351 U.S. 915 (1956); Adams v. Lucy, 351 U.S. 931 (1956).

52. Key v. McDonald, 350 U.S. 895 (1955) (ballots); Holmes v. Atlanta, 350 U.S. 879 (1955) (public parks); Mayor of Baltimore v. Dawson, 350 U.S. 877 (1955) (public beaches); see South Carolina Elec. & Gas Co. v. Fleming, 351 U.S. 901 (1956) (intrastate carriers). But see Charlotte Park and Recreation Comm'n v. Barringer, 242 N.C. 311, 88 S.E.2d 114 (1955), *cert. denied sub nom.* Leeper v. Charlotte Park and Recreation Comm'n, 350 U.S. 983 (1956); Naim v. Naim, 197 Va. 80, 87 S.E.2d 749, *vacated and remanded per curiam,* 350 U.S. 891 (1955), *on remand,* 197 Va. 734, 90 S.E.2d 849 (1956).

53. 351 U.S. 12 (1956).

proceedings—represents a significant extension of the rights of the accused. And Justice Frankfurter's concurring suggestion that such rulings be limited to *prospective* application[54] could, if followed, remove a road-block that has played no small part in discouraging the advance of like doctrines in the past.[55] In *United States ex rel. Toth* v. *Quarles,*[56] the Court took the unusual step of invalidating an act of Congress in order to guard the procedural rights of an individual against the hazards of military trial, holding that an ex-serviceman could not be retrospectively deprived of his civilian status and tried by court martial for a crime allegedly committed during his term of military duty.

As for labor judgments (again excluding those involving a question of subversion), a case possibly indicative of a trend is *United Automobile Workers, CIO* v. *Wisconsin Employment Relations Bd.,*[57] in which it was held that Wisconsin could enjoin mass picketing accompanied by violence, although the same conduct was forbidden by the Taft-Hartley Act. In the opinion of Justice Douglas, who dissented, this marked a retreat from *Garner* v. *Teamster's Union, AFL,*[58] which had disallowed such duplication of remedies. Like the line of cases hedging on *Thornhill* v. *Alabama,*[59] this decision suggests that organized labor no longer enjoys the favored position in the Supreme Court's value system that it occupied during the brave days of judicial New Dealism. In spite of this (or perhaps partly because of it) the general impression conveyed by all these results is that of a Court alive to values such as federalism, but equally alive to the need for protecting and extending the range of individual justice in a world that has recently seen that ideal so gravely challenged.

54. 351 U.S. at 26.
55. See Green, *The Bill of Rights, the Fourteenth Amendment and the Supreme Court,* 46 MICH. L. REV. 869, 906 (1948), referring specifically to the proposal that indictment by information be forbidden in state criminal procedures: "The greatest problem would consist of the thousands of prisoners who lie in state penitentiaries as a result of convictions following information rather than indictment."
56. 350 U.S. 11 (1955).
57. 351 U.S. 266 1(956).
58. 346 U.S. 485 (1935).
59. 310 U.S. 88 (1940); see Price, *Picketing—A Legal Cinderella,* 7 U. FLA. L. REV. 143 (1954).

Much more significant in terms of the special point of this paper are a group of decisions that raised more or less directly the "mixed" issue of the subversive problem and individual rights. Here the Court hesitantly, but still more forthrightly than before, devoted itself to the self-assigned function of considering the non-substantive questions raised by such governmental action, leaving the great question of power to the determination of the legislature.

In most of these cases, procedural niceties were at issue, and two of them raising the problem of the fifth amendment should be considered together. *Ullmann* v. *United States*[60] involved the Immunity Act of 1954,[61] which in certain circumstances qualifies the right against self-incrimination by requiring testimony and concurrently providing that the witness shall be exempt from prosecution or "any penalty or forfeiture" as a result of his testimony. The Court upheld the law against the dissent of Justice Douglas in which Justice Black joined (Justice Reed concurred in the substance of the decision). Justice Frankfurter, for the Court, was faced with two especially significant constitutional problems. One was presented by the argument that Congress did not and could not grant immunity from state prosecutions in the Immunity Act. The Court found no difficulty in holding that it did and could, surely a conclusion that should astonish no one considering the modern scope of the necessary and proper clause, not to mention *Brown* v. *Walker*,[62] but an important conclusion nonetheless. Another problem was more difficult. Petitioner had urged that the law did not grant him immunity from non-criminal disabilities "such as loss of job, expulsion from labor unions, state registration and investigation statutes, passport eligibility, and general public opprobrium."[63] Justice Douglas in dissent suggested that the majority was perhaps reading the statute to provide such immunities (though "public opprobrium" could hardly be forfended by congressional act), but the suggestion appears to be disingenuous, and Justice Frankfurter made it sufficiently clear that the law

60. 350 U.S. 422 (1956).
61. 18 U.S.C. § 3486 (Supp. III 1956).
62. 161 U.S. 591 (1896). See particularly the discussion at pp. 607–608.
63. 350 U.S. at 435.

as he read it protected the witness only from *criminal* penalties arising from his testimony and that even read in this way the law was not unconstitutional.[64]

The majority opinion is infused throughout with a precept that is obviously an important element in Justice Frankfurter's constitutional creed—that the "specific provisions" of the Constitution, such as the right against self-incrimination, should be constant in their meaning, as distinguished from great concepts such as commerce, due process, and liberty, which "were purposely left to gather meaning from experience."[65] *Brown* v. *Walker* and cases following it have for him settled the point that the self-incrimination immunity applies only to the threat of criminal prosecution.

Justice Douglas' dissent, largely devoted to arguing that this interpretation is too narrow, is a powerful one, and it would be idle to pretend that the witness under this law has as much immunity as he might enjoy if he kept silent, though the public "infamy" and other informal penalties that he incurs by speaking would probably be no less if he were allowed to stand mute and claim the privilege against self-incrimination. Nevertheless the decision does not represent a backward step, but only a refusal to go forward, and it should certainly not be thought of as an indication that the Court is disrespectful of the self-incrimination guarantee. Justice Frankfurter's insistence that he approached the problem in the "spirit of strict, not lax, observance of the constitutional protection of the individual"[66] must be taken seriously.

That it should be so taken became apparent in *Slochower* v. *Board of Higher Educ.*,[67] where a five-man majority, including Justice Frankfurter, held that a state violated the due process clause when it discharged an employee *merely* because he had invoked the Fifth Amendment before a committee of the United States Senate. Under the challenged provision of the city charter "the assertion of the privilege against self-incrimination is

64. 350 U.S. at 431.
65. National Mut. Ins. Co. v. Tidewater Transfer Co. 337 U.S. 582, 646 (1949) (dissenting opinion).
66. U.S. at 429.
67. 350 U.S. 551 (1956).

equivalent to a resignation . . . [and the employee loses his job without] notice, hearing or opportunity to explain."[68]

The Supreme Court's decision is very carefully restricted to a narrow range. The Court leaves open the possibility that Slochower could have been dismissed if the refusal to answer had occurred in the course of an inquiry into an employee's fitness by the city officials themselves[69] or if, having invoked the privilege before any body, he was unable to provide a satisfactory explanation when given an opportunity to do so.[70] The most that can be said confidently is that the fact of invoking the privilege before a federal committee cannot be made the sole ground for dismissal, for the terms of government employment must be "reasonable, lawful, and non-discriminatory"[71] to satisfy the requirements of due process.

The particular reasons for holding that the New York charter provision violates these requirements are not free from ambiguity. Justice Clark seems to lean rather heavily on the idea that the charter provision improperly takes the questions asked as confessed, yet as the dissenters point out, the New York Court of Appeals had authoritatively ruled otherwise.[72] If this basis for finding a vice in the provision is discarded, what remains is the suggestion that, whatever the city may choose to infer, the right to invoke a constitutional right is protected by due process. There is language in the opinion that might warrant such an interpretation,[73] but the reliance on the idea that the law sets up an inference of guilt muddies the waters so much that it is hard to be sure. Justice Reed, dissenting, contends that New York was not here inferring Communist party membership, but only imposing on its employees the "public duty" to furnish facts pertinent to

68. 350 U.S. at 554.
69. 350 U.S. at 556.
70. 350 U.S. at 555.
71. *Ibid.*
72. Daniman v. Board of Educ., 306 N.Y. 532, 538, 119 N.E2d 373, 377 (1954).
73. "The heavy hand of the statute falls alike on all who exercise their constitutional privilege, the full enjoyment of which every person is entitled to receive." 350 U.S. at 558.

official inquiries.[74] If the Court by way of reply meant to suggest that the state cannot impose a "public duty" to surrender a constitutional right, it is a pity that the Justice did not say so plainly. Nevertheless this may have been meant, since the logic of the opinion is hard to understand on any other premise. And, adding to this possible gloss of the decision's import the indubitable fact that it flatly condemns any imputations of guilt based on Fifth Amendment invocation, the general impression is indeed that of "strict, not lax, observance of the constitutional protection of the individual."[75] It is true that the decision leaves open the possibility that a board of education might discharge a teacher for standing mute before a board inquiry, or even perhaps for inadequately explaining his invocation of the right elsewhere; the decision therefore does not, as Justice Reed charged, "strike deep"[76] into the authority of the state. In fact, it leaves the state so much leeway that its limiting effect may be more moral than practical. But moral guidance too has its place in a system of constitutional restraints.

In *Communist Party* v. *Subversive Activities Control Bd.,*[77] the Court carried its fastidious concern for procedural regularity in this field to somewhat extraordinary lengths, and incidentally postponed the determination of thorny constitutional questions. The case involved an order of the Board that the Party register as a "communist action organization" under the Subversive Activities Control Act of 1950.[78] Among the grounds asserted by the Party for challenging the order was the argument that three of the witnesses on whom the Board relied in determining that the party merited the designation had been perjurers. The court of appeals had concluded that the evidence supporting the order was ample without reference to the testimony of these three, who included the ubiquitous Harvey Matusow;[79] but the Supreme

74. 350 U.S. at 561.
75. Ullmann v. United States, 350 U.S. 422, 429 (1956).
76. 350 U.S. at 559–560.
77. 351 U.S. 115 (1956).
78. 50 U.S.C. § 781 (1952).
79. 223 F.2d 531, 565 (D.C. Cir. 1954).

Court, speaking by Justice Frankfurter, declared that it could not "pass upon a record containing such challenged testimony,"[80] so the case was returned to the Board "to make certain that the Board bases its findings on untainted evidence."[81]

The argument of the dissenters that the Board's new judgment would precisely duplicate the old and that the remand would accomplish nothing beyond extending an already heavy-footed process of inquiry and review has a certain common-sense appeal about it. But seeming common sense is often delusive, and the nub of this decision lies, not in the legal rule it propounded, which was almost negligible, but in its spirit and the judicial purpose that underlay that spirit. As Justice Frankfurter said:

The untainted administration of justice is certainly one of the most cherished aspects of our institutions. Its observance is one of our proudest boasts. This Court is charged with supervisory functions in relation to proceedings in the federal courts. . . . Therefore, fastidious regard for the honor of the administration of justice requires the Court to make certain that the doing of justice be made so manifest that only irrational or perverse claims of its disregard can be asserted.[82]

These words might be taken as a text for the Court's attitude toward governmental action aimed at subversion. The judiciary may hesitate to substitute its judgment for that of Congress in deciding whether laws like these should be passed. But it can make sure that no one, Communist or not, is able to say that the laws were enforced unfairly in American courts. The Court perhaps leans over backward to clinch that result, but the result may be worth it.

The policy of avoiding substantive constitutional issues was further exemplified in *Black* v. *Cutter Laboratories*,[83] though here, as in the *Slochower* case, the logic of Mr. Justice Clark's majority opinion is not without its mysteries. The Cutter laboratories had discharged an employee on the stated ground, among others, that she was an active Communist party member, but an arbitration

80. 351 U.S. at 125.
81. *Ibid.*
82. 351 U.S. at 124.
83. 351 U.S. 292 (1956).

board had found this charge "stale" and had concluded that she was in fact being discharged for union activity. Apparently the collective bargaining agreement between company and union did recognize Communist party membership as "just cause" for dismissal, but the board pointed out that the company had known of the alleged affiliation for two years and argued that the right to invoke this cause had been waived by the delay in doing so. Upon affirmation by a lower court, the Supreme Court of California reversed, holding that the employee had been discharged for her Communist party activities and that it was against the public policy of the state to apply the doctrine of waiver in a case involving discharge for that reason.

For the Supreme Court of the United States, Justice Clark dismissed the writ, declaring that the state supreme court had merely construed a local contract under local law and that the cause therefore raised no federal question. But the difficulty, as Mr. Justice Douglas insists in dissent, is that the state decision seemed to involve enforcement of a contract barring members of the party from employment; if that reading is correct, the question is raised as to whether this state action violates the Fourteenth Amendment. It is hard to be sure why Clark believes the question is not presented. Surely, considering *Shelley* v. *Kraemer*,[84] he cannot doubt that state court action is "state action" within the meaning of the amendment. Perhaps what is meant is that the state court had left undecided the question of whether it would or would not command specific performance of such a contract and had limited itself to interpreting the meaning of the contract itself. Since there is no doubt that private parties may make such an agreement, and the state was not being asked to enforce anything but only to refrain from preventing the contract from being carried out, no federal constitutional question arises. If this is the explanation of the opinion's perplexities, the sequiturs that might clarify the argument are undoubtedly missing, and it is hardly surprising that both the dissenters and others assume the Court was approving state court enforcement of a contract that barred Communists and thus deciding a significant constitutional question

84. 334 U.S. 1 (1948).

sub silentio.[85] Yet it is at least doubtful that a constitutional point can be established by a decision in which the Court explicitly states that no constitutional question is presented. *Black* v. *Cutter Laboratories* is therefore a slender reed of constitutional precedent; the most that can be said is that it leaves the issue of enforcing non-Communist provisions of collective bargaining agreements in suspense. Once more the Court has gone the long way around in order to bypass the substantive problem presented by subversion and the law.

In two of the most publicized cases of the term the Court employed still another technique that enabled it to side-step the direct question of substantive power in this field. *Pennsylvania* v. *Nelson*[86] and *Cole* v. *Young*[87] both had the practical effect of contracting the scope of anti-subversive government actions, and both rested largely on the interpretation of congressional laws.

In the *Nelson* case, the Court struck down the Pennsylvania Sedition Act[88] on the ground that congressional action bearing on this matter superseded state laws. Four arguments are advanced by Mr. Chief Justice Warren to support the holding. In the first place he contends that Congress had intended, when it passed the Smith Act,[89] the Internal Security Act of 1950,[90] and the Communist Control Act of 1954[91] to "occupy the field," leaving no room for the states to supplement national efforts. This is of course an application of the occupancy doctrine long familiar in other areas, most particularly interstate commerce; and apparently no amount of logic-chopping can reduce it to an objective formula.[92] Neither the Chief Justice who finds a preclusive intent nor Mr. Justice Reed, who does not, is entirely convincing in sup-

85. 25 U.S.L. WEEK at 3026 (1956): "the opinion justifying dismissal of the writ of certiorari definitely established that there is no constitutional bar to state-court enforcement of a provision in a collective bargaining agreement prohibiting the employment of Communists."

86. 350 U.S. 497 (1956).

87. 351 U.S. 536 (1956).

88. PA. STAT. ANN. tit. 18 § 4207 (Purdon 1939).

89. 18 U.S.C. § 2385 (1952).

90. 50 U.S.C. § 781 (1952).

91. 50 U.S.C. §§ 841, 843 (Supp. III, 1956).

92. See Note, *Occupation of the Field in Commerce Clause Cases 1936–1946: Ten Years of Federalism,* 60 HARV. L. REV. 262 (1946).

porting his position in this case, and one is reminded of the jocosities of H. W. Biklé[93] and T. R. Powell[94] about the wonderful things Congress says by remaining silent. Second, the Court holds that the "enforcement of State sedition acts presents a serious danger of conflict with the administration of the federal program," and again the supposed intent of Congress helps determine the issue, the idea being that the vast number of state laws, often loosely worded and administered, may defeat the congressional purpose " 'to protect freedom from those who would destroy it without infringing on the freedom of all our people.' "[95]

Third, the Chief Justice adumbrates an argument prefigured by *Hines* v. *Davidowitz*[96] and *Rice* v. *Santa Fe Elevator Corp.*[97] that the federal laws " 'touch a field in which the federal interest is so dominant that the federal system [must] be assumed to preclude enforcement of state laws on the same subject.' "[98] The suggestion is that the sedition issue is part of the overall national problem of "resistance to the various forms of totalitarian aggression"[99] and therefore inappropriate for local regulation. Without a specific disclaimer, this might be taken as a flat ruling under the *Cooley*[100] doctrine that the states must eschew the sedition field whether or not Congress has entered it. However, since the Court abjures that interpretation,[101] the conclusion seems to be that Cooleyesque emanations from the "federal system" are called into being by Congress' decision to do something about the threat of totalitarianism, quite apart from any specific intent Congress might have to allow or disallow state laws on the subject. To the uninitiated this might further suggest that state action in the field would be invalid even if Congress should pass an act permitting it, so long as the federal sedition laws stand. But however

---

93. Biklé, *The Silence of Congress*, 41 HARV. L. REV. 200 (1927).
94. Powell, *The Still Small Voice of the Commerce Clause*, in 3 SELECTED ESSAYS ON CONSTITUTIONAL LAW 931 (1938).
95. 350 U.S. at 508.
96. 312 U.S. 52 (1941).
97. 331 U.S. 218, 230 (1947).
98. 350 U.S. at 504.
99. *Ibid.*
100. Cooley v. Board of Wardens, 53 U.S. (12 How.) 229 (1851).
101. 350 U.S. at 500.

logical such a conclusion may appear, it is patently wrong; a series of decisions beginning with *Leisy* v. *Hardin* in 1890[102] put it beyond much doubt that Congress can reverse the Court's holding of federal exclusiveness if it is so inclined.[103]

Finally, at the close of the Chief Justice's opinion he mentions a point that seems to have played a part in shaping those that went before. State sedition laws, he says, raise the threat that a man may be prosecuted twice for the same act, and "without compelling indication to the contrary, we will not assume that Congress intended to permit the possibility of double punishment."[104] This factor appears to be an important make-weight in swinging the scales of statutory interpretation here, and it should not be overlooked. Double punishment, the court seems to suggest, while by no means unknown,[105] is unusual enough and severe enough to warrant a presumption that Congress did not intend to provide for it; that presumption helps settle the question of whether state laws were superseded, and it buttresses the judgment that they were. Just as Congress will not be presumed to act unconstitutionally,[106] it will not be presumed to act with a harshness that seems at variance with normal practice.

A similar approach seems inferable from *Cole* v. *Young*,[107] in which the Court held invalid a dismissal under Executive Order 10450[108] and sharply restricted the scope of the Federal Loyalty Program. Mr. Justice Harlan, speaking for a six-man majority, argued that the order prescribed summary dismissal whether or not the dismissed employee was engaged in work "affected with the 'national security' ";[109] that the 1950 Act[110] under which the

102. 135 U.S. 100 (1890).
103. Prudential Ins. Co. v. Benjamin, 328 U.S. 408 (1946); Whitfield v. Ohio, 297 U.S. 431 (1936); Clark Distilling Co. v. Western Md. Ry., 242 U.S. 311 (1917); *In re* Rahrer, 140 U.S. 545 (1891); see Dowling, *Interstate Commerce and State Power—Revised Version*, 47 COLUM. L. REV. 547 (1947).
104. 350 U.S. at 509–510.
105. See United States v. Lanza, 260 U.S. 377 (1922).
106. Ogden v. Saunders, 25 U.S. (12 Wheat.) 213, 270 (1827).
107. 351 U.S. 536 (1956).
108. 3 C.F.R. 72 (Supp. 1953).
109. 351 U.S. at 543.
110. 5 U.S.C. §§ 22–1, 22–3 (1952).

order was promulgated authorized such dismissal only when the employee occupies a "sensitive" position; and that a dismissal made without considering the special sensitivity of the position violated the Veterans Preference Act.[111] The crux of the matter was of course the Court's determination that the summary procedures of the 1950 Act (which excluded the right of appeal normally available under the Veterans Preference Act) were meant by Congress to extend only to a special class of sensitive positions. Congress had specifically named eleven agencies to which the procedures applied and had provided for the president to extend them to such other agencies of the government as the president might from time to time find necessary in the interest of national security. The President had accordingly extended the act to all other departments and agencies of the government without regard for any criteria of sensitivity. In the Court's opinion this wholesale extension was at variance with congressional intent as revealed on both the face of the act and in its legislative history.

Leaving aside the inference from legislative history, which is at best debatable, the controlling principle seems to be one closely related to those made in *Pennsylvania* v. *Nelson:* that the face of the act makes the Court's narrow interpretation reasonable, and that in view of the doubtful necessity of extending the act to non-sensitive positions and in view of the "stigma attached to persons dismissed on loyalty grounds . . . [the Court] will not lightly assume"[112] that Congress meant to abolish usual procedural safeguards on an undiscriminating basis. Again Congress is solicitously endowed with presumptive good intentions and especially is invested with the same concern for procedural regularity that is felt by the Court itself.[113]

111. 5 U.S.C. § 863 (1952).

112. 351 U.S. at 546–547.

113. The Court did not question the authority to dismiss employees on loyalty grounds, but "only the extent to which the summary *procedures* authorized by the 1950 Act are available," 351 U.S. at 544. Nor, incidentally, did the decision meet the problem of whether the Order might be sustainable under the executive power alone; for, said the Court, the President expressly confined his action to the limits of the statute. 351 U.S. at 557, n. 20.

It is certainly possible that the Congress was surprised to learn of the intentions imputed to it by the Court in both the *Nelson* and *Cole* cases. The dissenters (Reed, Burton, and Minton in *Nelson;* Clark, Reed, and Minton in *Cole*) obviously had no doubt about the matter, but one feels that they rested their judgment rather too much on a layman's hunch about the mood of the congressmen who passed these laws. It is not a mood but a statute that became the law of the land; and it is hard to criticize the Court for assuming that Congress was more sensible than some of the public utterances of its members might indicate, or for requiring it to speak plainly if it means to endorse those utterances.

The civil liberty cases of the 1955 Term, particularly the six just discussed, strongly affirm the impression that judicial purposes in reference to the problem of totalitarianism have begun to crystallize into a matured concept of the judicial role. Mindful of both the importance and the limitations of its function in the American system, the Court is judiciously extending the concepts of freedom and equality in fields unrelated to the problem of subversion. Meanwhile, in connection with that problem, the Court contents itself with a sharp scrutiny of procedural requirements and of the legislative warranty for oppressive governmental actions. The whole approach is characterized by a tendency to confront the smaller questions rather than the larger in each case that presents itself, but the net effect is to cast the Court's weight on the side of moderating anti-subversive laws.

That result is not unqualified, nor should it be expected to be. The *Ullmann* and *Black* cases, to which perhaps should be added *Jay* v. *Boyd*,[114] were decided adversely to the individual rights claimed by alleged "subversives." But as suggested above, the *Ullmann* opinion accompanied its denial of certain claimed rights with a reaffirmation of certain others; the *Black* decision seems to decide nothing except the specific controversy; and though one may deeply regret the Court's refusal in the *Jay* case to bar the testimony of "faceless informers" in an application for discretionary relief from a deportation order,[115] that holding is counter-

114. 351 U.S. 345 (1956).
115. See the dissenting opinion of Mr. Justice Douglas, 351 U.S. at 347.

balanced by the requirement of *United States* v. *Zucca*[116] that an affidavit of "good cause" is a procedural prerequisite to the maintenance of denaturalization proceedings. As for *Slochower, Subversive Activities Control Board, Nelson,* and *Cole,* each of them in some degree whittled away the procedural asperities of anti-subversive measures, serving notice to the governments of the United States and to observers at home and abroad that awareness of the totalitarian threat has not overwhelmed the tradition of fair play.

A word is in order about the specific response of individual justices to the issues presented by these cases and about the lineup of the Court behind the judicial attitude described here. In this discussion "the Court" has been spoken of as if it were a single entity, and of course such usage has only limited validity. "The Court," like any group, consists of individuals prone to individual diversities; when we say that "it" did this we may mean no more than that a certain majority agreed to a decision, and when we say that "it" displayed an attitude or decided on an approach we must be especially careful to avoid semantic error. In fact, the Supreme Court at any given time is likely to be unanimous or nearly so in its adherence to certain broad value premises but is likely to split over their application and in its acceptance of certain sub-premises. The modern Court, it is suggested, has been substantially unanimous in its high regard for the values of what has here been called "humane democracy." As Mr. Justice Frankfurter remarked in 1943: "All members of the Court are ... equally zealous to enforce the constitutional protection of the free play of human spirit."[117] In recent years at least the Court has also been largely agreed about the nature and dimensions of the totalitarian threat. In these connections it is perfectly justifiable to treat the Court's attitude as if the Court were a unit.

But disagreement has arisen and still persists over the question of how the judicial process should implement these general evaluations, and when it is said that the Court seems for the moment to

116. 351 U.S. 91 (1956).
117. Murdock v. Pennsylvania, 319 U.S. 105, 139 (1943) (dissenting opinion).

have chosen the road of what might be called "non-substantive scrutiny" with respect to the laws aimed at subversion, the statement subsumes a variety of differences and compromises.

Old classifications of the justices into liberals and conservatives no longer have discriminatory value; but, without insisting on rigid categories, some analysis of the divisions can be illuminating. In the six major cases discussed Justices Reed and Minton were uniformly in favor of upholding the anti-subversive measure, and it is perhaps fair to assume that they flatly oppose the policy of non-substantive scrutiny. Justices Black and Douglas support it as far as it goes but, judging by their dissents in *Ullmann* and *Cutter* and their concurrence in *Slochower,* would push it farther and would, moreover, be readier to meet the substantive question than their brethren are. The most impressive single fact, however, is that Justice Frankfurter, and he alone, was with the majority in all six of these cases, so that he seems to represent with remarkable faithfulness the "sense of the meeting" on the whole question. The remaining justices sometimes joined him and sometimes opposed him, but in each case enough leaned his way to fill out a majority. Yet the point is that it is a majority, and although some members of the Court may disagree on special points or agree for special reasons, this does not vitiate the fact that the effective result was to ratify the general approach outlined above.

And it seems almost unescapable to conclude, considering what we know of his attitudes and considering the pivotal nature of his position in the 1955 Term, that the adoption of a policy of non-substantive scrutiny constitutes a triumph for Justice Frankfurter. A complex judicial personality cannot be summarized in a few catch-phrases, but surely anyone who has pondered this jurist's record off and on the Court must have discerned an abiding concern for individual liberty, a concept of the judiciary "at the same time exalted and self-moderating,"[118] and an intense preoccupation with the procedural and interpretive niceties that are close to the essence of a judge's craft. These qualities are aptly reflected in the private rights decision of the 1955 Term.

118. Jaffe, *The Judicial Universe of Mr. Justice Frankfurter,* 62 HARV. L. REV. 357, 359 (1949).

The concept of judicial responsibility that seems to underlie the sedition cases of the 1955 Term is not wholly satisfying to all the members of the Court itself; nor will it satisfy all the observers, lay and professional, who take an interest in the Supreme Court's doings. The "libertarian judicial activists," to use Mr. Justice Jackson's term, will feel, with Justices Douglas and Black, that the Court should be bolder in laying substantive inhibitions on government's power to control free expression. Others may believe, with Justices Reed and Minton, that the majority has insisted too scrupulously on procedural hair-splitting. They will remind us with lofty authority of Mr. Chief Justice Stone that "it is not the function of this Court to disregard the will of Congress in the exercise of its constitutional power"[119] or, with particular reference to the *Nelson* case, that "due regard for the maintenance of our dual system of government demands that the courts do not diminish state powers . . . by reference to their own conceptions of a policy which Congress has not expressed and is not plainly to be inferred from the legislation which it has enacted."[120]

Of course it is always open to argue that the Court has done too little or too much, and it may be that a later bench in different circumstances will heed one or another of these admonitions. One reason it is so difficult to define the Court's role in America is that the role has an inconsiderate habit of changing. But in the context of 1955–56 the policy of non-substantive scrutiny has much to be said for it. If the last ten years of world events have taught us nothing else, they should have taught us to be wary of easy answers when a threat of totalitarianism is under consideration; foolishly ill-advised as much anti-subversive action may have been, only the greatest self-certainty would warrant a judgment that government lacks altogether the power to take that action. Moreover, those who urge on the Court a policy of substantive negativism in this field have never quite been able to explain how they allay the misgivings about overweening judicial power expressed by Judge Learned Hand,[121] among many others. "Courts," we

119. Girouard v. United States, 328 U.S. 61, 79 (1946).
120. Cloverleaf Butter Co. v. Patterson, 315 U.S. 148, 176–177 (1942).
121. HAND, THE SPIRIT OF LIBERTY 180 (1953).

were once compellingly told, "are not the only agency of government that must be assumed to have capacity to govern."[122]

On the other hand the American political tradition does assume, for better or worse, that the judiciary will have a hand in guiding the republic, and a Court that abdicates is no more comportable with that tradition than one that rules too strictly. The judiciary cannot ignore the problem posed by the conflict between our libertarian premises and the totalitarian fact without shirking its historic duty; it must play a part. The question is what part it can best play. And the choice of roles that is implied by the cases of the 1955 Term seems peculiarly well suited to the actor's capacities as well as to the circumstances of the drama. As Judge Hastie has remarked, the judge is especially "at home" in the realm of procedure; his training and his disinterest "qualify him preeminently for judgment whether there has been an intolerable sacrifice of decent and trustworthy modes on the altar of expediency."[123] Here if anywhere judicial wisdom has the weight of authority, and here the Court of the 1955 Term has elected to draw its lines. Even the 1955 statutory constructions in such cases as *Nelson* are strengthened by similar considerations of judicial competency, for the reading of statutes is the judge's special art, and he must be granted an ipse dixit here that would be more doubtful if he were judging substantive issues of policy. The crucial point is, of course, that he is not so judging. The power of the legislative arm to accomplish its objectives still exists if those objectives still recommend themselves and if their sponsors are willing to observe the canons of procedural decency. Meanwhile, the Court decisions have given the nation and its representatives a chance for a second look and have given them and the world at large a salutary reminder that the American tradition prescribes fair play, even in nervous times like the present. This may not be quite all a Court could have done. But it is a lot to have done nonetheless.

122. United States v. Butler, 297 U.S. 1, 87 (1936).
123. Hastie, *Judicial Method in Due Process Inquiry,* in GOVERNMENT UNDER LAW 181, 194 (1955).

USEFUL TOIL OR THE PATHS OF GLORY?*

[This article first appeared in the *Virginia Law Review*, 43, no. 6 (October 1957), 803–835.]

I have suggested[1] that the Supreme Court had at length developed, out of the vicissitudes and ambiguities of the post-1937 period, a matured concept of its current role in the American polity. With respect at least to the broad area loosely called "civil rights," the Court's posture, it was said, might be understood in terms of the relationship between three factors: the urge to protect the values of humane democracy; the fact that totalitarianism is a formidable threat to those values; and the awareness that judicial supervision is confined by certain natural limits. Government infringements on individual rights, such as racial equality, fair trial, and free expression, will encounter more severe judicial scrutiny than a Court of thirty years ago might have accorded them. But, in the first place, considerations of judicial modesty will deter the Court in all these fields from automatically converting its own views that laws are "futile or even noxious"[2] into the law of the land. And in the second place, the deterrent effect of these considerations will be accentuated when the government action is aimed at the totalitarian problem. For some judges feel, not without a certain color of reason, that the main task of judgment about this problem should be assigned where the main responsibility lies—to the political branches.

The upshot in judicial policy is two-fold: in fields not directly concerned with the subversion issue the frontiers of civil rights are pushed ahead fairly steadily, though not precipitously; in fields that do impinge on that issue, the Court satisfies itself with a more restrained role and merely holds the government to a rather strict

---

* Thanks are due Morton M. Maneker for valuable contributions to the substance of this paper and help in preparation of the manuscript.

1. In the previous section. *The Supreme Court Finds a Role.*

2. Truax v. Corrigan, 257 U.S. 312, 344 (1921) (dissenting opinion of Mr. Justice Holmes).

standard of procedural regularity and statutory authority. The crucial difference is perhaps that in areas like racial equality or religious liberty the substantive power of government is actually curtailed; but in areas like subversion the Court seeks to temper power without denying it. This, compendiously stated, is the pattern that seems to have emerged from the past few years of judicial history and to have culminated in the civil rights cases of the 1955 Term. It was a pattern in which the Court appeared as a significant but not dominant partner in the American governmental enterprise. It placed the Court not at the center, but neither at the periphery of the arena in which the great political decisions of America are made.

This was a comparatively modest version of the doctrine of judicial supremacy. The political storms of the 1930's and the scoldings of the legal realists had impelled some American judges to reread the commissions they held and to construe them more narrowly than had many of their predecessors. Yet it would have taken a bold man to predict, as this writer did not, that the Supreme Court was permanently self-constrained to the role defined by its 1955 Term decisions—that the shift in 1937 and after marked an irreversible retreat from the centers of political power. American constitutional courts, like acorns, have a tradition of expansionism, and tradition as an historical force is never to be taken lightly. Mr. Chief Justice Warren and his brethren inherit mantles worn by the tribunal that produced *Chisholm* v. *Georgia*,[3] *Pollock* v. *Farmers' Loan and Trust Co.*,[4] and *United States* v. *Butler*,[5] to name but three decisions that presumed to settle great questions of American social policy. They sit in the chairs of the men who, a few short years after the judicial disaster of the *Dred Scott* case,[6] ventured to set drastic limits on the currency[7] and war powers[8] of Congress and to challenge the vengeful program of the Radical Republicans both in Congress and in the

3. 2 U.S. (2 Dall.) 419 (1793).
4. 158 U.S. 601 (1895).
5. 297 U.S. 1 (1936).
6. Dred Scott v. Sandford, 60 U.S. (19 How.) 393 (1857).
7. Legal Tender Cases, 79 U.S. (12 Wall.) 457 (1871).
8. Ex parte Milligan, 71 U.S. (4 Wall.) 2 (1866).

states.[9] These same mantles once adorned, these chairs were adorned by, John Marshall, Stephen J. Field, and Rufus W. Peckham, again to name just three who helped enlarge the bounds of judicial supervision. "The first duty of a good judge is to extend his jurisdiction," David Henshaw once jeered with the great Chief Justice in mind,[10] and whether entirely fair or not, the charge was surely not frivolous. It would hardly be surprising that a Court with such a history should show signs of nostalgia; those who have played Hamlet are unlikely to be wholly content with the part of Horatio even though their friends and their own best judgment tell them it is more appropriate.

As might be expected, the years since 1937 have not been empty of hints that the Supreme Court remembers its venturesome past and is sometimes tempted to revisit it. Certain bold declarations of doctrine in the free speech field in the early 1940's suggested to some observers that the Court would hold government action aimed at speech to the kind of strict substantive limits that had formerly been applied to inhibitions on "freedom of contract."[11] When the chips were down in *Douds*[12] and *Dennis*,[13] that promise of *Thomas* v. *Collins*[14] and its fellows was not fulfilled; but this should not obscure the significance of the fact that the promise had once been made. In 1952 came the Steel Seizure case[15] and an opinion of the Court which chose to meet the great constitutional issue of inherent presidential power, even though a narrower basis for the decision was ready at hand. It is true that the broad restrictions laid down by Mr. Justice Black's opinion were hard to find in the concurrences (except that of Mr. Justice Douglas), but the impression of judicial boldness remained; even the decision to take jurisdiction and thus mediate a conflict between

9. Ex parte Garland, 71 U.S. (4 Wall.) 333 (1867); Cummings v. Missouri, 71 U.S. (4 Wall.) 277 (1876).
10. SOCIAL THEORIES OF JACKSONIAN DEMOCRACY 172 (Blau ed. 1954).
11. *E.g.*, L. Hand, *Chief Justice Stone's Conception of the Judicial Function*, 46 COLUM. L. REV. 696, 698 (1946).
12. American Communications Ass'n., CIO v. Douds, 339 U.S. 382 (1950).
13. Dennis v. United States, 341 U.S. 494 (1951).
14. 323 U.S. 516 (1945).
15. Youngstown Sheet & Tube Co. v. Sawyer, 343 U.S. 579 (1952).

the great economic interests of the realm and the most powerful chief executive in the Western world seemed incongruous with a stance of judicial humility. And in 1954, most impressive of all, came the Public School Segregation decision[16] which, its merits apart, involved a breathtaking assumption of judicial responsibility. Evidently the impulse to mount the heights of power was not wholly scotched by the chastening experiences of the 1930's and the sobering advice of a generation of judicial and non-judicial critics. For always in the background there is the beguiling illusion that a tribunal entrusted with defining its own power may define it as it likes.

The great question for a student of contemporary constitutional history is this: can the Court rest satisfied with the important but subsidiary place in government which the main course of its post-1937 decisions seemed to imply? Or were the judicial events just mentioned forewarnings of a new era of *gouvernement des juges* in which the Court will strive once more to bring the central problems of American political life under close surveillance? To put the questions more specifically: did the decisions of the 1955 Term, with their carefully limited admonitions against reckless invasion of individual rights, represent a settled judicial policy with some pretensions to endurance? Or are they to be understood as marking a transition between the extreme forbearance of the Vinson Court and a future period of fullscale judicial activism? An observer thinks of *Mugler* v. *Kansas*[17] in 1887 with its curious portents of the *Lochner*[18] doctrine; or of *Meyer* v. *Nebraska*,[19] in which Justice McReynolds presaged *Gitlow* v. *New York*[20] without apparently being quite aware that he was doing so. Were the 1955 Term cases comparable to these? If so, or even if not, we may be poised at one of those moments in constitutional history that later are seen to have been decisive. Whether the Court is preparing to move ahead to dubious battle or settle for the lesser

16. Brown v. Board of Educ., 347 U.S. 483 (1954).
17. 123 U.S. 623 (1887).
18. Lochner v. New York, 198 U.S. 45 (1905).
19. 262 U.S. 390 (1923).
20. 268 U.S. 652 (1925).

glory and risk may be a difficult question precisely because it is now in process of determination.

In the light of this supposition that the Court is currently standing on the banks of the Rubicon, the 1956 Term decisions involving civil rights assume a very special interest for students of American constitutionalism. If the Term is to be judged by the noise it evoked and the public bolts that have been hurled from certain high circulation quarters, it must be concluded that the river has already been crossed, that the general is hurrying toward Rome and may indeed already have arrived. Leaving aside the violent but geographically specialized reaction to the segregation decision, no term for over twenty years has set going such a chorus of resentment. The old charge that an overweening judiciary has handcuffed government in vital areas has been brought out of the retirement it has enjoyed since 1937. The Court, we are told, "may have tied the hands of our country and have rendered it incapable of carrying out the first law of mankind—the right of self-preservation."[21] The decisions, it is said, are "in many respects . . . more devastating and more destructive of the rights of Congress to function as a coordinate branch of government than any decisions ever rendered by our highest Court in its entire history."[22] Even one of the Court's own members accuses the majority of crippling the committee system of Congress "beyond workability."[23] Proposals for curtailing the Court's appellate jurisdiction, an anti-judicial program as old as the Republic itself, are heard once more.[24] Plainly enough, the Court of the 1956 Term has been stirring a good many embers.

But is there actual fire behind these clouds of public smoke?

21. Statement of Herbert R. O'Conor, Chairman of the Committee on Communist Tactics, Strategy and Objectives of the American Bar Association, New York Times, July 26, 1957, p. 1, col. 1.

22. Lawrence, *Treason's Biggest Victory*, U.S. News & World Report, June 28, 1957, p. 152.

23. Watkins v. United States, 354 U.S. 178, 222 (1957) (dissenting opinion of Mr. Justice Clark).

24. See S.2646, 85th Cong., 1st Sess. (1957), which excepts from the appellate jurisdiction of the Supreme Court several classes of cases involving attempts of the federal government and the states to root out subversives; recently recommended by the Senate Subcommittee on Internal Security.

Has the Court embarked on a program of nay-saying that is really analogous, or faintly comparable, to the 1935-36 period which gave us such landmarks of judicial governance as *Railroad Retirement Bd.* v. *Alton R.R.*,[25] *Schechter Poultry Corp.* v. *United States*,[26] and *Carter* v. *Carter Coal Co.*,[27] or to 1895, which saw the Court produce both the Sugar Trust[28] and Income Tax decisions?[29] Do the 1956 Term decisions really challenge the power of the other branches to deal with the subversive threat; do they shackle government? Or are they instead still consonant with the policy of restrained supervision that seemed to underly the decisions of the 1955 Term—reading statutes strictly, insisting on reasonable procedural regularity, but leaving the substance of power basically intact? Only a careful examination of the cases themselves can supply answers to these questions; and those answers may, in turn, shed light on the earlier queries about the overall direction of the present Supreme Court.

Most of the public sound and fury in the 1956 term was generated by cases involving the issue of subversion, but meanwhile the Court was quietly following in non-subversion fields a course broadly consistent with its recent trends. Since the point of this paper is mainly directed to the Court's reaction to the subversion issue, other decisions must be passed over rapidly, but their relatively hasty treatment should not be taken as suggesting that they are insignificant.

The holding in *United States* v. *E. I. duPont de Nemours & Co.*,[30] that Du Pont's substantial acquisition of stock in General Motors violated the Clayton Act, is far too intricate for analysis here, and is perhaps principally relevant as an illustration of the fact that the Court feels free to interpret federal economic regulation broadly, comforted by the realization that Congress may correct the interpretation if it likes. The same attitude appears to underly such Taft-Hartley decisions as *Textile Workers Union* v.

25. 295 U.S. 330 (1935).
26. 295 U.S. 495 (1935).
27. 298 U.S. 238 (1936).
28. United States v. E. C. Knight Co., 156 U.S. 1 (1895).
29. Pollock v. Farmers' Loan and Trust Co., 158 U.S. 601 (1895).
30. 353 U.S. 586 (1957).

Lincoln Mills,[31] *Goodall-Sandford, Inc.* v. *Local 1802, United Textile Workers, AFL,*[32] and *General Elec. Co.* v. *Local 205, United Elec. Workers,*[33] in which the Court found that section 301(a) of the law grants district courts jurisdiction over labor contract controversies whether diversity of citizenship is present or not, and went on to hold that these courts were further authorized to apply federal law fashioned by them "from the policy of our national labor laws."[34] It is hard to escape the feeling that Mr. Justice Douglas was drawn to this result partly because he so reads the law and partly because he prefers so to read it. But if, as Mr. Justice Frankfurter suggests in dissent, this strains "the alchemy of construction,"[35] the legislative remedy is always available. Such considerations cannot excuse a reading that is really untenable, but they may allow some play within the borders of tenability. The reverse of the shield is, of course, that national statutes regulating ideas will be read narrowly, also subject to congressional correction.

In other non-subversion cases, the Court added doctrinal layers to the law in connection with racial segregation, state criminal procedures, obscenity, military trials, and labor picketing. The tortuous implications of the Court's desegregation policy were further revealed when it was held, *per curiam,* that a school operated by a city with funds from a testamentary trust could not exclude Negroes, although the will spoke only of educating "poor white male orphans"; this, said the Court, would be discrimination by the state and therefore in conflict with the Fourteenth Amendment.[36] The right to counsel was advanced somewhat by the holding in *Chessman* v. *Teets*[37] that a petitioner had been denied procedural due process when a seriously disputed transcript on appeal was used as the basis for affirming his conviction without

31. 353 U.S. 448 (1957).
32. 353 U.S. 550 (1957).
33. 353 U.S. 547 (1957).
34. Textile Workers Union v. Lincoln Mills, 353 U.S. 448, 456 (1957) (dictum).
35. *Id.* at 462.
36. Pennsylvania v. Board of Directors of City Trusts, 353 U.S. 230 (1957).
37. 354 U.S. 156 (1957).

allowing petitioner to appear in proceedings determining the validity of the transcript, or appointing counsel to appear for him. *Butler* v. *Michigan*[38] set a salutary limit on state laws aimed at "obscene" literature; the state cannot, said Frankfurter for the Court, prohibit the distribution of a book to the general reading public on the ground that it has a potentially deleterious effect on youth. "Surely, this is to burn the house to roast the pig."[39] On the other hand, the Court in *Roth* v. *United States* and *Alberts* v. *California*[40] squarely faced for the first time the question of whether true "obscenity" is protected by either the first or fourteenth amendments, and held that it was not.[41] This conclusion was hardly surprising, but Mr. Justice Brennan for the Court then proceeded to lay down an interpretation of obscenity that seemed to leave a rather wide latitude for suppression of literature. The meaning of the word turns, said the Court, on "whether to the average person, applying contemporary community standards, the dominant theme of the material taken as a whole appeals to prurient interest."[42] One trouble with this standard, as Douglas, dissenting, saw it, was that it allowed suppression for the impurity of the thoughts provoked, rather than for the "overt acts" or "anti-social conduct" that a publication might threaten to engender.[43] How far government can go under this standard will perhaps be spelled out in later decisions, and the effect of the holding may not be as permissive as it sounds; but any attempt to narrow it much will be embarrassed by the Court's approval of the trial instruction in *Roth* that "the common conscience of the community"[44] is the test for determining a book's allowability.

In *Reid* v. *Covert*[45] the Court held that, at least in capital cases, civilian dependents of members of the armed forces outside the continental United States could not be subjected to court-martial,

38. 353 U.S. 380 (1957).
39. *Id.* at 383.
40. 354 U.S. 476 (1957).
41. *Id.* at 485.
42. *Id.* at 489.
43. *Id.* at 508–509.
44. *Id.* at 490.
45. 354 U.S. 1 (1957).

a reversal of two decisions handed down a year ago.[46] The four-man opinion of Mr. Justice Black ventured some broad generalizations on the subservience of the treaty power to constitutional prohibitions, and these should go far to set at rest the apprehensions arising out of *Missouri* v. *Holland*[47] that helped create that hardy perennial bridesmaid, the Bricker Amendment. The decision also disposes of *In re Ross*[48] and its doctrine that the Constitution has no applicability abroad.

Finally, in a case involving state power and labor picketing,[49] the Court set the final capstone on a conclusion described here a year ago—that organized labor no longer enjoys the fatherly protection lavished on it by the doctrine of *Thornhill* v. *Alabama*.[50] The purpose of the picketing, said the Court, was to coerce the employer to coerce his employees to join a union in violation of the state's declared policy, and the state may enjoin such picketing at its pleasure. As Douglas, dissenting, points out, this result has been implicit in the Court's decisions since *Local 309, Int'l Brotherhood of Teamsters* v. *Hanke*,[51] and the dissent can be taken as a kind of funeral oration for the *Thornhill* doctrine: "Today, the Court signs the formal surrender. State courts and state legislatures cannot fashion blanket prohibitions on all picketing. But, for practical purposes, the situation now is as it was when *Senn* v. *Tile Layers Union* . . . was decided. State courts and state legislatures are free to decide whether to permit or suppress any particular picket line for any reason other than a blanket policy against all picketing."[52]

The general tendency of the non-subversion decisions of this term, like the last, is that of movement—slow and wavering, but reasonably sure. Little by little, the scope of civil rights protection

46. Reid v. Covert, 351 U.S. 487 (1956); Kinsella v. Krueger, 351 U.S. 470 (1956).
47. 252 U.S. 416 (1920).
48. 140 U.S. 453 (1891).
49. Local 695, Int'l Brotherhood of Teamsters, AFL v. Vogt, Inc., 354 U.S. 284 (1957).
50. 310 U.S. 88 (1940).
51. 339 U.S. 470 (1950).
52. Local 695, Int'l Brotherhood of Teamsters, AFL v. Vogt, Inc., 354 U.S. 284, 297 (1957).

is widened in this area and that; the range of statutory economic regulation is extended; doctrines the Court deems no longer relevant are sloughed away. This is not the militant and doctrinaire "Old Court" of pre-1937 days, nor yet is it the crusading New Deal Court of the late 1930's and early 1940's; but it is a Court that has tuned its instruments to the different world of 1957.

In connection with each case involving subversion, it is well to distinguish between the strict effect of the holding and its possible implications. *Service* v. *Dulles*[53] merits only passing attention; for, like *Peters* v. *Hobby*[54] two terms ago, it rested on extremely narrow grounds and did not promulgate new doctrine. Mr. Service's discharge from the Foreign Service was invalid, said the Court unanimously (Mr. Justice Clark not participating) because the Secretary of State had violated his own regulations when he took the action. Under *United States ex rel. Accardi* v. *Shaughnessy*,[55] valid regulations are binding on the administrator who makes them, as well as on others; and the "McCarran Rider"[56] was interpreted as not exempting the Secretary from this requirement. The decision is chiefly significant for its confirmation of the recent trend to interpret the Federal Loyalty Program authority strictly.[57]

A good deal more important were two decisions that overturned state denials of bar admission on grounds linked to subversion. *Schware* v. *Board of Bar Examiners*[58] was one of those comparatively rare cases that must gladden judicial hearts because the scales of justice seem so heavily weighted in favor of one conclusion, and the choice is fairly easy. The petitioner had been refused permission to take the bar examination on the ground that he lacked "good moral character"—the bases for this finding being that he had used aliases, had been arrested several times, and had allegedly

53. 354 U.S. 363 (1957).
54. 349 U.S. 331 (1955).
55. 347 U.S. 260 (1954).
56. See Department of State Appropriation Act, 1953, c. 651, § 103, 66 STAT. 555 (1952). A similar provision was attached to each of the State Department appropriation acts for 1948 through 1952. All these provisions are referred to in the opinion as "the McCarran Rider."
57. See Cole v. Young, 351 U.S. 536 (1956); Peters v. Hobby, 349 U.S. 331 (1955).
58. 353 U.S. 232 (1957).

once been a member of the Communist party. But he testified that
the aliases had been used to avoid anti-Semitic prejudice; the arrests had been for "suspicion of criminal syndicalism" and for
recruiting men to fight on the Loyalist side in the Spanish Civil
War, and in all cases the charges had been dropped. The Communist party membership had terminated in 1940; there was no evidence that the petitioner had even then engaged in or advocated
violent action against the government; and the Communist party
at the time of his membership was lawful in most states. Schware
had testified freely about all these facts and had presented abun-
dant evidence of a blameless life since he had abandoned the
aberrations of his youth.

The Court—Mr. Justice Black writing its official opinion—had
little difficulty reaching the unanimous conclusion that Schware
had been denied due process of law. Since the use of the aliases,
when explained, seemed quite irrelevant and since, as the Court
says, mere arrests without conviction have little if any probative
value, the crux of the issue was the Communist party affiliation.
And, strictly read, the Court's holding simply means that Communist membership fifteen years in the past, unsupplemented by
evidence of unlawful action even in that remote time and rebutted
by more recent evidence, cannot alone justify a finding of bad
moral character. Thus stated, the decision sounds almost self-
evident.

But easy cases sometimes have a way of making more law than
the unwary might suspect.[59] It is well to read them carefully, and
there are two aspects of the *Schware* decision that warrant special
consideration. The first is the flat declaration that freedom of occupation is protected by the due process clause,[60] together with
the intimation that the "privilege doctrine" is no longer available
as a defense for arbitrary state licensing requirements. This clears
up an old and gaping ambiguity in American constitutional law.
It has long been contended, both with respect to public employ-

59. Compare the pristine statement of the clear and present danger test
in Schenck v. United States, 249 U.S. 47 (1919), with the contemporary
doctrine as enunciated in Dennis v. United States, 341 U.S. 494 (1951).
60. 353 U.S. at 238.

ment and with respect to "public professions" like the law that, since the privilege to engage in them is granted by the state, it can be taken away at the state's pleasure.[61] *Wieman* v. *Updegraff*[62] and *Slochower* v. *Board of Higher Educ.*[63] disposed of this contention as to actual civil servants; now *Schware* accomplishes a like result in relation to professional men. The qualifications the state sets for lawyers "must have a rational connection with the applicant's fitness or capacity to practice law."[64] It remains to be seen whether the Court will implement its new solicitude[65] for occupational freedom by wide-ranging review of license requirements in the professions and trades. What is presently clear is that the doctrinal way is open.

Some problems of judicial housekeeping that might be raised by such a course are suggested when we turn to the second noteworthy aspect of the decision: its implications concerning what is or is not reviewable in state determinations. Here Frankfurter, concurring in company with Clark and Harlan, assumes an artful role that brings to mind the famous Brandeis concurrence in *Whitney* v. *California*;[66] that is, he agrees with the Court's judgment but seeks to limit its range by the force of his own independent analysis. He is patently well aware that this decision verges on the danger line that separates questions of law from questions of fact; and he is at pains to insist that the state holding is overturned because it employed an unallowable legal standard, not because the ʔupreme Court disagrees with the particular result.[67] The state court had set up the apparently irrebuttable presumption that Communist party membership in young adulthood establishes the joiner for the rest of his life as of questionable character.[68] The facts of history, says Mr. Justice Frankfurter, prove this presumption unwarranted; since the state court "*as a matter of law* took a

61. See Yeiser v. Dysart, 267 U.S. 540 (1925); Cummings v. Missouri, 71 U.S. (4 Wall.) 277 (1867) (dissenting opinion).
62. 344 U.S. 183 (1952).
63. 350 U.S. 551 (1956).
64. 353 U.S. at 239.
65. See *In re* Summers, 325 U.S. 561 (1945).
66. 274 U.S. 357 (1927).
67. See 353 U.S. at 248–249.
68. See *id.* at 251.

contrary view . . . it denied him due process of law"[69] (emphasis added). For him it does not follow that the Supreme Court will now attempt the impossible task of reassessing the facts in all state administrative and judicial findings. There is no denying that the fact-law distinction in this case is a slippery one, and the Frankfurter opinion, though emphasizing it, may not wholly clarify its obscurities. Nevertheless the emphasis is important, for it serves notice that, if he has his way, state exercise of judgment will still receive respectful consideration.

Conceivably, as Frankfurter seems to hope, the same distinction can be squeezed from the opinion of the Court; but no such measured caution is evident in its language. The question, says Black, "is whether the Supreme Court of New Mexico on the record before us could reasonably find that [the petitioner] had not shown good moral character."[70] And he concludes that the record is bare of evidence "which rationally justifies"[71] the finding. Unless the sweep of these words is qualified in subsequent decisions, it is hard to see what limits are set on the Supreme Court's willingness to review factual determinations. Perhaps controversies involving the question of "good moral character" and alleged subversive connections are, like the forced confession cases, a quasi exception to the principle that the facts are in the states' domains.[72] But the Court majority advances no reasoning for assigning them this special status, and until it does the range of potential review seems wide indeed.

The impression that Mr. Justice Black is judging the facts in such cases is not dispelled by his majority opinion in *Konigsberg* v. *State Bar*.[73] This petitioner's case was a good deal muddier than

69. *Ibid.*
70. *Id.* at 239.
71. *Id.* at 246–247.
72. See Watts v. Indiana, 338 U.S. 49 (1949), and cases there cited. "But 'issue of fact' is a coat of many colors. It does not cover a conclusion drawn from uncontroverted happenings, when that conclusion incorporates standards of conduct or criteria for judgment which in themselves are decisive of constitutional rights. Such standards and criteria, measured against the requirements drown from constitutional provisions, and their proper applications, are issues for this Court's adjudication." *Id.* at 51.
73. 353 U.S. 252 (1957).

that of Schware. He had been refused certification to state practice on the ground that he had not met the burden of proving that he was of good moral character and did not advocate the overthrow of government by "unconstitutional means."[74] The rub was that Konigsberg—when questioned about such matters as Communist party membership, certain editorials he had written, and beliefs he held—refused to answer, arguing that the First and Fourteenth Amendments forbade the inquiries. Without upholding or denying this claim of privilege, the Supreme Court addressed itself to the question of whether the record supported any reasonable doubt as to the petitioner's good character or loyalty[75] and concluded that it did not. On the petitioner's side was substantial character testimony and an unblemished professional, military, and academic record. The State, said Black, could not draw unfavorable inferences from his refusals to answer if those refusals were based on his conviction, not frivolous, that the questions invaded a constitutionally privileged area. The remaining evidence, such as it was —testimony that Konigsberg had been a Communist party member in 1941 and the fact that he had published criticisms of government officials—must therefore stand alone and, standing alone, was insufficient to support the finding.

On its face then, the decision might be interpreted as merely holding that past party membership coupled with an expressed low opinion of public officials is inadequate grounds for doubt about character or loyalty, especially in the face of undiscredited favorable evidence. If so understood, *Konigsberg* would be pretty much on all fours with *Schware*. But this result is achieved by excluding all inferences based on refusal to answer, and this exclusion does imply a doctrinal advance. Although the Court denies that it is treating the matter of political belief and association as privileged, in fact it does so left-handedly by holding that no negative conclusions can be drawn from the self-imposed silence. Until the claims of constitutional privilege are formally decided one way or another, it would seem that a kind of tentative privilege does exist.

The net of the bar examination cases is this: (1) neither re-

74. *Id.* at 253.
75. *Id.* at 262.

mote, youthful Communist membership, nor refusal to answer questions about political connections, nor both together can be used as a sufficient basis for a finding of bad moral character; (2) state occupational requirements must comply with the due process clause; (3) to an uncertain degree state factual determinations will be reviewed as to the validity of the standards used and perhaps the actual correctness of their results. The first point seems moderate enough, since there is no intimation that present or even recent party membership might not warrant the adverse finding, if the fact of such membership can be established without forcing the applicant to talk in the face of his constitutional doubts. Points (2) and (3) are potentially far-reaching, but it is notorious in constitutional history that the road between potentiality and reality is often long.

The only other case of the Term concerning state power and the subversion issue was *Sweezy* v. *New Hampshire;*[76] but since that decision was linked with and in a way dependent on *Watkins* v. *United States,*[77] which involved national authority, it is best to consider *Watkins* first. The petitioner had been convicted of "contempt of Congress" under a statute penalizing the refusal to answer "pertinent questions" propounded by a Congressional committee.[78] Although he had testified willingly enough about himself, Watkins had challenged the authority of a subcommittee of the House of Representatives Committee on Un-American Activities to ask him questions about past associates whom he did not believe were presently members of the Communist party. His challenge was generally based on the argument that the investigation served no public purpose but was designed to expose individuals solely for the sake of exposure.[79]

The Court's opinion by Mr. Chief Justice Warren, dismissing the indictment, can be divided into three phases for purposes of analysis. In the first place, it offers a series of observations on the general theme that legislative investigations should rest on a valid

76. 354 U.S. 234 (1957).
77. 354 U.S. 178 (1957).
78. 2 U.S.C. § 192 (1952).
79. 354 U.S. at 199.

legislative purpose set forth with some degree of clarity by the legislature itself. Starting from the conceded premise of *Kilbourn* v. *Thompson*[80] that a legislative purpose must be present, the Chief Justice declares that Congress has no general power "to expose for the sake of exposure."[81] Then he goes on to suggest that a broad authorization like that enjoyed by the Un-American Activities Committee makes it impossible for anyone to know whether Congress really wanted the information being gathered: the House itself is insulated from the specific inquiry by the "wide gulf" separating "the responsibility for the use of investigative power and the actual exercise of that power."[82]

Second, the Chief Justice advances some broad animadversions concerning the impact of legislative investigations on the freedoms of the First Amendment. A long-standing uncertainty is dissipated by his statement that the investigatory power is subject to First Amendment limitations because it is "part of lawmaking."[83] This conclusion has been at least logically implicit in the Court's doctrine since *Quinn* v. *United States*[84] assumed that the privilege against self-incrimination was available to congressional witnesses, for if one provision of the Bill of Rights was applicable there seemed no good reason for assuming that others were not. But the outright affirmance of the implication is a milestone of no trivial importance nonetheless.[85] And, continues the Chief Justice, where the investigatory power bumps up against freedom of expression, the aforementioned need for a clear-cut congressional mandate is all the greater.

At this point a reader might well assume that the opinion lays

---

80. 103 U.S. 168 (1881).
81. 354 U.S. at 200.
82. *Id.* at 205.
83. *Id.* at 197.
84. 349 U.S. 155 (1955).
85. United States v. Rumely, 345 U.S. 41 (1953), raised the question of First Amendment relevance to the investigatory power; but the Court found a statutory basis for deciding the question of rights. As late as 1957 a writer could say: "To the extent that its decisions thus far are a criterion, a majority of the highest Court appears to be of the view that there are few, if any, constitutional restrictions of consequence upon the permissible scope of Congressional inquiries." SCHWARTZ, THE SUPREME COURT 56 (1957).

the basis for a holding of broad dimensions. If vague and over-extensive mandates from Congress to its committees are as pernicious as has been said, and if their vice is enhanced when a committee entrenches on First Amendment rights, then the Court must be preparing to hold that compulsory process is unavailable except when the committee mandate is both clear and reasonably circumscribed. Congress is about to be deprived of the power to assign its committee a "roving commission to inquire into evils,"[86] or at any rate to use compulsory process when it does.

But now the Chief Justice turns to the third phase, or aspect, of his decision. The indictment must fall, he says, because the statutory penalty applies only to the refusal to answer questions "pertinent to the question under inquiry;"[87] due process requires that a person in jeopardy of such a penalty "have knowledge of the subject to which the interrogation is deemed pertinent"[88] so that he can have some idea of when he is about to transgress the law; no such knowledge was available to Watkins because neither the House, the subcommittee chairman, nor the intrinsic character of the hearing clarified the subject of inquiry; therefore the indictment violates the due process clause. In short, the vices of breadth and vagueness which have been so roundly criticized can apparently be remedied by a mere statement from the chairman or the full committee or even, failing such a statement, by inference drawn from "the nature of the proceedings themselves." Congress can still send its committees forth on fishing expeditions, and the pertinency of its questions for the purposes of compulsory process can be established so long as it is clear what particular waters are being fished at any given time! The suggestion that the original legislative mandate must be clear and specific, the discussion of First Amendment rights, the dictum against the "power of exposure" seem almost wholly irrelevant in the light of this modest result. Again Justice Frankfurter, concurring, plays the part we observed in the *Schware* case. "I deem it important," he says, "to

86. A. L. A. Schechter Poultry Corp. v. United States, 295 U.S. 495, 551 (1935) (concurring opinion).
87. 354 U.S. at 208.
88. *Ibid.*

state what I understand to be the Court's holding."[89] He then proceeds to set forth what has been called here the third phase of the Court's opinion, treating the issue as involving the application of due process to a penal statute, leaving out all references to other large matters, and getting the job done in just three paragraphs of medium size.

The Court's opinion in *Sweezy* v. *New Hampshire* is pervaded with the same disapprobation of wide-ranging mandates to investigate that was found in *Watkins,* but here the Court's strictures may have a little more to do with the case result. The legislature of New Hampshire had directed the Attorney General of that state to conduct an investigation in hope of determining whether "subversive persons are presently located" within the borders of New Hampshire; he was directed to report back to the legislature on the results of his reconnaissance. To aid him in the quest he was armed with subpoena power and with the power to call on the state superior court to hold recalcitrant witnesses in contempt. The petitioner, summoned before the Attorney General, had been otherwise responsive but had declined to answer two groups of questions: those relating to his knowledge of and association with the Progressive party in New Hampshire and those relating to a lecture he had delivered at faculty invitation to a class at the University of New Hampshire in 1954. His contention was that these questions were not pertinent to the matter under inquiry and were in conflict with the First Amendment.

The Chief Justice's opinion, for himself and Justices Douglas, Clark, and Brennan, lays the ground for its conclusion by setting down at the outset a sharp critique of the term "subversive person" —which was defined by the state law so loosely that it included one who, even without *scienter,* assisted an assistant of a person who attempted violent overthrow of the government. Next he reaffirms the doctrine of *Watkins* that legislative investigations, like laws themselves, may encroach on the right of free expression, and he declares that this one has so encroached "in the areas of

89. *Id.* at 216.

academic freedom and political expression."[90] The third step is to assert, with ample argument, that these freedoms are of very special importance.

Here is a turning point similar to the one in *Watkins,* though it is followed by a rather different conclusion. The Chief Justice's opinion so far has cleared the way, or seemed to clear the way, for a judicial determination of whether the state need to discover the facts it seeks outweighs the deprivation of constitutional rights in these important areas.[91] He comes perilously close to answering the question negatively in this rather startling sentence: "We do not now conceive of any circumstance wherein a state interest would justify infringement of rights in these fields."[92]

But, he continues, this task of the imagination need not be essayed because it is impossible to know here what facts the legislature sought and therefore what state need the discovery of those facts might be said to serve. This is true because the mandate to investigate subversive persons is too broad to be meaningful. If the legislature has not told us what it wants, we cannot decide that what it wants is important. The uncertainty as to what the legislature seeks involves equal uncertainty as to whether it needs what it seeks; and without a knowledge of some state need, we cannot allow the abridgement of fundamental liberties.

The short answer to all this is that the legislature has delegated to the Attorney General the power to decide what it seeks, and the opinion is understandable only if we assume that the legislature is being denied the right thus to delegate its power. Readers familiar with such famous cases as *Hampton*[93] and *Panama Refining,*[94] not to mention John Locke's *Second Treatise on Government,* will be tempted to think that this is their old friend, the doctrine of separation of powers, now applied to the states. But the Chief Justice flatly repudiates the idea that his ruling is related to the

90. 354 U.S. at 250.
91. Cf. American Communications Ass'n, CIO v. Douds, 339 U.S. 382 (1950).
92. 354 U.S. at 251.
93. J. W. Hampton, Jr., & Co. v. United States, 276 U.S. 394 (1928).
94. Panama Refining Co. v. Ryan, 293 U.S. 388 (1935).

classic doctrine. His concern is with "separation of the power of a state legislature to conduct investigations from the responsibility to direct the use of that power."[95] This language is taken almost verbatim from *Watkins*.

Whatever may be the merits of this distinction between two kinds of separation of power, they apparently evade the understanding of Mr. Justice Frankfurter. He sees the Chief Justice's opinion as a resort to the classic doctrine and thus in conflict with *Dreyer* v. *People*,[96] which held that the states were not bound by the separation of powers requirement. He accepts the idea that the Attorney General's demand is the legislature's demand and goes on to ask the next logical question: does a state need warrant this invasion of individual rights, bearing in mind that the rights are very precious and that to override them "the subordinating interest of the State must be compelling."[97] The threats to the security of New Hampshire involved in the matters being inquired into here were, he holds, too remote and shadowy to justify the queries. In spite of his frequent warnings against too much judicial zeal in the free speech field, Justice Frankfurter has always conceded that when legislative action passes a certain extreme margin of reason it must encounter the judicial veto. This presumably is one of those governmental acts which lacks "rational justification"[98] or is "outside the pale of fair judgment."[99]

In sum, *Watkins* and *Sweezy*, in their strict holdings, leave the legislature's power to investigate subversion not many millimeters from where they found it. As for Congress, the kind of procedural flaw that was condemned in the treatment of Watkins can probably be mended if the investigators merely define the subject under inquiry at any particular time. It is possible, though by no means certain, that the House might also be required to clarify to some degree its mandates to the investigators, but apparently "a measure

95. 354 U.S. at 255.
96. 187 U.S. 71 (1902).
97. 234 U.S. at 265 (concurring opinion).
98. West Virginia State Bd. of Educ. v. Barnette, 319 U.S. 624, 666 (1943) (dissenting opinion).
99. Dennis v. United States, 341 U.S. 494, 540 (1951) (concurring opinion).

of added care"[100] would be enough. As for the states, the mandates of their legislative bodies are held somewhat more explicitly to the requirement of specificity by the opinion of the Chief Justice and his associates. But in the first place, he speaks for only four members of the Court (Justice Whittaker took no part; Justices Frankfurter and Harlan concurred in the judgment but not in the opinion; Justices Clark and Burton dissented). And in the second place, there is no reason to doubt that a modicum of tidiness in drafting resolutions would answer the need. Finally, the declaration that First Amendment rights may be claimed against legislative committees opens doors but supplies no guarantee that the Court will enter them in the future more often than it has in the past.

Among all the cases of the 1956 Term dealing with subversion, *Jencks* v. *United States*[101] probably excited the greatest public furor for the smallest cause.[102] The petitioner had been convicted under an indictment charging that he had falsely sworn in a Taft-Hartley "non-Communist affidavit" that he was neither a member nor an affiliate of the Communist party. In the trial two government witnesses, J. W. Ford and Harvey F. Matusow, had testified concerning petitioner's alleged party activity during the relevant period. The trial court had denied a motion to produce for inspection FBI records containing contemporaneous reports by these witnesses about the facts to which they later testified. Petitioner claimed error in denial of the motion and in the instructions as to the meaning of "affiliation." Only the first challenge was considered by the Court.

The majority opinion, by Mr. Justice Brennan, held that the trial court, as well as the court of appeals which sustained it,[103] had

100. 354 U.S. at 215.
101. 353 U.S. 657 (1957).
102. Three weeks after the decision a bill was introduced in the Senate declaring that, "any rule of court or procedure to the contrary notwithstanding," only the actual reports of witnesses themselves relating to the subject matter of testimony shall be made available to the defense. S. 2377, 85th Cong., 1st Sess. (1957). It is doubtful that the bill is more than declaratory of the judgment of the Court.
103. Jencks v. United States, 226 F.2d 540 (5th Cir. 1955), *rev'd*, 353 U.S. 657 (1957).

erred. Both government opposition to the motion and the court of appeals holding had rested on the ground that a preliminary foundation of inconsistency between the reports and the testimony had not been laid. Such a foundation, said the Supreme Court, is unnecessary. If the reports "were of the events and activities related in their testimony"[104] they must be produced. Moreover, they must be produced to the defendant and not merely to the trial judge. If the reports touch "the events and activities as to which they [the witnesses] testified at the trial," the petitioner may inspect them to decide whether to use them in his defense.[105] The Government therefore has two alternatives. It may produce the records to the defense or it may drop the case; there is no third choice.

The opinion, read as a whole, suggests beyond much likelihood of misunderstanding that the files which must be produced are no more than those concerning the testimony of the adverse witnesses and quite probably only the particular reports the witnesses themselves made concerning the facts they described in testimony. Yet two or three sentences, if read unwarily and out of context, might hint that a broader foray into FBI files is permitted, and it is this trap that seems to have ensnared a few lay and professional commentators, the latter including Mr. Justice Clark. Says the Court:

The practice of producing government documents to the trial judge for his determination of relevancy and materiality, without hearing the accused, is disapproved. Relevancy and materiality for the purposes of production and inspection, with a view to use on cross examination, are established when the reports are shown to relate to the testimony of the witness. Only after inspection of the reports by the accused must the trial judge determine admissibility—*e.g.,* evidentiary questions of inconsistency, materiality and relevancy—of the contents and the method to be employed for the elimination of parts immaterial or irrelevant.[106]

These words may convey the impression that the files of government intelligence agencies are "opened . . . to the criminal," thus

104. 353 U.S. at 666.
105. *Id.* at 668.
106. *Id.* at 669.

affording him "a Roman holiday of rummaging through confidential information."[107] But it is most improbable that they were meant to do so. The uncertainties arising from this language could be two. First, the statement that the trial judge may not make prior determination of relevancy and materiality might suggest that the files in general are open to the defendant for him to examine in the hope of finding something that has to do with the testified facts.[108] Second, the statement that "relevancy and materiality for the purposes of production . . . are established when the reports are shown to relate to the testimony" might suggest that other reports than those of the witnesses must be made available, provided only that they pertained to the testified facts—for example, a report of another nontestifying agent on the same facts. But neither of these interpretations seems tenable when earlier language is taken into account. As for the first confusion:

a sufficient foundation was established by the testimony of Matusow and Ford that their reports were *of the events and activities related in their testimony.*[109]

We now hold that the petitioner was entitled to an order directing the Government to produce for inspection all reports of Matusow and Ford . . . *touching the events and activities as to which they testified at the trial.*[110]

As for the second: "Nor was this a demand for statements taken from persons or informants *not offered as witnesses.*"[111] "[T]he petitioner was entitled to an order directing the Government to produce for inspection all reports of *Matusow and Ford.*"[112]

It is hardly probable that the Court, after phrasing the points in such limited terms, meant to discard the limitations by innuendo in the later sentences quoted. While the Court does not say explicitly that the trial judge may first examine and withhold from

107. *Id.* at 681–682 (dissenting opinion).
108. But see Simms v. United States, Cr. No. 13658, D. C. Cir., July 8, 1957.
109. 353 U.S. at 666. (Emphasis added.)
110. *Id.* at 688. (Emphasis added.)
111. *Id.* at 667. (Emphasis added.)
112. *Id.* at 668. (Emphasis added.)

the defense any material that is unrelated to the testified facts, as well as any reports by persons other than the witnesses, both inferences appear almost unmistakable. In such a case, the government may keep from the stand witnesses who have made previous reports of their testimony, or it may produce to the defense the witness's reports having to do with the testified facts, or it may withhold the reports and drop the case. When seen in this modest light the *Jencks* case seems indeed a molehill promoted to the status of a mountain. It is a minor procedural advance, a slight extension of the rights of accused persons (whether "loyal" or "subversive") and no more.

Another decision that appears to have set pulses racing with doubtful reason was *Yates* v. *United States*,[113] though of all the holdings of the 1956 Term this was perhaps the most ambiguous. It involved fourteen persons convicted of conspiring to advocate and teach overthrow of the government by force and violence and of conspiring to organize, as the Communist party of the United States, a society dedicated to such advocacy.[114] The Court, through Mr. Justice Harlan, held that the conviction on the second charge could not be sustained because the term "organize" referred only to "act entering into the creation of a new organization, and not to acts thereafter performed in carrying out its activities, even though such acts may loosely be termed organizational."[115] Since the legislative history of the Smith Act was unilluminating as to the precise meaning of the term, and since the term was susceptible of both interpretations, the Court followed "the familiar rule that criminal statutes are to be strictly construed. . . ."[116] The Communist Party having been "organized" in this strict sense in 1945 and the indictment having been returned in 1951, the charge was barred by the three-year statute of limitations.

All of this was straightforward enough and is interesting for the purposes of this paper mainly because it exemplifies the Court's policy of interpreting anti-subversive laws narrowly, a policy re-

113. 354 U.S. 298 (1957).
114. See *id.* at 300–302 for exact terms of indictment.
115. *Id.* at 310.
116. *Ibid.*

vealed two years ago in *Peters* v. *Hobby* and carried on in such 1955 Term cases as *Pennsylvania* v. *Nelson*[117] and *Cole* v. *Young*,[118] and in *Service* v. *Dulles* in this term. In *Yates* as in those cases, the blow to the substantive power of government is far from mortal, for Congress can quite properly change the law if it prefers the broader interpretation; meantime, there seems no good reason why the Court should be expected to assume the legislative burden of amendment. Moreover, there is little danger, even if this interpretation stands, that malefactors will thereby slip through the Smith Act's net. The Government still has the "membership clause"[119] and the clauses prohibiting advocacy, either of which might be applied to organizational activity in the broad sense urged by the prosecution.

Having disposed of that matter in the case, however, the Court now turned to the question of whether the advocacy charge could stand, and here the underbrush is a little thicker. The trial judge had rejected jury instructions proposed by both defense and prosecution and based on those approved by the Supreme Court in *Dennis* v. *United States.* In the present Supreme Court's view, the instructions which the trial judge had preferred failed to distinguish between "advocacy of forcible overthrow as an abstract doctrine and advocacy of action to that end."[120] Congress did not intend to punish the former kind of activity; therefore the conviction on this charge must fall.

The meaning of this part of the decision is open to two interpretations, and unfortunately both can find some support in the words of the Court. The Court might be understood as suggesting that the proscribed advocacy must aim not only at the generalized object of overthrowing the government, but at some specific action to that end—in other words, there is a difference between telling a man that he ought to try to overthrow the government and telling him that he ought to repair to a particular barricade armed with appropriate musketry. Mr. Justice Harlan speaks of Congress'

117. 350 U.S. 497 (1956).
118. 351 U.S. 536 (1956).
119. 18 U.S.C. § 2385 (1952).
120. 354 U.S. at 320.

awareness of the "distinction between advocacy or teaching of abstract doctrine and advocacy of action"[121] and elsewhere phrases the problem of discrimination in similar terms.[122] Because it was agreed that the advocacy must in any case be done with specific intent to accomplish overthrow, this reading would suggest a second order of specific intent: the *very* specific intent to send listeners to the barricades. A reader of the Court's opinion might be excused for thinking that this other level of intent was already subsumed under the rubric of specific intent to accomplish overthrow, and some of the arguments of Mr. Justice Reed in *Hartzel* v. *United States*[123] come to mind. If the jury has already found beyond reasonable doubt the specific intent to accomplish overthrow, then there is nothing "abstract" about the advocacy, and it is gilding the lily to require yet another order of proof.

But there is a second and more likely interpretation: that the Court was really focussing on the distinction between "the statement of an idea which may prompt its hearers to take unlawful action, and advocacy that such action be taken"[124]—that its concern was not with the intent of the advocacy (since that was taken care of by the finding of specific intent to cause overthrow), but with its probable effect. The inadequacy of the jury charge was that it withdrew from consideration "any issue as to the character of the advocacy in terms of its capacity to stir listeners to forcible action."[125] Of course in considering this question of probable effect, the jury might be more impressed by a call to the barricades than by a more generalized appeal, but that is another matter. The Court was obviously worried that the jury might confuse abstract discussion and incitement, and the difficulty about interpreting this worry reliably is that the term "incitement" may imply both the

121. *Ibid.*
122. "We are thus faced with the question whether the Smith Act prohibits advocacy and teaching of forcible overthrow as an abstract principle, divorced from any *effort to instigate* action to that end, so long as such advocacy or teaching is engaged in with evil intent." *Id.* at 318. (Emphasis added.)
123. 322 U.S. 680, 693, 694 (1944) (dissenting opinion).
124. 354 U.S. at 322.
125. *Id.* at 315.

intent and the probability of an evil result.[126] But in this situation the intent aspect is covered by the requirement to find specific intent to attempt overthrow, and it seems logical to infer that the chief objection of the Court is to the fact that the issue of reasonable and probable result was withdrawn from the jury. The jury would thus be left free to find punishable under the Smith Act words that were likely to leave hearers quite unmoved, provided their intent was evil. One thinks of a professorial disquisition on the necessity of revolution which its academic author fondly hopes will foment bloodshed but which is in fact more likely to foment ennui. Under the judge's charge, the jury might find guilt in the publication of such a tract, and the Court is obviously perturbed by that interpretation. Its perturbation is hardly surprising, since a holding that Congress could punish advocacy unaccompanied by probability of dangerous action would ignore constitutional doctrine that has been building since *Schenck* v. *United States.*

But it must be conceded that the language is cloudy on this point, and it is conceivable that the Court had both a requirement of "super-specific intent" and of probable effect in mind. Even if it did, however, this part of the decision establishes no very rigid limitations on congressional power. There is no reason to believe that it inhibits Congress any more than did *Dennis* v. *United States,* for the clear drift is that the same instructions as those used in the *Dennis* trial would have been approved. Moreover, here as before, the Court is merely construing the Smith Act, and Congress may change that law if it likes. It is true that the opinion suggests that a "constitutional danger zone" would be reached if Congress attempted to punish abstract doctrine; but, as suggested earlier, that danger zone has been known to exist for almost forty years. If *Yates* enlarges it at all, it does not enlarge it much.

Such was the civil rights record of the Supreme Court during its 1956 Term; these were the breezes that caused the gale. What do they add up to? Has the Court departed from the role in which it cast itself in other recent years? Have the justices turned back

126. See Gitlow v. New York, 268 U.S. 652, 664, 665 (1925); Whitney v. California, 274 U.S. 357, 376 (1927) (concurring opinion).

the clock two decades to a civil rights version of the judicial activism of Mr. Justice Sutherland?

Before these questions are answered even tentatively, a word about judicial ambiguity may be in order. A student of the Court's history, past and present, has no right to ask that his task of analysis and interpretation be discharged *a priori* by opinions so lucidly intelligible that they leave no room for doubt. The world which the justices rule is a pertinaciously complex one; its blacks and whites have a disconcerting tendency to dissolve into various shadings of gray. It is hard to write simply about intricate and subtle matters, and often it is quite impossible to write so that those who run may read. But even those who are prepared to sit still and ponder might feel that some of the 1956 Term opinions carry the enigmatic a few ells beyond strict necessity. The Chief Justice's opinions in *Watkins* and *Sweezy* tease the understanding partly because significant sequiturs appear to be omitted and partly because he insists that what seems to be the old spade "separation of powers" be called something else. If the difference is real rather than semantic, it badly needs clarification. By the same token, the opinions of Mr. Justice Brennan and Mr. Justice Harlan in *Jencks* and *Yates,* respectively, leave highly significant strings untied.

But ambiguity has its uses, and the model for a certain form of studied opacity is no less than the great Chief Justice himself. The question of whether *Fletcher* v. *Peck*[127] rested on the contract clause or natural law, the question of whether *Gibbons* v. *Ogden*[128] condemned the state law because of conflict with a federal statute or with the "dormant" commerce power—these questions are not reliably answerable from John Marshall's opinions. Each was left for history to determine. Meantime a case result had been achieved; a lecture had been read to those who cared to listen (and some who did not); a seed had been sown, to wither or prosper. Perhaps the elusiveness of points in some of the 1956 Term decisions was designed with this prototype in mind.

127. 10 U.S. (6 Cranch) *87 (1810).
128. 22 U.S. (9 Wheat.) *1 (1824).

Solacing as these speculations may be, they make it no easier to declare with perfect confidence what the subversion cases of the Term add up to. Yet the uncertainties, though present, are not so great or so many as to obscure the overall results. Surely it is clear that the strict holdings in these cases are neither very startling nor very menacing to the substance of governmental power in this field. The bar examination cases forbid a standard of proof based on an absurd anachronism and set up a narrow implied privilege of silence that might be relevant to one bar applicant in a hundred thousand. The *Watkins* decision is ultimately so narrow that it seems to bypass the very evils of uninhibited inquisition against which the opponents of the investigatory power most complain. *Sweezy* evades the substantive issue that even the fastidious Justice Frankfurter felt required to decide and erects a procedural requirement that can probably be met by the most modest feat of legislative draftsmanship. *Jencks* and *Yates* bite only a trifle, if any, deeper. On the most likely interpretation, *Jencks* allows the defense discovery of the few reports of government witnesses concerning the facts they have testified about. If the facts are already in testimony, it is hard to see why the government should wish to withhold the reports about them—unless indeed the testimony and the reports are in conflict. In the far-fetched event that these particular reports contain government secrets so inextricably associated with the testimony that they cannot be separated, the witness can be kept from the stand and the files will remain sacrosanct as before. These inconveniences seem small in return for the assurance that justice is being done. As for *Yates,* the narrow definition of "organize" simply expunges a kind of redundancy from the law and is, in any event, subject to congressional revision; the holding on the "advocacy" charge, however interpreted, apparently creates no difficulties that were not met by the prosecution with the approval of the Court in *Dennis* v. *United States.* If the critics wanted the Court to approve *any* prosecution under the Smith Act, no matter how conducted, their hopes have been dashed. But this was a good deal to ask of the highest judicial body in a nation that still respects the rule of law.

In short, the Supreme Court of the 1956 Term, when judged in terms of its strict holdings is still comfortably within the limits described in the preceding section. That these holdings erect no important substantive bars in the subversion field is an evaluation too obvious to merit much further belaboring. Procedural fault-finding and statutory interpretation are still the order of the day. But, as everyone knows, procedural restrictions may proliferate into a maze of harassments and delays that amount to substantive paralysis; statutory interpretation may cloak a policy of stubborn judicial negativism. Is this perhaps the case here? Has government's power to deal with subversion been covertly whittled away or indirectly challenged? Again the plain answer is that it has not. There is no apparent reason to believe that meeting the procedural requirements will even impose a very serious inconvenience, or to suspect that the avenues of legislative amendment have been significantly straitened. The campaign against subversives can go on, subject only to the proviso that the campaigners observe, as contest-makers say, "a few easy rules."

Much less does the record of the term support the suggestion that the Court's current interdictions are cognate with the judicial nihilisms of the early 1930's. The nature of the great anti-New Deal decisions has been aptly described by the late Justice Jackson:

Had the decision of the Court been confined to the limited issues actually involved in the immediate controversies and the way left clear for the Congress to improve and perfect its remedies, no irrepressible conflict would have arisen.

But in striking at New Deal laws, the Court allowed its language to run riot . . . In overthrowing the A.A.A. the Court cast doubt upon all federal aid to agriculture; in laying low the N.R.A., the Court struck at all national effort to maintain fair labor standards; and in outlawing the New York Minimum Wage Law . . . the Court deliberately attempted to outlaw any form of state legislation to protect minimum-wage standards. The Court not merely challenged the policies of the New Deal but erected judicial barriers to the reasonable exercise of legislative powers, both state and national, to meet the urgent needs of a twentieth-century community.[129]

129. JACKSON, THE STRUGGLE FOR JUDICIAL SUPREMACY 174-175 (1941).

This is an almost perfect description of what the Supreme Court has *not* done in connection with the issue of subversion, in either the 1956 Term or those that immediately preceded it.

In examining some of the incidental results, dicta, and implication of the Term, the landscape may assume a somewhat different aspect—though not different enough to lend color to the canards that have been fashioned from it. Some of these corollate developments have the effect of extending the judicial purview without necessarily implying very stringent limitations. The premise of the bar examination cases, that arbitrary occupational requirements cannot be justified on the ground that the state is granting a "privilege," punctures a legal sophistry that never had much excuse for being. The concession in *Watkins* that investigatory action *may* infringe freedom of expression simply stamps constitutional recognition on a fact of life. Both these pronouncements may be regarded as ironing out lines of constitutional logic which had been distorted beyond good sense. The hints in *Schware* and *Konigsberg,* that the Court may reassess state factual determinations, is mildly disturbing, but it bears not so much on the subversion problem as on the general problem of "span of control," and the judges will no doubt take steps to insure that their reach does not exceed their grasp.

Other developments raise somewhat stronger misgivings. The *Watkins* denunciation of exposure "for the sake of exposure" impales a congressional abuse that may deserve censure; and the denunciation has no apparent bearing on the present holding. Perhaps it can be taken as a non-operative homiletic, like Marshall's famous sermon against the Jeffersonian party before he denied jurisdiction in *Marbury* v. *Madison.*[130] On the other hand, it could be a kind of finger exercise for a future decision that a congressional inquiry was backed by no valid legislative purpose. If it portends the opening of that Pandora's box, a long and thoughtful pause is in order. And similar qualms are provoked by some of the reasoning in *Sweezy,* if it is pressed to its potential. Is the Court preparing to furbish a remodelled version of the

130. 5 U.S. (1 Cranch) 137 (1803).

doctrine of separation of powers and apply it to the states? If so, a whole body of new constitutional law is implied, and it could make, as Justice Frankfurter says, "the deepest inroads upon our federal system."[131]

There is no way of being sure whether these hints cast up by the 1956 Term Court are meant to serve as moral admonitions only or to foreshadow a renascence of judicial supremacy in the civil rights field. Quite possibly, the judges, or some of them, are themselves unsure. But it may be reasonable to infer that much of the rhetoric, seemingly meaningless to the decisions of the cases, does indicate a certain restlessness on the bench, a lingering dissatisfaction with the role of modest grandeur that has been its lot in recent years, a nascent tendency to sway the rod of empire once more.

This tendency or temptation, if it is one, is stimulated by certain contemporary factors whose aggregate force is not unimpressive. In the first place, on the Court itself are Justices Black and Douglas, who have consistently urged that the power to punish "subversion" should be sharply and substantively curtailed. Justice Black, concurring in part and dissenting in part, reiterates their position in *Yates*:

Unless there is complete freedom for expression of all ideas, whether we like them or not, concerning the way government should be run and who shall run it, I doubt if any views in the long run can be secured against the censor. The First Amendment provides the only kind of security system that can preserve a free government—one that leaves the way wide open for people to favor, discuss, advocate, or incite causes and doctrines however obnoxious and antagonistic such views may be the rest of us.[132]

These are wise words and good words for citizens to hear, but when they are put forward as a standard for judicial supervision they beg a most important question: whether they impose on the

131. 354 U.S. at 256.
132. 354 U.S. at 344. In its flat-footed hostility to legislative adventures like the Smith Act, this view smacks of the argument advanced by the philosopher Alexander Meiklejohn a few years ago, that First Amendment freedoms should be absolutely, not relatively, immune from government interference. MEIKLEJOHN, FREE SPEECH AND ITS RELATION TO SELF-GOVERNMENT (1948).

courts a responsibility greater than courts can bear. Nevertheless there is some reason to suspect that they attract the Chief Justice and Mr. Justice Brennan without altogether convincing them. In the six decisions that have been given main attention here— *Schware, Konigsberg, Watkins, Sweezy, Jencks,* and *Yates*—these four judges stood together with the majority opinion in all but *Yates,* in which the Chief Justice joined Justices Harlan and Frankfurter and Justice Brennan did not participate. Without pressing the point too hard, it might be fairly inferrable that Justice Frankfurter holds solidly in favor of the moderate supervisory role the Court assumed a year ago and is often joined by Burton and Harlan; Black and Douglas exert their influence to carry the Court to much bolder negativisms; Brennan and the Chief may be drawn a little way along that road, but so far on the judicial record they stand closer to the Frankfurter position than to that of Douglas and Black. But these are powerful advocates, and their possible impact on the course of judicial development should not be taken lightly. Justice Clark, it should be added, seems immune to their importunings; and since Justice Whittaker took no part in any of these cases, he remains a comparatively imponderable quantity.

A second factor which may tend to inspire judicial temerity in the civil rights field is the encouragement of what may loosely be called the liberal community. For years now the Court has been urged to take a stronger line against governmental suppression of First Amendment freedoms. When such urgings are rooted in an awareness that the judicial range of choice has limits, they merit respectful consideration; but it is still worth remembering that cheerleaders are exempt from the responsibility for wrong decisions, while players are not. Still a third factor might be the chorus of dispraise in the past two terms from the branch of American opinion which David Riesman identifies as "pseudo-conservative."[133] A good deal of this criticism has been intemperate

133. *New Critics of the Court,* New Republic, July 29, 1957, p. 9. The author suggests, not without justice, that Justice Clark "spoke in the recent civil liberties cases with the forceful and unambiguous simplicities of the pseudo-conservative."

and thoughtless and has suggested all too clearly the idea that the Court and the rule of law should knuckle under whenever they happen to displease us. In the existing climate, it is entirely possible that such criticism from such sources would embolden, rather than daunt, the Supreme Court. Justice Frankfurter once remarked that as a result of such execration "a judge, proud of his independence, may unconsciously have his back stiffened, and thereby his mind."[134]

Such factors, combined with the tradition of supremacy it inherits, not to mention the human propensity to right a wrong, could dislodge the Court from its carefully considered pose of recent years and send it forth on a new career of derring-do. That it has not yet embarked on that career is indisputable; not even a clear intention to do so can be wrung from the opinions of the 1956 Term. The most that can be inferred is an underlying note of impatience with this business of self-restraint, a flagging of what Keats called "negative capability."

Nevertheless, it is not perhaps too early to sound a soft note of alarm, to urge that the Court's existing role in the American polity is a noble and appropriate one, to hope that the justices will go slow in reasserting their sometime place at the vortex of politics. No one but a prophet can know whether the imperium once lost can be regained and held, assuming that it was more than an illusory possession in the first place. Was the control the Supreme Court once exercised in the economic sphere real sovereignty, or did it rest on the substantial devotion of the nation to the principle of laissez-faire? How long did it last after that devotion faded? How many chapters in judicial history, carefully read, reveal the Court successfully thwarting a determined Congress where major issues were concerned? Not many, and they involve a Court that still professed the myth of Olympian self-certainty. It is at least doubtful that a judicial power, once committed to the mordant common sense of Holmes in *Baldwin* v. *Missouri*[135] or Stone in *United States* v. *Butler*,[136] can recover

134. Craig v. Harney, 331 U.S. 367, 392 (1947).
135. 281 U.S. 586, 595 (1930) (dissenting opinion).
136. 297 U.S. 1, 87–88 (1936) (dissenting opinion).

the carte blanche it so firmly relinquished. Both "the inner republic of bench and bar" and the educated American community
are more sophisticated about the judiciary than they were a couple
of generations ago.

But quite beyond the question of whether the Court can return
to the custodial ways of the past is the question of whether it
should return to them. The finest hours of the Court have not been
those in which it flatly opposed the substantive power of the other
branches, confident that judges understand better than all others
the process of balancing necessity and justice. On the contrary,
the Court has served both the judicial tradition and the American
republic most usefully when it has kept to a path of duty more
consistent with its real expertise— insisting upon a decent regard
for regularity and fairness, enforcing the plain command of the
Constitution when it was really plain, but respecting the judgment of the other branches always, and most especially in those
matters of high political decision that are the peculiar responsibility of the legislative and executive authorities. No doubt those
authorities often err and have erred in their assessment of the
subversion threat and what to do about it. Insofar as such error
is almost wholly irrational, as in the *Sweezy* situation, the Court
must assume the burden of correcting it, as Justice Frankfurter
did. Insofar as it violates the procedural imperatives of the Constitution, as in *Jencks,* the Court should call a halt. Insofar as it
rests on a loose interpretation of a statute, as in *Yates,* the Court
can adopt a more restrictive gloss and give Congress a chance to
look again at its policy. These judicial actions preserve the vitality
of constitutionalism while keeping the Court within the limits of
a fitting role. It would be regrettable if the Court, having done
all this, should try to occupy the plains of heaven too.

TOOLS, STUMBLING BLOCKS, AND
STEPPING STONES*

[This article first appeared in the *Virginia Law Review*, 44, no. 7 (November 1958), 1029–1055.]

> Each is given a bag of tools,
> A shapeless mass,
> A book of rules;
> And each must make,
> Ere life is flown,
> A stumbling block
> Or a stepping stone.
>
> R. L. Sharpe

From 1937 to 1958 the Court has accommodated itself and its doctrines to the new juridical order whose advent was signalized by the dramatic decisions of 1937 and to the new world order which was even then coming into being. The major premises of the new jurisprudence were reduced concern for protecting economic rights, increased concern for protecting the other rights of individuals, and acceptance of the idea of judicial self-restraint. The egregious facts of the new world order were war, the threat of war, and modern totalitarianism. During these twenty years the Court's problem has been to formulate a role which brings these assorted premises and facts into some kind of viable relationship; yet for a time it seemed that this task of synthesis would go unperformed. It was temptingly (though speciously) satisfying in particular cases to forget this premise or to ignore that fact, rather than to make an adjustment between them; justices are not necessarily immune to the American illusion that hard questions can be resolved by pretending they are easy. And the Court often appeared divided in these years between those who recognized one half of the problem and those who recognized the other half.

* Thanks are due Donald R. Reich and Mary Messer for aid in preparing this paper.

But in the 1955 Term it was possible to find evidence that the Court had at last put these facile ways aside and had evolved a role which took due account of both facts and premises. The decisions of the Term suggested a fairly coherent judicial policy. Civil rights were being protected; the solicitude for the individual which distinguished the post-1937 Court from its predecessor was still on full display. But the justices were tacitly employing a kind of double standard, depending on whether or not the galling and explosive issue of "subversion" was raised. When that issue was involved, the Court's veto was couched in terms of procedural caveat and statutory interpretation, and the substantive power of government remained unchallenged. When the subversion issue was not involved, the frontiers of constitutional liberty were pushed ahead more boldly, even to the extent of inhibiting governmental power in fundamental ways. Such a dualism seemed to imply that the Court majority, though mindful of the individual, was also aware that judicial governance must be bounded by the limits of judicial capacity. It preferred to play a modest role in connection with an issue so near the political storm center. Then other issues, less politically charged but no less important in the long run to the atmosphere of freedom, could—it was hoped—be dealt with all the more effectively. For the Court's balance and prestige would not have been impaired by a bout of windmill-tilting.

If the justices who took up this scrupulously modest position did hope that their self-restraint would be noted and appreciated, they must now be nursing a sense of injured innocence. The trouble was, of course, that the decisions involving racial discrimination, particularly *Brown* v. *Board of Education*,[1] had created an atmosphere of sectional hostility and laid the basis for an alliance between the proponents of segregation and the proponents of harsh anti-subversion laws. As a result, the decisions touching the subversion problem in the 1955 and 1956 Terms evoked a noisy chorus of denunciation and a formidable array of legislative proposals designed to rebuke the judiciary and gratify the constituents.

1. 347 U.S. 483 (1954).

Some of these proposals have been mischievous to the point of imbecility.[2] Others which would merely correct the Court's specific interpretations of congressional intent[3] also seem unwise, though well within the range of the legislative prerogative. But from the point of view of this paper the significant thing is that even such a circumspect judicial foray into the subversion question should have troubled the waters so considerably. The decisions of the 1955 Term simply held the governmental campaign against subversion to a rather strict standard of procedural regularity and statutory authority. In the 1956 Term, in spite of some sonorous dicta,[4] the Court's actual holdings were equally discreet. Yet these slender provocations were enough to set off an ominous and nearly successful anti-judicial campaign. What might have been the proportions, and the prospects, of that campaign if the Court had heeded the cheerleaders on and off the bench who have urged that government's power to punish subversion be flatly denied?

Of course, congressional attacks on judicial power have been going on since the birth of the republic, and most of them have failed.[5] The present campaign is not likely to cripple the judiciary. Excessive alarm about criticism could itself immobilize the Court and thus subvert the rule of law. If John Marshall's Court had recoiled whenever opposition in Congress seemed probable, the cornerstones of American constitutionalism would never have been laid. In the law, as in the world at large, one must venture in order to gain. But to say that the Court must sometimes take a stand is not to say that it must take the most extreme stand. Marshall's pre-eminence among builders of the American constitutional tradition rests not only on his well-known boldness—

2. See S. 337, 85th Cong., 1st Sess. (1957), which would enact in part that "no Act of Congress shall be construed as indicating an intent on the part of Congress to occupy the field in which such Act operates, to the exclusion of any State laws on the same subject matter, unless such Act contains an express provision to that effect."

3. See S. 2646, 85th Cong., 2d Sess., § 3 (a) (1957), which would reinstate state subversion laws held repugnant to federal legislation in Pennsylvania v. Nelson, 350 U.S. 497 (1956).

4. See Sweezy v. New Hampshire, 354 U.S. 234 (1957); Watkins v. United States, 354 U.S. 178 (1957).

5. See Warren, *Legislative and Judicial Attacks on the Supreme Court of the United States*, 47 AM. L. REV. 1 (1913).

his "tiger instinct for the jugular vein,"[6] as an enthusiastic metaphorist once called it—but also on his less noticed sense of self-restraint. The great prestige of the Taney Court, before the tragic issue of slavery demolished it, was founded on a carefully moderate jurisprudence which took full account of both the potentialities and the limits of judicial power.[7] The recent policy of the Supreme Court toward the subversion issue has excited antagonism, as might have been expected, but the Court can face that opposition with assurance that the controverted decisions in fact respect the claims of other branches of government to govern —that the charges of excessive judicial imperialism are really baseless. It has done its part to spell out a fair and sensible approach to the subversion problem, but it has not tried to play all the roles in the drama. When the winds on Capitol Hill are howling, this is a comforting assurance.

Not the least of the advantages of such a course of moderation is that it does leave the judiciary free to get on with other business not so spectacular but perhaps more fit for judicial supervision. There is a broad range of individual rights questions which do not involve the superheated issue of subversion, or involve it only incidentally. The post-1937 Court has steadily, though gradually, widened the concept of constitutional privilege in such fields. The Court has been able to do this partly because it has not been gambling its prestige too cavalierly in other, more perilous arenas at the same time. Similarly, the Taney Court was able to increase the incidence of judicial control in certain vital fields by moderating judicial dogmas in others.[8]

The two previous sections of this book have emphasized the decisions clustering around the subversion issue because those decisions bulked so large in the 1955 and 1956 Terms and because

6. CORWIN, JOHN MARSHALL AND THE CONSTITUTION 130 (1919).

7. See HAINES & SHERWOOD, THE ROLE OF THE SUPREME COURT IN AMERICAN GOVERNMENT AND POLITICS 1835–64 (1957); 2 WARREN, THE SUPREME COURT IN UNITED STATES HISTORY 1–38 (1937).

8. Compare Rhode Island v. Massachusetts, 37 U.S. (12 Pet.) 657 (1838), and Louisville, C. & C. R.R. v. Letson, 43 U.S. (2 How.) 497 (1844), with Mayor of New York v. Miln, 36 U.S. (11 Pet.) 102 (1837), and Brisco v. President of the Bank of Ky., 36 U.S. (11 Pet.) 257 (1837).

judicial policy toward that issue seemed to call imperatively for analysis. In the civil liberties decisions of the 1957 Term, subversion is not so dominant a theme; and the Court's attitude on the subject is not significantly different from the attitude which emerged in the two previous terms. Consequently, the 1957 Term provides an occasion for paying special attention to judicial policy in non-subversion fields—specifically how, and how well, the Court has been discharging certain other civil rights assignments.

Of the 1957 Term cases which did involve the problem of subversion, three groups merit special consideration: those concerning the alien-born, those raising the now well-worn question of self-incrimination, and those concerning the "right to travel."

In the first series of decisions, the Court performed some mildly impressive gymnastics to soften the asperities of federal laws providing for deportation and denaturalization. In *Heikkinen* v. *United States*,[9] the Justices found it easy to conclude that the petitioner could not be punished for "willfully" lingering in the United States after a deportation order when no other country was willing to receive him, and when the Immigration and Naturalization Service had given him reason to believe that arrangements for departure were being made on his behalf. But *Rowoldt* v. *Perfetto*[10] and *Bonetti* v. *Rogers*[11] made them strain a bit harder. In the first, the Court refused to ratify the deportation of a man who, twenty years before, had belonged to the Communist party for less than a year, who seemed to have only the vaguest notion about the party's doctrines or purposes, and who may have been "affiliated" in order to eat. The Subversive Activities Control Act of 1950, prescribing deportation for aliens who "at the time of entering the United States, or . . . at any time thereafter" have been affiliated with the party,[12] was read in the light of "the alleviating Amendment of 1951"[13] to apply only to those who have been guilty of "meaningful association."[14] The second case

9. 355 U.S. 273 (1958).
10. 355 U.S. 115 (1957).
11. 356 U.S. 691 (1958).
12. 64 Stat. 987, 1008 (1950).
13. 355 U.S. at 120.
14. *Ibid.*

involved an alien who had been a party member after his original entry to the United States in 1923, but who had left and reentered in 1938 and was not a communist thereafter. The entry referred to in the law, said the Court, was the "adjudicated lawful admission"[15] in 1938; the petitioner, having eschewed the party since that time, was not now deportable. Both these interpretations are highly debatable; the second is perhaps especially so because it leads to the paradox that an alien who has continuously remained in the country can be deported while this petitioner, merely because he broke his continuous residence, cannot. Yet they are not so far-fetched as to be unreasonable glosses of a law which is itself fairly called "cloudy";[16] they proceed on the basis of the salutary principle that, in legislation which trenches on a right so precious, " 'ambiguity should be resolved in favor of lenity.' "[17]

The citizen who seeks something to criticize might well address himself to the legislative spirit which gave rise to such shotgun enactments or, even better, the administrative witlessness which brought these cases into court. Similar thoughts are evoked by two denaturalization decisions, *Nowak* v. *United States*[18] and *Maisenberg* v. *United States*.[19] The Court held that the government, seeking to show that citizenship had been fraudulently or illegally procured, had not met the burden of proving its case by " 'clear, unequivocal, and convincing' evidence."[20] The mere fact that the petitioners had been party members and functionaries before naturalization was not enough to establish lack of attachment to the Constitution in light of the standard laid down in *Schneiderman* v. *United States*;[21] and the statements attributed to the petitioners, again in view of that strict standard, were too equivocal to prove knowledge that the party advocated violent overthrow. Again the conduct aimed at by the government's action is chronologically remote (pre-1938 in both cases), and it seems reasonable

15. 356 U.S. at 696.
16. *Id.* at 699.
17. *Id.* at 699.
18. 356 U.S. 660 (1958).
19. 356 U.S. 670 (1958).
20. Nowak v. United States, 356 U.S. 660, 668 (1958).
21. 320 U.S. 118, 158 (1943).

to suspect that the Court's outlook reflects this fact. Whatever might be thought about applying the full *Schneiderman* reasoning to conduct in the 1950's, this version of it seems pretty appropriate to these twenty-year-old events, which can hardly be said to imperil our present security. It is perhaps noteworthy that Mr. Justice Frankfurter, who joined the powerful dissent of Mr. Chief Justice Stone in *Schneiderman*, is here, silently, on the side of the majority.

Among the cases presenting the issue of self-incrimination, one involved federal proceedings and the others state action. *Brown* v. *United States*[22] posed a vexing problem. The petitioner had been found in contempt by a district court when she refused to answer, on Fifth Amendment grounds, questions asked in cross-examination about Communist connections since 1946, the date of her naturalization. But she had voluntarily taken the stand in her own behalf and had testified on direct examination, *inter alia*, that she was now attached to the Constitution. The Court, through Justice Frankfurter, held that by so testifying she had waived her privilege of rejecting questions relevant to the testimony; the breadth of the waiver "is determined by the scope of the relevant cross-examination."[23] One difficulty with this rule, as Mr. Justice Black points out in dissent, is that it was designed for criminal cases in which failure to take the stand cannot be made a subject for comment by judge or prosecutor nor used as the basis for inference of guilt. Denaturalization is, of course, a civil proceeding. Thus, under the Court's rule a party may be forced to choose between taking the stand at risk of incrimination or having his failure to do so "used against him." It is true that the Court's rule might occasionally force a party into this dilemma, and to that extent he might be indirectly "coerced" to take the stand, although the coercion seems conjectural and rather tenuous. But the alternative would be to let him testify in his own behalf without fear of cross-examination on that testimony, and the Court evidently feels that the government's interest in preventing such an anomaly[24] justifies a narrow construction of the constitutional right.

22. 356 U.S. 148 (1958).
23. *Id.* at 154–155.
24. See *id.* at 156 n. 5.

The path marked out by the state cases was equally restricted. *Lerner* v. *Casey*[25] and *Beilan* v. *Board of Educ.*[26] involved the dismissal of public employees who had refused to answer questions about Communist affiliations. Lerner, a subway conductor in New York City, had been dismissed after invoking the Fifth Amendment in the course of an investigation by the city Commissioner of Investigation. The Transit Authority felt he had thus created doubt as to his reliability and that this merited dismissal under the state's Security Risk Law.[27] Lerner argued, among other things, that his discharge rested on an inference of Communist party membership drawn from his invocation of the Fifth Amendment, and that such an inference is barred. But the Court held that no such inference had been made and that, in any event, "the federal privilege against self-incrimination was not available to appellant"[28] in this state investigation. It is hard to see why the Court, if it is going to make the second point, bothers with the first, which is exceedingly slippery: it requires the Court to argue that the finding of unreliability rests on the lack of candor itself, rather than on inferences drawn from that lack of candor—a somewhat puzzling, not to say unrealistic, distinction.[29] Indeed, the realism of Mr. Justice Douglas' dissent is hardly greater, for he simply contends that the state must suffer in silence when an employee refuses to answer a question like this, apparently on the ground that the question concerns an area "where government may not probe."[30] Since the Court has frequently held that the government *may* probe the area in ques-

25. 357 U.S. 468 (1958).

26. 357 U.S. 399 (1958).

27. N.Y. Sess. Laws 1951, ch. 233, as amended, N.Y. Sess. Laws 1954, ch. 105.

28. 357 U.S. at 478. This point had been foreshadowed in Knapp v. Schweitzer, 357 U.S. 371 (1958), decided the same day.

29. Of course the Court may have felt obliged to meet the general point that "due process" precludes adverse inferences, even if the self-incrimination clause does not apply. But would it not be more reasonable to admit that some inferences are being drawn, *e.g.*, the inference that the employee *may* be hiding some evidence of disqualification? If the self-incrimination clause were applicable, such an inference might be forbidden; but since that clause is not applicable, the inference seems "reasonable" enough to satisfy the requirements of due process.

30. 357 U.S. at 414 (dissenting opinion).

tion,[31] this dissent appears to be another variation on the all-out libertarian theme so often sounded by Douglas and Black; whatever else may be said for it, it does not contribute much to an argument based on the present Court's presuppositions.

The *Beilan* case presents a similar problem. The petitioner, a Pennsylvania school teacher, had been discharged for "incompetency" when he declined to answer questions about Communist affiliations. The discharge was upheld against due process attack on the theory that the state is not constitutionally precluded from defining incompetency to include deliberate refusal to answer a question of his administrative superior in a " 'vitally important matter related to his fitness.' "[32] The Chief Justice and Mr. Justice Brennan argued in dissent that the incompetency charge was a pretext and that Beilan was actually being punished for invoking the Fifth Amendment before a congressional committee at another time. This may be true, but it is hard to see how the Supreme Court could properly turn its decision on this point in view of the state supreme court's holding that the incompetency charge was alone sufficient. And, if that point does fall, the case is fairly easy—unless, again, we expect the Court to abandon the settled doctrines of the last ten years and hold that inquiry into these matters is simply irrelevant. Assuming *arguendum* that the question is *not* irrelevant to fitness, a teacher can hardly refuse to answer with impunity any more than he could refuse to answer a question about his ability to teach algebra.

There is no doubt that these decisions confine the right against self-incrimination to a very narrow room. This conclusion is further reinforced by *Knapp* v. *Schweitzer*,[33] which held, following *Feldman* v. *United States*,[34] that the federal right was not available in a state proceeding even though the compelled testimony might later be used in a federal criminal case. The alarm expressed two years ago that *Slochower* v. *Board of Educ.*[35] would "strike deep"[36]

31. Adler v. Board of Educ., 342 U.S. 485 (1952); Dennis v. United States, 341 U.S. 494 (1951).
32. 357 U.S. at 408.
33. 357 U.S. 371 (1958).
34. 322 U.S. 487 (1944).
35. 350 U.S. 551 (1956).
36. *Id.* at 559–560 (dissenting opinion).

into the authority of the state was never very comprehensible to one who had read the majority opinion, but any lingering doubts must surely be put to rest by *Lerner*. For there the Court simply gives effect to the clear implication of *Slochower*—that the privilege of the Fifth Amendment does not protect from discharge a state employee who stands mute before an inquiry by his own superiors, even though the state cannot discharge him *merely* for invoking the right before a federal authority, like a congressional committee.[37] Adding to all this the *Brown* decision of this term and *Ullman* v. *United States* in 1956,[38] a well-marked judicial attitude appears: the Court will adhere scrupulously to what it deems the explicit command of the self-incrimination clause, but will not extend the right a fraction of an inch beyond those strict limits. Most certainly it will not enlarge the protection into a general "right to silence" or apply it in any form as a restriction on the states.

It is difficult and in some ways meaningless to try to evaluate specific holdings about the self-incrimination privilege without first considering the merits of this general attitude. Two basic notions are reflected in the attitude: one, that the privilege is not so fundamental as to be ranked an "immutable principle of justice which is the inalienable possession of every citizen of a free government,"[39] and two, that the clause is one of those "specific provisions" whose meaning was "defined by history" (unlike, for example, "equal protection of the laws") and which allow little scope for "individual legal judgment."[40] A further consideration is the idea that the right to privacy about one's opinions and associations, which is sometimes loosely equated with the self-incrimination clause, can be better and more appropriately protected by the free expression guarantees of the Constitution.[41] These arguments seem rather compelling in view of the fact that no judge

37. It was suggested earlier that the limiting effect of *Slochower* "may be more moral than practical."

38. 350 U.S. 422 (1956).

39. Twining v. New Jersey, 211 U.S. 78, 113 (1908).

40. United States v. Lovett, 328 U.S. 303, 321 (1946) (concurring opinion); *accord* Ullman v. United States, 350 U.S. 422, 438 (1956).

41. See Sweezy v. New Hampshire, 354 U.S. 234, 255–68 (1957) (concurring opinion); West Va. Bd. of Educ. v. Barnette, 319 U.S. 624 (1943).

who takes a contrary stand has so far succeeded very well in refuting them. They do not warrant a "lax"[42] interpretation of the privilege, and the *Feldman* doctrine comes close to meriting that adjective. For, admitting that the Fifth Amendment was not designed to limit the states, it surely was designed to limit the federal government; yet under *Feldman* compelled testimony can lead to federal incrimination. But the arguments do make out a strong justification for the Court's refusal to overpass the strict mandates of the Constitution.

The passport problem provoked some of the most publicized decisions of the Term. *Kent* v. *Dulles,*[43] the principal case, involved the refusal to grant passports to two men on the ground, *inter alia,* that they were alleged to be Communists. The Secretary of State, in denying the passports, purported to act under the authority of a law codified in 1926, which states that he "may grant and issue passports . . . under such rules as the President shall designate."[44] The majority decision by Mr. Justice Douglas denies him this discretionary authority, and in the course of reaching that conclusion makes an important point by way of dicta. "The right to travel is a part of the 'liberty' of which the citizen cannot be deprived without the due process of law under the Fifth Amendment."[45] Though not, perhaps, very surprising, this is the first flat declaration by the Supreme Court to this effect, and it thus represents a significant milestone in constitutional history. Another salient right is now within the potential range of judicial protection. However, the Court utilizes the right in this case only as an aid to statutory construction. A holding that the Secretary had been granted the power to withhold passports to citizens on the basis of beliefs and associations would raise "important constitutional questions";[46] therefore, the Court avoids the constitutional questions and holds that the power was not granted by the law.

Unfortunately, Justice Douglas has a weighty argument to cope with before he reaches this congenial conclusion. It was urged that

42. Ullman v. United States, 350 U.S. 422, 429 (1956).
43. 357 U.S. 116 (1958).
44. 22 U.S.C. § 211a (1952).
45. 357 U.S. at 125.
46. *Id.* at 130.

the Secretary had often used his discretion for "protection of this country's internal security"[47] both before and after the codification of 1926, and that Congress, by repeatedly enacting a statute forbidding those without passports to enter or leave the United States, had impliedly approved this administrative practice. Douglas does his very competent best to dispose of the point, arguing that wartime practices do not determine this problem of statutory construction, that such administrative rulings in peacetime are "scattered" and uninstructive before 1926, and that this date is the one that matters most because it was then that the "may grant and issue" law took final form. But he is struggling with recalcitrant material, and Justice Clark, who dissents for himself and three others, seems to have the better of the argument over administrative practices.

This is by no means to agree with the dissenters that the Court erred in interpreting the law as it did. Congress, after all, has never spoken directly on the subject of the Secretary's power to use his discretion in this way. Absent a previous Supreme Court declaration that the right to travel is constitutionally protected, it is fairly likely that Congress did not consider the constitutional question when it passed the "may grant and issue" law and the various laws restricting entrance and exit, and that it might have decided differently if it had. The administrative practices point is strong, but hardly strong enough to bear the weight of the rather shocking idea that the Secretary is empowered to deny an important constitutional right at his unfettered discretion. No doubt the government can restrict the right to some extent, and quite possibly those who have been found by some regular process to be actual Communists can fall under such a ban. But meantime there is no good reason to grant the Secretary such a praetorian authority by judicial inference.

Of other decisions involving subversion, only *Dayton* v. *Dulles*[48] and *Harmon* v. *Brucker*[49] need be noted here. The first raised the potentially interesting question of whether a passport denial could,

47. *Id.* at 135 (dissenting opinion).
48. 357 U.S. 144 (1958).
49. 355 U.S. 579 (1958).

consistently with due process, rest on a confidential file which was not disclosed to the applicant; but the Court preferred not to reach this constitutional question and merely held, on the authority of *Kent,* that the denial exceeded the Secretary's statutory authority. In *Harmon* the Court held per curiam that the Secretary of the Army lacked statutory authority to issue a less-than-honorable discharge on the basis of an inductee's preinduction activities. *Speiser* v. *Randall,*[50] treated below, also raised the subversion issue.

Disregarding *Speiser* for the moment, what generalizations can be drawn from the subversion decisions of the 1957 Term? In the first place, an overall view suggests that the Court is adhering to the carefully modest concept of its functions which has infused decisions in this field for at least the past three years. Not one of the decisions significantly impairs the substantive power of government; in fact, not one of the decisions which favor the individual actually turns directly on a constitutional claim.[51] The self-incrimination right has been confined to a bed which, if not Procrustean, is surely far from roomy. The right to travel has been granted constitutional status, but the Court has fastidiously declined to decide now to what extent the government's power to infringe the right will be curtailed. It was suggested in the preceding section that the Court in the 1956 Term, though substantially holding to a modest course in this field, displayed some signs of restlessness. Scattered dicta seemed to imply faintly that a majority might be yearning to play a bigger part in the affairs of the nation. Those hints, such as they were, have emphatically not been brought closer to reality in the subversion decisions of the 1957 Term. If the Court of a year ago was hesitating between self-restraint and rashness, the proponents of the more circumspect course seem now to have won the day. Even the lofty pulpit tone of some of last year's decisions is missing in the majority opinions of the past year.

This point should need no further belaboring. But those familiar with American constitutional history will remember how many

50. 357 U.S. 513 (1958).
51. Unless, as is doubtful, the "clear, unequivocal and convincing" standard of *Schneiderman* is to be so regarded.

times in the past the Court has been assailed for doing what it has not done, and will not be astonished by the current campaign of willful or ingenuous misrepresentation. Mr. Chief Justice Taney's opinion in the *Dred Scott* case is only the most famous example of a judicial pronouncement that suffered such a fate,[52] but perhaps it is salutary to bring this particular example to the attention of certain present critics. Beyond that, it may be worthwhile to say once more as plainly as possible that in the subversion field the Court has recently been interpreting statutes and correcting minor procedural faults, not setting up impassable barriers to governmental action. The critic has a right to argue that the interpretations have been mistaken, but he has no moral right to assert what is flatly untrue—that the Court has delivered America bound into the hands of its enemies or has exceeded the traditional limits of its jurisdiction. If he wants the interpretation externally corrected, he has a right to seek a change in the law (though the failure of such laws to pass in recent congressional sessions suggests that the Court's constructions of legislative intent may not have been so outrageous after all), but he has no moral right to undermine the institution of judicial review itself—unless, indeed, he would prefer an America without the rule of law. If that is our critic's premise today, I wonder if he will enjoy living with it in a tomorrow when the shoe may be on the other foot.

The judicial mill has also been grinding out a series of judgments in cases which involve civil rights questions unassociated with communism and related menaces. For the past twenty years the Court has been following a line (whose beginnings, of course, go back a good deal farther than that) characterized by alert consideration for the rights of the individual. If we can speak of dominant judicial concerns (and, with appropriate reservations, we can), it might be said that the Court from 1789 to the Civil War was preoccupied with protecting the union against the forces of parochialism; that from the 1870's to 1937 it sought to protect business from government; and that the distinguishing mark of the

52. See SWISHER, ROGER B. TANEY 511–523 (1936); CORWIN, THE DOCTRINE OF JUDICIAL REVIEW 129–157 (1914).

modern period has been a concern for protecting "the dignity and intrinsic importance of the individual man"[53] against encroachment. To be sure these time periods overlap; nor should our awareness of the prominent differences between them obscure the great underlying continuities. Yet in general the distinctions hold, and they shed light on the doctrinal developments of recent years.

The modern judiciary, encountering an essentially novel range of problems at the start of this third great era of Court history, has had to reshape the doctrines which are the tools of its trade. The 1937–1958 period has been analogous to the years before 1820 when Marshall and his predecessors were fashioning the instruments of judicial control over the states; or the years after 1877 when the slow accumulation of precedent was transmuting the due process clause and the commerce clause into the legal embodiments of a laissez-faire philosophy. In each period the Court has had to work out (whether consciously or not) a view of its own place in the American body politic. Then it has had to build the doctrinal bridges—or whittle away the barriers—along the paths it will follow. The first of these processes has already received attention here; the second needs further treatment, with special reference to the 1957 Term.

One cardinal development deserves special examination, partly because of its general significance in the modern period and partly because it is well exemplified in the 1957 Term decisions: the tendency to clear the way for judicial supervision of subjects which had once seemed more or less immune. The extent to which this has been done by the modern Court in the civil rights field is genuinely impressive. For example, the Court has opened up the primary election process to control[54] by erasing the old ideas that primaries are not, constitutionally speaking, elections,[55] and that the acts of "private" groups like political parties are not "state action."[56] It has rejected the precedent[57] that exempted movie cen-

53. GRISWOLD, THE FIFTH AMENDMENT TODAY 7 (1955).
54. See Smith v. Allwright, 321 U.S. 649, *amended*, 322 U.S. 718 (1944); United States v. Classic, 313 U.S. 299 (1941).
55. Newberry v. United States, 256 U.S. 232 (1901).
56. Grovey v. Townsend, 295 U.S. 45 (1935), *overruled*, 321 U.S. 649 (1944).
57. Mutual Film Corp. v. Industrial Comm'n, 236 U.S. 230 (1915).

sors from constitutional surveillance[58] and the notion that book censors could throw their weight about without fear of federal judicial interference.[59] It has erased the idea that public employment is a "privilege" which the state can abrogate at its unfettered whim,[60] and it seems to have also brought state occupational requirements under some potential constitutional control.[61] It has held that the government's power to deport aliens, though undoubtedly great, is subject to the requirements of due process,[62] and that the action taken by legislative committees may unwarrantably infringe freedom of expression.[63] It has even declared that the Court's purview may extend, under special circumstances, to "issues of fact" (or what would strike many as issues of fact) in state criminal proceedings.[64] And in the 1957 Term itself the right to travel has been recognized as constitutionally protected.[65]

All of these decisions and others like them open up the possibility of judicial control over subjects with which pre-1937 Courts were not wont to deal. Most of them provide us with no solid assurance as to how the Court will exercise that control—whether any given case will be decided in favor of the claims of the individual or the government. That question must be determined in specific situations by criteria which will be gradually spelled out. But these decisions create the enabling conditions for judicial protection of individual rights; they make it less likely that constitutional remedies will be barred *a priori* on the ground that the subject is beyond judicial cognizance. They represent a necessary step in the modern Court's development of new tools in the field of civil liberties.

Three decisions, or sets of decisions, of the 1957 Term involve this problem of whether particular subjects shall be brought within

58. See Joseph Burstyn, Inc., v. Wilson, 343 U.S. 495 (1952).
59. See Butler v. Michigan, 352 U.S. 380, *motion to intervene or consolidate denied,* 352 U.S. 922 (1956).
60. See Wieman v. Updegraff, 344 U.S. 183 (1952).
61. See Schware v. Board of Bar Examiners, 353 U.S. 232 (1957).
62. Jordan v. DeGeorge, 341 U.S. 223 (1951).
63. Watkins v. United States, 354 U.S. 178 (1957); Sweezey v. New Hampshire, 354 U.S. 234 (1957).
64. Watts v. Indiana, 338 U.S. 49, 51 (1949) (dictum).
65. See Kent v. Dulles, 357 U.S. 116 (1958).

the span of judicial control. *NAACP* v. *Alabama*[66] presented an intriguing issue: does the compulsory disclosure of members of associations violate a constitutional right? Alabama had brought suit to enjoin the NAACP from operating within the state without qualifying under a statute which regulates foreign corporations. Petitioner argued that the statute did not apply, and the state moved for production of records, including membership lists, maintaining that this information was essential to a hearing on the question of the statute's application. The state court ordered the information produced, and when the Association failed to comply it was adjudged in contempt and fined $100,000.

It cannot be denied that a good deal of loose thinking in the past supported Alabama's position. State and federal lobbyist and registration laws had been advocated without much regard to the constitutional liberties they might infringe.[67] And in 1947 the President's Committee on Civil Rights gave what sounded like unqualified approval to the "principle of disclosure" in order to counter "totalitarianisms of all kinds."[68] In 1928 the Supreme Court had upheld a New York registration requirement as applied to the Ku Klux Klan[69] without really responding "to the argument that exposure is repressive, that it was only to achieve this repression that the act was passed, and that the state legislature had thereby indirectly achieved a goal which it could not have achieved directly—legislating the Klan out of existence."[70] It is not entirely strange that Southern states might have thought they could extirpate the NAACP.

But other, more recent judicial straws in the wind[71] should have suggested quite a different conclusion: that a Court heavily concerned with civil rights is not likely to tolerate a doctrine which permits such rights to be frustrated indirectly. The Supreme Court,

66. 357 U.S. 449 (1958).
67. BLAISDELL, AMERICAN DEMOCRACY UNDER PRESSURE 84 (1957).
68. PRESIDENT'S COMM. ON CIVIL RIGHTS, TO SECURE THESE RIGHTS 52–53 (1947).
69. See Bryant v. Zimmerman, 278 U.S. 63 (1928).
70. Robison, *Protection of Associations from Compulsory Disclosure of Membership*, 58 COLUM. L. REV. 614, 644 (1958).
71. United States v. Harriss, 347 U.S. 612 (1954); United States v. Rumely, 345 U.S. 41 (1953); Thomas v. Collins, 323 U.S. 516 (1945).

through Mr. Justice Harlan, unanimously held that the right to privacy is constitutionally protected because it is often indispensable to freedom of association and that "Alabama has fallen short of showing a controlling justification for the deterrent effect on the free enjoyment of the right to associate which disclosure of membership lists is likely to have."[72] In the light of reality no other result would have made sense. Yet well-rooted illusions are sometimes remarkably hard to dispel, and the flat, unanimous statement that associational privacy is constitutionally protected is thus a needed, and important, advance.

The problem raised by the tax exemption cases, *First Unitarian Church* v. *County of Los Angeles*[73] and *Speiser* v. *Randall*,[74] is in many ways similar. Two war veterans and two churches had claimed property tax exemptions under the California constitution.[75] However, state law provides that applicants for such exemption must take oath that they do not advocate violent overthrow of the government or the support of a foreign government against the United States in a war.[76] The applicants had refused to subscribe the oath, and the assessors denied the exemptions. The Supreme Court, by Mr. Justice Brennan, limited itself to the question of whether the state provisions deny "freedom of speech without the procedural safeguards required by the Due Process Clause of the Fourteenth Amendment."[77] It was held that "a discriminatory denial of a tax exemption for engaging in speech is a limitation on free speech";[78] that the provisions of the California tax exemption laws impose on the taxpayer the burden of proving that he belongs in the exempt category; and that this allocation of the burden of proof on an issue concerning free speech is a denial of due process.

But this short way of putting the conclusions takes no account of the difficulties the Court encounters before arriving at them.

72. NAACP v. Alabama, 357 U.S. 449, 466 (1958).
73. 357 U.S. 545 (1958).
74. 357 U.S. 513 (1958).
75. CAL. CONST. art. 13, §§ 1 1/4, 1 1/2; art. 20, § 19.
76. The full oath is set forth in Speiser v. Randall, 357 U.S. 513, 515 (1958).
77. *Id.* at 517.
78. *Id.* at 518.

One problem, as Mr. Justice Clark points out in dissent, is that the Court must squeeze the California law a bit in order to reach the federal constitutional question which it considers. The Court assumes that the oath is not conclusive and that the assesor, even if the oath has been taken, has a duty to proceed to further investigation of the facts. Throughout these proceedings, including any judicial review of administrative findings, "the burden lies on the taxpayer of persuading the assessor, or the court,"[79] and this is the vice which invalidates the law. The dissent argues that under California law the oath is conclusive; that, even if the state law is ambiguous on this point, the Supreme Court should so construe the law as to avoid a constitutional question; and that the "burden of proof" issue would not then arise. This seems fairly persuasive. But the point is that the Court, if it did so construe the law, would avoid a minor issue only to face a major one—whether the oath requirement for tax exemption can be valid at all in view of *Pennsylvania* v. *Nelson*.[80] Brennan and the majority are following the well-marked road in cases involving subversion: they are seeking procedural rather than substantive flaws; they are answering the lesser questions in preference to the greater.

The other problem faced in the tax exemption decisions is a more general one: the contention that exemption from taxation "is a bounty or gratuity on the part of the sovereign and when once granted may be withdrawn."[81] This is the old point, often made in connection with such subjects as the postal power and public employment, that the state may grant or withhold "privileges" at its whim without confronting a constitutional question[82] (since the state need grant no tax exemptions at all, it may grant them to whom it likes). T. R. Powell once trenchantly exposed the weakness of this whole line of argument,[83] and the modern Court has been consistently backing away from it. The states are

79. *Id.* at 522.
80. 350 U.S. 497 (1956).
81. Speiser v. Randall, 357 U.S. 513, 541 (1958) (as expressed by the California court and in Justice Clark's dissent).
82. See Public Clearing House v. Coyne, 194 U.S. 497, 506–507 (1904); Atkin v. Kansas, 191 U.S. 207, 223 (1903).
83. Powell, *The Right to Work for the State*, 16 COLUM. L. REV. 99, 107 (1916).

finding it harder and harder to do indirectly under the shelter of such sophistries what they may not do directly.

The expatriation decisions, involving as they do the "awesome power"[84] of invalidating an act of Congress, raise an issue of somewhat different dimension but not unrelated to the *NAACP* and *Speiser* problems. What is the extent, if any, of Congress' power to deprive persons of their American nationality? This question arose under the Nationality Act of 1940,[85] which prescribes loss of citizenship under certain conditions. *Nishikawa* v. *Dulles*[86] was relatively simple. An American citizen of Japanese descent had gone to Japan in 1939 and in 1941 was inducted into the Japanese army. Although the act provides loss of citizenship for merely "entering, or serving in, the armed forces of a foreign state,"[87] the majority assumes that the conduct must be voluntary and then goes on to hold that the government has not met its burden of proving voluntariness. The Chief Justice and four others assert that the government always bears this burden in expatriation cases and that the standard must be the "clear, unequivocal and convincing evidence" of *Schneiderman*[88] if "voluntariness" is put in issue (for example, by showing that the petitioner was "conscripted in a totalitarian country to whose conscription law, with its penal sanctions, he was subject"[89]). Justice Frankfurter, joined by Justice Burton, objects to the rule that this standard applies whenever voluntariness is put in issue; but he agrees that it should apply in this case, where the critical fact of a mandatory criminal law is readily provable. Though not perhaps entirely plain sailing (see the dissent shared by Justices Harlan and Clark), this set of facts did not tax the judicial yachtsmen unduly.

But in the other expatriation cases the water became considerably more choppy. *Perez* v. *Brownell*[90] involved the pro-

---

84. Trop v. Dulles, 356 U.S. 86, 128 (1958) (dissenting opinion).

85. Now incorporated into Immigration and Nationality Act of 1952, 8 U.S.C. § 1481 (1952).

86. 356 U.S. 129 (1958).

87. 54 STAT. 1168, 1169 (1940), as incorporated into 8 U.S.C. § 1481 (a) (3) (1952).

88. Schneiderman v. United States, 320 U.S. 118, 125 (1943).

89. Nishikawa v. Dulles, 356 U.S. 129, 137 (1958).

90. 356 U.S. 44 (1958).

vision that nationality shall be forfeited by voting in a foreign election,[91] *Trop* v. *Dulles* the provision that it shall be forfeited by one who has been convicted by court martial for deserting the armed forces in time of war and has been dismissed or dishonorably discharged as a result.[92] The law is upheld in the first as a permissible exercise of Congress' power over foreign affairs and struck down in the second as exceeding the boundaries of the war powers. But the interesting aspects of the cases from the viewpoint of this paper are the assumptions guiding the judges who reach these seemingly contradictory results.

Mr. Justice Frankfurter, speaking for the Court in *Perez* and dissenting in *Trop,* takes an extremely permissive approach to the problem of congressional power. For him, the expatriation statutes raise a question under the necessary and proper clause as qualified—though not much—by the due process clause.[93] If the means chosen (denationalization) bears a rational relation to the end sought (for example, "regulation of foreign affairs"[94]), the law is constitutional. This unadorned language does suggest a sort of plenary indulgence for Congress to expatriate at will, and it causes Mr. Justice Douglas to propound a list of horrific eventualities which might proceed from this logic. Could Congress expatriate those who "disputed the position of the Secretary of State" or "pleaded for recognition of Red China"[95] on the theory that they "embarrassed" our foreign relations? Surely there would be in one sense of the word a "rational" nexus between such penalties and the conduct of foreign policy; no doubt the lot of diplomats would often be a happier one if their fellow citizens would keep quiet. One feels that Frankfurter in his zeal to avow a policy of judicial self-restraint has spoken in more sweeping terms than are needed, and that at first blush Douglas' alarms are not without some color of plausibility. But an examination of previous Frankfurter opinions reveals clearly enough that the

91. 8 U.S.C. § 1481(a)(5) (1952).
92. 8 U.S.C. § 1481(a)(8).
93. See Trop v. Dulles, 356 U.S. 86, 119–120 (1958) (dissenting opinion).
94. Perez v. Brownell, 356 U.S. 44, 58 (1958).
95. *Id.* at 81, 82 (dissenting opinion).

word "rational" bears for him a meaning which makes such dark forebodings quite unwarranted. Ultimately it involves balancing the individual right in question against "the subordinating interest"[96] of the state and a conclusion that the latter outweighs the former. To be sure, the state's "subordinating interest" becomes a strong factor in this calculus when the connection between means chosen and end sought is arguably close rather than "remote" and "shadowy."[97] To be sure, the calculus will be conducted "in a [greater] spirit of humility"[98] when it concerns a congressional act.[99] But, with these reservations, the constitutional lines will be drawn when they must be drawn. The logic of this position does not leave the expatriation power untrammelled; it does not open the door to arbitrary lawmaking.

It must be admitted that these qualifications of the seemingly uncompromising Frankfurter language have to be inferred, and it is fair to wish they had been stated more explicitly. And we must also concede that the position he takes, even with these inferred qualifications, is still very permissive. No one has been more concerned than he to avoid sweeping negative pronouncements which might unduly rigidify constitutional adjudication in the future; perhaps it is no less important to beware of wholesale affirmations which could equally cramp judicial discretion in situations now unforeseen. However, his temptation to lean far backwards and dig in his heels is understandable when we turn to examine the position he sought to controvert. For his brethren Warren, Douglas, and Black (and, to an undeterminable extent, Whittaker) advanced a doctrine so inflexible that an observer stands awestruck before their self-certainty.

In a word, this doctrine seems to be that Congress has no power whatever to deprive a person of citizenship against his will.[100] A more flat-footed negation is hardly to be found in the

96. Sweezy v. New Hampshire, 354 U.S. 234, 265 (1957) (concurring opinion).

97. *Ibid.*

98. *Id.* at 267.

99. See Trop v. Dulles, 356 U.S. 86, 128 (1958) (dissenting opinion).

100. "The power to denationalize is not within the letter or the spirit of the powers with which our Government was endowed." Perez v. Brownell, 356 U.S. 44, 78 (1958) (dissenting opinion). "Citizenship, like freedom of

annals of the Court. Fortunately for common sense, this ultra-extreme dogma is evidently shared by only three justices, all of whom dissent in *Perez*. But in *Trop* Mr. Justice Whittaker joins the three in endorsing a position only slightly less austere—that, at all events, Congress has no power to prescribe denationalization as a punishment for crime, for this is a "cruel and unusual punishment" forbidden by the Eighth Amendment.[101] There is no suggestion here, such as one finds in Mr. Justice Field's dissent in *O'Neil* v. *Vermont*[102] or the majority opinion in *Weems* v. *United States*,[103] that the punishment is invalid when and because it is disproportionate to the crime. In the black-and-white constitutional universe posited by these opinions, Congress could not denationalize a malefactor who combined the iniquities of Vidkun Quisling and Jack the Ripper.

Surely denationalization is a dire penalty and statelessness can be a pitiable condition. One may follow Mr. Justice Frankfurter's contention that "expatriation under the Nationality Act of 1940 is not 'punishment' in any valid constitutional sense"[104] but still disagree with it. If the conventional rhetoric of constitutional law allows us to argue that Trop was not being punished, then the rhetorical principles had better be changed in the name of realism and humanity. But it is a seven-league step farther, into the mimsy world of Humpty-Dumpty and the Mock Turtle, to declare that Congress may hang or electrocute but may not denationalize under any circumstances, that "loss of citizenship is a fate worse than death."[105] And, quite apart from its divorcement from

speech, press, and religion, occupies a preferred position in our written Constitution, because it is a grant absolute in terms. The power of Congress to withhold it, modify it, or cancel it does not exist." *Id.* at 84 (dissenting opinion). Editor's note: this became the position of a majority of the Court in Afroyim v. Rusk, 387 U.S. 253 (1967) except perhaps where the citizen consents to the deprivation. But the Court began to narrow the doctrine again in Rogers v. Bellei, 91 S.Ct. 1060 (1971).

101. 356 U.S. at 101.
102. 144 U.S. 323, 339–340 (1892).
103. 217 U.S. 349, 371 (1910).
104. Trop v. Dulles, 356 U.S. 86, 124 (1958) (dissenting opinion).
105. The words are Mr. Justice Frankfurter's; *id.* at 125 (dissenting opinion).

logic,[106] this doctrine is distressing because it is gratuitous—because its sponsors seem so pertinaciously bent on absolutism even though a more contingent formulation would do just as well. The Constitution is not Mount Sinai, and the justices of the Supreme Court, august though they may be, have seldom been comfortable for long in the robes of Moses.

It is therefore gratifying to be able to report that this extreme position does not reflect the views of the Court majority, and that the prevailing doctrine of the denationalization cases seems to fall somewhere between the broadly permissive spirit of Mr. Justice Frankfurter's opinion and the astringent negativism of the Chief Justice and his cohorts. Mr. Justice Brennan tips the scales against the government in *Trop,* but he does so, not on the theory that citizenship is absolutely immune, but because he concludes that "the requisite rational relation between this statute and the war power does not appear."[107] The remote chance that the threat of expatriation will further the war effort does not warrant so harsh a penalty. The reasoning of this opinion could stand some clarification, but its upshot is clear enough—Congress can divest citizenship under special circumstances but will be held to a rather strict standard of rational justification when it seeks to do so. And since Mr. Justice Brennan is the swing man on this issue, that seems to be (for the present) the operative doctrine of the Court. The power to expatriate, like other powers gravely affecting individual rights, must be exercised within judicially prescribed constitutional limits.

The civil liberties developments chronicled in this section represent a slowly accumulating judicial appreciation of the problems and duties thrust upon the Supreme Court by the post-1937 world. Little by little, for almost twenty years, the Court has been edging toward a mature position in relation to the subversion problem: in the 1955 Term the justices seemed to find that position at last, and in the 1957 Term they have reconfirmed it. And mean-

106. But cf. Roche, *The Loss of American Nationality: The Development of Statutory Expatriation,* 99 U. PA. L. REV. 25, 70 (1950).

107. 356 U.S. at 114.

while the Court has been delineating, little by little, a stand with respect to a broader range of individual rights issues not involving subversion, exerting its power somewhat more boldly in this area, and working out a jurisprudence which will reflect the new concern for civil rights and enable the judiciary to protect them within the range of its capacity. The particular development focused on here is the extension of *potential* judicial control, and the 1957 Term was from this point of view highly significant. It was made clear during that term that the right to travel and the right of associational privacy can be claimed as constitutional rights, and that government may not adopt an arbitrary policy in relation to either tax exemption or expatriation. These are important advances, even though their implications remain to be spelled out; hereafter the government cannot effectively contend that its activities in these fields raise no constitutional question.

The historical parallels which might be drawn are striking, and instructive enough to justify a little further emphasis. The story of "how laissez faire came to the Supreme Court"[108] has usually been told with a pejorative overtone by modern critics, but we need not either condemn or condone that historic phenomenon when we note that it bore certain similarities to what is going on today. Surely the doctrine of the *NAACP* case finds some analogy in the *Minnesota Commission*[109] case of 1890, where the issue of rate regulation was brought within judicial surveillance despite a strong intimation in *Munn* v. *Illinois*[110] that this would be a matter of legislative discretion. The expatriation cases, and particularly Mr. Justice Brennan's opinion, bring to mind—for better or for worse—the "reasonableness" doctrine glorified in *Lochner* v. *New York*.[111] The tax exemption decision invites comparison with the *Child Labor Tax Case*,[112] for now, as in the earlier case, the Court is alert to prevent devious as well as direct infringement on the rights it has chosen to protect.

108. TWISS, LAWYERS AND THE CONSTITUTION: HOW LAISSEZ FAIRE CAME TO THE SUPREME COURT (1942).
109. Chicago, M. & St. P. Ry. v. Minnesota, 134 U.S. 418 (1890).
110. 94 U.S. 113 (1877).
111. 198 U.S. 45 (1905).
112. 259 U.S. 20 (1922).

The point is, of course, that a Court which had elected to defend economic liberty against arbitrary abridgment had to close up the doctrinal loopholes which would make such abridgment possible. Similarly, a Court which exalts civil liberties to the status of a primary judicial concern must take care that it be able to reach and supervise the governmental devices by which civil liberties may be infringed. That is what the Court has been doing in the cases here described; it is what the Court has always done as the shifting historical scenery presented constitutional law with new problems and the Court with new preoccupations.

But the uses of the past are not exhausted when it is noted that these parallels exist; history also suggests some clues for an evaluation of contemporary judicial behavior. As remarked, modern scholarship generally deplores the Court's record in the heyday of judicial laissez-faire. This is sufficiently well known to be self-evident, but it is worthwhile to note that this critical attitude can rest on more than one ground. What *was* so objectionable about the Court's attitude toward economic legislation in the 1890–1937 era? The answers are various. For one thing, it might be, and was, contended that economic liberty is not a value entitled to special consideration, and that the Court erred at the outset when it chose to build up a system of jurisprudence dedicated to "laissez faire." But this root-and-branch critique of the "Old Court" was not the only one. It was also possible to argue, even assuming that the Court should play some part in defending economic liberty, that it had sometimes overplayed or played badly. From this point of view the defect of a decision like *New State Ice Co.* v. *Liebmann*,[113] for example, was not that the Court was interfering in business-government relationships, but that it was employing an absolutist doctrine in doing so. The rubric of "business affected with a public interest" had become, in the hands of Mr. Justice Sutherland, a straitjacket. And the objection to decisions like *Schechter Poultry Corp.* v. *United States*[114] was not their assumption that the Court had some discretion in approving or disapproving economic regulation, but the fact that

113. 285 U.S. 262 (1932).
114. 295 U.S. 495 (1935).

the justices had abused that discretion by interfering in matters too immediate and momentous for effective judicial control.

Such a backward glance can help clarify assessment of the judicial conflicts which have characterized recent constitutional history, including the 1957 Term. On the basis of his votes and written opinions, Mr. Justice Clark seems almost to reject entirely the idea that the Court should prescribe boundaries between governmental power and civil liberties.[115] This fundamental challenge to the modern Court's presuppositions has at any rate the merit of clarity; when a man tells us that the community's demands are nearly always more imperative than the individual's rights, we know what he means, even though we may not concur. Acceptance of the root-and-branch critique of judicial values would devitalize the concept of constitutional freedom in the United States, but judging by recent outbursts there are a fair number of seemingly responsible people who are eager for this devitalization process to occur.

Happily, however, not many of them are on the Supreme Court. The majority of justices have gone on assuming that the judiciary has an important part to play in protecting civil freedoms and lengthening the list of relevant subjects which may be brought within the judicial purview. And, given such assumptions, this course is unexceptionable; for the Court must have the doctrinal tools necessary to do the job. But the question of how those tools are to be used is not settled by the declaration that they exist, any more than it was settled that the Old Court would use its authority wisely once the gaps in that system of authority were filled.

With all respect, it is suggested that the civil liberties position adopted by the Chief Justice and Justices Black and Douglas smacks strongly of the judicial absolutism of the pre-1937 era. As their expatriation opinions are read, one can fairly hear Mr. Justice Butler saying: "the State is without power by any form of legislation to prohibit, change or nullify contracts between employers and adult women workers as to the amount of wages to be

---

115. Except, of course, in the area of race relations, where he has consistently stood with the unanimous Court.

paid."[116] These resounding pronouncements, foreclosing all possible eventualities, have an engagingly forthright ring, but they find little place in a jurisprudence based on Marshall's famous aphorism that "it is a *constitution* we are expounding." And in the flat Douglas-Black contention, reiterated in *Lerner,* that "government has no business penalizing a citizen merely for his beliefs or associations,"[117] one can detect the spirit of judicial superiority to other branches which prompted Mr. Justice McReynolds to say: "Grave concern for embarrassed farmers is everywhere, but this should neither obscure the rights of others nor obstruct judicial appraisement of measures proposed for relief. The ultimate welfare of the producer, like that of every other class, requires dominance of the Constitution. And zealously to uphold this in all parts is the highest duty intrusted to the courts."[118] Surely the fault of this attitude was not merely that it was applied to a milk control law.

The most troubling thing about all this is not that the Court seems for the moment likely to be drawn along such a path of doctrine, for as this and the two preceeding sections indicate, a working majority seems firmly planted on a middle ground between this contingent on the one extreme and Mr. Justice Clark on the other. The major cause for regret is that these justices—and particularly of course the two brilliant veterans, Douglas and Black—have, because of their intransigent position, failed to contribute as much as they might have to the recent development of American constitutional law. It is easy to write eulogies of civil freedom (though not perhaps to write them so eloquently as these men sometimes have). It is easy to declare as Mr. Justice Douglas does in *Perez* that the power of Congress to "withhold," "modify," or "cancel" citizenship, freedom of speech, press, and religion "does not exist."[119] But there is little in American political or constitutional history to suggest that such unqualified pronouncements will do service as operative rules of law; that they will deter legislative unwisdom in moments of stress, or recommend them-

116. Morehead v. New York *ex rel.* Tipaldo, 298 U.S. 587, 611 (1936).
117. Lerner v. Casey, 357 U.S. 468, 479, 414 (1958) (dissenting opinion).
118. Nebbia v. New York, 291 U.S. 502, 559 (1934) (dissenting opinion).
119. 356 U.S. at 84 (dissenting opinion).

selves to courts of the future as guides to construction. What might serve that purpose is a carefully reasoned doctrine, infused with the love of liberty but alert to the realities of American political life and the limits of judicial capacity. This is the doctrinal bequest which these justices, with their undoubted talents of heart and mind, might well have helped to prepare for posterity. It is one of the tragedies of modern judicial history that they have so far failed to do so.

DEEDS WITHOUT DOCTRINES

[This article first appeared in the *American Political Science Review*, 56, no. 1 (March 1962), 71–89.]

In 1898, Mr. Justice Brewer measurably strengthened his claim to immortality by publicly inviting criticism of the Supreme Court.[1] His words are well worn now, for generations of professors have gratefully quoted them in journal and classroom;[2] and during the twentieth century the challenge he issued has evoked a response that may give his shade occasional second thoughts. The Supreme Court has had many problems in the years since he spoke, but a shortage of critics has not been one of them. Journalists, academicians, and politicians have, in their several ways, poured out a steady stream of reproach which from time to time has swelled into a torrent.

The most recent of these outbreaks was set going by the desegregation decisions of 1954 and 1955 and a spate of mildly libertarian pronouncements involving the "subversion issue" in 1956 and 1957. The protest movement and its results have been ably recounted and evaluated elsewhere.[3] For present purposes it is enough to note that a vengeful and foolish anti-Court law almost passed Congress in the summer of 1958, that the Court in subsequent years has stood absolutely firm on the desegregation question, but that the controversial doctrines in the subversion field have been held to extremely narrow implications. In the latter area there is room for argument as to whether the Court has

1. For a full review of the work of the 1960 term, including civil rights decisions, see "The Supreme Court: 1960 Term," *Harvard Law Review*, Vol. 75, pp. 40–244 (Nov., 1961); and Philip B. Kurland, ed., *1961 The Supreme Court Review* (Chicago, 1962).

2. The most recent seems to be G. A. Schubert, *Constitutional Politics* (New York, 1960), p. 18.

3. C. H. Pritchett, *Congress versus the Supreme Court 1957–1960* (Minneapolis, 1961); Anthony Lewis, "The Supreme Court and its Critics," *Minnesota Law Review*, Vol. 45, pp. 305–332 (Jan., 1961); P. A. Freund, *The Supreme Court of the United States: Its Business, Purposes and Performance* (Cleveland, 1961).

significantly back-tracked; at any rate, the broadly libertarian promises that might have been inferred from some of the language in such decisions as *Watkins,*[4] *Sweezy,*[5] *Slochower,*[6] and *Konigsberg*[7] were surely not fulfilled. If the judges were tempted three years ago to launch an all-out onslaught against subversive activities laws, a majority of them have now rather convincingly mastered the impulse.

This self-restraint, whatever else may be said about it, has helped to temper the critical climate. The segregationist critics are still fairly robust, but their northern support among the Smith and McCarran Acts crowd has attenuated a good deal, and they miss it. On the extreme right the anti-Court cacophony goes on; David Lawrence has not quite given up. But the congressional temperature chart has returned to normal, and the danger of punitive action has subsided.

One man's meat is notoriously another man's poison, however, and it is not strange that the Court's recent gestures of self-denial have displeased some while placating others. Liberals, or some of them, feel that the current majority is derelict when it refuses to shackle the power of legislative investigation, or strike down our national sedition laws. Most of the critics from this new quarter have been, to their credit, more level-headed than the Jenners and Butlers of yesteryear. Indeed, some of the most extreme protests have been voiced by two members of the Court itself, Justices Black and Douglas; liberal commentary has in general been milder than they.[8] But there is enough disquiet in this camp to merit notice. The Court, yesterday criticized for defending liberty too much, is today chided for defending it too little.

4. Watkins v. United States, 354 U.S. 178 (1957).
5. Sweezy v. New Hampshire, 354 U.S. 234 (1957).
6. Slochower v. Board of Education, 350 U.S. 551 (1956).
7. Konigsberg v. State Bar, 353 U.S. 252 (1957).
8. See: "Retreat from Freedom," *Christian Century,* Vol. 78, pp. 163–4 (Feb. 8, 1961); "Free Speech and Movies," *Commonweal,* Vol. 73, pp. 495–6 (Feb. 10, 1961); "The Court and the Committee," *ibid.,* pp. 624–5 (March 17, 1961); "Security and Civil Rights," *id.,* Vol. 74, pp. 316–17 (June 23, 1961); "Neither Clear Nor Present," *Nation,* Vol. 192, pp. 509–10 (June 17, 1961); "Censorship of Movies," *New Republic,* Vol. 144, p. 8 (Feb. 27, 1961); "Un-American Activities," *ibid.,* pp. 5–6 (March 13, 1961); "No Decision," *Reporter,* Vol. 25, p. 12 (July 6, 1961).

So much, for the moment, about what have been called the "result-oriented"[9] critiques of the Court's performance. Meanwhile still another plaint has been heard, largely from the groves of academe: that the judges, results aside, have been fudging their obligations as craftsmen. The point seems to be that in one way or another the Court has failed to produce doctrines that rest on the "exercise of reason":[10] the rhetorical flourish or the *ipse dixit* is found where we ought to find explicit principles rationally justified and applied.[11] These strictures are not backed, as the vendetta of 1958 was, by the threat of political retribution. Nevertheless they claim the respect of the Court and those who study it because their authors are defenders of judicial review who speak more in sorrow than in anger.

The aim of this paper is to review, in terms of these two criticisms, the 1960–61 record of the Supreme Court in the field of civil rights. What is the actual pattern of results? Did the Court of the 1960 Term do less than it ought to have done to buttress the liberties of the individual? And did it at the same time maintain the standards of legal craftsmanship that ought to be maintained by the supreme tribunal of a constitutional democracy? In short, to what extent are either the "result-oriented" or the "reason-oriented" critiques warranted? It happens that the 1960 Term was unusually rich in significant pronouncements involving civil rights; it should provide, therefore, a fairly adequate test of both indictments.

The decisions that excited the gravest misgivings among libertarians were those having to do with alleged subversion. One of them, so Mr. Justice Douglas said, signalized "a sharp break with traditional concepts of First Amendment rights."[12] Others caused

9. Lewis, *op. cit.,* p. 306.

10. Herbert Wechsler, *Principles, Politics, and Fundamental Law* (Cambridge, Mass., 1961) p. 16.

11. H. M. Hart, Jr., "Foreword: The Time Chart of the Justices," *Harvard Law Review,* Vol. 73, pp. 84–125 (Nov., 1959); A. M. Bickel and H. H. Wellington, "Legislative Purpose and the Judicial Process: The Lincoln Mills Case," *id.,* Vol. 71, pp. 1–39 (Nov., 1957); E. N. Griswold, "Foreword: Of Time and Attitudes—Professor Hart and Judge Arnold," *id.,* Vol. 74, pp. 81–94 (Nov., 1960).

12. Scales v. United States, 367 U.S. 203 (1961).

Mr. Justice Black to fear that the Court had adopted a deliberate policy of sacrificing individual freedom to governmental control,[13] that the boundaries of the Bill of Rights have been "all but obliterated,"[14] that the liberties of America "must be fast disappearing,"[15] and that, "if the present trend continues ... government by consent will disappear to be replaced by government by intimidation."[16] If these forebodings are plausible, the 1960 Term does indeed mark "a fateful moment in the history of a free country."[17]

Wilkinson and *Braden* involved the old, intractable problem of legislative investigations, specifically some recent antics of the House Un-American Activities Committee. A subcommittee of that egregious agency had invaded Atlanta armed with a Committee resolution authorizing investigation of Communist infiltration into southern industry, Communist propaganda activity, and "any other matter within the jurisdiction of the Committee." Both Wilkinson and Braden had publicly criticized this proposed inquiry and had then been brought before the subcommittee, queried about party membership, and duly indicted when they refused to answer. They justified their refusal mainly by a challenge to the pertinency of the questions, and by an appeal to the First Amendment and to the doctrine of "valid legislative purpose."

With the best will in the world it was hard to argue that the questions had not been pertinent to the subject under inquiry, or that the witness had not been informed of the subject matter so that he could judge its pertinence. Since *Watkins* the Committee has framed its resolutions carefully and instructed its victims thoroughly, and as Mr. Justice Stewart says, it would be hard to imagine a preliminary question *more* pertinent to the topics under investigation. Moreover, *Barenblatt* v. *United States*[18] in 1959

13. Braden v. United States, 365 U.S. 431 (1961).
14. *Ibid.*
15. *Ibid.*
16. Wilkinson v. United States, 365 U.S. 399 (1961).
17. Communist Party v. Subversive Activities Control Board, 367 U.S. 1 (1961).
18. 360 U.S. 109.

had apparently decided that such inquiries are within the range of valid legislative purpose and do not infringe the First Amendment. But, it was said, the situation in the present cases is different; for Wilkinson and Braden have been called and questioned, not for the sake of gaining public information, but with the aim of punishing them because they assailed the Committee. A legislative purpose that might otherwise be valid is corrupted by this punitive motive.

This was the only significant contention not quite covered by *Barenblatt* or other precedents. Mr. Justice Stewart, upholding the convictions, replied that the Committee's behavior did not inescapably imply an intent to punish the witness, and that even if it did the inquiry would be valid. For, quoting *Watkins,* "motives alone would not vitiate an investigation . . . by a House of Congress if that assembly's legislative purpose is being served." And in these instances the subcommittee had "probable cause" to believe that the witnesses had information that would serve that purpose.

This implied requirement of probable cause may be a slender ray of libertarian promise in an otherwise somber landscape, but it is slender indeed. For, as Mr. Justice Black remarked in dissent, each witness had been identified as a Communist, so far as the record shows, only by a single paid informer's flat statement; if that is enough to satisfy the requirement, its value as a curb on Committee excesses is negligible. As for the pertinency requirement, the legislators can obviously meet it by modest care in drafting resolutions and instructing witnesses. And the claim that the interest in individual freedom may outbalance the state's interest in procuring information is apparently answered by the *Barenblatt* assumptions that the state interest is nothing less than the preservation of the nation, admittedly a rather awesome interest to contend with. Justice Black, and others, would insist that the destruction of America is not materially forestalled by the harassment of men like Braden and Wilkinson, and that the majority, while pretending to apply the "balancing test" in cases of this kind, has weighted the government's side so heavily (and artificially) as to preordain the result.

There is some justice in the charge—which becomes even

stronger in *Wilkinson,* where, as Justice Black says, the Court even "disclaims any power to determine whether the Committee is in fact interested in the information at all." To be sure, the balancing formula cannot be expected to produce certain and precise results. But we can fairly ask that the users of the test weigh realities against realities insofar as imperfect man can discern them.

As an exercise in reason, then, the majority opinions here are marred by an evasion: the supposed key issue—the balancing of private rights and public need—is handled by referring us back to an earlier opinion in which the heart of the matter is likewise evaded. And the net result of these pronouncements is that congressional committees remain unfettered by significant constitutional restraints. Add the latest chapter in the saga of Willard Uphaus[19] in which the Court adhered to a similarly expansive view of state investigatory power, and it becomes clear that the judiciary offers chilly comfort these days to the shorn lambs who face governmental inquisition.

Yet it cannot be said that the dissenters suggest alternative criteria that would meet the difficulties inherent in the problem. Justice Black's opinion in *Wilkinson* makes a powerful assault on the majority position, but can it be seriously proposed that the judiciary should look behind every ostensible legislative purpose and evaluate the latent motives it finds there? Is there any way to insure that such an evaluation would represent anything but the subjective bias of the judges who made it? How *does* one assess the weight of the public need for particular information when, in the nature of the investigatory process, the information is not yet known? Some tightening up of the probable cause standard might serve a symbolic purpose, but an investigator cannot be asked to prove in advance what he is supposedly trying to find out. And surely the standards that guide us in this field should not be determined by the performance of the *HUAC.* They must be applicable to other committees, past and future, whose quest might indeed be relevant to the republic's welfare. Such standards may

19. Uphaus v. Wyman, 364 U.S. 388 (1960).

be devisable, but they do not emerge from the minority opinions here. And the result of *Wilkinson* and *Braden* should be judged with that fact in mind.

Wilkinson and *Braden* were decided in February; the judges thoughtfully waited until June to deliver the next one-two punch in the subversion field. Again by votes of five to four, the Court held that the Communist party must register under the McCarran Act and that the membership clause of the Smith Act had been validly applied to Junius Scales.[20]

The registration case presented a problem well calculated to tax the ingenuity of a judge who prefers not to invalidate a federal statute. The McCarran Act requires the registration of "Communist action" organizations with the Attorney General, and the registration statement must contain a variety of information including the names of officers and members. Once registered, or validly ordered to do so, the organization and its members become subject to certain obligations and disabilities. After hearings and appeals extending back to 1950, the American Communist party now faced such an order to register, and the Supreme Court faced the question of that order's validity.

The statutory and constitutional challenges to the order were several, but perhaps the most weighty were those based on the First and Fifth Amendments. The Court has held that registration requirements may sometimes unconstitutionally constrict freedom of expression and association. Does not the McCarran Act applied to the party have this effect? The Court has also held that the government cannot compel divulgence of Communist party membership. Do not the act's disclosure requirements force the officers to incriminate themselves?

The first of these objections could not be expected to prevail in the light of such holdings as *Dennis* v. *United States*[21] and such undoubtedly valid statutes as the Corrupt Practices Act and the Lobbying Act. Justice Frankfurter for the majority found that the registration order did not violate the First Amendment. The balancing formula was duly stated—impediments on freedom

20. Above, notes 12 and 17.
21. 341 U.S. 494 (1951).

against public need—but the public-need side of the scale was heavily and decisively weighted by the idea that Congress has the primary responsibility for our security against foreign danger and that its choice of means for dealing with such threats must be respected unless the choice is rooted in "unfounded or irrational imaginings." In short, it would seem that no federal law aimed at a foreign-directed menace can fail to pass the balancing test: in this area the principle of legislative deference predetermines the result.

The Fifth Amendment is another matter. But its protection cannot be invoked by the party on behalf of its officers; they must invoke it themselves, and they had not yet, as individuals, done so. It will be time to consider their privilege when they do refuse to register, citing the Fifth Amendment as their justification. Until then the challenge is premature. The *party* is now required to register. Whether a given officer can escape the burden of the requirement is a matter for the future, as is the question of the validity of the disabilities imposed on those who are required to register under the act. The Court thus managed adroitly to postpone the really ticklish Fifth Amendment issue, deciding only the narrow and relatively easy question of whether the Party was altogether immune from the obligation to identify itself.[22] Only Justice Black was prepared to say it was. The Chief Justice wanted to postpone the whole decision by sending the case back once again to the Subversive Activities Control Board to tidy up some procedural loose ends. But, if constitutional issues were to be met, he agreed with Justice Brennan that the act did violate the Fifth Amendment.

Justice Brennan's argument on this point was formidable. The Court had admitted *arguendo* that the Act would be invalid if it imposed on officials the obligation of answering in such a form as effectively to nullify the privilege against self-incrimination. But, said the Court, the question of whether the statute does contain this vice can wait until the party or its officers are prosecuted for

22. Editor's note: the Court subsequently held that officers of the party were protected by the Fifth Amendment from prosecution for failure to register the party.

failure to register. Meanwhile the order to register stands. The Brennan point was that this puts the official in a cleft stick: he may register and thus surrender his possible privilege or refrain from registering and expose himself to the possibility of the grave criminal penalties provided for non-compliance. He is thus coerced to give up his privilege, and this amounts to an erosion of the amendment's guaranties. These contentions were not fully answered by Justice Frankfurter's majority opinion. Plainly, he was animated by a previously expressed conviction that the privilege against self-incrimination should be rigidly enforced within its traditional limits but not extended an iota beyond them.[23] In this instance, however, even the traditional limits seemed narrowed, for the official was being pressured to waive his rights in much the way that a defendant is pressured if the prosecutor comments on his failure to take the stand.[24]

In the *Scales* decision the majority again revealed its great reluctance to challenge the power of Congress in the subversion field. Scales had been convicted of being a member of the Communist party with knowledge of its illegal purposes and with a specific intent to overthrow the government. The most serious contentions urged in his defense were three: that "guilt by association" violates the Fifth Amendment, which prescribes that guilt must be personal; that the First Amendment immunizes such activities and associations; and that the McCarran Act of 1950 repealed the membership clause of the Smith Act.

The Court, by Justice Harlan, conceded that the Fifth Amendment argument had weight. Due process does require that guilt be personal, and membership alone, even in an illegal organization, may indeed be constitutionally protected. But the statute here was interpreted as punishing membership only if the petitioner was an "active" member who knew the party was engaged in illegal activity and who had himself a specific intent to bring about the illegal results. The standard objection to the concept of guilt by association is that it may lead to punishment of the innocent

23. Ullman v. United States, 350 U.S. 422 (1956).
24. See In re Opinion of the Justices, 300 Mass. 620 (1938); State v. Wolfe, 64 S.D. 178 (1936).

or confused,[25] but the Court argued that these restrictive interpretations forfend that danger.

As for the First Amendment question, that too was pretty well disposed of simply by citing *Dennis*. Justice Harlan's only problem was the argument that the law discourages freedom of association by frightening the potential member whose aims are wholly innocent and legal. This objection is met, he said, by the requirement of *knowing* membership.

This may be, so far as it goes, a sufficient answer to the particular point, but the use of *Dennis* as a kind of *vade mecum* is beginning to be disturbing. The idea of that decision—and of such predecessors as *Schenck*[26]—was that the "clear and present [or probable] danger" determination depended on the circumstances "in every case." Whether the Court employs the clear and present danger rubric or its contemporary surrogate, the balancing test, may not matter very much. In either event, the test, if it is one, must be applied to new contexts as new cases arise;[27] that is, *Dennis* did *not* settle "that the advocacy with which we are here concerned" is unprotected speech. It may be answered that the Court is unequal to the task of deciding in a field related to national defense whether "the gravity of the 'evil,' discounted by its improbability justifies such invasion of free speech as is necessary to avoid the danger,"[28] and that the majority was tacitly conceding this. If so, would it not be better to acknowledge the fact by explicitly giving the congressional judgment conclusive weight, as Justice Frankfurter did in the registration case? There is little to be said for retaining the appearance of a reasoned, independent judgment without the reality. If both the clear and present danger and the balancing tests are defunct for all practical purposes in cases of this kind, then in the name of reason it would be well to say so.

There remained for the Court a nice problem of statutory con-

25. Zechariah Chafee, Jr., *Free Speech in the United States* (Cambridge, Mass., 1946), pp. 470–483.

26. Schenck v. United States, 249 U.S. 47 (1919).

27. The relevant period in Dennis was 1945 to 1948, in Scales 1946 to 1954.

28. Dennis v. United States, 183 F.2d 201, 212 (1950).

struction which had to be met before Scales could be locked away. The McCarran Act of 1950 provides that "neither the holding of office nor membership in any Communist organization . . . shall constitute *per se* a violation . . . of this section or of any other criminal statute." Does not this wipe out the membership clause of the Smith Act, passed ten years earlier? No, said Justice Harlan; this simply requires us to construe the Smith Act so as to apply only to active, knowing membership. The quoted phrase declares that *mere* membership is not criminal, but Congress did not intend to immunize membership of a purposeful sort. This interpretation was supported, as he saw it, by the context of the clause and by legislative history. Justice Brennan, on the other hand, argued in dissent that the law immunizes against prosecution for any kind of membership. The language is: "membership . . . shall [not] constitute *per se*" a crime, rather than "membership *per se* shall not constitute a crime." The position of "*per se*" makes a crucial difference; and without better knowledge of congressional intent than we have, we should assume that the law means what it says —that membership alone of whatever kind is not forbidden.

These were the main decisions of the term involving federal power and the Red Menace. Certainly their result is to make it clear that the substantive authority of Congress in this field will not be challenged by the Court. But this has been tolerably obvious at least since 1951, and in fact no federal sedition law has ever been held unconstitutional. Like it or not, the policy of judicial acquiescence on this point can hardly be called surprising. What is rather dismaying is the Court's failure to make more use of certain judicial options which have enabled it in the past to take a hand in matters of this kind without running head-on into Congress' basic power to govern. The registration issue might have been evaded altogether by returning the case to the board, as the Chief Justice suggested. The membership clause might have been bucked back to Congress by construing it in the way Justice Brennan proposed, for the construction was surely not unreasonable. By these expedients, as one acute observer has remarked,[29] the Court could have

29. A. M. Bickel, "The Communist Cases," *New Republic,* Vol. 144, pp. 15–16 (June 19, 1961).

at least deferred an outright holding that two dubious, repressive statutes are sanctioned by the Constitution. And it seems particularly unfortunate to uphold both statutes, for they look in different directions, and even a modest Court is warranted in telling Congress that it cannot have it both ways, that it must choose between the ventilation of the McCarran Act or the prohibition of the Smith Act. The Court would be on particularly strong ground in enforcing this choice, for the judges would rest squarely on the procedural right against self-incrimination, and procedure is a well-recognized judicial domain. By such techniques—the judicious use of the power to remand, the power to interpret statutes, and the power to enforce procedural regularity—the Court has performed usefully in this field in the past, and it would be a pity if it now chose to abandon even this carefully self-restrained function.

Fortunately there is evidence even in these cases that such a course of inaction has not been irrevocably set. For one thing, the Court did make it clear in *Scales* that the government is bound to prove active, knowing, purposeful membership in each prosecution, and this requirement should not only mitigate individual injustice, but also hold the number of such prosecutions to a minimum. For another thing, Justice Harlan reiterated the *Yates*[30] doctrine that the government must show advocacy of illegal action, not merely "abstract doctrine," and further explained that very strict standards of proof are required. These pronouncements caused a conservative magazine, loath to approve the Supreme Court's behavior even when anti-subversive laws were upheld, to suggest that the proof requirement would make the cause virtually unenforceable.[31] This is probably too optimistic—or pessimistic as the reader prefers. But in *Noto* v. *United States*[32] the Court did void a membership clause conviction because the evidence of illegal advocacy by the Party was inadequate by these strict standards. Add *Communist Party* v. *Catherwood*,[33] which held, as against a

30. Yates v. United States, 354 U.S. 298 (1957).
31. "Let the Intellectuals Take it From Here," *National Review*, Vol. 10, p. 371 (June 17, 1961).
32. 367 U.S. 290 (1961).
33. 367 U.S. 389 (1961).

state determination, that the Party need not be deprived of the benefits of unemployment compensation, and *Deutch* v. *United States*,[34] which freed a recalcitrant HUAC witness under the pertinency rule; and the faint glimmer of a silver lining may be descried. The Court is probably going to behave unobtrusively in this field, but it has not yet wholly abdicated.

Apart from the after-echoes of the *Uphaus* problem, the only significant state cases involving the "Communist question" were *In re Anastaplo*[35] and *Konigsberg* v. *State Bar*.[36] Both involved state refusals to admit to the bar candidates who would not answer questions about Communist party membership. In Illinois and California, where the cases arose, the bar examiners must be satisfied that aspirants are of good moral character, and California specifically denies bar admission to those who advocate violent overthrow of government. The committees argued that Anastaplo and Konigsberg had, by their refusals to answer, obstructed full investigation of their qualifications; it was this obstruction of a relevant inquiry that justified their rejection as members of the bar.

The Supreme Court, by Mr. Justice Harlan, upheld the committees over sharp dissenting opinions by Justices Black and Brennan. Mr. Justice Black insisted, *inter alia,* that compelling answers to such questions was an unconstitutional impingement on speech and association; and both he and Justice Brennan contended that the states were imposing upon applicants the burden of proving that they did not advocate violent overthrow—a shifting of the burden condemned three years earlier in *Speiser* v. *Randall*.[37] The Court answered the first objection by invoking the balancing test: "the State's interest in having lawyers who are devoted to the law in its broadest sense, including . . . its procedures for orderly change" is "sufficient to outweigh the minimal effect upon free association occasioned by compulsory disclosure in the circumstances here presented." As for *Speiser*, Justice Harlan was able to distinguish it. Unlike *Speiser*, the present cases involve the denial of positions of responsibility to "a limited class of persons" re-

34. 367 U.S. 456 (1961).
35. 366 U.S. 82 (1961).
36. 366 U.S. 36 (1961).
37. 357 U.S. 513 (1958).

garded as dangerous "because the position might be used to the detriment of the public." Moreover, there is no evidence that the state here shifted the burden of proof to the petitioner; rather, it seems that the state assumed the burden itself and was prevented from discharging that burden by the refusals to answer.

No cloud of words can conceal the fact that a lawyer may now be required to answer questions about Communist party membership as a precondition to practicing his profession; and it seems equally clear from the Court's language that a state may deny bar admission if advocacy of violent overthrow can be demonstrated. No doubt it is unwise to levy such gratuitous pains and penalties on those who believe, like Shelley, in their right to silence, or even on those who still adhere to the miserable remnant that is now the American Communist party. But wisdom and constitutionality are different matters, and—as in the investigation cases—the question is where a viable line might be drawn. Can it be held that the state is *unreasonable* in believing that advocacy of illegal means to change the form of government is an important consideration in determining the fitness of lawyers "in whose hands so largely lies the safekeeping of this country's legal and political institutions?" And if this is a reasonable belief, can the applicant be allowed to thwart the inquiry designed to implement it? Justice Brennan would apparently concede, *arguendum,* that the belief is reasonable, but would require that the state assume the burden of proving a *prima facie* case against the applicant before denying him admission. This suggestion may have promise; these decisions do not altogether close the door on it. Yet such a rule would apparently be at odds with standing procedures in most states, and the Court seems justified in at least postponing so drastic a departure from custom.

Meanwhile, it must be said of the bar examination cases, like the cases just discussed involving federal power, that they contain few surprises. Some years ago the Court began to hint that it might take a hand when the urge to persecute unorthodox opinion impinged on freedom of occupation. The hints were very tentative, the limitations on state power were cautiously drawn, and the development had to be understood in the light of a line of cases that upheld such impingement when the occupation was that of a specially placed group such as public employees.[38] The bar examination cases surely make no libertarian advance in this field; but neither do they depart significantly from lines long since established.

One of the justest criticisms of the Communist registration case and *Scales* is that they gave positive sanction to repressive acts, even though the issues might have been avoided. A rather similar point can be made about *Times Film Corporation* v. *Chicago.*[39]

The issue was movie censorship, and a few words of background are in order. In 1952, the Court repudiated the old doctrine[40] that movie censorship is immune from challenge under the free expression clauses of the Constitution.[41] However, although he conceded that movies raise First Amendment questions, Mr. Justice Clark for the majority was careful not to condemn all regulation of this medium of expression, nor was he even prepared to rule that all "prior restraint" was forbidden. In subsequent cases,[42] Justices Black and Douglas began to urge that the Court take at least this minimum step of outlawing prior restraint, which has been traditionally regarded as peculiarly objectionable in the free speech field; but the majority steadily refrained from doing so. The case-by-case approach that was adopted had this to be said for it: the whole subject was novel as a constitutional issue; the argument against censorship may depend in part on such variables as the means of communication and the form of the restriction; and judges, like lesser mortals, sometimes need the aid of time to ripen their understanding. Not even the "priorness" of the repression settles the matter. Even before *Burstyn,* Paul A. Freund had persuasively argued that there are kinds and kinds of prior restraint;[43]

38. Adler v. Board of Education, 342 U.S. 485 (1952); Garner v. Los Angeles Board, 341 U.S. 716 (1951); Barenblatt v. United States, 360 U.S. 109 (1959).

39. 365 U.S. 43 (1961).

40. Mutual Film Corp. v. Ohio Industrial Comm., 236 U.S. 230 (1915).

41. Burstyn v. Wilson, 343 U.S. 495 (1952).

42. Kingsley Pictures v. Regents, 360 U.S. 684 (1959); Superior Films v. Ohio, 346 U.S. 587 (1954).

43. "The Supreme Court and Civil Liberties," *Vanderbilt Law Review,* Vol. 4, pp. 533–554 (Apr., 1951).

the Court, charting new seas, must go slowly while such insights are evaluated and digested.

But in the 1960 term, the majority seemed to lose patience with this tortoise-like pursuit of wisdom. Chicago requires that movies must be submitted, before showing, to the police commissioner, who may grant or withold a permit subject only to review by the mayor. The Times Film Corporation had refused altogether to submit a film, arguing that—quite apart from the standards the commissioner might employ—this system of administrative prior restraint was void on its face. The Court, by Mr. Justice Clark, saw this as presenting the question of whether an exhibitor has "complete and absolute freedom to exhibit, at least once, any and every kind of motion picture." The answer, said the Court, is no. Very well. Given this formulation of the issue, the answer is not astonishing. But the result is to uphold the principle of administrative censorship, which is, as the Chief Justice said, prior restraint in its "purest and most far-reaching form." From refusing to condemn prior restraint of all kinds, the Court seems to have taken the long stride to a policy of approving a particularly vicious kind. Of course review will still be granted as to the legitimacy of the standards police chiefs may employ. But the concept of administrative licensing itself has apparently been constitutionally ratified.

The mischief of such a concept was exposed by the Chief Justice in his strong but somewhat diffuse dissent. The administrative censor operates in comparative privacy, free from the procedural safeguards that would prevail in a court of law. Though his decisions may be theoretically subject to judicial review, this is likely to be a hollow consolation in practice because of the delays of the adjudicative process—the present case had been pending for three years. Meantime the would-be exhibitor is trapped because he cannot show the film until the license issues. He is likely therefore to knuckle under to the censor's whim, even though it is based on plainly arbitrary standards.

Mr. Justice Clark's opinion proceeds as if the only alternative to this arrangement would be utter freedom to show any film—however obscene—at least once. But this is a false view of the options available. The Court in 1957 had upheld a system of book regulation which permitted New York City to seek in court a "limited injunctive remedy" under close procedural safeguards, including the right of the book-seller to immediate trial.[44] This procedure mitigates to a considerable degree the objections to administrative censorship mentioned in the last paragraph, and is a far cry from the Chicago arrangements. Perhaps the Court is not ready to prescribe the New York method as a universal rule; perhaps movies present problems of control different from those imposed by books. But the *Kingsley Books* case does at least suggest that there is a middle ground between the evils of administrative censorship and complete abandonment of the principle that condemns prior restraint.

The trouble is that Justice Clark's tendency to think in polarized terms on one side of such issues is matched by a similar tendency on the Black-Douglas side of the courtroom. Justice Douglas had denounced the New York ordinance as "censorship at its worst," which it patently was not. The Chicago arrangement was in fact a good deal worse, and it is this kind of refusal to acknowledge differences in degree that impedes the development of a workable jurisprudence in the civil rights field.

There is some possibility that the implications of *Times Film* are less deplorable than they seem. A later court might hold that the case merely rejected the claim of an absolute right against all prior restraint. That may be what Justice Clark meant when he said "It is that question alone that we decide." The question of the procedural sufficiency of any particular system could then still be raised. But if this was what was meant, nothing would have been easier than to say so, and the cloudiness of the majority reasoning leaves room for the lamentable inference that administrative censorship is constitutionally approved. That inference may serve as the basis for a substantial revival of censorship before the Court in its deliberate majesty gets around to facing the issue again.

So far the tale of the 1960 Term is a rather dreary one. In the cases involving the subversion issue, the Court has added another layer or two to the long-standing but growing impression that it

44. Kingsley Books v. Brown, 354 U.S. 436 (1957).

will deal only with the extreme periphery of the problem. In *Times Film,* it has marred a ten-year record of cautious but effective discouragement to the spirit of Mrs. Grundy. Despite the cross-threads and reservations that have been duly noted, an observer might understandably doubt that this is a Court whose members are all "equally zealous to enforce the constitutional protection of the free play of the human spirit."[45] But a term— like a book, or a life—must be judged in the round, and there are further deeds to be recorded.

The decisions that probably caused the most general excitement were those in the Sunday law cases.[46] No doubt this unwonted public concern for a constitutional issue came about partly because of the widespread impact of Sunday closing laws: there is hardly an American who has not been mildly inconvenienced by such statutes, while most have never so much as seen a Communist except in television dramas. But partly the interest must be explained as an aspect of that curious and anachronistic fascination our people have for disputes with a religious undertone. No matter how secular we may become in spirit and practice, the mention of religion can still make dogmatists out of citizens and mountains out of molehills.

The issues posed in these cases were whether Sunday closing laws violated the equal protection and religious freedom guaranties and the prohibition against laws "respecting an establishment of religion."·The short answer is that they do not. But brevity was hardly the watchword for the judges in this litigation. The opinions on both sides consumed, by rough count, 58,000 words— 47,000 more than it took Marshall to decide *McCulloch* v. *Maryland.*

The four cases varied both in the circumstances of the persons involved and in the nature of the statutes challenged, but certain constitutional issues were common to all. For one thing, it was

45. Frankfurter, J., Murdoch v. Pennsylvania, 319 U.S. 105, 129 (1943) (diss.).
46. Braunfeld v. Brown, 366 U.S. 599 (1961); Gallagher v. Crown Kosher Super Market of Mass., Inc., 366 U.S. 617 (1961); McGowan v. Maryland, 366 U.S. 420 (1961); Two Guys from Harrison-Allentown, Inc. v. McGinley, 366 U.S. 582 (1961).

argued that the laws' purpose and effect was to aid religion and that this violated the "no establishment" principle. On the contrary, said the Chief Justice, who spoke for the Court in all four, the *present* purpose of the legislation is to set aside "a day of rest, repose, recreation and tranquillity." The original purpose may have been religious, but in the course of time this basis has been replaced by a secular objective which is, constitutionally speaking, unexceptionable. In each case the Chief Justice conducted an examination of the laws in question and warned that Sunday laws would be struck down if they betrayed a religious motive. But surely it would be a modest feat of legislative draftsmanship to avoid such pitfalls, and it may be assumed that the basic power to establish a "day of tranquillity" is now safe from constitutional assault. Only Justice Douglas seems to disagree.

The second major objection to the laws was that they violated the equal protection clause because of the eccentricity and arbitrariness of the exceptions they granted: Maryland forbids oyster-gathering but permits the playing of pinball machines; Massachusetts allows the sale of ice cream at retail and of dressed poultry at wholesale but prohibits (presumably) the wholesaling of the former and the retailing of the latter. And so on. The pattern in Massachusetts had been called by the district court an "unbelievable hodgepodge." But the possibility of overthrowing the laws on this ground was thin to the vanishing point once it was conceded that they aimed at a legitimate secular objective. For years the Court has steadily held that a statutory discrimination will not be set aside if any state of facts reasonably may be conceived to justify it.[47] These laws may have stretched a little the judicial capacity to conceive, but not more than some others have. A religious (or racial) basis for the classification would, of course, damn it. But absent that factor, the Court found no difficulty in imagining reasonable grounds for the distinctions.

The final question was not so easy. The Sunday laws may be secular in their motivation, but suppose they have the incidental effect of imposing a discriminatory burden on certain religions—

47. Railway Express Inc. v. New York, 336 U.S. 106 (1949); Queenside Hills Realty Co. v. Saxl, 328 U.S. 80 (1946).

Orthodox Jews, for example, whose faith forbids them to work on Saturday. Is this not a restriction or penalty on religious freedom? The Chief Justice admitted that it is. The Orthodox may be forced to a choice between abandoning Sabbatarianism or suffering the economic disadvantage of a five-day week for their shops as against a six-day week for their competitors. But, said the Chief Justice, the state is sometimes permitted to restrict or burden religious practices in the course of seeking a legitimate secular objective. This law does not forbid Saturday observance; it merely makes it inconvenient. Such a law is valid "unless the State may accomplish its purpose by means which do not impose such a burden."

But for Justice Brennan, who dissented on this issue, the quoted phrase was precisely the sticking point. Why not require the state to allow an exception for anyone whose *bona fide* religious beliefs require him to rest on Saturday? Many states do grant this exception which eliminates the burden on religious freedom yet keeps the "day of tranquillity" substantially intact. This might indeed be the wiser solution, said the Court, but we are not prepared to impose it as a constitutional requirement. Such exceptions could create enforcement problems, since the state might have more difficulty in keeping track of violations. The Sunday observers might arguably claim that *they* were disadvantaged. And finally, such a system would plunge the state into the vexing business of distinguishing between sincere and spurious claims of religious scruple. The state may choose to enter such a hornet's nest if it likes, but the Constitution does not require it.

It should be emphasized that this question of allowing exceptions for Sabbatarians was the only one that was close enough to attract as many as three dissenters. Even if such a rule had been imposed, it would have been a minor qualification of the general holding that Sunday laws are valid; for only the Sabbatarians themselves would have standing to raise the issue, and their number is not great. Perhaps that fact alone argues for the rule. As Justice Brennan said, Sundays might be a little noisier and the task of enforcement a little more difficult, but this price is worth paying in order to avoid discriminating against religion. Yet the objections raised by the Chief Justice—and Justice Frankfurter's concurring opinion—were more substantial than Justice Brennan conceded. In fact, the arguments on both sides in these cases have a thoughtful, cogent quality, so that the reader is held delicately poised between agreement and disagreement. The Sunday Law decisions provide us with one of those all-too-rare instances in which reason seems to have played a significant part in the result.

Why is this so? Perhaps because the Sunday laws cut across the categories into which the Court's thinking has tended to crystallize in recent times. Such a problem as this is not answerable in terms of simplistic pro-individual or pro-government concepts, and the judges are therefore led to look beyond their prepossessions for guidance. How would the results of these cases be assessed in any pro and con enumeration? How do we weigh the individual right of A to enjoy a tranquil Sunday against the individual right of B to pursue his trade free from discrimination on account of his religion—and incidentally to mar A's tranquillity? Certainly it is hard to classify as anti-libertarian holdings so equivocal as these, particularly when they are supported by Justices Warren, Black, and, except for the special question of Sabbatarians, Brennan. The vitality of the Court's concern for religious freedom is evinced not only by the warnings embodied in the language of the Sunday law decisions, but by *Torcaso* v. *Watkins*,[48] which unanimously overthrew a requirement of the Maryland constitution that public officers declare their belief in God.

The doctrinal history of the modern Supreme Court in the area of criminal procedure has been extremely complex, partly because procedural and substantive questions are often intertwined and partly because even the cases involving "pure" criminal procedure issues are very numerous. Since the early 1930's, when the judges began to display a new sensitivity for the rights of the accused, such cases have bulked large on the Court's docket, and the pattern of decision-making is labyrinthian. Nevertheless, allowing for cross-threads and convolutions, it can be said that there has been a broad tendency to go forward (that is, to extend the constitutional rights of accused persons), moderated by a disposition to

48. 367 U.S. 488 (1961).

hold the line in certain areas such as the right to counsel in state courts[49] and the right against eavesdropping.[50] Except for the brief period of the Vinson Court, when such holdings as *Trupiano* v. *United States*[51] were spawned, relatively few important backward steps have been taken. Perhaps no other field, except racial discrimination, so clearly illustrates the general concord of the judges on a basic ideal of fairness to the individual. The disagreement has usually been between those who would go slow in extending this ideal and those who would go somewhat faster. Between these mild extremes the majority has forged gradually ahead.

The 1960 term was marked by a distinct spurt forward in this field; not, indeed, the kind of headlong advance that Justice Douglas would favor, but a brisk one nonetheless. Leaving aside decisions already treated, like *Wilkinson* and the Communist registration case, in which procedural questions were linked to major substantive issues, the Court upheld the government in only a handful of cases. Chief among these were a pair involving the claim of double jeopardy[52] and another pair involving the question whether federal courts should enjoin the use of illegally obtained evidence in state courts.[53] The first three simply represent a refusal to go forward; certainly they could not be regarded as retreats from settled libertarian positions. *Wilson* v. *Schnettler* may be a little cloudier, for in *Rea* v. *United States*[54] the Court had held that a federal court injunction could issue to prevent federal agents from presenting in state court evidence illegally seized, and Wilson was invoking that holding. But there were factual differences between the two situations; and the Court in *Wilson,* though rejecting the petitioner's claim, did not depart from *Rea's* basic holding that illegal search can warrant federal court intervention. And at all events, *Mapp* v. *Ohio*[55] (discussed below) seems to obviate the

49. Betts v. Brady, 316 U.S. 455 (1942).
50. Goldman v. United States, 316 U.S. 129 (1942).
51. 334 U.S. 699 (1948).
52. Gori v. United States, 367 U.S. 364 (1961); Callahan v. United States, 364 U.S. 587 (1961).
53. Pugach v. Dollinger, 365 U.S. 458 (1961); Wilson v. Schnettler, 365 U.S. 381 (1961).
54. 350 U.S. 214 (1956).
55. 367 U.S. 643 (1961).

whole question by holding that *all* unconstitutionally seized evidence is excludable in state courts, so that hereafter a defendant like Wilson could simply invoke that rule and an injunctive remedy would be unnecessary. In short, the spirit of these decisions seems at most static rather than retrogressive.

In any case, they are greatly overbalanced on the libertarian side by other criminal procedure decisions of the term. Not only is it true that a heavy proportion of the cases were decided in favor of the accused. More important, two of these decisions must be regarded as landmarks in the history of modern constitutional doctrine.

The lesser of them was nevertheless highly significant, not because it carved out new doctrine but because it adhered so scrupulously to the limits of the old. Since *Goldman* v. *United States* permitted admission of "detectaphone" evidence, there has seemed reason to fear lack of constitutional protection against the ingenious electronic eavesdropping made possible by modern science. Such fears were not entirely stilled by *Silverman* v. *United States*,[56] but they were confined within borders. In this, the "spike-mike" case, the Court held inadmissible evidence obtained by driving a spike attached to an amplifier into the wall of a house until it hit a heating duct; the entire heating system thereby became a giant microphone. The detectaphone in the *Goldman* case had not penetrated the house wall, and this, said the Court, made a crucial difference. Eavesdropping accomplished by an "unauthorized physical penetration" of this private house invaded the rights secured by the Fourth Amendment. The petitioner had asked for reconsideration of *Goldman*, but Justice Stewart found this unnecessary in light of the difference in the facts. However, the language of his majority opinion reveals alertness to the threat of "frightening paraphernalia" to the right to privacy, and the determination not to go beyond *Goldman* "by even a fraction of an inch." There may in fact be reason to doubt that *Goldman* itself could now survive direct constitutional attack, especially when it is remembered that Justice Frankfurter was among the dissenters in that case.

56. 365 U.S. 505 (1961). Editor's note: the Court subsequently overruled Goldman in Katz v. United States, 389 U.S. 347 (1967).

The second and even more striking decision was *Mapp* v. *Ohio,* which held that evidence obtained by unconstitutional search is inadmissible in state prosecutions, thus overruling one of the most controversial procedural cases of the modern era, *Wolf* v. *Colorado.*[57] This development is so spectacularly libertarian, especially when viewed against the background of *Wolf,* that it must play a major part in any evaluation of the term's results. Yet not even a staunch advocate of forward movement in this field could allow himself more than two cheers, unless he were so result-oriented as to be entirely indifferent to the need for reasoned decision.

Mapp must surely rank as one of the untidiest decisions in which the modern Court has announced a salient constitutional doctrine, which is saying a good deal. The case had arisen from a state prosecution for the possession of "lewd and lascivious" books and pictures, and the main issue briefed and argued concerned the validity of the Ohio law which punishes mere possession of such material so long as the possessor knows it to be obscene. The evidence had admittedly been seized illegally, but the *Wolf* doctrine of course controlled this question, and the suggestion to overrule *Wolf* came in the course of an *amicus curiae* brief and was hardly argued at all. As Justice Harlan remarked, dissenting, an important change in constitutional law should be preceded by full-dress argument, insuring the most sober kind of judicial consideration, especially when the prevailing rule has been laid down comparatively recently and the issue is one of some intricacy. Even more, it seems unfortunate to decide a constitutional question of such moment when the case might have been disposed of by reference to another clearer question that had been fully briefed. Cases involving illegally obtained evidence are common enough, and if the Court was resolved to overthrow *Wolf* it would not have had to wait long for a more felicitous opportunity.

Unhappily, the faults of Justice Clark's majority opinion did not stop here. His arguments for overthrowing *Wolf* revealed the need for what Justice Harlan called the "aid which adequate briefing and argument lends to the determination of an important issue."

57. 338 U.S. 25 (1949).

The Court's basic point was that *Wolf* recognized that the Fourth Amendment's right to privacy applies to the states and that it is therefore anomalous not to apply the constitutionally derived *Weeks* rule,[58] which excludes illegally obtained evidence from federal trials, to the states as well. But this begs at least three important questions: is the *Weeks* rule of constitutional origin or, rather, a rule of evidence imposed by the Supreme Court in pursuance of its power to supervise the federal judicial system? Was it the Fourth Amendment that was applied to the states in *Wolf,* or the "principle of privacy," which might have a different meaning in the Fourteenth than it has in the Fourth? Is it always anomalous that state courts are allowed more room for variation than federal courts, or does the concept of federalism warrant just such leeway?

Each of these questions needed careful consideration even if they were all to be answered as the Court answered them. And failure to consider them weakened the Court's other arguments, one of which was that the passage of time since *Wolf* had undermined the case against exclusion, partly because "more than half" of the states passing on the question since then had adopted the exclusionary principle. As Justice Harlan said, half of all states still do admit such evidence, and in any case state autonomy is not to be overridden simply because a slight tendency has developed to regard one rule as more desirable than another. Another of Justice Clark's points was that we exclude involuntary confessions in state courts, and the exclusion of illegally seized evidence is analogous. But Justice Harlan gravely impaired this argument by pointing to a crucial difference. Forced confessions are excluded because they may infect the fairness of the trial itself, not because of something the police did before the trial. To admit such evidence would make the trial a farce; the strongest evidence of innocence might be overborne by a confession that was coerced and thus quite possibly false. On the other hand, illegally obtained evidence is excluded, when it is, not because the *trial* has been rendered unfair (the evidence may be perfectly convincing, though illegally pro-

58. Weeks v. United States, 232 U.S. 383 (1914).

cured), but to deter police from unconstitutional conduct. The Supreme Court has the authority thus to supervise the conduct of federal police, but under the federal system it has no such power to discipline the police of the states.

The point is not whether the majority's assumptions can be defended or whether Justice Harlan's strictures are unanswerable. Nothing the latter says quite disposes of Justice Murphy's contention in *Wolf* that only the exclusionary rule can make the right to privacy real. And even in connection with the argument canvassed above, one might well ask whether the Court is in fact limited to concerns bearing on the trial itself. The Fourteenth Amendment speaks of due process of *law*, and it might be contended that this touches the whole process by which criminals are brought in and punished. But the point is that the majority opinion did not effectively state the case for overruling *Wolf;* it did not meet the burden of justifying a departure from *stare decisis*. The dissenting opinion was in fact far more effective than the prevailing one. *Wolf* may have deserved to be buried, but it merited a more persuasive funeral oration.

Whatever the infirmities of the reasoning, *Wolf* is decisively overthrown, and the *"Mapp* doctrine" takes an important place among the rules that insure uniform fair play to the individual, as does the "spike-mike" doctrine of *Silverman*. Other decisions of the term, while less spectacular, add to the impression of judicial resolution in this field. For example, the Court reconfirmed and strengthened the doctrine of *Griffin* v. *Illinois*[59] that financial hurdles must not bar an indigent's right to review of his conviction;[60] a state trial prejudiced by newspaper publicity with the prosecutor's connivance was held violative of due process:[61] and an indigent convicted of felony was held entitled to a hearing to determine whether the state denial of counsel offended due process.[62] The interesting thing about this last case was not its result, but Justice Douglas' concurring plea for reconsideration of *Betts* v. *Brady,*

59. 351 U.S. 12 (1956).
60. Smith v. Bennett, 365 U.S. 708 (1961).
61. Irvin v. Dowd, 366 U.S. 717 (1961).
62. McNeal v. Culver, 365 U.S. 109 (1961).

which allowed the state to dispense with counsel in some felony cases. "I cannot believe," he said, "that a majority of the present Court would agree to *Betts* v. *Brady* were it here *de novo*." If his guess about the temper of the present Court is correct, there may be further startling events to come in the near future. Has the present majority resolved the old misgivings about the wisdom of imposing procedural rules on the states? Has Justice Frankfurter's concern for flexible federalism lost out to those who contend for a more uniform standard of due process? The answer, as Justice Story would say, is "locked up in the inscrutable purposes of Providence"—and in the bosoms of five members of the Court; the chances are that it will emerge gradually, if at all. But *Mapp* is a very considerable straw in the breeze; and there can on the whole be little doubt about the direction of wind currents during the 1960 Term at least.

Since 1954, as every schoolboy knows, the Supreme Court—and even more the lower federal courts which it supervises[63]—has been heavily preoccupied with the problem of public school integration. After the seven-league stride of the *Brown*[64] decision, the Court has moved steadily but not hastily forward against other forms of racial discrimination. The implications of the *Brown* doctrine were applied in per curiam holdings against segregation in such facilities as public recreation grounds[65] and intrastate buses;[66] the states that sought to take retributive action against the NAACP were stymied;[67] the concept of "state action" was extended so as to make it a little harder to maintain a discriminatory policy.[68] With the possible exception of this last case, these developments might be said to be logically inherent in the broad disapproval of racial discrimination that was exemplified by the *Brown* doctrine.

In the 1960 Term there began to be signs that the Court was approaching, though not yet reaching, the limits of that logic. For

63. See J. W. Peltason, *Fifty-Eight Lonely Men: Southern Federal Judges and School Desegregation* (New York, 1961).
64. Brown v. Board of Education, 347 U.S. 483 (1954).
65. Baltimore v. Dawson, 350 U.S. 877 (1955).
66. Gayle v. Browder, 352 U.S. 903 (1956).
67. NAACP v. Alabama, 357 U.S. 449 (1958).
68. Pennsylvania v. Board of Directors, 353 U.S. 230 (1957).

one thing, there is in some of the cases the first real break in the unanimous front recently maintained by the Court on such questions. In *Shelton* v. *Tucker*[69] the majority held invalid an Arkansas law requiring schoolteachers to list all organizations they have belonged to for five years. What troubled the dissenters here was the problem of reconciling this holding with such precedents as *Adler,* in which a state's right to inquire into its employees' associations had been upheld. Mr. Justice Stewart's point, for the majority, was that the state could have no legitimate interest in all associational ties and that it must therefore draw such statutes more narrowly if it hopes to meet judicial inspection. This doctrine may be a good one but it is also somewhat novel, and its implications may require careful examination if the Court is to keep its lines of logic straight.

Again, in *Boynton* v. *Virginia,*[70] the Interstate Commerce Act was held to bar a trespass action against a Negro who refused to leave a bus terminal restaurant. The act forbids "unjust discrimination" in facilities "operated or controlled" by a motor carrier, and the whole Court agreed that this would prohibit racial discrimination in a bus company's own restaurant. But this restaurant was owned by a local Virginia corporation and leased to a private operator. Nevertheless, said Justice Black for the Court, it is subject to the act, without regard to niceties of title, if the bus company has volunteered to provide terminal facilities and "the terminal and restaurant have acquiesced in and cooperated in this undertaking." This feat of constructive alchemy was too much for Justices Whittaker and Clark, who dissented.

In another line, *Burton* v. *Wilmington Parking Authority*[71] raised similar misgivings, this time about the elasticity of the "state action" concept of the Fourteenth Amendment. The Court held that a restaurant privately operated but leased from the city was engaged in state action and thus subject to the equal protection clause. But the grounds for so deciding were far from clear in Justice Clark's majority opinion, which threw together, as Justice

69. 364 U.S. 479 (1960).
70. 364 U.S. 454 (1960).
71. 365 U.S. 715 (1961).

Harlan said, "various factual bits and pieces" and then undermined "the resulting structure by an equally vague disclaimer." Since there was some basis for believing that the state law might specifically authorize the racial discrimination in question, which would flatly contravene the Fourteenth Amendment, three members of the Court wanted to seek an authoritative interpretation from the state court before deciding the case. They preferred to avoid the tortuous question of state action until it was forced upon them. Sooner or later that question will have to be faced, but its resolution would strain the powers of Daniel himself. Meantime there is little to be said for such ad hoc formulations as this majority opinion offers, however congenial the immediate results may be.

The minority qualms expressed in these cases reflect an awareness that the problems have not been entirely thought through and that pragmatic decisions in defense of the shared value of racial equality may close portals in other areas where an open-door policy has so far prevailed. These reflections are relevant to *Gomillion* v. *Lightfoot*,[72] which was probably the most surprising racial rights decision of the term and may have the most significant implications. It concerned Tuskegee, Alabama, which had allegedly been gerrymandered so as to exclude from voting in city elections all but four or five of its four hundred Negro former voters. The state hoped, relying on *Hunter* v. *Pittsburg*[73] and *Colegrove* v. *Green*,[74] that this stratagem would be beyond the reach of the federal courts and that the disadvantaged Negroes would thus be unable to raise the claim of constitutional rights.

But the Supreme Court thought otherwise. If the allegations could be proved, the act would be an invalid racial discrimination affecting the right to vote as protected by the Fifteenth Amendment. *Hunter* and related cases did not hold that the state has plenary power to manipulate municipal borders at will, but only that the particular constitutional clauses there invoked could not avail to limit the power in those particular contexts. As for *Cole-*

72. 364 U.S. 339 (1960).
73. 207 U.S. 161 (1907).
74. 328 U.S. 549 (1946).

grove, the Court there held that the dilution of appellants' voting strength because of the legislature's failure to reapportion presented a "political question." *Gomillion* was different because the legislature here had affirmatively acted to deny the vote on *racial* grounds, specifically forbidden by the Fifteenth Amendment.

This opinion was carefully and neatly wrought so as to permit the Court to checkmate racially discriminatory gerrymanders without opening up the whole vast question of apportionment. Justice Whittaker, concurring, would rely on the equal protection clause, but he too felt that *Colegrove* was distinguishable.

The case is important enough if its emanations go no further than this: that electoral apportionment is subject to challenge on the ground of racial discrimination. But it may prove difficult to confine it to those limits, and the case nicely illustrates the problem of logical consistency posed by some of these decisions in the racial field. The Court is obviously determined to nullify "sophisticated as well as simple-minded modes of discrimination"[75] and must therefore be alert against indirect action with a segregationist motive. But that kind of action may take forms that would apparently immunize it from attack under previously announced constitutional doctrine—most readers of *Adler* v. *Board of Education* would think that it authorized Little Rock to query schoolteachers about organizational ties; most readers of *Colegrove* would think that Tuskegee's gerrymander presented a non-justiciable question. In correcting these misunderstandings, as it did in *Shelton* and *Gomillion,* the Court has two choices: to declare in effect that there are special rules for situations that involve the hint of racial discrimination, or to fashion a new general rule that will cover the situation. If it takes the former course, it will be holding that the right against racial discrimination enjoys a super-"preferred position" in our system of constitutional restraints. That seems to be the idea of Justice Frankfurter in *Gomillion* (though he would of course ardently reject the phrase): electoral inequality is forbidden if based on racial grounds, but other kinds of inequality do not offend the Constitution. This double standard may have some war-

75. Lane v. Wilson, 307 U.S. 268, 275 (1939).

rant, as he implies, in the precise language of the Fifteenth Amendment. But the equal protection clause of the Fourteenth speaks in more general terms, and the question is whether the concept of equality, so strictly conceived to protect the Negro, can go on being interpreted permissively when the rights of men in general are at issue. There is some reason to suspect that *Gomillion* may become an entering wedge for reconsideration of the whole apportionment problem.[76] Whatever may be the truth about this, the fact remains that hard judicial soul-searching impends in this field. If a double standard is to prevail, it requires careful exposition and justification. If on the other hand general constitutional doctrines are to be reinterpreted so as to accommodate decisions like these, the task of synthesis will be a formidable one. So far, it seems fair to say, neither job has been done.

Only brief attention will be paid here to a scattering of other civil rights decisions, though some of them might well have attracted more notice in a term less crowded with momentous developments in this field.

The nasty question of arbitrary security dismissals was raised by the case of one Rachel Brawner, a short-order cook in a privately operated cafeteria in a naval weapons plant.[77] This installation was under military command, and Mrs. Brawner lost her job when the commanding officer withdrew, without specific charges or a hearing, her identification badge on the ground that she failed to meet security requirements. The Supreme Court might have held that such action was unauthorized by statute[78] or that it violated procedural due process; Mr. Justice Stewart, for the majority, chose to do neither. Though he admitted that dismissed government employees may have constitutional rights in some circumstances, there was no right to notice and hearing here, where the reasons for her exclusion were not "patently arbitrary or discriminatory." This reasoning bypassed the sticky issue, which was that the "security risk" badge of infamy was involved. To recognize a constitutional right to a hearing for all dismissed government em-

76. Baker v. Carr, 364 U.S. 898 (1960), prob. juris. noted.
77. Cafeteria Workers v. McElroy, 376 U.S. 886 (1961).
78. Greene v. McElroy, 360 U.S. 474 (1959).

ployees would plunge both the law and public personnel administration into endless difficulties. But the security risk tag is so damaging to the individual that its use should, at the very least, be accompanied by some procedural protections. One can only hope that a later Court will be able to confine this precedent very narrowly to its specific facts and minimize its potential damage to the tradition of procedural fairness.

Two potentially interesting and important constitutional issues were evaded by the Court in the 1960 Term. One was the issue of whether a man coerced by law to join and pay dues to an association can object if his money is used to further political purposes uncongenial to him. In a federal case, the Railway Labor Act as amended was interpreted to forbid a union so to spend a member's money;[79] in a state case involving a bar association, a plurality of four believed that the record did not present the facts "as leanly and as sharply" as necessary to justify decision of the constitutional question.[80]

The other issue was birth control.[81] The Connecticut statute in question forbids the *use*—not the sale—of contraceptives and makes possible the punishment of those who counsel such use (physicians, for example). Plaintiffs had assailed the law under a state declaratory judgment act. But the fact seemed to be that the law was not currently being enforced; and until it is, said the Court, the constitutional issues are not ripe for our consideration. The plaintiffs' supposed fear of prosecution was deemed chimerical in light of the non-enforcement record.

There were dubious elements in the opinions supporting these evasive results: the federal statute had to be tortured cruelly to produce *Street;* five justices thought the constitutional issue was properly before them in *Lathrop,* so the curious result is that the evasion was supported by only a minority of the Court; the grounds for dismissal in the birth control case were somewhat novel and very debatable, as Justice Harlan's dissent shows. But it is not surprising if the judges began to feel by this time (these

79. International Association of Machinists v. Street, 367 U.S. 740 (1961).
80. Lathrop v. Donohue, 367 U.S. 820 (1961).
81. Poe v. Ullman, 376 U.S. 497 (1961).

were end of term decisions) that enough was enough. There may be such a thing as domestic economy even within a Supreme Court, and the 1960 Term had already produced enough significant civil liberty decisions to overfill any reasonable quota. The questions of dues and politics and birth control will no doubt be back again, and in short order. Meanwhile they remain open, and these decisions could not be recorded either pro or con in a charting of the Court's record in the field of constitutional rights.

Finally, in two significant cases with constitutional undertones the Court construed federal law so as to protect individual rights. *Monroe* v. *Pape*[82] held that the 1875 Civil Rights Act provides a civil remedy for those deprived of federal rights by state officers, even though the officers have violated state law. The statute provided a federal remedy only where the state officer acted "under color of state law." It had been argued that where the officer's action actually violated state law, he could hardly be said to be acting "under color" of it. The solid majority reconfirmed the *Classic*[83] and *Screws*[84] doctrine that "misuse of power . . . made possible because the wrongdoer is clothed with the authority of state law, is action taken 'under color of' state law" in the meaning of the statute. In short, state police who violate Fourteenth Amendment rights can now be sued in federal court by the injured party —who need not, by the way, carry the heavy burden of proving a willful deprivation of constitutional rights. In the other case the Court held that railroad publicity programs designed to influence legislation could not be made a basis for suit under the Sherman Act, even though the legislation sought was economically advantageous to the railroads and injurious to their trucker competitors and even though "reprehensible" and "deceptive" publicity techniques were employed.[85] A contrary construction would "raise important constitutional questions" involving the right of petition.

This then is the 1960–61 civil rights record of the Supreme Court—or enough of it to permit evaluation. A few words of sum-

82. 365 U.S. 167 (1961).
83. United States v. Classic, 313 U.S. 299 (1941).
84. Screws v. United States, 325 U.S. 91 (1945).
85. Eastern Railroad Presidents Conference v. Noerr Motor Freight, 365 U.S. 127 (1961).

mary may sharpen the picture. In the cases involving the Communist menace, real or imaginary, the Court with minor exceptions held against the individual and in favor of governmental power. This spirit of judicial permissiveness was most striking in the field of legislative investigations: it seems obvious that such inquisitions into the subject are now immune from any very meaningful substantive restraints. And pretty much the same statement can be made about government-imposed qualifications for professional practice, at least as applied to "a limited class of persons" in positions of public responsibility. With respect to punishment for party membership and the registration requirements of the McCarran Act, the Court's attitude was a little more ambiguous. Old, mildly restrictive interpretations of the Smith Act were adhered to, and the government was put to a rigorous standard of proof in enforcing the membership clause; the Fifth Amendment may still be available as an individual defense against the order to register, even though its value may be somewhat attenuated by the time the issue is finally faced. But there is no doubt that a determined government can make things warm for Communists and suspected Communists if it has the time and energy to spare, and that the plea of "security risk" carries great weight in the judicial mind.

Apart from these political offender cases, the most noteworthy anti-libertarian development of the term was the apparent ratification of administrative movie censorship in *Times Film*. But then the impression of the term begins to change. The Sunday law decisions defy classification; but surely little evidence can be wrung from them that the Court has flagged in its concern for religious freedom. The decisions involving dues and politics and birth control were indecisive. On the other hand, the signs of forward movement in the field of criminal procedure and Negro rights seem unmistakable. In the former area the *Mapp* decision stands out like a beacon, perhaps even portending a general erosion of the scruples about federalism that have heretofore retarded movement of this kind. But the pattern of other, less spectacular cases reveals a similarly "progressive" trend. And the Negro rights cases also suggest a tendency to mark out new frontiers, not so dramatic as those of 1954, but salient nonetheless.

What kind of term was it? Was it a "libertarian term," or did its results justify the dark misgivings of Justices Black and Douglas quoted above? The answer will depend, broadly, on how one weighs the pro-government spirit of the political offender cases and *Times Film* against the pro-individual record in the criminal procedure and racial equality decisions. But even conceding such subjective variations in outlook it is hard to see how it could be contended that this was, in balance, a retrogressive term. It must be remembered that a few short years ago such matters as legislative investigations, public employment standards, and movie censorship seemed arguably immune from all constitutional restraints. The doctrines correcting these misapprehensions are still in relative infancy. One may wish that the Court would push them toward adulthood a little faster, but this is a quite different thing from charging that they are old and seasoned constitutional traditions, now dead by the Court's hand. In fact, they are neither old nor dead. And a similar point can be made about *Scales*. The present Court is far more scrupulous about requiring personal knowledge and intent than its predecessor was in *Whitney* v. *California*.[86] True, it has refused to throw out guilt by association altogether, but it never said that it would. True, it has refused to invalidate the Smith Act, but neither has any previous Court overthrown a national sedition law; and at least this Court has construed the law so as to retain some measure of sense and justice.

The truth is that most of these cases represent refusals to advance, not retreats. They may be no less regrettable for that, but it is well to know what we are talking about. In recent years Justices Black and Douglas seem to have themselves developed a libertarian position that is more uncompromising than some of their earlier opinions would suggest.[87] This may create an illusion,

---

86. 274 U.S. 357 (1927).

87. Both of them seem to have taken leave of the clear and present danger doctrine at one end while the majority was taking leave of it at another. Both had invoked it in earlier cases (Bridges v. California, 314 U.S. 252 [1941] and Craig v. Harney, 331 U.S. 367 [1947]), though Justice Black had declared in the former case that it was only a "minimum compulsion," which left the way open for him to begin applying a more absolutist standard with Breard v. Alexandria, 341 U.S. 622 (1951).

even in their own minds, that the majority has retrogressed, but an illusion it is. It is they who have moved "forward," not the Court that has moved "back."

The Court's propensity generally in the last decade—as exemplified by the 1960 Term—has been to extend the concept of civil rights fairly steadily in certain selected but vital fields, to stand relatively still in certain others (notably those involving the security issue), and to retreat, if that is the word, only in the sense that such implied half-promises as those in *Watkins* are unredeemed. By common sense reckoning, this pattern of large pluses and small minuses would seem to yield a substantial gain for civil liberties.

Is this, to pose the result-oriented question, "enough" for the Court to do? Or is it failing the nation in the hour of need? The question is slippery and incurably non-objective, but it is the kind that is hard to avoid in discussing political institutions. And surely even the beginning of any answer must center around some preliminary assumptions about the range of judicial capacity. No one would contend that the Court can correct all the errors, big and small, that a great, dynamic democracy commits. The stock of prestige that supports judicial review is substantial but not inexhaustible. That stock has been drawn on heavily in recent years, as the 1958 counter-attack attested. Probably it is going to be further taxed as the judges continue to press forward ideals like racial equality and fair treatment of the accused, to name only two. There is no known perpetual inventory system that infallibly warns us when the limit has been approached. All that can be offered here is one observer's judgment that (to drop the metaphor) the Court of the 1960 Term did or seemed in the process of doing about as much on behalf of civil rights as we can reasonably expect nine men to do.

When we turn from the "result-oriented" to the "reason-oriented" line of evaluation the spectacle is a little different. To be sure, the matter must again be viewed relatively. We cannot demand that a living institution, dealing with living problems, achieve perfect logical symmetry; for logic overdone can stultify all it touches. Nor is it clear that Courts of the past have followed the ideal of reasoned decision more than has the present one.

What of the opinions of the 1920's and early 1930's—for example, those that T. R. Powell used to dissect so mercilessly? What of such masterpieces of inner contradiction as *Munn* v. *Illinois*[88] or *Hurtado* v. *California?*[89]

Yet admitting all this, and admitting further that the modern Court faces riddles of unexampled complexity, it still seems fair to wish that more progress could be made in ordering and solving them. And it must be ruefully said that very little such progress marked the 1960 Term. The balancing test begins to seem more and more a "fiction intended to beautify what is disagreeable to the sufferers,"[90] at least in subversion cases. The opinions in *Times Film* and *Burton* leave the reader in grave doubt as to what was decided and why. The conclusion of *Mapp* v. *Ohio* is fairly plain, but the route to it is murky.

Nevertheless, the main complaint on this score is a more general one—that the Court is not confronting the task of intellectual architecture that is posed by its modern jurisdictional claims in the field of civil rights. In 1951, Mr. Justice Jackson remarked that the Court's prior decisions "will be searched in vain for clear standards"[91] governing civil liberties questions. The remonstrance seems just about equally valid ten years later, though it covers an even wider ground, for since then the Court has in important respects extended its power to supervise. The state action problem, the problem of censorship, occupational freedom, legislative inquisitions, the general right of the government to inform itself and ventilate facts, the right against self-incrimination, the problem of scientific eavesdropping and other unreasonable searches, the limits of statutory flexibility, racial discrimination in the determination of voting units—all these and many more were within the judicial ambit in the 1960 Term. Future terms may see new departures bearing on such matters as legislative apportionment and the right to counsel in state courts. These problems are not discrete; the resolution of one touches most of the others. To

---

88. 94 U.S. 113 (1877).
89. 110 U.S. 516 (1884).
90. Tyson Bros. v. Banton, 273 U.S. 418, 446 (1927).
91. Kunz v. New York, 340 U.S. 290, 299 (1951).

quote Justice Frankfurter, speaking ten years ago, "there are now so many of these decisions, arrived at by the *ad hoc* process of adjudication, that it is desirable to make a cruise of the timber."[92]

Why has the Court as a whole never taken that cruise? Why has it done so little to develop a reasoned, connected set of doctrines in the field of civil rights? Partly no doubt because this is easier said than done—it is one thing to call for reasoned principles and quite another thing to devise them. But though this might account for some inadequacy in doctrinal structure, it does not fully explain the failure to develop any such structure at all.

That failure seems to be caused by a certain fragmenting and hardening of attitudes that characterize the modern Court, making it impossible to achieve a consensus of reason even when an agreement on result does exist. Even with respect to results the Court has been of course far from unanimous, but the steady expansion of civil rights jurisdiction attests that a majority united by this common concern can frequently be assembled. But the dissensus as to the reasons for the holdings is far more stubborn. As the pattern of concurrences and dissents shows, there is a tendency for such pairs as Warren-Brennan, Frankfurter-Harlan and Clark-Whittaker to produce separate reasons for the positions they take. But the dissensus goes farther than that. Doctrinal idiosyncrasies often require individual statement. Justice Black's special ideas about the absolutism of the First Amendment, and his equally special ideas about search and seizure, produce personal reasoning in such cases as *Noto* and *Mapp*. Justice Clark seems to worry more about procedural regularity in state courts than in federal, while Justice Frankfurter feels quite the other way. Justice Douglas felt called on to speak separately in cases like *Lathrop* and *Scales*.

What has happened is that certain members have frozen into attitudes unacceptable to most of their brethren, and they are hence unable to join in a reasoned statement of doctrine. They can perhaps agree *a fortiori* with results, as Justice Douglas does in *Gomillion* or Justice Frankfurter does in *Irvin,* but their reasoning fails to persuade a majority and sometimes persuades only themselves. The justice who seems most nearly free from this

92. Niemotko v. Maryland, 340 U.S. 268, 276 (1951).

quality of dogmatic separatism is Stewart, the swing man in these cases. Justices Black and Douglas have taken a view toward many of these issues that appears irreconcilable with the view of any possible majority. Justices Frankfurter and Harlan can sometimes attract four others to their reasoning, but solid doctrine is hard to build on five-to-four decisions. Justices Warren and Brennan show some tendency to seek a middle ground; they seem more flexible than Black and Douglas, at any rate. But they too can seldom carry a solid majority for their opinions in disputed cases.

This multiple stalemate has an incidental effect that is worth noting: it diminishes the contribution to constitutional law of those best qualified by experience and ability to make such a contribution. In the cases discussed above, Justice Black wrote the majority opinion in only three, two of them easy decisions exciting no serious question. Justice Douglas wrote only one. Justice Frankfurter wrote his share, five, but it cannot be said that any of them except perhaps *Gomillion* stated new and viable doctrine. How much more impressive and convincing *Mapp* and *Cafeteria Workers* v. *McElroy* could have been, for example, if these men had not been precluded, for one reason or another, from framing the Court opinions.

The main point is that these conflicting dogmatisms have, for a long time, impeded the growth of doctrine in general. Worse, there are signs that the divisions have further crystallized with age. There seems small chance that they will soften enough, given existing personnel, to permit the development of a system of reasoned criteria in the civil rights field.

This circumstance is profoundly relevant to the question of future appointments to the supreme bench. There may have been times in history when a loyal henchman or a good journeyman would be appropriate enough, but that time is not now. The Court's present need is for a man or men with the master craftsman's intellectual capacity to weave the disparate strands of civil rights doctrine into a coherent tapestry, and a spirit of moderation that can marshal assent among those who are open to persuasion. It is an exacting set of requirements. But the plea for reasoned doctrine is not likely to be answered until it is filled.

V THE LATER WARREN COURT

The notes to Chapter IV, "The Early Warren Court," and Chapter V, "The Later Warren Court," remain in the same form as when they appeared as notes to articles.

THE REAPPORTIONMENT CASE

[This article first appeared in the *Harvard Law Review*, 76, no. 1 (November 1962), 54–74. Copyright 1962 by The Harvard Law Review Association.]

On March 26, 1962, the Supreme Court startled the nation with the announcement of its long-awaited decision in *Baker* v. *Carr*,[1] the Reapportionment case. The alarums and excursions that ensued in the legal-political world exceeded anything evoked by a Supreme Court decision since 1954, and memory would have to reach back a good many years more to find another adequate comparison. Indeed, if we did not know better we might suspect the justices of a conscious taste for the dramatic. The decision came after several months of a term that had been, constitutionally speaking, rather uneventful, and the watchers in the stalls might have begun to feel that the author-players would coast for this term after the very considerable exertions of the last. This seemed a reasonable possibility; but it is the ability to transcend the obvious and confound our expectations in such a moment that marks the authentic dramatist.

The judgment was attended by six separate opinions, including three concurrences and two dissents in addition to the opinion of the Court. This forest of prose will be explored more fully a little later. But it is well to have some of the main features of Mr. Justice Brennan's majority opinion before us at the outset.

The case involved an action under the Civil Rights Act[2] brought by certain Tennessee voters on their own behalf and on behalf of others similarly situated and alleging that the present apportionment of the state legislature deprived them of their federal constitutional right to equal protection of the laws. A district court was asked for a declaratory judgment invalidating the 1901 state legislation on which the apportionment was based; for an injunction restraining the defendant election officials from holding

1. 369 U.S. 186 (1962).
2. REV. STAT. §§ 722, 1979 (1875), 42 U.S.C. §§ 1988, 1983 (1958).

an election under the existing system; and for a decree reapportioning the legislature or, in the alternative, an order that the next election be held at large.[3] The argument, as ultimately presented by the complainants and by the United States appearing as *amicus curiae,* was in essence that, although the Tennessee constitution provided for decennial apportionment of representatives and senators among counties and districts according to their respective numbers, the legislature had failed to make such a reapportionment since 1901; that because of population changes in the past sixty years the votes of the appellants had been unconstitutionally debased, since the equal protection clause forbids arbitrary and unreasonable apportionment of legislative seats. The starting point, it was said, for measuring an apportionment against this prohibition is *"per capita* equality of representation,"[4] and departures from that standard must rest on a rational foundation. The action had been dismissed by the district court on the grounds that the court lacked jurisdiction of the subject matter and that the complaint failed to state a claim upon which relief could be granted. These stated grounds reflected the district court's understanding of the "federal rule, as enunciated . . . by the Supreme Court . . . that the federal courts, whether from a lack of jurisdiction or from the inappropriateness of the subject matter for judicial consideration, will not intervene in cases of this type to compel legislative reapportionment."[5]

The Supreme Court held that the dismissal was error. The federal courts do possess jurisdiction of the subject matter; the appellants have stated a justiciable cause of action upon which they "would be entitled to appropriate relief"; and they do have standing to challenge the statute.[6] The issue presented is not, as the district court thought, a "political question" immune from judicial control. *Colegrove* v. *Green* and other supposed precedents have been misread on that point.[7] And the claim does not

3. Brief for the United States as Amicus Curiae on Reargument, pp. 2–6, Baker v. Carr, 369 U.S. 186 (1962).
4. *Id.* at 26.
5. Baker v. Carr, 179 F. Supp. 824, 826 (M.D. Tenn. 1959).
6. 369 U.S. at 197–198.
7. *Id.* at 232–234.

involve any of the characteristics that have caused the Court in the past to label a question "political" and deny jurisdiction. The cause was therefore remanded for trial and decision. It is perhaps worth emphasizing that the Supreme Court offered the lower court no standards by which the decision should be reached and no hints about the remedy that might be appropriate if the plaintiffs prevailed. "Judicial standards under the Equal Protection clause," Justice Brennan said, "are well developed and familiar"[8] and it would be "improper now to consider what remedy would be most appropriate."[9]

History can be an intractable wench, going her own way without regard to the paths we have envisioned for her, and one who writes contemporaneously about a Supreme Court term is uneasily aware of her capriciousness. There is no assurance that posterity will see the term as the present sees it, will concur with us in singling out the events that are noteworthy. Some little-observed horseshoe nail may have dropped by the way in the spring of 1962, and the future, with its advantage of hindsight, may decide that this was the really consequential incident of the season.

But with these concessions to an uncertain world duly registered, by almost any criterion for assaying such matters it seems a fair conjecture that 1962 will appear to historians of the Supreme Court as the Year of the Reapportionment Case.[10] For one thing, no development since the Segregation Cases[11] has so focused the public eye on the doings of the Court. The publicity and popular interest evoked by a court decision may be among the less dependable of indices for evaluating its importance, but they cannot be left altogether out of the account. Those who are to wear the boot are not, perhaps, the only judges of whether it will pinch when broken in, but their judgment commands our attention. Especially does this seem so when we reflect that a court decision can become, in a sense, what the public thinks it is. The public

8. *Id.* at 226.
9. *Id.* at 198.
10. The nearest competitor as a prospect for fame—or notoriety—was probably Engel v. Vitale, 370 U.S. 421 (1962); see Sutherland, *Establishment According to Engel,* 76 HARV. L. REV. 25 (1962).
11. Brown v. Board of Educ., 347 U.S. 483 (1954); Bolling v. Sharpe, 347 U.S. 497 (1954).

version of the Chief Justice's opinion in *Dred Scott*[12] was a very different thing from the opinion that he wrote, but it was the public version that helped to kindle the Civil War.[13]

For another thing, it is hard to recall a decision in modern history which has had such an immediate and significant effect on the practical course of events, or—again excepting the Segregation cases—which seems to contain such a potential for influencing that course in the future. The short-term response has been nothing short of astonishing.[14] It has been as if the decision catalyzed a new political synthesis that was already straining to come into being. Not only federal judges, but state judges as well, have taken the inch or so of encouragement offered by the Supreme Court and stretched it out to a mile. Legislatures all over the country have been bidden to redistrict or to face the prospect of having the judiciary do the job for them. Under this spur, and sometimes in anticipation of it, a number of them have set going their laborious machinery of conflict and compromise. The shape of the apportionment plans that will emerge from this strange confluence of judicial and legislative power remains to be seen, but there can be no doubt that the American political world is stirring.

The long-term results are, of course, even more speculative, but the immediate reaction just described may cast a few shadows ahead. Court decisions have not always generated such a ready—almost over-ready—spirit of compliance. When a decision fails to strike a responsive chord in the public breast, the tendency is at best to abide by its minimum compulsion grudgingly interpreted.[15] The tendency suggested by early reactions to the reapportionment decision seems very different from this, and it may warrant the conjecture that the Court here happened to hit upon what students of public opinion might call a latent consensus.[16] It is quite true,

12. Scott v. Sandford, 60 U.S. (19 How.) 393 (1857).
13. SWISHER, ROGER B. TANEY 511–523 (1935); 2 WARREN, THE SUPREME COURT IN UNITED STATES HISTORY 300–317 (rev. ed. 1926).
14. The general pattern of response is discussed in DIXON, DEMOCRATIC REPRESENTATION: REAPPORTIONMENT IN LAW AND POLITICS (1969).
15. Patric, *The Impact of a Court Decision: Aftermath of the McCollum Case,* 6 J. PUB. L. 455 (1957).
16. KEY, PUBLIC OPINION AND AMERICAN DEMOCRACY 263–287 (1961).

as Justice Frankfurter reminds us,[17] that neither our past nor our present political institutions have treated numbers as the "basic" principle of representation. But institutions sometimes lag behind opinion, and it may be that most Americans have come to think of some version of the majority principle as at least the presumptive democratic standard.[18] If so, the implied ratification of the standard in the Reapportionment case may have struck them, in Jefferson's terms, as "the common sense of the subject," commanding their assent as "an expression of the American mind."[19] And the decision, even without further adumbration, may precipitate a train of events that will alter profoundly the nature of representation in American politics.

But this is speculation, not premonition, much less confident prophecy. For the present, there is no way of being sure about these and other possibly enduring effects—which political party will gain and which lose; whether the increment of electoral strength will be greater for suburbia or for central cities; whether the vitality of state government will be augmented or diminished; whether the cause of racial equality will be significantly advanced. The nature and scale of such repercussions will depend on imponderables and unforeseeables, including the substantial question whether and how the Supreme Court itself will elaborate the jurisdictional potential this decision created. The one thing that seems fairly certain is that seismic events will be continuing for some years to come.

The decision is also important to those who ply the lonely, slighted trade of tracing and unraveling the strands of Supreme Court doctrines, for it writes a new and salient chapter in the time-worn history of "political questions."[20] In fact, although it

17. 369 U.S. at 301 (dissenting opinion).
18. Prothro & Grigg, *Fundamental Principles of Democracy: Bases of Agreement and Disagreement,* 22 J. POLITICS 276 (1960).
19. BECKER, THE DECLARATION OF INDEPENDENCE 25–26 (2d ed. 1958), quoting from 7 THE WRITINGS OF THOMAS JEFFERSON 304 (1869).
20. Standard works on the doctrine are: POST, THE SUPREME COURT AND POLITICAL QUESTIONS (1936); Field, *The Doctrine of Political Questions in the Federal Courts,* 8 MINN. L. REV. 485 (1924); Finkelstein, *Judicial Self-Limitation,* 37 HARV. L. REV. 338 (1924); Finkelstein, *Further Notes*

would be too much to say that the chapter closes the book, we may legitimately wonder whether the doctrine it treats will now have a very lively future, for its viability as an aid to a policy of judicial self-restraint would seem to have diminished considerably.

This brings us back to Justice Brennan's majority opinion and to some of the dissents and concurrences that flanked it. The opening question for the Court was, of course, whether federal courts were barred altogether from entertaining such a suit, either at the threshold because of lack of jurisdiction of the subject matter or lack of standing, or just beyond the threshold because no judicially determinable duty had been asserted or no judicial protection for the claimed right could be devised. The first of these possible grounds for forebearance raised issues of constitutional and statutory authorization and of standing. The second plunged the Court explicitly into the issue of whether this cause, in light of the Court's precedents and traditions, should be regarded as a "political question"; and that becomes the crux of the dialogue between the majority and the dissenters.[21]

Justice Brennan's reading of the political question tradition contains a mystery or two, but it seems to run somewhat as follows. To begin with, he says, the record shows that a question has been recognized as political and therefore nonjusticiable only when it involves the problem of separation of powers—"the relationship between the judiciary and the co-ordinate branches of the Federal Government"[22]—or when there is "a lack of judicially discoverable and manageable standards for resolving it."[23] Indeed, some of his language might suggest that applicability of the doctrine is strictly limited to causes which concern the power of the federal judiciary as against the power of the president or Congress; that the relationship between the federal judiciary and the state governments can-

---

on Judicial Self-Limitation, 39 HARV. L. REV. 221 (1926); Weston, Political Questions, 38 HARV. L. REV. 296 (1925).

21. Of course the two kinds of issues sometimes overlap: factors that might have identified the question as "political" are influential in deciding that standing must be denied (see Massachusetts v. Mellon, 262 U.S. 447 [1923]) or in holding that no substantial federal question has been presented (see Colegrove v. Barrett, 330 U.S. 804 [1947]).

22. 369 U.S. at 210.

23. Id. at 217.

not raise a political question.[24] But this can hardly be what is meant, for he elsewhere speaks of the possible lack of judicially discoverable standards as a factor to be considered in *Baker* v. *Carr* itself,[25] which concerned, of course, no coordinate branch of the federal government. So it must be that this is an independent factor: the absence of such standards could cause the Supreme Court to stamp a question as "political" no matter what branch of government—state or federal—was involved.

Nevertheless it seems fairly clear that for Justice Brennan "the lack of judicially discoverable and manageable standards" is the *only* reason for the Court to call a question involving state governmental arrangements a political question. He is at pains to emphasize that claims do not become nonjusticiable simply because they touch upon matters of state governmental organization.[26] And the "formulations" he lists that may describe a political question seem all (again with the exception of the unmanageable standards item) concerned with intrafederal relationships,[27] as

24. "In the Guaranty Clause cases and in the other 'political questions' cases, it is the relationship between the judiciary and the coordinate branches of the Federal Government, and not the federal judiciary's relationship to the States, which gives rise to the 'political question.' " *Id.* at 210.
"The nonjusticiability of a political question is primarily a function of the separation of powers." *Ibid.*
"The nonjusticiability of such claims [under the guaranty clause] has nothing to do with their touching upon matters of state governmental organization." *Id.* at 218.
25. *Id.* at 226.
26. See *id.* at 218.
27. "It is apparent that several formulations which vary slightly according to the settings in which the questions arise may describe a political question, although each has one or more elements which identify it as essentially a function of the separation of powers. Prominent on the surface of any case held to involve a political question is found a textually demonstrable constitutional commitment of the issue to *a coordinate political department;* or a lack of judicially discoverable and manageable standards for resolving it; or the impossibility of deciding without an initial policy determination of a kind clearly for nonjudicial discretion; or the impossibility of a court's undertaking independent resolution without expressing lack of the respect due *coordinate branches* of government; or an unusual need for unquestioning adherence to a political decision already made; or the potentiality of embarrassment from multifarious pronouncements by various *departments* on one question." 369 U.S. at 217 (emphasis added).
This list is not always easy to relate to Brennan's surrounding discussion of specific political question cases, nor is it entirely clear that the six cate-

are the precedents he examines in such fields as foreign affairs, the duration of hostilities, "validity of enactments," and the status of Indian tribes.[28] The precedents treating the claim that state governmental forms violated the guaranty of a republican form of government[29] might seem to point in the other direction, for such claims have been uniformly held nonjusticiable.[30] But the reason for this, as Justice Brennan sees it, has been that guaranty clause claims "involve those elements which define a 'political question.' "[31] These are unmanageable standards or the problem of intrafederal relationships; that is, the Court has withheld its hand out of a feeling that the guaranty clause was for Congress to enforce, and not out of a feeling that matters of state governmental organization were intrinsically unfit for judicial control.

If the Court's analysis means what it appears to mean, the scope of the political question doctrine has been significantly narrowed. Admitting that the contours of the doctrine have been desperately hard to ascertain with confidence, three underlying ideas seem to run through it: the idea that the courts should not intervene in areas which, either by their nature or by constitutional language, are peculiarly committed to the president or Congress;[32] or in which "standards meet for judicial judgment" cannot be framed;[33] or in which the "framework and political character" of government (state or national) are called in question.[34] No doubt the three have sometimes tended to run together—for example, the reluctance to interfere with the framework of government or to

---

gories are separable one from another. What, for example, is the distinction between the last three? It is hard to be confident; but the italicized words, taken together with the last clause of the opening sentence, suggest strongly that the political question doctrine is pretty largely a matter of intrafederal relationships.

28. See cases cited *id.* at 211–216.

29. U.S. CONST. art. IV, § 4.

30. See cases cited 369 U.S. at 218–226.

31. *Id.* at 218.

32. See, *e.g.*, Coleman v. Miller, 307 U.S. 433 (1939); Luther v. Borden, 48 U.S. (7 How.) 1 (1849).

33. 369 U.S. at 289 (dissenting opinion of Frankfurter, J.).

34. See, *e.g.*, Pacific States Tel. & Tel. Co. v. Oregon, 223 U.S. 118, 150 (1912); Walton v. House of Representatives, 265 U.S. 487 (1924); Wilson v. North Carolina, 169 U.S. 586 (1898); *In re* Sawyer, 124 U.S. 200 (1888).

challenge Congress in a particular field is influenced by the uncertainty about standards to implement a policy of judicial supervision. But at the same time each of them has been thought to have a measure of independent force—the policy of letting "the people and their political representatives"[35] decide the root questions of the political framework has mirrored the feeling that these matters are too "high,"[36] too nakedly power-oriented, and perhaps too explosive for judicial control, quite apart from whether armchair ingenuity could devise standards that sounded plausibly applicable. It amounts to respect, either prudential or normative in origin, for the arrangements worked out by the political process for shaping the political process. It now appears that this respect will henceforth operate as a separate determinant only when the federal courts confront their peers—the President and Congress—not when they confront the states.

No doubt this amputation will make the analytic problem somewhat simpler, for the idea just discussed has always been elusive and impalpable. The Court has taken jurisdiction in the past in a number of cases involving apportionment and other problems of state governmental organization;[37] and though many of these are arguably distinguishable, as Justice Frankfurter, dissenting, shows, their cumulative effect has been to weaken the premise that such problems are judicially ungovernable.[38] Moreover, the Court has from time to time plunged into maelstroms at least as "political" and turbulent as questions of state governmental organization are likely to be.[39] Of course the conception has been that there is a subtle difference between the sense in which questions

35. Luther v. Borden, 48 U.S. (7 How.) 1, 51 (1849) (dissenting opinion of Woodbury, J.), quoted in Baker v. Carr, 369 U.S. at 296 (dissenting opinion of Frankfurter, J.).

36. McCloskey, *The McCarran Act and the Doctrine of Arbitrary Power,* 4 PUBLIC POLICY 228, 244–245 (Friedrich & Galbraith ed. 1953); Finkelstein, *Judicial Self-Limitation,* 37 HARV. L. REV. 338, 345 (1924).

37. *E.g.,* Gomillion v. Lightfoot, 364 U.S. 339 (1960); Smiley v. Holm, 285 U.S. 355 (1932); Carroll v. Becker, 285 U.S. 380 (1932); Koenig v. Flynn, 285 U.S. 375 (1932).

38. See Brief for the United States as Amicus Curiae on Reargument, pp. 54–61, Baker v. Carr, 369 U.S. 186 (1962).

39. *E.g.,* Youngstown Sheet & Tube Co. v. Sawyer, 343 U.S. 579 (1952) (holding unconstitutional the President's seizure of part of the steel industry without statutory warrant); Carter v. Carter Coal Co., 298 U.S.

of national power to regulate commerce are "political" and the sense in which questions of apportionment are "political." Justice Frankfurter would presumably concede the Court's historic power to entertain the former questions, but would insist on drawing the line against judicial intrusion into "those large contests of policy . . . by which governments and the actions of governments are made and unmade."[40] But he himself admits that these are differences of degree and that "within a certain range of cases on a continuum, no standard of distinction can be found to tell between them."[41] They are differences that depend on "feel," on intuitions; and those who do not sense them cannot be persuaded of their meaningful existence. It is simpler to say that the mere fact of involvement in state governmental arrangements is irrelevant to the political question doctrine and go on to the residual inquiries: whether the matter under consideration involves a possible conflict with other branches of the federal government, or whether appropriate judicial standards are lacking. The former query answers itself with respect to the present case: *Baker* v. *Carr* does not present a "question decided, or to be decided, by a political branch of government coequal with this Court."[42] So the sole and determinative issue remaining is that of "judicially discoverable and manageable standards."[43]

But that issue, *mirabile dictu,* is not treated at all in the opinion of the Court. One sentence suffices to dismiss it: "Judicial standards under the Equal Protection Clause are well developed and familiar, and it has been open to courts since the enactment of the Fourteenth Amendment to determine, if on the particular facts they must, that a discrimination reflects *no* policy, but simply arbitrary and capricious action."[44] This is the moment toward which the

---

238 (1936) holding unconstitutional the Bituminous Coal Conservation Act of 1935, which provided in part for the negotiation of agreements to set minimum wages); Railroad Retirement Bd. v. Alton R.R., 295 U.S. 330 (1935) (holding unconstitutional an act which established compulsory retirement and pension systems for railroad workers and others)·
40. 369 U.S. at 287 (dissenting opinion).
41. *Id.* at 283.
42. *Id.* at 226.
43. *Id.* at 217.
44. *Id.* at 226.

whole course of the analysis has been directed. The cases have been reviewed, the citations have been multiplied so that other possible factors in the judgment can be cleared away and this factor stand forth as the only one that need be considered. And then it is not considered. The very question on which the whole judgment has been made to hang is whether standards *are* "well developed and familiar" in this field; and now that question is answered by a simple and wonderfully pregnant "yes."

Whether this keystone sentence quite carries the argumentative burden that falls on it or not, its implications for the future of the "political question" doctrine are sufficiently devastating. If the problem of state governmental organization as such no longer calls that doctrine into being, and if the problem of judicially manageable standards is obviated by an incantatory reference to terms like "equal protection," there is not a great deal left. Presumably it may survive in connection with the relationship of the federal courts to the president and Congress, in foreign relations for example. And for Justice Brennan at least, the guaranty clause is still confided to the care of Congress. But even this inference is somewhat clouded if we press the logic of *Baker* v. *Carr,* for if the guaranty clause intrinsically raises political questions, this cannot be because it "is not a repository of judicially manageable standards."[45] Its standards are not any more nebulous than those of the equal protection clause in this context.[46] Indeed, as Justice Frankfurter says, the republican form of government issue and the equal protection issue are inextricably related halves of the same question, because the Court must decide what is the basic republican norm before deciding whether departures from it are unreasonable. So what exempts guaranty clause claims from judicial reach must be the possibility of conflict with "a political branch of government coequal with this Court"[47] and nothing else, since that is the only political question criterion not undermined by the opinion.

45. *Id.* at 223.
46. See Bonfield, *Baker* v. *Carr: New Light on the Constitutional Guarantee of Republican Government,* 50 CALIF. L. REV. 245 (1962); Bonfield, *The Guarantee Clause of Article IV, Section 4: A Study in Constitutional Desuetude,* 46 MINN. L. REV. 513 (1962).
47. 369 U.S. at 226.

While that criterion lasts[48] the doctrine of political questions may retain some remnants of vitality, but its status as a major doctrine of our constitutional jurisprudence seems to be impaired beyond recovery.

With all respect to its age and ancestry, this may not be altogether a bad thing. The political question doctrine has been used in the past as a talismanic phrase to signal the fact that a subject was thought, for a variety of reasons, to be inappropriate for judicial control. It has been, that is, a kind of verbal redundancy in a general theory of judicial self-restraint, much as the old doctrine of "business affected with a public interest" was merely another way of saying that a price regulation was deemed "reasonable" under the due process clause. Such fictions designed to "beautify what is disagreeable to the sufferers,"[49] may once have been useful in that they allowed the Court to express an intuitive conclusion to abstain without explaining it. But as *Baker* v. *Carr* shows, they are two-edged because they also permit a court to intervene, equally without explanation. Their mischief is, in short, that they may encourage those who live by them to bypass the thought process that is supposed to underlie them. In *Baker,* the focus on whether apportionment presented a "political question" enabled the Court to talk about everything but the real issue—which was whether the courts *ought* to enter this thicket. It is hard to mourn the enfeeblement of a doctrine that has served this obscurantist purpose.

Now to the final reason for regarding *Baker* v. *Carr* as a momentous occasion in constitutional history: its relevance to the developing contemporary debate over the proper scope of judicial review. In a sense, of course, that debate has been continuous since 1789, but in earlier days it has often been hampered by the insistence of the Court and many of its defenders that there was no choice, that the range and nature of judicial power were simply

48. That it may not last indefinitely is suggested by Justice Douglas: "The statements in *Luther* v. *Borden*, 7 How. I, 42, that this guaranty is enforceable only by Congress or the Chief Executive is not maintainable." *Id.* at 242 n.2.

49. Tyson & Bro. v. Banton, 273 U.S. 418, 446 (1927) (dissenting opinion of Holmes, J.).

determined by the inescapable imperatives of the Constitution.[50] A discussion can hardly proceed when the participants thus challenge the very premise of its existence. But in the twentieth century this hindrance has been at least partially eroded by scholarly skepticism, much of it from the justices themselves. After Holmes and Brandeis and Stone, to mention only the dead, it was difficult to contend that the sovereign prerogative of choice between self-restraint and intervention was nonexistent. Although there might still be room to argue about the extent of the leeway the Court enjoyed, the way was open for fruitful consideration of how it ought to use the leeway it plainly had. The need for such considerations was all the more pressing after 1937, when it became evident that the Court, having abandoned most of its old authority in the economic field, was proceeding to stake out a substantial dominion in the area of civil rights. New tasks in a new historical context made it desirable to think anew the question of the Court's role in relation to the other branches of government.

Even so, the dialogue was slow to get going; from the Court itself Justices Stone and Frankfurter gave it a promising start in the first Flag Salute case,[51] but thereafter in that forum it developed fitfully and not very productively. Perhaps the Court is not the best place to carry on such a discussion, partly because the mystique of this venerable institution sometimes still inhibits plain talk, and partly because the adversary relationship between concurrers and dissenters encourages each side to argue as if the rightness of its own view is almost too obvious for discussion. At any rate, instead of proceeding as a dialogue should, in the direction of increased understanding and ultimate synthesis, the dispute has carried the participants farther apart to a point where competing assertions take the place of discussion. Justice Frankfurter has tried to join the issue more determinedly than most of the others, and his opinion in *Baker* is, as far as it goes, brilliant argu-

50. *E.g.,* West Coast Hotel Co. v. Parrish, 300 U.S. 379, 400–405 (1937) (dissenting opinion of Sutherland, J.); United States v. Butler, 297 U.S. 1, 62 (1936) (Roberts, J., for the Court).
51. Minersville School Dist. v. Gobitis, 310 U.S. 586, 601 (1940) (Frankfurter, J., for the Court, Stone, J., in dissent), overruled by West Virginia State Bd. of Educ. v. Barnette, 319 U.S. 624 (1943).

mentation. But even he stops short of really explaining why courts should not tamper with legislative apportionment, why the standards devisable in this field are not "meet for judicial judgment." The evaluation evidently rests on his heavily documented insistence that history argues for a policy of judicial restraint and on his educated revulsion against such meddling with the stuff of politics. But the Court in recent times has shown little disposition to bear the yoke of history against its own inclinations, and even one who respects the past may not be willing to surrender judgment to it. And revulsion is often incommunicable to those who do not already share it.

Outside the Court, the dialogue was at length propelled into its present, active phase by Judge Learned Hand.[52] Uniquely well-cast for the part as one of the most respected of American jurists, he was sure to be heeded when he declared that the Court has a choice, that the question of "when a court should intervene"[53] merits discussion; not being himself on the Supreme Court, he could speak his mind freely. The most widely noticed rejoinder to Judge Hand came from Herbert Wechsler.[54] He tried in a sense to cut the discussion off before it was well begun by arguing that both the duty and the limits of judicial intervention are predetermined by organic law; even the apparent discretion to abstain implied in the doctrine of political questions is, he said, illusory; the only justifiable basis for invoking that doctrine is that the constitutional text commits the subject to the political branches. But as Alexander Bickel has remarked, the political question doctrine cannot be "domesticated" in this manner,[55] and neither can the broad issue of "when a court should intervene." It would set the understanding of constitutional law back several decades to contend that courts really do act, or fail to act, in response to inescapable external commands; and it is not likely that Wechsler

52. HAND, THE BILL OF RIGHTS (1958). See also FREUND, *Concord and Discord,* in THE SUPREME COURT OF THE UNITED STATES 28 (1961).
53. THE BILL OF RIGHTS 1.
54. Wechsler, *Toward Neutral Principles of Constitutional Law,* 73 HARV. L. REV. 1 (1959).
55. Bickel, *Foreword: The Passive Virtues, The Supreme Court,* 1960 *Term,* 75 HARV. L. REV. 40, 46 (1961).

was offering this as an empirical observation. Rather, he seemed to be saying that courts *ought* to proceed only in these terms. This is an interesting proposition, but it is doubtful that a tribunal so constrained could have played the Supreme Court's historical part; it is equally doubtful that any future Court would bridle itself in such a fashion.

Nevertheless Wechsler, whatever his intentions, further animated the dialogue Hand had begun[56] by going on to urge that the Court, when it does intervene, should make its judgments on the basis of "neutral principles." For him of course this prescription is logically related to his belief that the Court's jurisdiction is ordained rather than moulded, but the relationship is not necessarily inevitable. The demand for "neutral principles" is a special way of saying that the Court should work only with "standards meet for judicial judgment," and the question whether such standards are discernible is, as *Baker* v. *Carr* shows, a major factor in the question of "when a court should intervene." It may be legitimate for the Court to base a decision to abstain on the inarticulable hunches that often define "prudence."[57] But the decision to intervene must rest on a predetermination that the subject will turn out to be judicially manageable. In short, one can believe that the Court has substantial discretion in defining the areas it will supervise and still believe that its discretion should confine it to those areas where appropriate judicial criteria can be contrived.

The question is then, to get back to the case at hand, whether the Court embarked in *Baker* v. *Carr* on a course in which such criteria are lacking. An answer to this would depend in turn on the answer to two other questions: how is it decided whether a standard is meet for judgment by the Supreme Court of the United

---

56. The responses to Wechsler include: Black, *The Lawfulness of the Segregation Decisions*, 69 YALE L.J. 421 (1960); Givens, *The Impartial Constitutional Principles Supporting Brown v. Board of Education*, 6 HOW. L.J. 179 (1960); Miller & Howell, *The Myth of Neutrality in Constitutional Adjudication*, 27 U. CHI. L. REV. 661 (1960); Mueller & Schwartz, *The Principle of Neutral Principles*, 7 U.C.L.A. L. REV. 571 (1960); Pollak, *Racial Discrimination and Judicial Integrity: A Reply to Professor Wechsler*, 108 U. PA. L. REV. 1 (1959); Wright, *The Supreme Court Cannot Be Neutral*, 40 TEXAS L. REV. 599 (1962).

57. Bickel, *supra note* 55, at 46.

States, and what *is* the course of development that *Baker* portends?

Surely the starting point for an answer to the first question is a conception that might be called "differentiation of function." In Justice Frankfurter's words: "The Court's authority—possessed neither of the purse nor the sword—ultimately rests on sustained public confidence in its moral sanction."[58] This confidence itself depends heavily on the idea that what judicial review adds to the governmental process is significantly different from what the political branches contribute. We need not pause now to inquire whether or to what degree this idea may be delusion; delusion or not, the idea is vital to the Court's position as "the ultimate organ of 'the supreme Law of the Land.' "[59] If the public should ever become convinced that the Court is merely another legislature, that judicial review is only a euphemism for an additional layer in the legislative process, the Court's future as a constitutional tribunal would be cast in grave doubt.

Nor need we decide here what all the factors are that contribute to this idea of the Court's differences. For present purposes the relevant point is the supposition that the Court works with decision standards that are really, not just rhetorically, distinguishable from those a legislature characteristically applies. The distinction is elusive, and no single word can quite express it. "Impartial," "disinterested," "impersonal," "general"—all of which Mr. Wechsler tells us he considered[60]—will not quite serve. Nor will "neutral," which was his final choice; nor "detached,"[61] nor "objective."[62] Wechsler himself comes closer to the crux of the matter when he says that judicial criteria should be capable of being "framed and tested as an exercise of reason and not merely as an act of willfulness or will."[63] But even this formulation must be taken with the understanding that it involves "a matter of de-

58. 369 U.S. at 267 (dissenting opinion).
59. *Ibid.*
60. WECHSLER, PRINCIPLES, POLITICS AND FUNDAMENTAL LAW at xiii (1961).
61. 369 U.S. at 267 (dissenting opinion of Frankfurter, J.; his word is "detachment."
62. Braden, *The Search for Objectivity in Constitutional Law,* 57 YALE L.J. 571 (1948).
63. Wechsler, *supra* note 54, at 11.

gree."[64] Legislators are not always strangers to the reasoning process; judges cannot always eliminate all quality of fiat from their decisions.[65] Perhaps the most we can say is that judges should be thought of as striving more determinedly to reduce the element of fiat; that they must be more reluctant to reach the point where will alone rules.

The nature of this misty ideal can be clarified a little by briefly revisiting a decision that has probably received more nearly unanimous criticism than any other in the twentieth century: *Lochner* v. *New York*.[66] What, after all, was so bad about it apart from the fact that it reflected an economic theory later generations find distasteful? Two of its vices, apposite to our present problem, stand out. In the first place, it promulgated a constitutional value for which there was little or no detectable constitutional warrant: the value of freedom of contract, of laissez-faire. Neither the language nor the intent of the Constitution supported this interpretation of its meaning. Indeed, it was arguable that the kind of restraint it imposed was alien to the spirit in which the Constitution was framed. This objection is summarized aphoristically in two famous sentences of Justice Holmes's dissent: "The Fourteenth Amendment does not enact Mr. Herbert Spencer's Social Statics" and "a constitution is not intended to embody a particular economic theory, whether of paternalism and the organic relation of the citizen to the State or of *laissez faire*."[67]

The second fault of *Lochner* was that it propounded a rule that could not be applied as "an exercise of reason." The Court did not lay it down that working hours were entirely exempt from state control; that would have been a palpable enough standard all right, but not even Justice Peckham could think it feasible. Under the "rule" announced, the regulation of hours was valid if the Court thought it reasonable and invalid if the Court thought it unreasonable; and no guidance whatever was provided for objectifying this discrimination. The only standard was the Court's

64. 369 U.S. at 283 (dissenting opinion of Frankfurter, J.).
65. Fuller, *Reason and Fiat in Case Law*, 59 HARV. L. REV. 376 (1946).
66. 198 U.S. 45 (1905).
67. *Id.* at 75.

value-loaded intuition that "the limit of the police power has been reached and passed."[68]

The point is that the judgment criteria here employed are indistinguishable, even in degree, from those that characterize the legislative process. The ideal of "standards meet for judicial judgment" is that they possess the qualities the *Lochner* standards did not—that they be somehow plausibly rooted in constitutional language or intent, and that their application can be to some significant degree an "exercise of reason."

It would be idle to pretend that the Court has always adhered to this ideal, though to be sure many of the apparent departures from it can be extenuated. A specific intent to forbid racial segregation in public education cannot be wrung from the language or history of the Fourteenth Amendment; but history does suggest a general purpose hostile to legally enforced racial distinctions, and it further suggests that the differentiation in function between the Court and Congress in the implementation of this purpose was left to posterity for decision.[69] In light of the nature of American constitutional history it is reasonable to assume that the Court was expected to play a part in effectuating this purpose. And the Court's fiat, if it is one, is more warrantable in such a field.[70] Similar considerations may be relevant to the Court's disposition of controversies between states in a case like *Nebraska* v. *Wyoming,*[71] which Justice Douglas cites in support of his contention that "adjudication is often perplexing and complicated."[72] For these cases there is often no other means of resolution; deference to the political

68. *Id.* at 58.

69. Bickel, *The Original Understanding and the Segregation Decision,* 69 HARV. L. REV. 1 (1955).

70. While the determination of municipal boundaries involves standards as ineffable as those involved in legislative redistricting, and any court should pause before second-guessing political branches on such a matter, the Court in Gomillion v. Lightfoot, 364 U.S. 339 (1960), was not faced with this question; rather, the question was whether an ordinance upsetting the status quo was discriminatory. Enforcement of the doctrine that the states may not use race as a basis for discriminatory legislation of this character seems rather clearly within the field consigned to the Court's care by the Civil War amendments.

71. 325 U.S. 589 (1945).

72. 369 U.S. at 245 (concurring opinion).

processes is not feasible. Here the justices can fairly say that they act "not by authority of our competence but by force of our commissions."[73] It might even be contended that long-standing judicial custom can also have a bearing on the issue. The criteria historically employed to judge state laws impinging on interstate commerce—the "direct" or "undue" burden concepts, for example[74] —are hardly amenable to precise, reasoned application. As an original question, it might be doubted whether judges were uniquely qualified to make such evaluations, but their assumption of authority to do so is more than a century old;[75] the passage of years may validate a power that would be hard to justify on other grounds.

Nevertheless there have, of course, been salient occasions in constitutional history when the Court has, without the benefit of such extenuating considerations, imposed on the other branches of government a standard which was neither inferable from the constitutional text nor capable of objective, "reasoned" application. *Lochner* itself and its relatives in the field of substantive due process provide one such example. Another, more congenial to the post-1937 judicial generation, is the line of cases in which freedom of speech has been protected, particularly against state actions. It cannot be said that freedom of speech is any more clearly embodied in the mandatory language of the due process clause than was freedom of contract; and the intent of the framers about such matters is, at best, ambiguous.[76] Moreover, the balancing formula,[77] which now enjoys ascendancy as the guiding standard in the field, is no more amenable to precise, reasoned application than were the old formulations like "business affected

73. West Virginia State Bd. of Educ. v. Barnette, 319 U.S. 624, 640 (1943).

74. Stern, *The Problems of Yesteryear—Commerce and Due Process* in ESSAYS IN CONSTITUTIONAL LAW 150 (McCloskey ed. 1957).

75. Wilson v. Black Bird Creek Marsh Co., 27 U.S. (2 Pet.) 245 (1829); Cooley v. Board of Wardens, 53 U.S. (12 How.) 299 (1851).

76. Fairman, *Does the Fourteenth Amendment Incorporate the Bill of Rights? The Original Understanding,* 2 STAN. L. REV. 5 (1949).

77. See Wilkinson v. United States, 365 U.S. 399, 414 (1961); Sweezy v. New Hampshire, 354 U.S. 234, 266–267 (1957) (Frankfurter, J., concurring in the result).

with a public interest."[78] The process of decision based on it is not easy to distinguish in principle from the legislative process.

The Court then has, it must be admitted, sometimes broken the ideal here described. This can serve as a reminder that an institution of such vitality and of such historic antecedents will never be entirely cribbed and confined by any prescriptions we write for it. When the men who hold these lofty commissions see an evil that they believe imperatively calls for redress, they will on occasion strike out, with little regard for consistency or caution. So it is; so it has been; and if history can validate their other prerogatives, it may validate this one as well. But even here a few qualifying points can still be made. For one thing, it is noteworthy that the modern Court has seemed a little uneasy about its jurisdiction in the free speech field. The balancing formula has been used primarily to uphold governmental authority.[79] In its free speech decisions invalidating governmental action the Court has often sought and found criteria that seemed more ponderable, more historical, more "judicial": the well-worn idea of federal preemption;[80] procedural concepts like vagueness; [81] familiar-sounding legal terms like "prior restraint."[82] Even Justice Black's insistence on "absolutes" in this area[83] is a left-handed acknowledgment that it is somehow inappropriate for the judiciary to operate free from the restrictions of concrete standards. And for another thing, it must be urged that a price is paid for each judicial venture into uncharted and unchartable seas, whether or not an analogue can be found in past or present judicial behavior. Each such venture tarnishes a little more the idea that the judicial process and the legislative process are distinguishable; and this idea

78. Munn v. Illinois, 94 U.S. 113 (1877); Tyson & Bro. v. Banton, 273 U.S. 418 (1927).

79. E.g., Braden v. United States, 365 U.S. 431 (1961); Wilkinson v. United States, 365 U.S. 399 (1961); Barenblatt v. United States, 360 U.S. 109 (1959); Uphaus v. Wyman, 360 U.S. 72 (1959); American Communications Ass'n v. Douds, 339 U.S. 382 (1950).

80. Pennsylvania v. Nelson, 350 U.S. 497 (1956).

81. Winters v. New York, 333 U.S. 507 (1948); Joseph Burstyn, Inc. v. Wilson, 343 U.S. 495 (1952).

82. Near v. Minnesota, 283 U.S. 697 (1931); Joseph Burstyn, Inc. v. Wilson, supra note 81.

83. Black, The Bill of Rights, 35 N.Y.U.L. REV. 865 (1960).

is indispensable to judicial review. The idea can survive—has survived—a certain amount of this treatment, but there is no reason to think it is ineradicable. A prudent court will seek always to minimize doctrinal developments that cut so close to the very fulcrum of judicial power.

The implications of *Baker* are for the moment almost completely uncertain. Strictly speaking, as Justice Stewart emphasizes in his concurrence,[84] the Court decided only that the appellants were entitled to present their claim that the equal protection clause was violated by the Tennessee apportionment: the federal courts were not barred from hearing it by the political question doctrine. Even the idea that the clause will be held to limit the states in some way is an inference, though an almost unavoidable one unless this whole elaborate structure of argument and counter-argument is to be thought of as an adventure in futility. If we can trust common sense we must conclude that the Court will sooner or later declare what standards will be imposed to implement the jurisdiction it has now embraced. The possibilities seem to fall in two broad categories.

First there is a set of considerations that are, broadly speaking, "procedural" in character; that is, they relate to the question of how the decision was reached to apportion in the challenged manner. Here, as the situation in Tennessee itself suggests, the heart of the inquiry might be whether the ultimate constituent power was being allowed an adequate opportunity to express itself. It is certainly untrue that "one man, one vote" was regarded by the framers of the Constitution as an imperative basic principle for carrying on the day-to-day, year-to-year process of government; and it is at least dubious that any such principle became embodied in our constitutional tradition in the years that followed.[85] But it is beyond doubt that the framers acknowledged popular consent as the indispensable basis for setting up that process of government in the first place.[86] Though the government might take

84. 369 U.S. at 265.
85. *Id.* at 301–324 (dissenting opinion of Frankfurter, J.).
86. Corwin, "*We, the People*" in THE DOCTRINE OF JUDICIAL REVIEW 81 (1914).

various forms and possess various powers, those characteristics were *derived* from the consent of the governed. If this central principle, so plain in the Declaration of Independence, was not expressed in the explicit language of the Constitution, it is because after 1776 it was taken for granted.[87] Its claim to be a fundamental principle of the Constitution is about as solid as any claim could be.

All this is relevant to the Tennessee case facts as alleged. There is, it seems, no provision for popular initiative in Tennessee.[88] The procedure for inaugurating a constitutional amendment is locked in the hands of the legislature chosen under the existing apportionment system. This might itself raise a question as to whether the channels of popular consent were being kept open; but in this case the doubt is compounded by the fact that the present apportionment, ordained by the legislature in 1901, is grossly at odds with the standard set by that last expression of popular will. The constituent power is not only being thwarted from re-expressing itself; it is being flouted.

It seems possible then that the standards ultimately established under the Fourteenth Amendment could be focused on matters like these. If there has been a significant passage of time since the last constituent decision on apportionment, and if population shifts in the interval have substantially altered the distribution of legislative seats, and if the channels of popular access to the issue are obstructed—the present apportionment might be held to violate the Fourteenth Amendment. But no constitutional question could be raised as to the actual, substantive nature of the apportionment if the popular will had expressed itself or possessed adequate means for doing so.

The second possibility is that the courts might go behind these procedural considerations and undertake to approve or disapprove the actual distribution of legislative seats. They might start, as has been suggested,[89] from a presumption in favor of per capita equal-

87. WRIGHT, CONSENSUS AND CONTINUITY, 1776–1787 (1958).

88. 369 U.S. at 193 n.14.

89. Brief for the United States as Amicus Curiae on Reargument, p. 26, Baker v. Carr, 369 U.S. 186 (1962); Lewis, *Legislative Apportionment and the Federal Courts,* 71 HARV. L. REV. 1057, 1086 (1958).

ity of representation and proceed to evaluate departures from that norm. Such departures would be required, however, to be "reasonable" both in basis and in degree. "Geography, economics, urban-rural conflict,"[90] and various other nonlegal bases can make some claim to historical support and might conceivably be allowable within limits. But it would be the responsibility of the courts to decide *how much* departure from the norm of equality would be "rational" and at what point such variations would become "arbitrary and capricious."

Either of these courses of judicial action is at least imaginable on the basis of the opinions in *Baker* v. *Carr*. Justice Brennan's majority opinion leaves the issue wide open. His only reference to the question of criteria is the statement that judicial standards under the equal protection clause are "well developed and familiar," but he goes on to remark that "it has been open to courts since the enactment of the Fourteenth Amendment to determine ... that a discrimination reflects *no* policy, but simply arbitrary and capricious action."[91] The italics are his, and they may be significant. They could mean that an apportionment will still be presumed valid if it reflects *some* policy determination by the state, and that the Court will undertake to judge the determination on substantive grounds. Even if this is too much to squeeze from a single italicized word, the fact remains that the Brennan opinion commits the Court to no particular kind of criteria in future cases. This is also true of Justice Stewart's opinion. And Justice Clark, though he embarks on a daring arithmetical enterprise in substantive standard-setting, plainly says that he would not do so if the people of the state had been given any other means for obtaining the apportionment they might want.[92] If he had put the horse before the cart, he would have had no need to reach the substantive question at all—an apportionment system's validity would depend on whether it had been established, or could be altered, by the popular will. Only Justice Douglas, among the majority, appears to have no hesitation at all about plunging into the question of

90. 369 U.S. at 269 (dissenting opinion of Frankfurter, J.).
91. *Id.* at 226.
92. *Id.* at 258–259.

substantive standards. The dissenters, Justice Frankfurter and Harlan, would, of course, prefer that the Court stay out of the apportionment quagmire altogether, but their strictures against the majority holding lean heavily on the conviction that courts are unequipped to weigh the substantive factors that enter into the question of political districting.

Assuming then that the question of standards is open, and yet assuming further that some standards will be adumbrated in pursuance of the doctrinal swerve in *Baker* v. *Carr,* what should those standards be? Should the Court undertake a Lochneresque responsibility for defining the substantive constitutional norm ("one man, one vote," for example), and for determining whether each departure from the norm is "rational" or "capricious"? Or might it better restrict itself to the "procedural" considerations outlined above, chiefly the question whether the constituent power had expressed itself or had been given fair opportunity to do so? Suppose, to be concrete about it, that an organic apportionment principle has recently been ratified by popular vote, or that adequate procedures for initiating such a principle are available if "an aroused popular conscience"[93] should develop. Or suppose, as in the Tennessee case, that the legislature is ignoring the constitutional mandate that does exist—but that there is, as there is not in Tennessee, a provision for direct popular legislation. Should the courts go beyond these assurances that the principle of popular consent is unthwarted, and judge the rationality of the apportionment system itself?

The reasons for believing they should not are weighty. The standards for such a judgment are not inferable from the constitutional language or purpose, nor is the judicial authority to prescribe them vindicated by custom. We must assume, as the majority of the Court seems to assume, that they might make room for some consideration of geography, of insular minorities, of economics, and of other historically familiar factors in establishing a noninvidious distribution of voting strength. It is hard to see how the

93. *Id.* at 270 (dissenting opinion of Frankfurter, J.).

process of balancing these complexities and subtleties could be reduced to anything even resembling "an exercise of reason," how it could reflect anything more than a subjective *ipse dixit*. It is equally hard to see how the judicial process thus conceived could differ from the legislative process unless it would be by virtue of an abstract moralism that ignored reality. If the courts are to invade the center of this thicket they must be prepared to grapple with the problems that inhabit it; and if they do, they are acting as legislators. As suggested above, the judiciary may sometimes feel constrained to act this part in pursuit of an ideal it regards as transcendent. But it should do so as seldom as a sober conscience will permit and only when a more "judicial," more restrained alternative is unavailable.

Here there is such an alternative. A rule that focused only on the opening up of the procedures of popular consent would not be above criticism. It would be novel in its application to this subject; but then, the subject itself is novel. It would pose ticklish problems of remedy, but the basic decision that the subject is justiciable is responsible for that; and at least this kind of rule would not thrust the judiciary into the anomalous task of remapping election districts on its own account.[94]

On the other hand, such an approach would rest on an arguably valid constitutional base; and it would provide the judiciary with palpable, fathomable criteria of decision. Questions of degree

---

94. In the case of a state with a present apportionment grossly at variance with the standard set by the last expression of the constituent power, as in Tennessee, the court might give the legislature reasonable time to conform with these standards, under threat of an alternative of holding the next election at large. If, because of population changes and shifts, there was reason to believe that the state constitutional standards might themselves be superannuated, and if the electorate had no access to a remedy, the court might require that the machinery of popular reconsideration be set in motion within a reasonable time, again under the threat that an election would otherwise be held at large. In the perhaps unlikely event that the legislature failed to act in response to that threat, the election would have to be held at large; but then the apportionment plan voted by a legislature so elected might itself be held to be a sufficiently reliable reflection of the popular will on the question. Drastic as the remedy of election at large is from the viewpoint of the state, its virtue from the judicial point of view is that it would spare the courts the inappropriate and burdensome task of acting as apportionment boards for the nation.

would still arise as they always must in the law: the judgment process would not become automatic. But the range of factors to be considered would be channeled and evaluation of them would be communicable. There is a vast difference between the question whether the constituent power has had a fair opportunity to make a decision and the question whether the decision itself was substantively fair. It is comparable to the difference between asking whether a man had a fair hearing before he was hanged, and asking whether it was just to hang him at all. The first question is the kind that courts can handle as well, and sometimes better, than the "political" agencies of government. The second question carries the judiciary into an uncircumscribed realm of moral and practical choices that is indistinguishable from the legislative realm and in which judiciary competence to judge wisely is something less than self-evident.

There is a further, final reason for believing that the Court should content itself with this approach to its newly assumed task. It has to do with an observation made in the opening paragraphs of this commentary: that the Reapportionment case seems to have generated an astonishing spirit of compliance and that this may indicate that the decision has activated a latent consensus in American opinion. It must be pleasant for the justices, who have been vilified so much in recent years, to find a major decision so kindly received. The preceptor is always gratified by willing students. But before they proceed to the next lesson, they would be well advised to speculate about the precise nature of this consensus they seem to have aroused. Speculation it must be, for there are few certainties about such matters. But if the past is any guide, one can guess that the agreement consists, not of dogmas about how government should be organized, but of the underlying dogma that the people should be free to establish the governmental forms they want. Insofar as the reapportionment decision implied an affirmation of that dogma, its reception is not surprising. But if the judiciary should go beyond the premise of popular consent and attempt to prescribe "from its own bosom"[95] what the popu-

95. Hand, *The Contribution of an Independent Judiciary to Civilization,* in THE SPIRIT OF LIBERTY 125 (1959).

lace may consent to, the climate might alter drastically. Then indeed it might turn out that this new development, which began with such bright promise, had impaired "the Court's position as the ultimate organ of the 'Supreme Law of the Land.' "⁹⁶

96. 369 U.S. at 267 (dissenting opinion of Frankfurter, J.).

PRINCIPLES, POWERS, AND VALUES

[This essay first appeared in *Religion and the Public Order: An Annual Review of Church and State and of Religion, Law, and Society, 1964*, ed. Donald A. Giannella (Villanova: © Villanova University, 1965). Reprinted by courtesy of the University of Chicago Press.]

American constitutional history has been in large part a spasmodic running debate over the behavior of the Supreme Court, but in a hundred seventy years we have made curiously little progress toward establishing the terms of this war of words, much less toward achieving concord. The justices themselves have usually felt obliged to confine their opinions to the more formalistic aspects of the matter—to the historical-technical dimension rather narrowly conceived. We sometimes get hints, usually in dissenting opinions, that the justices are aware of the possible relevancy of other considerations. When Mr. Justice Frankfurter warned the judiciary against "political thickets"[1] and spoke of subjects not "meet for judicial judgment,"[2] he surely was expressing doubts about the Court's power to supervise apportionment policies, as well as about the propriety of its doing so. When Mr. Justice Field equated the Fourteenth Amendment with his own ethic of economic liberty,[3] he was telling us what values the amendment ought to protect, not merely contending that it had been designed to protect them. But more often than not, such misgivings as those of Frankfurter have been either ignored by the majority or countered by ringing restatements of the doctrine of judicial supremacy, while value recommendations like those of Field have been met by appeals to history and technical legalism which, however sound, fail to touch his central point.

As for observers outside the chamber, those who endorse the

1. Colegrove v. Green, 328 U.S. 549, 556 (1946).
2. Baker v. Carr, 369 U.S. 186, 289 (1962) (dissenting opinion).
3. Butchers' Union Slaughter-House and Live-Stock Landing Co. v. Crescent City Live-Stock Landing and Slaughter-House Co., 111 U.S. 746, 756–757 (1884).

majority position at a given moment are often so pleased to find the Court with them on the ramparts that they are indisposed to ask whether it really belongs there. On the other hand, those who oppose the current judicial policy are likely themselves to be so result-oriented that they contribute little to an objective appraisal of the Court's performance. And even when both disputants are able to submerge their prepossessions to some degree, the dialogue remains confused because there is no common understanding of the terms of the discussion. The result is that these recurring constitutional debates resemble an endless series of re-matches between two club-boxers who have long since stopped developing their crafts autonomously and have nothing further to learn from each other. The same generalizations are launched from either side, to be met by the same evasions and parries. Familiar old ambiguities fog the controversy, and the contestants flounder among them for a while until history calls a close and it is time to retire from the arena and await the next installment. In the exchange of assertions and counter-assertions no one can be said to have won a decision on the merits, for small attempt has been made to arrive at an understanding of what the merits are.

So it has been to a very considerable extent with the modern revival of the ancient conflict. In the last decade the Supreme Court has laid claim to a range of power that is almost unexampled in judiciary history. Not even John Marshall was so bold about exerting his Court's prerogative to command the nation; and only the Court of the early 1930's seems fairly comparable in the extent of its will-to-govern. As might have been implicated, this has set the old debate going again in very much its traditional form. Once more, on the Court and elsewhere, there is the exchange of time-honored generalities, the suppression of premises, and the argument at cross-purposes. The complaint that the Court has wrenched historical intent to suit its preferences is met (or rather not met) by the contention that an ethical goal has been achieved. The reminder that the Court lacks power to cure all of the republic's social ills brings forth the counter-assertion that it is legally and ethically bound to cure this one. It is as if bridge were being played with a set of rules that permitted each player to change the trump suit at any stage. Everyone wins and everyone loses, but rational assessment of what goes on is a trifle difficult.

It is not suggested here that any calculus can provide automatic answers to the problem of evaluating the Court's performance. Ultimate assessment of that performance will depend on judgments more subtle than any articulate judgment categories, and even within each category imponderables will always be encountered. But it may be possible to push a little closer to the area where imponderables take over, to cut away at least the unnecessary ambiguities that cloud discussion. Though rational analysis cannot resolve the problem, perhaps it can identify the channels through which an observer might move on the way to his own resolution; and that would in itself carry us a step beyond the usual clash by night.

I propose in this paper to consider the modern Court's performance with respect to the establishment of religion clause of the Constitution, to attempt an orderly and comprehensive analysis of that performance, and to conclude with an appraisal based on the analysis. This program makes it necessary to begin by being as explicit as possible about the factors that may be relevant to such an analysis and appraisal, that is, to confront at the outset the issues that are usually not confronted at all.

I suggest that our evaluation of a Supreme Court decision—or of a whole line of judicial conduct—ordinarily depends on one or more of three different judgment components: the question of what have been called above historical-technical standards, the question of power, and the question of value. In other words, in criticizing a judicial action we say that the Court has misread the Constitution, or that it has overtaxed its power capabilities, or that it has chosen the wrong ethical solution. I further suggest that a great deal of the confusion in discussions about he Court arises from the failure to distinguish between these three factors, or to be clear about which is in mind at any given time. To be sure, the factors are related, and it is ultimately necessary to consider them in relation in order to appraise the Court comprehensively. But to treat them as identical is to confuse discussion; and to slip from one to another without notice is to make discussion impossible.

It may be necessary—though it should not be—to offer a justification of this tripartite approach to the analysis of judicial behavior. There are those who would confine all evaluation to the historical-technical category and would pronounce it illegitimate even to consider issues of power or ethics.[4] There are others so dedicated to a value-oriented assessment that they regard legalistic strictures as mere pettifoggery,[5] and probably still others who would prefer to think of the Court purely in terms of its power to govern. It might be sufficient comment on such viewpoints to say that, whatever our preferences, these three different judgment criteria persist in turning up in the debates over judicial behavior; we cannot tame the subject to our own liking, however pleasant this might be. Or it might be enough to rejoin that any man is welcome to restrict himself to the analytic boundaries he prefers; only that he is then obliged in the name of reason to make it clear that he is so restricting himself and must not wander outside his chosen perspectives.

But in fact both history and common sense suggest hat it is desirable to take account of each of these evaluative factors. The Court has been and must be to some extent a "courtlike" institution, trading in the orthodox legal coinage of textual analysis, precedent, and "the intent of the framers." But it has also been a value-judging agency, "a national conscience . . . a channel for moral imperatives";[6] and this role has thrust it inescapably into the arena of political policy, where power considerations cannot be ignored. Whether it should have assumed this role, with all it entails, is an old, hard question. But that it has done so seems

---

4. See the discussion of "atavistic regressions to the simplicities of *Marbury v. Madison,* to its concept of the self-applying Constitution and the self-evident function of judicial review" in BICKEL, THE LEAST DANGEROUS BRANCH 75–78 (1962); the quoted words are at 74.

5. FRANK, MARBLE PALACE: THE SUPREME COURT IN AMERICAN LIFE *passim* (1958); Arnold, *Professor Hart's Theology,* 73 HARV. L. REV. 1298 (1960).

6. Lewis, *Supreme Court Moves Again To Exert Its Powerful Influence,* N.Y. Times, June 21, 1964, §4, p. E3.

after the past fifty years of scholarship, beyond serious dispute; and the pattern of the past has shaped the expectations of the present. America does expect the Court to be both courtlike and statesmanlike, a law-finding and a value-judging agency, and the modern Court has enthusiastically endorsed that dual conception of its duty. Those who would like it otherwise are entitled to their tastes, but it would seem more useful to evaluate the Court as it is rather than as it never was. And since the Court we have is concerned with both the historical-technical and the ethical, and since that combination of concerns raises the issue of political power, we cannot fairly overlook any of these matters in seeking to judge how well and wisely the Court is doing its work.

Although it is necessary for the sake of clarity to recognize the separate identities of these three judgment components, it is also necessary to recognize that the ultimate appraisal of judicial performance depends on synthesis of the three. To put a complex matter very simply, each component is entitled to some weight in the evaluative process, and the final result will be a product of their cumulative force. Consider for example a hypothetical decision which is solidly based in constitutional text and precedent, which aims toward a clear ethical good, and which does not seriously tax the Court's power resources. The case for such a decision would be strong indeed. But now suppose that the historical-technical justification is more questionable. The case would be weaker, even though we might still approve the decision because of our belief in its value objective and our confidence about the Court's power to carry it off. And now suppose further that such confidence diminishes and that the ethical goal seems more cloudy and disputable: the case becomes weaker still. When we say that the Court has done well or ill, we are—or ought to be—expressing the result of such a multifactor judgment process.

It is worth emphasizing that this calculus is assumed to take place in a world where pluses and minuses are always relative. We need not consider the imaginary case in which there is no historical-technical argument for the Court's decision or, conversely, in which the constitutional mandate is unmistakable. No matter how dearly we prize, or bitterly deprecate, a supposedly ethical objective, we cannot ask that the Court do what is plainly forbidden or refrain from doing what is plainly commanded. Nor can we require it to essay a task that is inarguably beyond its power capacities: the Court cannot be expected to stop the tides from flowing, even though it might be good to stop them and even if the Constituion clearly authorized the issuance of such a command. To be sure there will always be critics who would denounce the Court for ruling that black is black, or failing to rule that black is white. But they are fortunately not yet a majority, and the real questions of evaluation arise in situations where the problem is to distinguish between a plausible and a less plausible historical-technical justification, a confident or a less confident estimate of the Court's power to effect its ends, and a greater or lesser belief in the value of those ends. Let us proceed to consider the Court's establishment-clause doctrines in those terms and in that order.

The discussion will be chiefly concerned with the decisions involving religion and the public schools—with the line of doctrine represented by the *Everson*,[7] *McCollum*[8] *Zorach*,[9] *Engel*,[10] and *Schempp*[11] decisions, although other cases bearing on this doctrinal development will be referred to when they seem germane. These school decisions are particularly appropriate for the kind of analysis proposed because they constitute a fairly well circumscribed package and raise sharp questions in all three of the judgment categories delineated above.

The story of the Court's performance in this area has been told so often and chewed over so much that it is unnecessary to do more than remind the reader of its outlines. The idea that the no establishment principle was applicable to the states by way of the Fourteenth Amendment was first seriously discussed by the Supreme Court in 1947, in *Everson*. Mr. Justice Black, for the majority, held that state payment of bus fares for parochial school students was a general welfare measure, not aid to religion. But before reaching that result he declared that actual state aid to

7. Everson v. Board of Educ., 330 U.S. 1 (1947).
8. Illinois *ex rel.* McCollum v. Board of Educ., 333 U.S. 203 (1948).
9. Zorach v. Clauson, 343 U.S. 306 (1952).
10. Engel v. Vitale, 370 U.S. 421 (1962).
11. School Dist. of Abington Township v. Schempp, 374 U.S. 203 (1963).

religion is indeed constitutionally forbidden; that no government in America "can pass laws which aid one religion, aid all religions, or prefer one religion over another."[12] This standard, literally applied, was quite enough to invalidate a religious instruction program conducted in public school buildings during school hours; and Black, for the Court, invoked it to strike down such a program in *McCollum*.

His opinion, however, emphasized certain factual circumstances —that the school buildings used for religious instruction were tax-supported and that the state was in a sense lending religion the coercive power of the compulsory education laws. This emphasis gave Mr. Justice Douglas an opening, albeit a very thin one, to hold for a new majority in *Zorach* that New York's "released time" religious instruction program was distinguishable from the arrangement condemned in *McCollum:* here tax-supported buildings were not being used and no coercion appeared on the record. Though not repudiating the unequivocal *Everson* standard quoted above, he proceeded to enunciate one that seems rationally irreconcilable with it: that state *encouragement* of and *cooperation* with religion is not state *aid,* that the difference between them is a question of degree, and that the question starts from the premise that "we are a religious people."[13] At this point then the Court was armed, as so often in the past, with two quite different constitutional yardsticks: the absolutist *Everson* standard forbidding all aid, and the pragmatic, "common sense" standard of *Zorach* permitting aid so long as it can be labeled encouragement or cooperation and so long as it does not exceed some undefined degree of state-church involvement. Both standards had been endorsed by a majority of the Court; neither had been nominally repudiated by a majority. The judges could take their choice between them when the next school religion case appeared.

The next important one was *Engel,* the school prayer decision; the majority, now again speaking through Justice Black, seem to have chosen in favor of the all-out *Everson* principle. Indeed, the opinion suggested a certain eagerness to reconfirm that principle,

12. 330 U.S. at 15.
13. 343 U.S. at 313.

whether or not the case required it. The Court explicitly refused to rest its judgment merely on the argument that the state-pre-scribed prayer was coercive, insisting that the "Establishment Clause . . . does not depend upon any showing of direct govern-mental compulsion."[14] And the only concession to *Zorach's* rela-tivism was a hint that patriotic ceremonies and hymns might still be allowed, even though they mention a supreme being, pre-sumably on the ground that their significance is primarily secular. The wall of separation now seemed nearly impassable once more, and Justice Douglas filed a puckish concurrence suggesting that observances like the supplications preceding sessions of the Su-preme Court and Congress were likewise unconstitutional govern-ment support of religion.

But a year later in *Schempp* the Court, though forbidding reci-tation of the Lord's Prayer and Bible-reading in public schools, again somewhat moderated the spirit, if not the actual letter, of its doctrine. The guiding principle, said Mr. Justice Clark for the Court, is that an enactment must have "a secular legislative pur-pose and a primary effect that neither advances nor inhibits re-ligion."[15] This might seem mere restatement of the *Everson* no-aid dogma, with the additional proviso that the Court is obliged to wrestle with the enigmatic distinction between primary and sec-ondary effects and to tread the "quicksands"[16] of legislative pur-pose before applying the dogma. But the proviso, precisely because of the slipperiness of those distinctions, may give the Court some leeway in judging practices that have a religious tinge.

Mr. Justice Brennan, who joined in both opinion and judgment, believed that the Court was still free to uphold provisions for army chaplains, invocational prayers in legislative bodies, non-devotional Bible study, tax exemptions for religious bodies, and other practices which do not import the dangers feared by the framers of the establishment clause. He even ventured "to suggest that the public schools present a unique problem,"[17] which at least

14. 370 U.S. at 430.
15. 374 U.S. at 222.
16. Pollak, *Foreword: Public Prayers in Public Schools*, 77 HARV. L. REV. 62, 67 (1963).
17. 374 U.S. at 294.

invites the inference that the no-aid principle could be construed less strictly outside the public school context. And Justices Goldberg and Harlan, also concurring in the Court's opinion, seemed to say that the establishment clause applied only to practices that have "meaningful and practical impact,"[18] that is, *de minimis non curat lex.*

It is true that these glosses do not appear plainly on Justice Clark's majority opinion, but the concurring justices seemed to believe they were compatible with it, and perhaps in some paralogical sense they are. If so the Court can be said to have reached in *Schempp* a position somewhere between the absolutism of *Engel* and the pragmatism of *Zorach.* The doctrine might be stated as follows: government action which "advances" religion is constitutionally objectionable if it creates in a substantial form the dangers the First Amendment was designed to prevent, unless its purpose and primary effect are secular or unless the effect of omitting the action would be to inhibit or discriminate against religion. A corollary point might be that the action will be viewed with special suspicion when it concerns the public schools, and with more latitude when only adults are involved.

Leaving aside for the moment, as far as possible, considerations of judicial power and ethical preference that usually intrude at this stage, how might this record of judicial doctrine-making be evaluated in historical-technical terms? Perhaps it can be agreed that the justification of a doctrine in this sense depends on two requirements: that it be plausibly based on constitutional language, intent, or custom; and that it be coherent enough for reasoned application, yet flexible enough so that it can be adapted to future and possibly unforeseen case situations.

The threshold question is whether the Court was warranted in grafting a broad disestablishment concept onto the Fourteenth Amendment in the first place. The only faintly relevant textual basis is the word "liberty" in the due process clause. This word would justify condemning a state-church involvement that directly infringed someone's religious liberty; but in that event the free exercise clause would invalidate the practice, and there would be

18. *Id.* at 308.

no need for the establishment clause at all. It requires a semantic leap to translate "liberty" into "disestablishment" when by definition the forbidden establishment need involve no restriction of the liberty of any individual.[19] As for the intent of the framers of the Fourteenth Amendment, it is hard indeed to find in the record convincing evidence that they had disestablishment in mind.[20] And even when that difficulty is hurdled we encounter the further one of determining whether the establishment clause of the First Amendment was itself designed to forbid anything more than government support of a particular religion in preference to others[21]—a far cry from the wide-ranging independent prohibition the modern Court seems agreed on.

The truth is that from neither constitutional text nor historical intent can we wring a positive mandate to the Court to outlaw non-discriminatory and non-compulsive state aid to religion, and even those who fervently endorse the broad disestablishment idea would be better off to admit this forthwith. As for precedent, since it has its effective beginning in the period under discussion, it can hardly be invoked as a basis for settling the discussion. Yet none of this is to say that the judicially arranged marriage between disestablishment and the Fourteenth Amendment is indefensible. If we ask not whether text and history require this union but whether they permit it, we get a very different answer. In the first place it is arguable that the framers of the establishment clause were aiming, not only at the direct encroachments on liberty which the free exercise clause would reach, but at the more ambiguous and indirect losses to liberty that may result from church-state involvement. The "dangers . . . the Framers feared,"[22] it might be contended, were the perversion of government to religion's ends, and

19. FREUND, THE SUPREME COURT OF THE UNITED STATES 58–59 (1961); Brown, *Quis Custodiet Ipsos Custodes?—The School Prayer Cases*, 1963 SUPREME COURT REV. 1, 27; Kauper, *Schempp and Sherbert: Studies in Neutrality and Accommodation*, 1963 RELIGION AND THE PUBLIC ORDER 3, 9 n.17.

20. CORWIN, A CONSTITUTION OF POWERS IN A SECULAR STATE 111–114 (1951); Fairman and Morison, *Does the Fourteenth Amendment Incorporate the Bill of Rights?* 2 STAN. L. REV. 5 (1949).

21. Murray, *Law or Prepossessions?* 14 LAW & CONTEMP. PROB. 23 (1949).

22. 374 U.S. at 295 (concurring opinion of Brennan, J.).

the consequent development of an atmosphere of persecutions and animosities which makes a free society impossible. Thus in this indirect sense the word "liberty" in the Fourteenth Amendment can be accommodated to the establishment clause's purpose without showing any specific threat to the freedom of a particular individual. And if such an interpretation is not precluded by examination of text and intent, the Court's license to adopt it is certified by the whole history of judicial review and the Fourteenth Amendment. From almost the first the Court has acted as if the due process clause had expressed a generalized desire that "liberty" be preserved and had authorized the judiciary to define and redefine the term as the future might seem to require; and the nation has acquiesced in this view of the matter. Surely it is too late to contend that an exercise of that function is unwarrantable, unless the new definition is plainly incompatible with the textual-historical record. A legal order that ingested substantive due process and the doctrine of the "corporation as person" need not strain unduly to swallow this morsel.

There appears, however, a formidable technical difficulty when the Court proceeds from this troublesome but perhaps allowable reinterpretation of "liberty" to the next step: to apply the doctrine to a concrete case. The difficulty is the problem of standing. Under orthodox principles only those whose rights have been infringed by a law in some specialized measurable way can challenge the law's constitutionality. A citizen, however aggrieved, cannot rest his claim merely on "a political concern which belongs to us all."[23] If a state-ordained religious practice coerces John Doe directly his standing can be established with relative ease; but if such coercion is not present he cannot—under orthodox principles—challenge the practice because he shares a general interest in holding government to the path of constitutional rectitude. Thus a state law "establishing" religion would be unchallengeable, except as it coerced someone specific; in which case it could be challenged under the free exercise clause, and the establishment clause would

23. Coleman v. Miller, 307 U.S. 433, 464 (concurring opinion of Frankfurter, J.).

be superfluous.[24] The Court's declaration that the establishment clause imposes an independent restriction on government must therefore—unless it is judicially meaningless—imply some relaxation of the normal standard requirements; indeed, both *Engel* and *Schempp* confirm this, for parents were permitted to assert rights not based on any claim of direct coercion.

This departure from orthodoxy may strengthen the case against the policy, but it does not conclude it. To be sure, grave questions would be raised if the relaxation of standing requirements were universalized: if any citizen could, apart from direct personal interest, sue whenever he doubted the validity of a governmental act, the judicial system might be smothered by an avalanche of abstract questions.[25] But if we assume that the Court is merely carving out a limited exception to the usual requirements, an exception restricted to establishment-clause issues and perhaps even further only to those involving the public schools, the departure is not so unsettling. It has been hinted in the past that religious liberty may be in a preferred position, even among the "preferred freedoms."[26] If the judges so believe, then perhaps their control over the "case or controversy" standard is wide enough to license this modification of *Frothingham* v. *Mellon*.[27] Under the strict *Frothingham* doctrine a congressional appropriation of one million dollars to support the Presbyterian church[28] could not be judicially challenged, and in such an event the Court's commitment to the no-establishment principle would bump up against its own past interpretation of the "case or controversy" barrier. A single, limited breach in that barrier is not so great an irregularity as to be insufferable. Of course it is open to argument that the breach is not warranted by the alleged threat, that the good supposedly accomplished by reaching "pure" establishment laws does not justify straining the "case or controversy" requirement. But that is another matter.

24. Brown, *supra,* note 19, at 15–31.
25. But see Jaffe, *Standing To Secure Judicial Review: Public Actions,* 74 HARV. L. REV. 1265, 1311–1312 (1961).
26. See Murdock v. Pennsylvania, 319 U.S. 105 (1943).
27. 262 U.S. 447 (1923).
28. The hypothetical example is offered by Brown, *supra,* note 19, at 17

The historical-technical case for the broad no-establishment policy seems to fall somewhere between "must" and "must not." Whether nearer the one than the other will depend on how the reader assesses the historical record and how seriously he takes the orthodox standing requirements. But surely the Court has not wandered far from its traditional range of discretion. It was certainly not bound by constitutional imperatives to reach this result, but neither was it strongly precluded from doing so. The next question is whether the judicially prescribed standards for implementing the policy are themselves justifiable in historical-technical terms. Here the initial difficulty is that the Court has prescribed not one standard but three: the flat and almost unqualified no-aid principle of *Engel;* the pragmatic, tolerant, question-of-degree approach of *Zorach;* and the elaborate compromise between these positions that seems to emerge from the multiple opinions in *Schempp.* As with the broader question just canvassed, history provides only general guidance to one who would choose among them, or rather it sets very broad boundaries within which choice may range. It is indeed doubtful that the New York Regents' Prayer "would have sent the Pilgrims to a stern and rockbound coast"[29] or that most of the framers of either the First or Fourteenth Amendments would have been repelled by school Bible-reading. Yet there is force in Mr. Justice Brennan's point in *Schempp* that "a too literal quest for the advice of the Founding Fathers" is "futile and misdirected,"[30] that the more fruitful inquiry is whether practices "threaten those consequences which the Framers deeply feared," that is, the "interdependence between religion and state which the First Amendment was designed to prevent."[31] But once we accept this not unreasonable conception of the inquiry we are free to roam widely among our prepossessions in deciding what does or does not threaten those consequences. Except at the extremes, it is hard to say that the Court is either right or wrong in condemning a practice on the ground that it threatens the dangers the First

29. Sutherland, *Establishment According to Engel,* 76 HARV. L. REV. 25, 36 (1962).
30. 374 U.S. at 237.
31. *Id.* at 236.

Amendment was designed to prevent. The more ponderable question is whether the tests the Court has offered us to identify such practices achieve—quite apart from their historical justification—the blending of coherence and flexibility requisite for a viable judicial standard.

Neither the strict no-aid principle of *Everson* and *Engel* nor the relativistic non-principle of *Zorach* seems satisfactory in these terms. The first has the appearance of coherence and predictability when it is stated boldly: no-aid means no aid and that is that. But thus stated it is so inflexible that it could not even be adhered to in the two opinions themselves. Justice Black felt obliged to admit an exception for "the benefits of public welfare legislation"[32] in *Everson* and for "patriotic or ceremonial occasions"[33] in *Engel,* though neither exception is compatible with the no-aid standard if that standard simply means what it says. On the other hand, the *Zorach* principle is flexible to the point of flaccidity. Although the opinion states that the First Amendment "studiously defines"[34] the specific barriers to state-church involvement, Justice Douglas provides no clue except "common sense" to help discover those studious definitions. It is hard to see how *Zorach* could provide any guidance at all to future reasoned adjudication.

In *Schempp,* however, the Court seemed to move toward a delineation that might be more promising. If we consider all the opinions, we detect an attempt to identify the criteria that merit consideration in an establishment-clause case: whether the practice has "meaningful and substantial impact"; whether the law is directly, purposefully, and primarily religious or secular; whether non-action would inhibit religious freedom; whether the persons affected by the practice are adults or children. To be sure, some of these questions may be ill-chosen; most of them involve a considerable element of subjectivity and require the Court to draw distinctions between more and less. But they may represent the end of the tendency to resolve the problem by absolutist statements or by sheer intuition and the beginning of an effort to

32. 330 U.S. at 16.
33. 370 U.S. at 435 n.21.
34. 343 U.S. at 312.

canalize the judgment process by identifying the factors that are relevant to its distinctions of degree. This would be a first, important step toward rational, yet flexible, adjudication standards. The next step is to articulate the factors more explicitly and to clear up such uncertainties as those left dangling by the bare pronouncements about standing. We may chide the Court for its tardiness in embarking on this course; but better late than never.

I turn now from the historical-technical question to the question of power. The literature of law, history, and political science contains very little systematic treatment of the nature and range of Supreme Court power, which is curious considering the interest of contemporary social scientists in power analysis[35] and the special application of such analysis to subjects like local government, the presidency, and foreign affairs.[36] No doubt this is partly explained by the long survival of Hamilton's old idea that the judiciary has neither force nor will, which survival is in turn explained by reluctance to acknowledge that the Court is a governing agency, facing some of the power problems that governors always face. There is a persistent feeling that it is somehow improper to ask whether the Court has the power to do a thing, as distinguished from the question whether it has the right to do it. Lord Milner was expressing this feeling in a different connection when he said in 1909, with respect to the House of Lords: "If we believe a thing to be bad, and if we have a right to prevent it, it is our duty to try to prevent it and to damn the consequences."[37]

There is reason to suspect that the justices of the Supreme Court have sometimes taken more account of consequences than Lord Milner and his American counterparts would approve. One thinks of Marshall's wariness after 1803,[38] of *Ex parte McCardle*,[39] of

35. *E.g.*, LASSWELL & KAPLAN, POWER AND SOCIETY (1950); Riker, *Some Ambiguities in the Notion of Power*, 58 AM. POL. SCI. REV. 341 (1964); Simon, *Notes on the Observation and Measurement of Political Power*, 15 J. POLITICS 500 (1953).

36. *E.g.*, BANFIELD, POLITICAL INFLUENCE (1961); NEUSTADT, PRESIDENTIAL POWER: THE POLITICS OF LEADERSHIP (1960); Ash, *An Analysis of Power, With Special Reference to International Politics*, 3 WORLD POLITICS 218 (1951).

37. OXFORD DICTIONARY OF QUOTATIONS 339 (1962).

38. 3 BEVERIDGE, THE LIFE OF JOHN MARSHALL 176–178 (1919).

39. 7 Wall. 506 (1869).

the "switch in time" in 1937; and of other occasions when discretion may have moderated valor. But in its official rhetoric the Court has usually felt obliged to ignore such matters, to cloak its awareness of them under euphemisms like the doctrine of political questions; or at most to utter broad generalities to the effect that no court has power to cure all the republic's major social ills,[40] or that judicial default of duty can weaken the law's power no less than judicial rashness.[41] Such statements are unexceptionable, but they are truisms that underline the power problem rather than resolve it. These conventions of judicial discourse are, and probably ought to be, unalterable: judicial opinions that articulated a calculus of power would be ludicrous and self-defeating. But even those outside the Court, bound by no such conventions, have been slow to press the appraisal much further. Although there is a growing body of empirical studies that should ultimately provide raw material for a better understanding of the Court's power,[42] analytic generalizations about the subject have been few and have, naturally enough, focused more on the Court of the past than the Court of the present.[43] These deficiencies cannot be wholly repaired here, if only because of limited space and time. But it seems both possible and worthwhile to set down a few observations that may improve perspectives on the power question and make it

40. Reynolds v. Sims, 377 U.S. 533, 589 (dissenting opinion of Harlan, J.).
41. Bell v. Maryland, 378 U.S. 226, 242 (concurring opinion of Douglas, J.).
42. See, *e.g.*, MURPHY, CONGRESS AND THE COURT (1962); PELTASON, 58 LONELY MEN: SOUTHERN FEDERAL JUDGES AND SCHOOL SEGREGATION (1961); Patric, *The Impact of a Court Decision: Aftermath of the McCollum Case*, 6 J. PUB. L. 455 (1957); Sorauf, *Zorach* v. *Clauson: The Impact of a Supreme Court Decision*, 53 AM. POL. SCI. REV. 777 (1959); Westin, *The Supreme Court, the Populist Movement and the Campaign of 1896*, 15 J. POLITICS 3 (1953); Note, *Congressional Reversal of Supreme Court Decisions: 1945–1957*, 71 HARV. L. REV. 1324 (1958).
43. In addition to the works cited in note 42 *supra*, see PELTASON, FEDERAL COURTS IN THE POLITICAL PROCESS (1955); PRITCHETT, CONGRESS VERSUS THE SUPREME COURT 1957–60 (1961); Dahl, *Decision-Making in a Democracy: The Supreme Court as a National Policy-Maker*, 6 J. PUB. L. 279 (1957); Latham, *The Supreme Court and the Supreme People*, 16 J. POLITICS 207 (1954); Mendelson, *Judicial Review and Party Politics*, 12 VAND. L. REV. 447 (1959); Roche, *Judicial Self-Restraint*, 49 AM. POL. SCI. REV. 762 (1955); and MURPHY, ELEMENTS OF JUDICIAL STRATEGY (1964), by far the most thorough discussion to date of the Supreme Court and the power question.

easier to appraise the Court's establishment-clause decisions in these terms.

To begin with, it is desirable to dissipate some of the ambiguities usually involved in a statement that the Court has, or has not, the power to get others to comply with its wish. One of these ambiguities is suggested when we inquire who those others are. The problem is that the Court's direct commands usually issue to a very special group of persons in a very special context, to lower court judges or, at one remove, to the litigants in a particular dispute, for example. These are "others" over whom the Court's influence, though not unlimited,[44] is obviously considerable. If we restrict ourselves to this level in assessing Court power, the inquiry is relatively simple. But the matter attains another dimension when we consider how the Court's pronouncements affect those outside the ambit of a specific litigation, for example, the school board in a district where no case has been brought, the legislator who may be contemplating an aid to religion program. Common sense suggests that the Court's power to obtain this general compliance with a given policy may be less than its power to control the results of a particular case, and it is important to be clear which idea of "others" we have in mind when we make an assertion about the Court's power capabilities.

Secondly, there are certain ambiguities in the notion of "compliance." The notion seems at first blush simple enough: a command issues and the "others" commanded either do or do not obey. But a little reflection reveals that the matter is more complicated than that. Even within the framework of formal litigation there can be disparities between the Court's mandate, fairly interpreted, and the actual result: lower courts may respond sluggishly or use the flexibility inherent in the remand process to reinterpret the mandate; litigants may take advantage of the law's delays and complexities to postpone and evade, even though they do not actually defy, the Court's behest.[45] Moreover, insofar as we think of

44. See Murphy, *Lower Court Checks on Supreme Court Power*, 53 AM. POL. SCI. REV. 1017 (1959).

45. Note, *State Court Evasion of United States Supreme Court Mandates*, 56 YALE L. J. 574 (1947).

the Court as seeking results beyond the formal limits of litigation, other possibilities appear. Response may take the form of enthusiastic cooperation, grudging submission, partial compliance, stubborn inaction, or defiance, and it may well simultaneously take one form in one section of the country and another elsewhere. Nor do the complications end there. So far we have been talking as if the responses to the Court's action were limited to a range between obedience and disobedience, but there is another possibility that transcends this range: political retaliation. It is quite possible to imagine a situation in which all those subject to a Court mandate might dutifully obey, but then mount a political counterattack designed to impair the whole basis of judicial authority. An observer might say with perfect truth that the Court possesses the power to obtain compliance with the mandate, but his statement would be misleading unless it reckoned the cost of obtaining the compliance; for the result of that reckoning might reveal a net power loss. Furthermore, while costs are being considered it is important to recognize that they may be cumulative. The Court may have the power to exact obedience to policy A and the prestige to withstand the resulting retaliatory backlash; but if it concurrently seeks to enforce policies B, C, and D, the force of the backlash may be augmented to a point where costs become prohibitive and even policy A becomes unfeasible. At the same time it should be recognized that the possibility of backlash implies its own opposite; resistance and retaliation from some quarters may tend to restrict the Court's power, but support from other quarters may simultaneously augment it.

One who is interested in adding up pro and con forces and judging the balance between them should bear in mind that not all potential supporters and defenders are of identical weight. Congress itself is the most dangerous foe because of its ultimate authority over such vital matters as appellate jurisdiction. It is also, of course, an invaluable ally. The president's acquiescence or positive support is essential to the enforcement of many judicial policies. His enmity is not in itself fatal, as Franklin Roosevelt learned, but it is not to be taken lightly. History suggests that an individual state government, or even a cluster of them, is no match for the

Court's prestige unless the sympathy of Congress or the president can be enlisted. Other public and private forces—the press, pressure groups, distinguished individuals, for example—will vary in weight depending on the intensity of their pro or con commitments and, again, on their capacity to influence congressional or presidential attitudes.

Much of this is simply to say that the Court's power is not entirely its own, that its capability depends in part on a preponderance of friends over enemies. This lineup, of course, varies somewhat from time to time and from issue to issue depending on whose oxen are being gored; but there are some secular trends that may have special significance for the modern Court. One of them is obvious enough, although its importance in this connection has not been widely remarked. Since 1937 the Court has to a considerable degree lost its most faithful historical ally, the conservative business-legal community.[46] Of course the modern Court, while losing old friends, has acquired new ones, but it remains to be seen if it has gained or lost—in power terms—by the exchange.

A final point is not unrelated: it is arguable that the modern Court stands in a novel relation to the American body politic, and that historically derived views about the range of judicial power are no longer reliable. The difference is not merely that the Old Court protected economic liberty and the New Court protects "humanistic" values like free speech, fair trial, and racial equality, although that difference is significant. Nor is it merely that the modern Court has more or less frankly acknowledged that it is a policy-making body, rather than the "powerless symbol of justice"[47] of historical myth, although that too may be important. There is another, less obvious, distinction that merits attention, a difference in the nature of what the historical Court and the modern Court have tried to accomplish. In a word, the Old Court usually tried to preserve the cake of custom; the New Court has been trying to break it. To put the matter in another way, the

---

46. BICKEL, *supra*, note 4, at 75.
47. MASON & BEANEY, THE SUPREME COURT IN A FREE SOCIETY 317 (1959).

Court of the past characteristically told people they must continue to do what they were accustomed to doing; the Court of today more often tells them they must *not* continue their accustomed ways, but must on the contrary do something else.[48] Plainly, the justices have conceived of themselves in the last decade as one of the chief initiative-supplying agencies in American government.[49] It seems probable that it is harder to compel people to break with their customs than it is to prevent them from doing so, and any appraisal of the modern Court's power problem should take account of this probability.

With these general considerations in mind, what can be said about the establishment-clause decisions and the question of judicial power? No very specialized knowledge is required to convince us that both the compliance problem and the backlash problem are substantial in this field. Any prohibition declared by the Court will be regarded by some as anti-religious and will awaken the spirit of piety from its usual Sunday-to-Sunday repose. Most Americans, though often secular enough in their weekday behavior, are accustomed to what Veblen called "devout observances" in public life; and they may be surprised and displeased to be told by the Court that these usages are at war with our constitutional tradition. Though it is very difficult to measure accurately the impact of a Supreme Court decision, evidence suggests that the *McCollum* rule against use of school buildings for religious instruction was

---

48. Marshall's Court was an arguable exception to these generalizations about Courts of the past. Certainly he would have liked to shake America out of its localist preconceptions and stimulate a bolder use of national power. But his commands to the states in such fields as the contract clause were largely negative, *i.e.*, they did not call on those affected to take affirmative action, as the modern desegregation and apportionment decisions do. And his decisions on the commerce clause and the necessary and proper clause offered the national government the opportunity to act nationally but did not require it to do so. In fact, of course, the invitation was not accepted in Marshall's lifetime.

49. " 'Our judges are not monks or scientists,' the Chief Justice wrote in 1955, 'but participants in the living stream of our national life, steering the law between the dangers of rigidity on the one hand and formlessness on the other . . .' As Thurman Arnold has observed, the Court under Chief Justice Warren, is becoming 'unified,' 'a Court of inspired choice and policy . . . rather than a Court of law as we used to know it.' " MASON & BEANEY, *supra*, note 47, at 318.

frequently ignored—"estimates of non-compliance ran from 15 per cent up to 40 and 50 per cent in some states."[50] I have found no comparable estimates of non-compliance with the prayer and Bible-reading prohibition, but considering the furor it aroused the response has probably been somewhat similar. As for backlash, the evidence is fresh and vivid. Within a few weeks after *Engel,* more than fifty proposals for constitutional amendments had been introduced in Congress; and the Court was denounced in journal and pulpit.[51] The *Schempp* decision produced a more mixed reaction, and influential voices were heard defending the Court and opposing the Becker amendment, which would override both *Engel* and *Schempp.*[52] Nevertheless, the House Judiciary Committee was in June 1964 still seriously considering the Becker proposal; and the 1964 Republican platform called for an amendment permitting religious exercises in "public places" so long as they were non-coercive and not state-prescribed.[53] Congress cut the salary increase for Supreme Court justices from $7,500 to $4,500, though other federal judges received the full $7,500 raise; the vote was attributed to congressional resentment over the prayer decisions, among others.[54] This last event, petty in itself, illustrates what was said above about the tendency of the backlash threat to be cumulative. The prayer issue alone was probably not enough to alienate more than a minority of congressmen, but with their number augmented by others disturbed about racial desegregation, apportionment, criminal procedures, or obscenity, a hostile majority could be formed. The more serious threat of the Dirksen-Mansfield

50. Sorauf, *supra,* note 42, at 784.
51. Sutherland, *supra,* note 29, at 50; Pollak, *W.B.R.: Some Reflections,* 71 YALE L. J. 1451, 1455–1456 n.17 (1962).
52. Spokesmen for the National Council of Churches, the Baptists, Lutherans, Presbyterians, Seventh-Day Adventists, Unitarians, and the United Church of Christ made declarations opposing the proposal; N.Y. Times, May 23, 1964, p. 22. The legal department of the National Catholic Welfare Conference advised Catholics to be "very cautious" about supporting proposals of this sort; N.Y. Times, June 23, 1964, p. 2. "223 Constitutional lawyers, including the deans of 55 law schools" petitioned Congress not to tamper with the Bill of Rights; N.Y. Herald Tribune, June 10, 1964, p. 22.
53. 110 CONG. REC. 16025 (daily ed. July 22, 1964). There is some reason to doubt that an amendment so worded would be incompatible with present Court doctrines.
54. N.Y. Times, Aug. 9, 1964, §4, p. 8E, col. 1.

amendment to stay court action in reapportionment cases was also felt to represent a reaction to multiple provocations.[55]

Since compliance is likely to be at best only partial and the backlash threat seems substantial, a cautious judiciary might have preferred to leave the religious-establishment issue severely alone and devote itself to more tractable and less dangerous tasks. Alternatively, the Court might have confined its rulings to religious practices that involved an element of coercion—an invasion of religious liberty.[56] Perhaps such a narrowing of the implications would diminish the backlash threat. But it would also, as Louis Pollak has pointed out, reduce the likelihood that the practices would be generally abandoned; for they would presumably be valid until challenged, and school boards would be "under no discernible legal obligation, as they assuredly now are, to suspend ongoing . . . programs on their own initiative."[57] In short, this approach, though lessening backlash, would also lessen the incidence of compliance with the policy against public religious practices. At any rate the Court has chosen to extend its reach to situations which are not directly coercive, and the practical question is how its various doctrines in pursuance of that choice should be evaluated in power terms.

The relativist doctrine of *Zorach* might at first appear to tax the Court's power capacities the least, but appearances are notoriously deceptive. Of course this doctrine would excite little anti-judicial feeling if it were always applied permissively as in *Zorach* itself. To quote Pollak again, "few major interest groups are deeply committed antagonists of official prayer."[58] But presumably a time

55. See Lewis, *Congress vs. the Court—Issue Joined on Redistricting*, N.Y. Times, Aug. 16, 1964, §4, p. E3. "What is about to be tested is whether the recent line of Supreme Court decisions protecting individual liberty has offended public opinion so much that the political forces arrayed against the apportionment decision will be able to limit or overcome it. On the answer depends not only a good measure of the states' future political makeup but the great role of the Supreme Court in the American system of government" (col. 8).

56. Paul Freund suggested that this would enable the Court "to put to one side all the problems of state aid on which feelings are now running high, and to limit the decision to the context of the school room." Quoted by Pollak, *supra*, note 16, at 70.

57. *Ibid.*

58. *Id.* at 62.

would come when considerations of degree would lead to a restrictive application, and in such event the Court might be disarmed by its own doctrine from defending itself adequately. The trouble with a completely relativist doctrine is that it gives the community no notice of what to expect and provides the Court with no legalistic refuge from its adversaries. It is a confession that cases are decided by purely subjective judicial hunches, and it invites an outraged citizen to question whether the hunches of nine men in Washington should be more binding than his own.

On the other hand, it seems possible that the strict no-aid principle of *Engel* would strain judicial power to something near the breaking point. Compliance with such an absolutist prohibition might be extremely spotty, and it is unhealthy for Court prestige that its policies be widely flouted. If the Court undertook to wipe out religious services in government hospitals and prisons, tax exemption for religious contributions, use of "In God We Trust" on coins, chaplains' salaries for Congress and for the armed forces, and all the other tradition-encrusted "aids" to religion that honeycomb our system, the retaliatory uprising in Congress and elsewhere is easy to imagine. A Court insistent on such a standard might gravely impair its power to govern in other areas as well as this one.

The more qualified and balanced doctrine that was beginning to take shape in *Schempp* seems more viable in power terms. To be sure, the assault on the Court for its "anti-religious" rulings continues as of this writing, but this merely confirms what has already been said—that public religious practices present a tender issue which a timid Court might elect not to prod at all. Having elected otherwise, a justice might nevertheless find a moral in the contrast between the reaction to *Engel* and the reaction to *Schempp*. No doubt the difference can in part be explained by the fact that *Schempp,* unlike *Engel,* was no surprise; and that the case against such practices in the schools had been canvassed in public debate during the interval between the two holdings. It turned out that some allies could be found to mitigate the thrust of the policy's adversaries. But it is also important that the decision carefully closed only the doors it meant to close, that it spelled out some reasoned exceptions to the no-aid barrier and hinted—especially in the concurrences—that there might be more. The way seems open for the development of a moderate but meaningful doctrine based on articulated judgment factors. The advantage of this, as has been well said in another connection, is "to focus the attention of all concerned on actualities and away from the never-never land of private, and perhaps unconscious, preconceptions."[59] No such balanced explication will sway those whose preconceptions are immovable or whose anti-judicial spirit is chiefly grounded on opposition to the Court's policy in quite different fields. Senator Eastland is probably unpersuadable. But a doctrine like this provides the best chance of maximizing results and minimizing cost in a situation that is at best fraught with risks for the judicial power.

The normative validity of the Court's aims in this field is our next concern. Disregarding for the moment the issue of historical-technical justification and the issue of power, how "good" are the policies the Court seeks to enforce—or, to turn the query around, how grave are the "evils" it seeks to correct? This matter is the one most difficult to judge with any semblance of objectivity. In spite of the proverb, what's sauce for the goose is often not sauce for the gander; this may not resign us to complete solipsism, but it moderates confidence about one's own "can't helps" and even more about one's abilities of persuasion in the realm of ethics.

Whether or not there exists some comprehensive and infallible system for dispelling such difficulties, no attempt will be made to present one here. At some point each of us will claim the right to his own peremptory dogmas. But there are perhaps a few things that can be said to those who are willing to postpone that point while they are making up their minds about the ethic of the establishment-clause decisions.

For one thing it serves little purpose to talk as if the evil against which the decisions are aimed is a seventeenth-century theocracy or the threat of pogroms or wars of religion. This is not the seventeenth century, nor even the eighteenth: America is not John Calvin's Geneva; it is in no peril from a new Inquisition or a new

59. Mendelson, *The First Amendment and the Judicial Process: A Reply to Mr. Frantz,* 17 VAND. L. REV. 479, 482 (1964).

Pilgrimage of Grace. The state-church involvements that the decisions touch upon are much less dramatic and horrendous: marginal relief from the financial burdens of parochial school attendance, a nudging of moppets in the direction of religious instruction classes, a modest amount of classroom praying and Bible-reading. This is not the stuff from which crusades and martyrs are made.

On the other hand, neither does it forward the discussion much to contend that such involvements are not noxious at all. They can, however slightly, entail results that most of us recognize as harmful. A child may feel to an extent coerced toward religiosity by a released-time program and toward a particular sectarian commitment by the classroom reading of the Lord's Prayer. He may be offended by the King James Bible, and his parents may be offended by the thought that their tax money or their government is supporting a religion they do not avow. Equally important, although a policy of judicial laissez-faire about such matters would not expose us to religious civil war, it might affect the political process regrettably. Religion has a special propensity to stir emotions and breed animosities when it becomes a subject of political controversy—ills that may be precluded if the organic law simply forbids the state to enact any laws respecting religion.

A rejoinder to all this might be that laws almost always coerce or offend someone and that most political questions are controversial by definition. Everyone endures some coercion he would like to avoid, sees his tax money used for policies that offend him, because the community has decided that the case for the policies is weightier than his objections. But of course the argument is that coercion in matters of religious belief is especially objectionable, that offenses to sensibilities are in this area especially exacerbating, that disagreement over religion is especially likely to embitter the political process and divert the community from its other common concerns. Perhaps the state can never altogether avoid these encroachments and diversions. Some of its secular policies may incidentally burden religion, as in the case of conscription laws. It must then choose whether or not to relieve these burdens by providing chaplain service and granting religious exemptions, and in either event consciences will be wounded and passions aroused.

The price must be paid to gain the secular end. But a religious law for a religious end can find no such external justification. It offends one religious conscience in the name of another, and unless we concede that some men's religious consciences are more worthy of the government's aid and comfort than others, we must find this blameworthy. Nor is such a law vindicated by the contention that it employs religious means to a secular end, that is, the development of a moral citizenry which will in turn produce a just and happy society. For whatever tendency the means have to accomplish that end may be canceled by their simultaneous tendency to generate the bitterness that makes such a society difficult.

Unless they are warranted by a secular purpose or by the need to avoid burdening religious freedom, all laws and state practices aiding religion seem to some degree objectionable. This verdict, as far as it goes, applies to the school prayers and Bible-reading in *Engel* and *Schempp* and to the religious instruction programs of *McCollum,* or for that matter *Zorach.* But having determined this (or having assumed it for the sake of the argument) we have not settled the evaluative issue. "Bad" like "good" is an adjective that can be compared. And even if we grant that these laws blemish our polity, it is hard to contend that the disfigurement is a very great one. School instruction programs and released-time programs may coerce some a little; they do not in themselves coerce many very much. The praying and Bible-reading involved in *Schempp* seem even less constraining; and the compulsiveness of *Engel's* Regents' Prayer is hardly visible to the naked eye. As for the tendency of such practices to embitter and distort political discourse, that threat too, though not imaginary, seems relatively mild.

My point is not that these injuries and dangers are negligible, but that they fall rather low on the scale of evils in our imperfect world. I am of course aware that judgments like these are ultimately subjective. Even the merest hint of coercion may seem insufferable to the extremely sensitive or timid; even a trace of religiosity in public life may offend some past all bearing. But most would admit that there is no comparison between the wrong of the Regents' Prayer and other wrongs that currently exercise our judicial system: racial discrimination in school and polling booth;

the "rationing" of criminal justice; arbitrary censorship of art and thought—to name only three. To be sure, it can be argued that the Regents' Prayer is a first step toward more palpable outrages to come. But this only means that we must be prepared to alter our estimate of evil when alteration is called for. It does not convert the prayer requirement itself into a serious present danger.

The final stage in this evaluative process is to reunite the categories which have so far been, for analytic purposes, kept artificially separate; to essay some synthetic judgments based on a summary view of the historical-technical, power, and value questions. Taking them all into account, how well has the Court performed in the establishment-clause field. What prescriptions are indicated for handling the subject in the future?

On the basis of power and value considerations taken together, a strong case could be made for judicial avoidance of the whole issue of state aid to religion, at least for the time being. The subject seems peculiarly well calculated to generate resistance and backlash and peculiarly ill calculated to enlist adequate countervailing support. Congressmen feel that defending prayer is like defending motherhood: it wins them some votes and costs them almost none. If the evil aimed at by the Court was a great one, this expenditure of judicial power might not be excessive. But the evil in its present manifestations is fairly moderate. Even so, judicial correction of it might be warranted if there were not other, graver wrongs simultaneously pressing for judicial attention and taxing the power capacities of the Court. But when we take into account that there are those other wrongs, the price of dealing with this one may seem very dear.

How much one worries about the prospect of these impairments depends on how near one thinks the Court of today is to the limits of its practical power. Those who believe that its potential is still not strained, that it has large unexpected reserves to call on, will shrug such apprehensions off; if their belief is correct, they are right to do so. But confidence on that score is open to question in the light of modern circumstances. The Court of present times has assumed a more creative place in American government than any of its predecessors; it has undertaken to defend a galaxy of values very different from those defended by Courts of the past; it has cast off its traditional "constituency," the business community. We cannot be sure about the net effect of all this, but we should at least consider the hypothesis that this highly ambitious Court is also proportionately vulnerable.

There have been some signs that anti-judicial sentiment may develop more readily today than it has usually done in the past. One such omen was the near-enactment in 1958 of a bill which would have seriously undermined Court authority by forbidding it to strike down state laws on "federal pre-emption" grounds.[60] The pettish discrimination against the Court in the salary bill of 1964 seems to be another. The congressional move to stay reapportionment judgments is one more. In short, evidence suggests that, although the Court has not yet passed the combustion point, it may be coming close to it. If so, the judiciary might have been better off to ignore such public religious observances as these and to husband itself for the tasks that matter more. It would not have baffled judicial ingenuity to keep the doctrinal way open for the time when a really malign establishment law might be presented —leaving the hot potato alone until then.

Such a policy of judicial self-restraint might be best if we were back in pre-*Everson* days and could foresee the manifold judicial

---

60. See MURPHY, *supra*, note 42, at 91, 193–223; PRITCHETT, *supra*, note 43, at 35–40. Although these two scholarly volumes have treated the 1958 counterattack in considerable detail, it seems fair to say that the incident has been inadequately noticed by even the informed public. Because only one of the "anti-court" bills considered in the summer of 1958 was actually passed, Pritchett is reassured about the modern Court's capacity to withstand such threats. That is one way to look at it. But the anti-pre-emption bill passed the House easily and was defeated in the Senate by only one vote. That such a mischievous measure could come so close to passage is the remarkable—and perhaps ominous—fact. The trouble is that, although we are accustomed to talk loosely about the "prestige" of the Court, we know very little about its nature or about what causes it to ebb and flow. I would suggest that when we use the term we usually have two somewhat different things in mind: the pro-judicial opinion that derives from approval of the Court's specific recent policy trends, and the pro-judicial opinion that rests on a belief in the value of the judicial institution, quite apart from the question of how that institution is currently behaving. Obviously the first variety is less constant and dependable than the second, and it would be useful (though perhaps impossible) for purposes of prediction to know what proportion of the Court's "prestige" at any given time is to be attributed to each.

problems of the 1950's and 1960's. But perfect foresight cannot be expected, and the judicial clock is hard to reverse. Once the Court decided, as it did in *Everson,* to subject state aid to judicial supervision it lost the option of complete forbearance, and the question was how best to handle the job to which it was now committed. Some insight into this matter may be achieved when the historical-technical dimension is added to the power and value factors that have just been discussed. When a Court elects to deal with a subject that may tax judicial power, it is prudent to ground itself on the firmest possible constitutional base. The firmer that base, the stronger the Court's claim to legitimacy for its mandates; the stronger that claim, the greater the Court's power capacities. A solid historical-technical justification will not mellow the wrath of a policy's really determined opponents, but it will weaken their arguments and decrease their capacity to enlist anti-judicial allies. In this field, it seems clear, the most convincing historical-technical case can be made for a holding that a state-aid program directly infringes personal liberty; for liberty is specifically named in the due process clause, and such a holding would require no distortion of orthodox standing requirements. Moreover, the value served by such a holding is one most of us would regard as precious and clear-cut. With a certain regard for the principle of *de minimis* the Court, having chosen to supervise state aid, might have been wiser to limit itself to cases challenging programs on individual freedom grounds.

To suggest that this course would have been wiser is not to contend that the argument for it is overwhelming, or that there is nothing to be said for the Court's chosen policy of bringing all religious aid within immediate judicial reach. That policy strains constitutional language and intent and disrupts orthodox procedural understandings, but it is not wholly unwarrantable in view of the Court's traditional, creative attitude toward constitutional interpretation. It helps to augment the contemporary drain on judicial power resources, but it does not plainly deplete those resources disastrously. The wrongs it aims at are not the worst we face, but they are wrongs nonetheless. With respect to each of these evaluative categories, I think the case against the policy is somewhat stronger than the case for it and that the cumulative appraisal falls on the negative side. Another might assess each category differently or assign them different relative weights. As I said earlier, these three judgment components provide no ready-made answers; they provide only channels within which our personal evaluative inquiries can proceed.

At any rate, the judges have not confined themselves to the boundaries here recommended and quite evidently have no intention of doing so. The remaining inquiry, then, is whether the Court has performed as well as it might have even within its chosen terrain. Very little can be said for the absolutist doctrine of *Everson* and *Engel* or the indefinite relativism of *Zorach*. The strict no-aid principle, coupled with an open door on the matter of standing and with no respect for the notion of *de minimis,* would plunge the judiciary into an endless, dangerous, and largely fruitless crusade against minor evils and deprive constitutional law of the flexibility that is one of its primary attributes. The *Zorach* doctrine, insofar as it can be called one, forsakes the juristic virtues of coherence and predictability and leaves the Court's flanks unguarded for the future. As for the judicial oscillation between these two approaches from 1947 to 1962, this seemed to offer the worst of both worlds and can hardly be regarded as a model policy.

Since the Court feels that it must oversee state-aid practices, the *Schempp* case—in its opinions but not necessarily in its result—comes nearest to achieving a viable position. If the implications of the several opinions are followed up, we can envision a set of standards elastic enough to give the judicial process some leeway, coherent enough to provide some guidance, and discriminating enough to distinguish between real and trivial wrongs. The concept of *de minimis,* which Mr. Justice Black seemed to extinguish out of hand in *Engel,* flickered a little in *Schempp;* and this concept alone, duly applied, would spare the Court gratuitous self-inflicted wounds in the state-aid field. The implied tolerance for religious enactments designed to protect freedom of worship—for example, provisions for army chaplains—would serve the same purpose and would help maintain a sensible balance among democratic values. The intimation that there may be a constitutionally significant difference between observances affecting adults and those affecting children suggests another basis for separating bad from less bad, and for circumscribing the arena of conflict with the political branches of government.

The distinction between a law that is directly, primarily, or purposefully religious and one that is not has its difficulties. Judicial experience in other fields with the notion of directness and with legislative motive is not reassuring. But the problem of determining whether or not a law's primary thrust is religious, though not subject to precise solution, would at least direct judicial attention toward realities and away from prepossessions.

No doubt other and better-thought-through criteria can be devised.[61] One of the recurrent lessons of judicial history is that the first, quick thoughts about constitutional doctrine are seldom the best, that viable standards must be evolved step by step as the complexities of a subject unfold, that unnecessarily sweeping pro-

---

61. Kurland suggests that the concept of "neutrality" will resolve the Court's decisional problems in this field: "The freedom and separation clauses should be read as stating a single precept: that government cannot utilize religion as a standard for action or inaction because these clauses, read together as they should be, prohibit classification in terms of religion either to confer a benefit or to impose a burden"; KURLAND, RELIGION AND THE LAW 112 (1961). I am inclined to agree that this principle, taken alone, would impose too rigid a standard; see Konvitz, *The Constitution or Neutral Principles,* 1963 RELIGION AND THE PUBLIC ORDER 99; Sherbert v. Verner, 374 U.S. 398, 422 (dissenting opinion of Harlan, J.). But as one factor, among others, in evaluating a religious law, the criterion could be viable and relevant. Kauper finds that *Schempp* and *Sherbert* yield the ideas of "accommodation" and "involvement" to modify and supplement a presumption in favor of "neutrality"; Kauper, *supra,* note 19. Though, as he says, these terms do not in themselves carry us very far, they point toward the kind of factors that must be considered when "balancing interests in arriving at responsible judgment"; *id.* at 39.

Another commentator proposes as principles of interpretation: "(1) The function of the Constitution is to exclude calculation of religious values, be they motives for deceit, or aid, or violation of statutes. (2) The Constitution also prevents the formulating or examining of the possible private ways of acting on religious beliefs"; Weiss, *Privilege, Posture and Protection: "Religion" in the Law,* 73 YALE L. J. 593, 619 (1964). The point of this paper has been that it is relatively easy to compose a formula that is coherent and internally consistent, or unlikely to overstrain the Court's power to command, or in accord with plausible value premises. The great difficulty is to construct one that takes account of all three of these desiderata. The variant analyses cited may all add layers to our understanding of the matter, however; and they suggest how important it is to let judgment ripen in judicial and scholarly discussion rather than to seize upon the first tidy absolute that comes to mind.

nouncements generate more political heat than legal light. This precept has been confirmed once more by modern experience with the establishment-clause cases. Perhaps there is reason to hope that the Court, while expanding and articulating the latent promises of *Schempp,* will not forget it again.

REFLECTIONS ON THE WARREN COURT*

[This article first appeared in the *Virginia Law Review*, 51, no. 7 (November 1965), 1229–1270.]

Anyone who studies government over a number of years notices that there are ups and downs in popular interest in his own pet branch of the subject. The march of events in the world of affairs casts shadows into libraries and seminar rooms. Belgium leaves the Congo and the Africanist, who has heretofore lived in tranquil solitude among his jujus and totems, suddenly finds his lore in popular demand. Castroism erupts in the Caribbean and universities, women's clubs, and government bureaus go hunting for scholars who "know something about Latin America." These bewildering variations in the intellectual stock exchange are doubtless inevitable in the policy-related sciences. Scholars distressed by such cycles might better have elected fields like medieval history or philology, where the market is presumably more stable.

Even a casual observer must realize that interest in the Supreme Court has been on an upswing during recent years. To the constitutional historian the boom is unmistakable. The *Index* of *The New York Times* listed 520 items (by rough count) under "Supreme Court" in the years 1949–1951; in 1962–1964 the number had climbed to 750. The *Public Affairs Information Service,* which indexes books and articles in learned and semi-learned periodicals, contained 51 entries under the same heading in its annual volumes for 1949–1951; the entries for 1962–1964 totalled 144, an increase of almost 200 per cent. No comparable figures are at hand to chart the rise of interest among students in colleges and universities, but an educated guess is that enrollment in constitutional law and history courses has kept pace with the increase in public concern. Surely not for many years, not at least

* Thanks are due Sanford Levinson for valuable contributions to the substance of this paper and aid in preparation of the manuscript.

since the constitutional crisis of 1937, have so many eyes been turned on the Supreme Court.

The reason for all this is not far to seek. The Court has been commanding the attention of the nation, and the command has been heeded. In the last dozen years the justices have written a spectacular new chapter in the history of constitutional law relating to individual rights. To be sure they have at the same time added some important paragraphs and displayed some interesting tendencies in other fields of public law.[1] But it is the drama of their civil liberties crusade that has captured the public mind and increased the flow of literature, learned and otherwise, about the judiciary—and that has provoked a new torrent of controversy and speculation about the "role" of the Supreme Court.

The controversy has been, or can be, subdivided into several often overlapping but analytically separable categories. In the first place there has been, as everyone knows, a sharp conflict of opinion over the ethical and policy objectives the modern Court has sought. It is this dispute that has predominated in the newspaper headlines and public oratory of the past decade. Although attacks on the Court's aims are frequently disguised as criticism of judicial methods, the disguise is penetrable. Governor Wallace, it seems fair to say, would be less concerned about judicial "usurpation" if he were less concerned about the substantive policies decreed in the desegregation cases; and Dr. King would perhaps be less zealous to defend judicial prerogatives if the Court had reaffirmed *Plessy* v. *Ferguson*[2] in 1954.

Second, there has developed, mostly in scholarly journals a voluminous debate over the legal craftsmanship of the modern Court's decisions.[3] In part this has been merely a continuation and

---

1. See generally SHAPIRO, LAW AND POLITICS IN THE SUPREME COURT 253–327 (1964).

2. 163 U.S. 537 (1896).

3. Critiques of the Court: Bickel & Wellington, *Legislative Purpose and the Judicial Process: The Lincoln Mills Case*, 71 HARV. L. REV. 1 (1957); Brown, *Quis Custodiet Ipos Custodes?—The School-Prayer Cases*, 1963 SUP. CT. REV. 1; Hart, *The Time Chart of the Justices, Foreword to The Supreme Court, 1958 Term*, 73 HARV. L. REV. 84 (1959); Kurland, *Equal in Origin and Equal in Title to the Legislative and Executive Branches of the Government, Foreword to The Supreme Court, 1963 Term*, 78 HARV. L. REV. 143

intensification of time-honored tradition: the law reviews have always analyzed the logic of Supreme Court opinions, both critically and approvingly. But in recent years criticism has accumulated until it amounts to a general charge that the Court has shirked its task of "reasoned exposition";[4] and judicial defenders have countered with a growing body of literature which seeks to refute the charge or—more often, I think—to supply a rationale which the Court's own opinions have failed to provide.

The values which the Court espouses and the craftsmanship of its opinions are both worthy subjects for analysis and debate. America is an "unfinished country."[5] Not even a pronouncement of the Supreme Court can or should close off discussion (as distinguished from defiance) of the norms on which the pronouncement is based; and the keystone of judicial review is the quasi-Platonic premise that reason can play a significant part in directing public conduct. These two points were summarized in 1932 in Mr. Justice Brandeis' familiar aphorism: "If we would guide by the light of reason, we must let our minds be bold."[6] They have lost none of their validity in the intervening years. But the rightness of the value system reflected in the modern Court's civil rights decisions is too vast and multi-hued an issue for condensed treatment; and the craftsmanship issue, though still very lively, has already attracted an ample volume of critical commentary.

Rather than pursue further either of these avenues, this article will focus mainly on certain other, less well-explored queries about the Warren Court. Recent years have seen a growing preoccupation among political scientists with two somewhat different ap-

---

(1964); Wechsler, *Toward Neutral Principles of Constitutional Law*, 73 HARV. L. REV. 1 (1959).

Defenses of the Court: BICKEL, THE LEAST DANGEROUS BRANCH—THE SUPREME COURT AT THE BAR OF POLITICS (1962); SHAPIRO, *supra*, note 1; Black, *The Lawfulness of the Segregation Decisions*, 69 YALE L. J. 421 (1960); Henkin, *Some Reflections on Current Constitutional Controversy*, 109 U. PA. L. REV. 637 (1961); Pollak, *Racial Discrimination and Judicial Integrity: A Reply to Professor Wechsler*, 108 U. PA. L. REV. 1 (1959).

4. Wechsler, *supra*, note 3, at 16.

5. The phrase is Max Lerner's (THE UNFINISHED COUNTRY [1959]).

6. New State Ice Co. v. Liebmann, 285 U.S. 262, 311 (1932) (Brandeis, J., dissenting).

proaches to the study of the governmental process: a concern simply to describe, as accurately as possible, the behavior of the "actors" in a governmental situation, and, concomitantly, an increased interest in analyzing political institutions in terms of the concept of "power." Of course neither of these currently fashionable approaches is by any means an innovation in the history of political thought. The idea of looking at things as they are was the essence of the revolt against medieval scholasticism, and the interest in understanding how power is achieved and lost can be traced back at least to Machiavelli. But old notions sometimes need new emphasis if only to remind us that there are many roads to Rome.

It happens that the rise of these interests among students of government coincides rather nicely with the period of the "Warren Court." The term is used for purposes of convenience, not to imply that the Chief Justice has dominated the bench of his time as Marshall once dominated his. The personal role of Earl Warren has been, one suspects, a good deal less magisterial. But the fact is that he came to the Court in 1953 and the years of his chieftainship have been something very special in Supreme Court history; enough of those years are now behind us to warrant some generalizations about the whole period. I shall therefore essay a synoptic view of the Court of the 1950's and 1960's, concentrating mainly on an analytic description of its behavior in the civil rights field, with some reference to the question of what accounts for that behavior, and culminating in some speculations about the problem of judicial power. I will not here join the debate over the righteousness of the Court's value objectives, but I believe the projected inquiry has a significant bearing on that issue. For both those who applaud recent judicial tendencies and those who deplore them, it is important to consider comprehensively what the Court has done and why, and to reflect a little about the question of judicial capability.

Historical generalizations are almost always either contestable or obvious. The first one offered here may strike some readers as open to doubt and others as self-evident. It is that the Court of the past dozen years has developed judicial activism[7] to a degree that at least matches the record of the Old Court of the 1920's and 1930's and that certainly exceeds the record of any other Court in our constitutional history. On reflection that the American Supreme Court has, since Marshall, been by long odds the most potent court in the world, this statement about modern judicial tendencies is seen in all its implications. One might say, paraphrasing Mr. Churchill, that only once before in history has a judicial tribunal tried to influence so many so much. This fact—assuming *arguendo* for the moment that it is a fact—has been referred to and lamented by critics of recent judicial tendencies, but their description has often been suspect because they so obviously object to the aims of the Court's activism rather than the activism itself. On the other hand the Court's champions, those who approve its policy aims, have tended to traverse or minimize the averment precisely because it was so frequently and angrily voiced by the Court's critics. The contention that the Court was exerting its authority in a way and to a degree not previously known sounded like and was often meant to be an assertion that the Court was exceeding the bounds of its legal mandate—a charge of judicial usurpation. In rejecting that charge, which I also reject, judicial defenders have also neglected the half-truth contained by the supposed indictment: that the Warren Court has used its legal authority more boldly than any Court has ever done before, again with the significant arguable exception of the 1920–1936 period.

The fact is that the remarkable degree of the Warren Court's activism has only become fully apparent in recent years. Writing in 1957, Bernard Schwartz declared: "Whatever else one may say of our governmental system during the past twenty years, it certainly can no longer be characterized as 'government by the judiciary.'" He quoted a North Dakota judge who in 1924 had complained: "We are governed by our judges and not by our

7. Like most broadly descriptive terms, "judicial activism" involves some ambiguities, but it is handy for the purpose of identifying a general tendency or point of view. It has been certified by both judicial and academic usage; see, *e.g.*, JACKSON, THE SUPREME COURT IN THE AMERICAN SYSTEM OF GOVERNMENT 57 (1955); PRITCHETT, THE ROOSEVELT COURT 277 (1948).

legislatures." "All of this," remarked Schwartz, "has been completely changed";[8] and he painted a picture of a modern Court which stressed its hesitancy to impose the veto, its deference to other branches of government, its doubts about the judicial capacity to direct the course of American society. In 1965 that picture seems curiously askew: could such a mild tribunal have launched the thousand ships of the current conflict over judicial doctrine? The point is not that Schwartz was lacking in insight, but that in 1957 we had not yet reached a juncture from which we could view the activism of the modern Court in perspective and judge its extent.[9] The tendencies were there, but they were still confusedly mixed with contrary tendencies, and it was perhaps necessary to wait until hindsight could clarify the design.

Now it appears that the years from 1940 to about 1953 were a period of irresolution marked by the alternate flowing and ebbing of judicial self-confidence. By 1940 the Old Court of the anti-New Deal crusade had been altered or superseded. The only one of the former intransigents remaining was Mr. Justice McReynolds, and he was soon to go; a solid majority of the justices were now Roosevelt appointees. The new Court had already made it plain that the laissez-faire values of the recent past were no longer constitutionally viable, and that the humanistic values loosely described by the term "civil liberties" were becoming a predominant judicial concern. The stage seemed set for a new jurisprudence and a new role for the judicial branch.

But civil liberties represented a comparatively novel and untried field of judicial endeavor, and the 1940's were a peculiarly difficult time for justices who were trying to learn new tricks. In the first place the justices were the proximate heirs of a political and intellectual movement which had sharply criticized over-

8. SCHWARTZ, THE SUPREME COURT 27 (1957), quoting BRUCE, THE AMERICAN JUDGE 6, 8 (1924).

9. The volatility of constitutional doctrine in recent years is strikingly illustrated by a consideration of the cases cited in Kadish, *Methodology and Criteria in Due Process Adjudication: A Survey and Criticism*, 66 YALE L. J. 319 (1957), to describe the then current status of doctrine in the criminal procedure field. Although the article was published only eight years ago, almost all of the holdings unfavorable to the accused have since been overruled.

weening judicial power and had elevated the majority will to new heights. They had heard deplored, and themselves had sometimes joined in deploring, the tendency of the courts to "roam at will in the limitless area of their own beliefs as to reasonableness and actually select policies, a responsibility which the Constitution entrusts to the legislative representatives of the people."[10] These sentiments were deeply ingrained in their thinking, and although some, like Mr. Justice Black, were able to persuade themselves that it was a different matter to enforce the "clearly defined protections contained in the Bill of Rights,"[11] others found the difference illusory.[12] Like most of the nation the members of the "Roosevelt Court" were conceptually prepared only to declare what the judicial branch should not do; what it should do and why had not been thought out.

In the second place the past offered little useful guidance as to how the new concern for civil rights should be specifically implemented. America had thought of itself as the land of the free since at least 1776 but had seldom inquired just how the self-image could be translated into legal doctrines for determining whether Government A could restrain Citizen B.[13] The literature of American democracy was replete with libertarian rhetorical flourishes, but these were material for anthologies, not legal casebooks. As Leonard Levy has shown,[14] even the framers of the First Amendment had only the dimmest idea of where liberty left

10. FPC v. Natural Gas Pipeline Co., 315 U.S. 575, 600–601 n.4 (1942) (Black, J., concurring).

11. *Ibid.*

12. Probably the classic statement of this position is Justice Frankfurter's dissent in West Virginia Bd. of Educ. v. Barnette, 319 U.S. 624, 646 (1943). See 648–649: "There is no warrant in the constitutional basis of this Court's authority for attributing different rôles to it depending upon the nature of the challenge to the legislation. Our power does not vary according to the particular provision of the Bill of Rights which is invoked . . . This Court's only and very narrow function is to determine whether within the broad grant of authority vested in legislatures they have exercised a judgment for which reasonable justification can be offered."

13. John Roche persuasively argues that it is only in the twentieth century that a concern for civil liberties has been a significant part of American institutional practice. See ROCHE, SHADOW AND SUBSTANCE (1964), especially the essay *American Liberty: An Examination of the Tradition of Freedom* at 3–38. See also ROCHE, THE QUEST FOR THE DREAM (1963)

14. LEVY, LEGACY OF SUPPRESSION (1960).

off and license began, and insofar as their notion of the range of free speech can be ascertained, it falls far short of the scope accepted by the post-1940 Court.

That not much progress had been made toward satisfactory definition in the next one hundred fifty years is evidenced by the fact that in 1941 Zachariah Chafee, surely among the most sophisticated of observers, set such store by the clear and present danger test as a standard for adjudication.[15] Today almost no one seems to believe that this formula can be very helpful in deciding concrete cases. As for the field of state criminal procedure which was to bulk so large in their future, the justices of 1940 had at hand the Palko rule[16] in all its vagueness, and not much else. In Palko and a dozen similar cases the Court had refused to find unconstitutional such state practices as the denial of counsel but had insisted that it would hold state trials to fundamental principles of liberty and justice. In the field of Negro rights the level of progress was represented by the separate but equal doctrine," now of inglorious memory. In short, the task of fashioning a meaningful jurisprudence of civil liberties was almost wholly yet to be done. The historical parallel that comes to mind is the 1880–1900 period and the judicial adumbration of the concept of economic freedom.[17] The concept had been familiar for many years as a vaguely understood premise of "the American way" but never translated into specific constitutional rules. Like the Court of the 1940's, the Waite-Fuller Court had to adjust both its outlook and it precedents when its members became convinced that business must have greater judicial protection. Such adjustments take time.

Perhaps more important than either of these considerations in explaining Court history in those years is the character of the era

15. See generally CHAFEE, FREE SPEECH IN THE UNITED STATES (1941).

16. Palko v. Connecticut, 302 U.S. 319 (1937). It is noteworthy and somewhat ironic that Justice Black joined in Justice Cardozo's majority opinion, while the only dissenter, without opinion, was the much maligned Justice Butler.

17. See Hamilton, *The Path of Due Process of Law*, in THE CONSTITUTION RECONSIDERED 167 (Read ed. 1938). See generally PAUL, CONSERVATIVE CRISIS AND THE RULE OF LAW (1960); TWISS, LAWYERS AND THE CONSTITUTION (1942).

itself. The first part of the period was overshadowed by the Second World War and its immediate aftermath; the second part by the Cold War, the Korean War, and that complex phenomenon usually called McCarthyism. It is hard enough to spell out workable civil rights doctrines in a tranquil era; but in a society at war, on the brink of war, or torn by inner antagonisms the difficulties are thrice compounded. The justices, or most of them, shared a common impulse to defend civil rights more than previous Courts had done; or to stick with the jargon, to be in this field more "activist" than their predecessors. But this impulse required them to deal with novel problems in a novel and constantly shifting historical context. It is not surprising that we can now see as we look back a pattern of false starts, stops, and retreats, of hesitation and discord.

To be sure, the net result of this process is a gradual gain for civil rights; in spite of the pauses and vacillations, a general tendency to broaden constitutionally protected personal liberty can be discerned. But the progress is meandering and painful; one moment's resolution yields to another's self-doubt. A compulsory school flag salute is upheld against religious scruples in the name of democratic self-education and national unity;[18] three years later the decision is overruled.[19] An eight-justice majority concurs in an opinion[20] which apparently endows labor picketing with the status of a "preferred freedom"; subsequent qualifying holdings whittle that freedom down to a near-nullity.[21] The right to counsel is required in state courts for some indigent defendants[22] but not for others;[23] a state may not affirmatively authorize arbi-

18. Minersville School Dist. v. Gobitis, 310 U.S. 586 (1940).
19. West Virginia Bd. of Educ. v. Barnette, 319 U.S. 624 (1943).
20. Thornhill v. Alabama, 310 U.S. 88 (1940).
21. Milk Wagon Drivers Union v. Meadowmoor Dairies, Inc., 312 U.S. 287 (1941); Carpenters Union v. Ritter's Cafe, 315 U.S. 722 (1942); Giboney v. Empire Storage & Ice Co., 336 U.S. 490 (1949); see SHAPIRO, *supra*, note 1, at 77; Tanenhaus, *Picketing-Free Speech: The Growth of the New Law of Picketing From 1940 to 1952*, 38 CORNELL L. Q. 1 (1952).
22. Williams v. Kaiser, 323 U.S. 471 (1945); Tompkins v. Missouri, 323 U.S. 485 (1945); Hawk v. Olson, 326 U.S. 271 (1945).
23. Betts v. Brady, 316 U.S. 455 (1942); Carter v. Illinois, 329 U.S. 173 (1946).

trary search and seizure, but it need not exclude evidence thus obtained from its courts.[24] "Neither a state nor the Federal Government . . . can pass laws which aid . . . religion,"[25] but on second thought if the aid can be called encouragement or cooperation it will pass muster.[26] Doctrinal indecisiveness appears at every hand: is the clear and present danger concept a *vade mecum*,[27] or a "literary phrase"?[28] Is federalism still a reigning value, or merely a practical inconvenience? Ar there preferred freedoms[29] or are there not?[30] The Court can be found at one time or another on both sides of all these questions, and the incertitude seems to exist not only as between different wings of the Court but within the hearts of individual justices. Was Justice Stone's outlook toward laws infringing speech the modest one attributed to him by Judge Learned Hand[31] or the alertly critical one described by George Braden?[32] More the latter than the former, no doubt, but there were enough cross-threads to create confusion. Was the "real" Robert Jackson the uncompromising defender of free expression who spoke in the second flag salute opinion,[33] or the man who acknowledged Caesar's claims in *Murdock* v. *Pennsylvania*[34] and *Martin* v. *Struthers*?[35] Even Justice Murphy, long regarded

24. Wolf v. Colorado, 338 U.S. 25 (1949).
25. Everson v. Board of Educ., 330 U.S. 1, 15 (1947).
26. Zorach v. Clauson, 343 U.S. 306, 314 (1952).
27. As in Pennekamp v. Florida, 328 U.S. 331 (1946); Thomas v. Collins, 323 U.S. 516 (1945); and Thornhill v. Alabama, 310 U.S. 88 (1940); majority opinions written by Justices Reed, Rutledge, and Murphy, respectively.
28. Pennekamp v. Florida, *id.* at 353 (Frankfurter, J., concurring).
29. See, *e.g.,* Kovacs v. Cooper, 336 U.S. 77, 88 (1949); Murdock v. Pennsylvania, 319 U.S. 105, 115 (1943). See also the recent attempt by Professors Hyman and Newhouse to construct a rationale for the "preferred freedoms concept" in *Standards for Preferred Freedoms: Beyond the First,* 60 Nw. U. L. REV. 1, 50–93 (1965).
30. For the most vigorous attack, see Mr. Justice Frankfurter's concurring opinion in Kovacs v. Cooper, *id.* at 89.
31. Hand, *Chief Justice Stone's Conception of the Judicial Function,* 46 COLUM. L. REV. 696, 697 (1946), in HAND, THE SPIRIT OF LIBERTY 204 (1960).
32. Braden, *The Search for Objectivity in Constitutional Law,* 57 YALE L. J. 571, 580–581 (1948).
33. West Virginia Bd. of Educ. v. Barnette, 319 U.S. 624 (1943).
34. 319 U.S. 105, 117 (1943) (dissenting opinion).
35. 319 U.S. 141, 166 (1943) (Jackson, J., joining in Justice Clark's dissenting opinion).

as the epitome of dogmatic libertarianism,[36] was, it now appears, far less sure of his bearings, at least in the beginning, than his voting record would suggest.[37] The Court was sailing uncharted seas, and most of the mariners knew it. Some of them indeed seemed able to develop the self-confidence to drive ahead steadily enough, but no consistently libertarian majority could be marshalled, and the overall effect was a civil rights jurisprudence in which libertarian impulses and misgivings seemed intricately mixed. Of course the proportions varied from time to time. The 1945 Term, for example, produced a larger number of noteworthy libertarian decisions than the 1946 Term. Pritchett has found that the Court majority favored the cause of liberty in 49 percent of the "non-unanimous personal liberty decisions" from the 1941 to 1946 Terms;[38] the proportion was only 35 percent in the 1946 to 1952 Terms.[39] This tends to confirm the impression, widespread among students of the Court, that the era of McCarthyism especially puzzled the will of the justices, as it did the will of America. Yet these cyclical variations do not nullify the general description here offered, that the era of the forties as a whole was one in which an urge toward a new civil rights constitutionalism was much retarded and sometimes halted by judicial self-doubts in the face of a novel situation.

With the 1950's there began to be signs of increasing boldness. The early rise of this temper can be marked in certain salient decisions which may now be regarded in retrospect as portents of things to come. The Steel Seizure Case in 1952[40] did not directly concern civil rights in the conventional sense, but a tribunal that dared to mediate a conflict between the President, the Congress, and one of the great economic interests of the realm did not seem to be overwhelmed by diffidence about its own capacity to govern.

36. ROCHE, SHADOW AND SUBSTANCE 162 (1964). "An ideological, even ritualistic liberal"; id. at 163.
37. See Howard, Justice Murphy: The Freshman Years, 18 VAND. L. REV. 473 (1965).
38. PRITCHETT, THE ROOSEVELT COURT 254 (1948).
39. PRITCHETT, CIVIL LIBERTIES AND THE VINSON COURT 190 (1954).
40. Youngstown Sheet & Tube Co. v. Sawyer, 343 U.S. 579 (1952).

In the same term, the *Burstyn*[41] decision held that movies were protected by the free speech guarantees and this, at least by implication, brought the vast field of artistic expression under judicial supervision. In 1953 came *Terry* v. *Adams*,[42] in which the Court displayed its zeal to stamp out racial discrimination in voting even though the "state action" concept had to be strained unmercifully to reach the desired result; and in 1952 there had been *Wieman* v. *Updegraff*,[43] in which a state loyalty oath was, for the first time, struck down. We must be careful that hindsight does not cause us to read more into these constitutional events than they contained at the time. Cross-threads were still present;[44] the judicial misgivings of the recent past had by no means been wholly allayed. With the exception of The Steel Seizure Case, none of the decisions mentioned above was really startling; each was arguably rooted in the evolving constitutional logic of the post-1940 Court. If they implied some increase in libertarian self-confidence, such implications had been detectable before (for example, in the 1943–1946 period), yet had been followed only by a new access of judicial modesty. They were no more than straws in the wind, and winds can change.

But in 1954 a far more momentous development suggested more strongly that an activist trend had truly set in: the public school desegregation decision, *Brown* v. *Board of Education*,[45] surely one of the most daring assertions of court authority in judicial history. So much has been said in the last dozen years about the policy and logic of this decision that we may tend to overlook its significance in the history of judicial review. In spite of its kinship with previous holdings like *Sweatt* v. *Painter*,[46] it represented not merely a continuation of past tendencies, but one of

41. Joseph Burstyn, Inc. v. Wilson, 343 U.S. 495 (1952).
42. 345 U.S. 461 (1953).
43. 344 U.S. 183 (1952).
44. In Irvine v. California, 347 U.S. 128 (1954), *e.g.*, which deals with search and seizure, the Court upheld the state's claim five to four, the majority including the new Chief Justice and the dissenters including Frankfurter and Burton.
45. 347 U.S. 483 (1954).
46. 339 U.S. 629 (1950).

those mutational leaps which occur from time to time in the evolution of species. The circumstance that it was unanimous has partially concealed[47]—when it should have underlined—the fact that the justices were hurdling the qualms about judicial capacity that had slowed them down in recent years. The concealment was furthered by the fact that the dialogue between the Black and Frankfurter wings of the Court—between activism and judicial modesty—continued unabated in other fields of constitutional doctrine. None of this is to say that the boldness of the Desegregation Case had made that dialogue irrelevant; activism and self-restraint are matters of degree, and the proper balance between them may vary from subject to subject. It is to say that the decision powerfully suggested a tipping of the scales in the direction of activism not only in the race relations field, but, by analogy, in other fields as well; and that this inference was likely to grow clearer in subsequent years as the social revolution inaugurated by the decision worked itself out. The justices themselves may not have realized all that their action augured. But whether they knew it or not they had crossed a watershed. A body of men who had attacked with telling effect perhaps the most difficult social problem in America were not likely to be overly modest about their powers thereafter. The desegregation decision was both an early symptom and a cause of the rising spirit of activism that characterized the Warren Court.

The most spectacular event of the following term was the "enforcement decision"[48] implementing the doctrine of the Desegregation Case. While the Court did not here go as far as some might have wished toward demanding immediate compliance, later events have dispelled any hopes or fears that the justices were backing down from their resolution to tackle race discrimination head-on. A trio of decisions recognizing a right against self-incrimination for congressional committee witnesses was modestly

---

47. But see Shapiro, *Judicial Modesty: Down With the Old!—Up With the New?*, 10 U.C.L.A. L. REV. 533–534 (1963): "Indeed, with the school segregation decision . . . [the Court] had begun to move toward judicial activism even when the enchantment with self-restraint was at its height."

48. Brown v. Board of Educ., 349 U.S. 294 (1955).

important, though unsurprising.[49] Otherwise this was a fairly quiet term, which is not surprising either. One long stride like *Brown* might well seem enough in any two-year period.

But in the 1955 Term the pace again accelerated and the 1956 Term was sensational, as constitutional historians judge sensations. These were the years of such anti-Red-scare decisions as *Pennsylvania* v. *Nelson*,[50] invalidating or greatly undermining most state subversion laws; *Yates* v. *United States*[51] and *Jencks* v. *United States*,[52] overthrowing federal convictions of alleged Communists; and *Watkins* v. *United States*[53] and *Sweezy* v. *New Hampshire*,[54] restricting the procedures of legislative investigating committees —to name only those most highly publicized. It is true that the Court in these holdings leaned heavily on statutory interpretations and procedural requirements, leaving the substantive power of Congress largely unimpaired.[55] But even this qualified venture into the delicate field of anti-subversion laws suggested that judicial self-assurance might be growing. Nor was this all. These were also the years in which the Court decided *Reid* v. *Covert*,[56] circumscribing congressional power to try by court martial civilian dependents living abroad; *Griffin* v. *Illinois*,[57] holding that states must provide indigent defendants who wish to appeal with transcripts of their trials; and *Roth* v. *United States*[58] and *Alberts* v. *California*, [59] explicitly holding for the first time that both state and federal laws banning "obscene" literature must meet First Amendment standards.

The 1957 to 1960 Terms present some intriguing problems for synoptic analysis. They were marked by a series of decisions in which the Court seemed to back down at least in spirit from its

49. Bart v. United States, 349 U.S. 219 (1955); Emspak v. United States, 349 U.S. 190 (1955); Quinn v. United States, 349 U.S. 155 (1955).
50. 350 U.S. 497 (1956).
51. 354 U.S. 298 (1957).
52. 353 U.S. 657 (1957).
53. 354 U.S. 178 (1957).
54. 354 U.S. 234 (1957).
55. See above, pp. 171–187.
56. 354 U.S. 1 (1957).
57. 351 U.S. 12 (1956).
58. 354 U.S. 476 (1957).
59. *Ibid.*

1956 Term stand against governmental harassment of supposed Communists.[60] Legislative investigators were, it turned out, freer to pursue their chosen purposes than the dicta of *Watkins* and *Sweezy* had seemed to imply;[61] a Smith Act conviction was sustained,[62] as was an order that the Communist party register under the McCarran Act.[63] These and a few other holdings of similar tenor produced a chorus of lamentations that the Court had reversed its libertarian course.[64] Mr. Justice Black was provoked to remonstrate that the protections of the Bill of Rights had been "all but obliterated"[65] and that "if the present trend continues . . . government by consent will disappear to be replaced by government by intimidation."[66]

This diagnosis, taken at face value, would present a distorted view of the state of constitutional rights at the time and of the tendencies of the Court during this four-year period. It is true that the justices seemed willing, perhaps over-willing, to tolerate measures aimed at "subversives" even though the measures plainly encroached on free expression. No Court had ever overthrown a national sedition law, and it is one of the ironies of recent constitutional history that "political speech," which has sometimes been regarded as the heart of the First Amendment guarantees,[67] has been relatively ill-protected, compared to several other forms of

60. MURPHY, CONGRESS AND THE COURT 238–241 (1962)· see above, p. 224.
61. See Barenblatt v. United States, 360 U.S. 109 (1959); Uphaus v. Wyman, 360 U.S. 72 (1959).
62. Scales v. United States, 367 U.S. 203 (1961).
63. Communist Party v. Subversive Activities Control Bd., 367 U.S. 1 (1961).
64. See *Retreat From Freedom,* 78 THE CHRISTIAN CENTURY 163 (1961); *Security and Civil Rights,* 74 THE COMMONWEAL 316 (1961); *The Court and the Committee,* 73 THE COMMONWEAL 624 (1961); *Free Speech and Movies,* 73 THE COMMONWEAL 495 (1961); *Neither Clear Nor Present,* 192 THE NATION 509 (1961); *Censorship of Movies,* New Republic, Feb. 27, 1961, p. 8; *Un-American Activities,* New Republic, Mar. 13, 1961, p. 5; *No Decision,* The Reporter, July 6, 1961, p. 12.
65. Braden v. United States, 365 U.S. 431, 445 (1961) (Black, J., dissenting).
66. Wilkinson v. United States, 365 U.S. 399, 421 (1961) (Black, J., dissenting). If the Court's cheerleaders were disappointed, some of its critics were greatly reassured. See MURPHY, *supra,* note 60, at 238 and citations therein.
67. See MEIKLEJOHN, FREE SPEECH AND ITS RELATION TO SELF-GOVERNMENT (1948).

expression. Some observers[68] had, wishfully or indignantly, read into *Watkins, Yates,* and other 1956 Term decisions a promise to curb congressional "inquisitors" and governmental "Red-baiters"; that promise, if it was one, was certainly unfulfilled. But the chagrin of libertarians over this disappointment may have caused them to overlook the fact that the Court's rate of progress in other civil rights fields had slackened little. *Kent* v. *Dulles*[69] gave the first explicit recognition to the idea that the "right to travel" is constitutionally protected. *Trop* v. *Dulles*[70] invalidated a section of the federal Nationality Act which expatriated wartime deserters. *Torcaso* v. *Watkins*[71] disapproved unanimously a Maryland requirement that a public official declare his belief in God. In the field of criminal procedure there were several noteworthy developments including the spike-mike case;[72] *Hudson* v. *North Carolina,*[73] which came very close to undermining the *Betts* rule that state courts need not provide counsel for indigents and partially foreshadowed *Gideon* v. *Wainwright;*[74] and, most striking of all, *Mapp* v. *Ohio,*[75] overruling *Wolf* v. *Colorado's*[76] rule that state courts could admit evidence obtained by unreasonable search or seizure. And in the field of race relations the Court was pushing ahead by the 1960 Term more determinedly than it had since 1955.[77] If constitutional liberties were being "obliterated," the majority was choosing a curious way to bring about that dire result.

But the activism of these four terms, robust though it still was, pales by comparison with the four that followed, which must surely rank as one of the most creative and daring periods in constitutional history. It is during this time that the remarkable extent of the Warren Court's will-to-govern becomes fully manifest.

68. *E.g.,* MURPHY, *supra,* note 60, at 112–117.
69. 357 U.S. 116 (1958).
70. 356 U.S. 86 (1958).
71 367 U.S. 488 (1961).
72. Silverman v. United States, 365 U.S. 505 (1961).
73. 363 U.S. 697 (1960).
74. 372 U.S. 335 (1963).
75. 367 U.S. 643 (1961).
76. 338 U.S. 25 (1949).
77. See Burton v. Wilmington Parking Authority, 365 U.S. 715 (1961); Shelton v. Tucker, 364 U.S. 479 (1960); Boynton v. Virginia, 364 U.S. 454 (1960); Gomillion v. Lightfoot, 364 U.S. 339 (1960).

This tendency is reflected not only in a handful of great, landmark decisions but in the cumulative effect of many others in which the justices chipped away at the doctrinal roadblocks to a judicially-defined good society. So many developments have occurred so recently that there is no need to describe them in detail. Perhaps it is enough to remind the reader of the Court's venture into the apportionment thicket[78] and the uncompromising "one-man-one-vote" standard imposed on both state legislatures and Congress;[79] of the dramatic extensions of the right to counsel in state criminal proceedings signalled by such holdings as *Douglas* v. *California,*[80] *Gideon* v. *Wainwright,*[81] and *Escobedo* v. *Illinois;*[82] of the school prayer decisions;[83] of the announcement of new constitutional standards in the fields of libel law[84] and movie censorship,[85] and with respect to state birth control[86] and anti-miscegenation statutes.[87] These years have been a fitting climax to the twelve-year trend of the Warren Court toward a position of extraordinary influence on the shape of the American polity.

This trend and its accelerating pace are evident enough from the kind of impressionistic, bird's-eye view just described. Tabulation and comparison seem to bear out the account faithfully, and this may comfort those with a taste for quantifiable data and a suspicion of intuitive conclusions.

"Judicial activism" is a slippery term, but perhaps one of its aspects can be acceptably defined as the Supreme Court's propensity to intervene in the governing process. If so, perhaps it will

78. Baker v. Carr, 369 U.S. 186 (1962).
79. Lucas v. 44th General Assembly, 377 U.S. 713 (1964); Reynolds v. Sims, 377 U.S. 533 (1964); Wesberry v. Sanders, 376 U.S. 1 (1964).
80. 372 U.S. 353 (1963). Concerning the importance of *Douglas,* which has been overshadowed by the attention given *Gideon,* see Kamisar, Book Review, 78 HARV. L. REV. 478 (1964); at 481: "I venture to say that twenty years from now, perhaps sooner, *Douglas,* not *Gideon,* will be regarded as 'the other' right-to-counsel case handed down on March 18, 1963."
81. 372 U.S. 335 (1963).
82. 378 U.S. 478 (1964).
83. School Dist. v. Schempp, 374 U.S. 203 (1963); Engel v. Vitale, 370 U.S. 421 (1962).
84. New York Times Co. v. Sullivan, 376 U.S. 254 (1964).
85. Freedman v. Maryland, 380 U.S. 51 (1965).
86. Griswold v. Connecticut, 381 U.S. 479 (1965).
87. McLaughlin v. Florida, 379 U.S. 184 (1964).

also be agreed that the proportion of cases decided against govern-ment is at least a crude indicator of the extent of that propensity. Table 1 shows all cases decided with opinion in the 1949 to 1964 Terms, giving the percentages of anti-government holdings.[88] Minor variations from year to year, or even fairly substantial ones, are of doubtful significance. They may be explained by coinci-

Table 1. Public law cases decided with full opinion

Term	For government	Against government	Total	Percentage against government
1948	60	30	90	33
1949	49	25	74	34
1950	53	32	85	38
1951	43	33	76	43
1952	52	32	84	38
1953	33	26	59	44
1954	34	24	58	41
1955	36	34	70	49
1956	40	47	87	54
1957	51	50	101	50
1958	53	32	85	38
1959	50	34	84	40
1960	59	43	102	42
1961	35	34	69	49
1962	38	48	86	56
1963	33	62	95	65
1964	47	38	85	45
[1965	42	43	85	51
1966	48	50	98	51
1967	43	56	99	57
1968	41	58	99	59]

88. The source of the data is the tabulation given in each November issue of *Harvard Law Review* since 1949 of cases decided with full opinion in which the decision was either "for" or "against" government (both state and federal).

dences that have nothing to do with the rise and fall of an activist judicial spirit. It is interesting to note the climb in the 1953–1956 period to a temporary high of 54 percent because this broadly conforms to the impression that judicial self-confidence was growing during these years. It is tempting to relate the sharp decline in the 1958 Term to the upsurge of anti-judicial criticism that reached its congressional apex in the summer of 1958 because the decline would seem to substantiate the idea that the justices pulled in their horns in the face of this threat. And the equally sharp rise in anti-government holdings during the last four terms taken as a whole at least coincides with what has been suggested above: that the self-confidence of the judiciary was only temporarily moderated in 1958–1959 and that it has been growing to new heights since then. But none of these detailed interpretations need be insisted on. The gross fact that does appear significant is the very substantial secular increase of anti-government holdings during the period of our concern. In the five terms for 1948–1952 the Court decided 257 cases for government and 152 against; in the five terms for 1960–1964 it decided 211 cases for and 222 against. The respective percentages of anti-government decisions are 37 and 51. This may not in itself "prove" that activism has greatly increased during the years of the Warren Court, but it does add weight to such an interpretation.

The picture is even more dramatic if tabulation is restricted to a smaller field in which there have nevertheless been enough decisions to permit arguably meaningful comparisons: the field of state criminal cases (Table 2). In the 1948 to 1952 Terms, 19 such cases were decided for government, 14 against; in the 1960 to 1964 Terms, 11 for, 64 against. In short, the state governments were losing 42 percent of their criminal cases before the Court during the first period, and in the last five terms 85 percent.

Corroboration of a related sort can be drawn from a chronology of state acts held unconstitutional by the Supreme Court. According to one recent enumeration,[89] in the eleven years 1942–1952

89. See *The Constitution of the United States of America: Analysis and Interpretation*, S. Doc. No. 39, 88th Cong., 1st Sess. 1491–1522 (Small ed. 1964). Tables begin at 1385 and 1403, which are respectively entitled "Acts

Table 2. State criminal cases

Term	For government	Against government	Total
1948	2	4	6
1949	2	1	3
1950	2	3	5
1951	7	3	10
1952	6	3	9
1953	2	2	4
1954	3	4	7
1955	2	4	6
1956	4	4	8
1957	5	7	12
1958	5	6	11
1959	1	6	7
1960	0	9	9
1961	4	10	14
1962	3	12	15
1963	1	15	16
1964	3	18	21
[1965	6	16	22
1966	8	23	31
1967	5	14	19
1968	4	18	22]

the Court invalidated 57 state acts; in 1953–1963 (the period of the Warren Court), the total was 83, and no less than 45 of them were clustered in the three years 1961–1963. It is perhaps also worthy of note that although only two acts of Congress were held unconstitutional from 1942 through 1952, the Warren Court from 1953 through 1963 struck down eight.

To summarize, the Warren Court appears to have succeeded

of Congress Held Unconstitutional in Whole or in Part by the Supreme Court of the United States" and "State Constitutional and Statutory Provisions and Municipal Ordinances Held Unconstitutional on Their Face or as Administered."

impressively in freeing itself from the self-doubts that deterred constitutional development during the 1940–1953 period. With a zeal that seems to have increased as the years went by, the justices have advanced boldly along the civil rights front. A variety of new subjects—for example, libel and censorship laws, the right to travel, the postal power—have been brought within their purview. Old doctrines that offered a pretext for judicial inaction, like the doctrine of "political questions"[90] or the "privilege doctrine,"[91] have been jettisoned or greatly eroded. Once lively value conflicts like the one between a Brandeisian concern for local autonomy and a Marshallian belief in centralized judicial control have apparently been resolved, at least by the majority, in favor of a unitary national standard, especially in the field of criminal procedure.[92] The incidence of judicial intervention in public affairs has increased markedly, and the importance of the Supreme Court as a factor in the American governmental and social process has reached lofty heights—heights of activism, as noted earlier, previously reached only by the Court of the 1920–1936 era. One thinks of the Marshall Court, which laid down the conceptual basis for national legislative power and national judicial control and which threw its weight against the rising states' rights movement of the times. These were great achievements in the history of judicial review. But the checks which Marshall actually imposed on the states are seen as few and light when we stop to examine them; and his pronouncements about congressional power and judicial supervision were very largely invitations to the future rather than immediately realized mandates.[93] The number and variety and weight of direct governmental functions which the modern Court has assigned to itself exceed anything the great Chief Justice ever shouldered.

Consider the record, not in terms of doctrinal development as above, but in terms of the voluntary assumption of substantive

90. Baker v. Carr, 369 U.S. 186, 208 (1962).
91. See Roth v. United States, 354 U.S. 476, 504 n.5 (1957) (Harlan, J., dissenting).
92. See the dialogue between Harlan on the one hand and his brethren, particularly Goldberg, on the other in Pointer v. Texas, 380 U.S. 400 (1965).
93. See MCCLOSKEY, THE AMERICAN SUPREME COURT 79 (1960).

tasks. The Warren Court has taken upon itself a major share of the responsibility for transforming a pattern of racial segregation deeply rooted in the social customs and laws of the nation. It has undertaken to stamp out or greatly alter the censorship arrangements that have prevailed in many of our states and cities. It has undertaken to eliminate, or reduce to a Court-defined limit, religious observances in government-supported activities. It has undertaken to supervise more closely than ever before our machinery of criminal law enforcement, including the pre-trial behavior of police. It has undertaken to modify in a fundamental way and to oversee the electoral apportionment systems of the several states and of Congress itself. It has asserted and enforced a measure of judicial control over certain national powers once largely immune from constitutional query—the postal power, the authority to issue passports, and the authority to define citizenship. It has sought, cautiously but unmistakably, to mitigate the asperities of governmental policies aimed at "subversives." What should be emphasized is that these tasks are largely new either in kind or degree: they have been assumed in addition to the already considerable responsibilities in civil rights and in other fields which the pre-1953 Court already bore. That earlier Court was indeed already trying to alter state criminal procedures and state patterns of racial discrimination, but it was moving toward those objectives more gradually. The modern judicial policies seek to push the United States along the paths of virtue a good deal faster, and the dimension of the judicial job has correspondingly increased. Other self-imposed functions—most notably the supervision of apportionment—are entirely novel. Even Marshall, with all his ambition and daring, might well be daunted by the prospect of governing a self-willed, dynamic nation in as many important ways as the Warren Court has sought to govern America.

This brings us to a consideration of the 1920–1936 Court, which has been regarded by constitutional historians as the very archetype of government by judiciary. How did its will-to-govern compare with the one implicit in the behavior of the Warren Court? The comparison is difficult, for it involves assigning weights to quasi-imponderables, but interesting questions are often vexing in this way. The 1920–1936 Court invalidated nearly 200 state acts: its batting average is distinctly the higher, although the Warren Court's performance in this category has improved, if that is the word, in very recent years. The 1920–1936 Court's record for overthrowing congressional laws is also of course unsurpassed. Beyond any doubt the tribunal of those years was playing an imposing part in the direction of public policy—whether for good or ill need not at present concern us.

But it is arguable that the role of the Warren Court is in some ways still more imposing, that it has attempted even more than its famous predecessor. If the argument is to be made, an exception must be recognized for those banner years 1935–1936; or rather, those years must be seen in relation to the one that followed. No Court ever challenged the national will as boldly as did the Old Court when it struck at the New Deal, but no Court ever so sharply and hastily backed down as that same tribunal did in 1937.[94] A sequence in which a throne is audaciously claimed in one moment and abdicated in the next can hardly be viewed on the whole as an example of judicial intrepidity.

On the other hand, in the years before the impetuous adventures of 1935–1936, the Court had exerted a less dramatic but powerful influence on the shaping of public policy. But that influence, it should be noted, was confined almost entirely to a single field: regulation of the economy. To be sure, this was a field of great importance; but the Court's title to deal with it had been established many years before, and the justices had the assurance (sound enough until the Depression changed the national temper) that their moderately laissez-faire position was fairly close to the American consensus. By contrast, the modern Court's civil rights doctrines have carried it into a variety of social and political areas; the Court's title to deal with them is new and comparatively untried; public attitudes about them are often uncertain or mixed. In some instances a consensus has seemed to take shape, not before, but after the Court laid down its own mandates.

94. See, e.g., WRIGHT, THE GROWTH OF AMERICAN CONSTITUTIONAL LAW 200–241 (194-).

Beyond that, there is another difference between the nature of the Warren Court's undertakings and those of any Court of the past, and the difference may be crucial to this comparison. The Warren Court has thought of itself as, and in an important sense has been, not the negative, restraining power of judicial tradition, but a major initiative-producing agency of modern government.[95] In the orthodox view of the judicial branch, resting heavily on Hamilton's 78th *Federalist* paper, it is assumed that Congress and perhaps the President will be the initiators, while the Court is seen as a check, a sheet anchor, against "momentary inclinations" and rapid change.[96] But when we reflect on the Warren Court's years, it becomes evident that this traditional allocation of functions has been to a significant extent altered, that the Court has emerged as a dynamic, initiating governmental force and that the negative function has been exercised, at least until very recently, by Congress. Since the advent of President Johnson, the legislative body —or rather the President with the legislature's cooperation— seems to have resumed a substantial share of the initiative for determining America's socio-political course. But in the decade 1953–1963, the paramount domestic innovations in public policy can be traced more to the Supreme Court than to either Congress or the President. Surely the Court was the major *governmental* instrumentality in the complex process which brought the issue of racial discrimination to public attention and inaugurated an upheaval in American customs and laws.[97] The precise impact of the reapportionment decisions on American political life is at present

95. See Miller, *The Changing Role of the United States Supreme Court,* 25 MODERN L. REV. 641 (1962); Murphy, *Deeds Under a Doctrine: Civil Liberties in the 1963 Term,* 59 AM. POL. SCI. REV. 64, 78 (1965).

96. THE FEDERALIST No. 78, at 494 (Wright ed. 1961) (Hamilton).

97. An interesting confirmation of this assertion is found in the data of Louis Harris, questioning Negroes, both rank and file and leaders, on "Who Has Done Most for Negro Rights." Of the governmental institutions named (and both rank and file and leadership assign the first two positions to the NAACP and Martin Luther King) the Supreme Court is cited by 10% of the leadership and President Kennedy only 1%; Congress is unmentioned. The rank and file place Kennedy third on their list with 9% naming him, but even here the Court is fourth with 5% first choices. BRINK & HARRIS, THE NEGRO REVOLUTION IN AMERICA 116 (1964).

unforeseeable,[98] but few question that it will be profound. Our standards of the permissible in literature and the other arts have altered considerably in the recent past; and while extra-governmental factors no doubt play a primary part in any such social change, the Supreme Court did more than any other public body to catalyze and legitimize this development. In these and other significant areas "the least dangerous branch,"[99] the branch with "neither force nor will,"[100] has been goading America forward while the legislative branch dragged its heels and the executive stood idly or helplessly by. This transformation of conventional understandings about the Founding Fathers' cherished separation of powers may be temporary. But it is striking enough while it lasts to lend color to the argument that the Warren Court has essayed a task more formidable and demanding than ever before attempted, even by the American Supreme Court.

The role that has just been described is the present culmination of the Warren Court. Before discussing the problems of power posed by this new form of judicial governance, perhaps it is in order to speculate a little about the question of causation. There have always been those who regard it as slightly improper to press this question at all—the Supreme Court acts thus because the Constitution, precedent, and ineluctable logic decree such a course of action; no more need be said. Probably few would subscribe to such an admirably simple view today. On the other hand it would be easy and no less spurious to slide to the other extreme and treat judicial history as a mere subdivision of political history in general, uninfluenced by the compulsions emphasized by the orthodox outlook. Since the truth of the matter lies somewhere in the middle, and since somewhere is almost as hard to locate as nowhere, the subject must be approached warily. But it must be approached if

98. CONGRESSIONAL QUARTERLY SERVICE, CONGRESS AND THE NATION 1945–1964, at 1525 (1965); see Pomfret, *States Accepting Court's Decision on Apportioning,* N.Y. Times, Dec. 28, 1964, p. 1, col. 1.

99. The phrase—the title of Professor Bickel's examination of the role of the Court, BICKEL, THE LEAST DANGEROUS BRANCH: THE SUPREME COURT AT THE BAR OF POLITICS (1962)—is suggested by Hamilton in the 78th Federalist Paper, *supra,* note 96, at 490.

100. *Ibid.*

we hope to understand, or begin to understand, the relation of the Supreme Court to the American polity. Some explanations of the modern Court's tendencies have been hinted at above; it is now time to probe the matter somewhat more deeply.

Admitting that the Court acts within an area circumscribed by constitutional text and precedent, yet recognizing that judicial leeway within those confines is broad, how can we account for the way the modern Court has used its leeway? If the question cannot be really answered, perhaps it is nevertheless possible to identify and comment on some possible categories which are relevant to an answer.

The most obvious of these categories is the one suggested by the word "personnel"—that is, by the idea that trends and shifts in Court behavior are determined by the happenstance that X, who had certain proclivities, was appointed to the bench at a given time, while Y, who had other proclivities, simultaneously retired. Of course there is something to this. The temporary weakening of the Court's libertarian thrust after the 1948 Term can be attributed in part to the fact that Justices Murphy and Rutledge were replaced by Justices Clark and Minton. The rate of the upsurge since the 1961 Term is no doubt related to the retirement of Justices Whittaker and Frankfurter and the appointment of Justice Goldberg. But explanations based on personnel changes must be examined carefully: they are not alone enough to account for the complex process in question. For example, they leave out of consideration shifts in the position of an individual justice. Sometimes these shifts simply amount to a change of mind which then becomes more or less permanent—for example, the famous about-face of Justice Roberts in 1937,[101] or the aforementioned hardening of Murphy's convictions after his novitiate on the Court. But sometimes the alterations of viewpoint are more subtle and protean. There is some reason to suspect that Mr. Justice Frankfurter thought of himself as a kind of balancing factor, striving to hold the Court and the country to what he thought was a golden mean. When there was

101. See WRIGHT, *supra*, note 94, at 203–208.

danger, as he saw it, that the majority might yield to "uncritical libertarianism,"[102] before the 1948 Term he often threw his weight against that tendency. But for several years after that, when the cause of civil liberty seemed to be threatened by a growing national mood of ruthlessness, and especially after the departure of Justices Murphy and Rutledge, he appeared to move toward the other side of the scales.[103] Comparable trends can be detectable in the outlook of even so staunch a libertarian as Mr. Justice Black in very recent years.[104] In a word, one difficulty with attributing Court tendencies to the mortality tables alone is that judges cannot be depended on to remain in the niches assigned to them. Evidently the movement of constitutional doctrine in the past twenty-five years must be explained by factors that go beyond a mere catalogue of arrivals and departures.

What are these factors? One of them may be simply the pressure of logic—or what the justices see as logic. This is no more than to say that when a basic position has been decided on there is a tendency for the decider to follow out that position's implications. Acceptance by the modern Court of the premise that civil rights were a special judicial concern generated an inclination to extend the

102. "We have greater responsibility for having given constitutional support, over repeated protests, to uncritical libertarian generalities." Dennis v. United States, 341 U.S. 494, 527 (1951) (concurring opinion).

103. See the tables in PRITCHETT, THE ROOSEVELT COURT 254, 257 (1948) and PRITCHETT, CIVIL LIBERTIES AND THE VINSON COURT 190 (1954). Frankfurter is found to have favored the individual in 34% of non-unanimous civil liberties cases during the 1941 to 1946 Terms and in 61% of such cases during the 1946 to 1952 Terms. Of course such figures are merely suggestive. The interpretation proposed in the text could only be verified by close analysis of individual cases and opinions.

104. In the 1964 Term, Black was the leading dissenter in state criminal trial cases, favoring the state's claim in 7 of 9 instances. Both pro-defendant votes involved the issue of *Mapp's* retroactivity, Angelet v. Fay, 381 U.S. 654, 656 (1965) and Linkletter v. Walker. 381 U.S. 618, 640 (1965). Otherwise, his dissents included cases involving search and seizure, Beck v. Ohio, 379 U.S. 89, 97 (1964); state criminal trial procedure, Henry v. Mississippi, 379 U.S. 443, 453 (1965); abatement of prosecution for sit-ins under the Civil Rights Act of 1964, McKinnie v. Tennessee, 380 U.S. 449 (1965) and Hamm v. City of Rock Hill, 379 U.S. 306, 318 (1964); a state obstruction of justice statute used against Negroes demonstrating in the area of a courthouse, Cox v. Louisiana, 379 U.S. 559, 575 (1965); use of contraceptives by married people, Griswold v. Connecticut, 381 U.S. 479, 507 (1965); use of television in a criminal trial, Estes v. Texas, 381 U.S. 532, 601 (1965). See also Murphy, *supra*, note 95, at 78.

Court's hand into all the areas arguably suggested by that premise and progressively to enlarge the list of "those liberties of the individual which history has attested as the indispensable conditions of an open . . . society."[105] The Court of 1915, unencumbered by such a premise, had no difficulty rejecting the claim that movies were free speech in the constitutional sense;[106] the 1952 Court, in light of the premise, felt impelled to reach an opposite conclusion.[107] And so it was in a number of other fields where the mere posing of a question, now that the premise had been established, seemed to dictate the result. As late as 1944 it had not been clear, that the Negro really had a constitutionally enforceable right to vote, in spite of the Fifteenth Amendment.[108] As late as 1955 it was contestable whether a Communist could invoke the privilege against self-incrimination before a congressional committee, despite the Fifth Amendment.[109] A Court dedicated to a general policy of enforcing personal rights could give only one answer to these uncertainties. Increasing activism was thus to a degree inherent in the policy. With more difficult questions the answers were less automatic. A value like federalism caused the Court to tolerate for some years the apparent anomaly that indigents need not always be provided counsel in state criminal trials; the traditional barrier of the political questions doctrine was permitted for even longer to stay judicial enforcement of a claimed right of equal representation.[110] But although arguments could be made in favor of such stopping-points, most of the justices obviously felt that the logical pull of the major premise was against them, and its force was ultimately too strong to be denied. The whole activist drift of the judiciary since about 1940 can be in part explained as a progressive outgrowth of the agreement about the Court's mission that had taken solid form at that time.

105. Kovacs v. Cooper, 336 U.S. 77, 95 (1949) (Frankfurter, J., concurring); see FRANKFURTER, MR. JUSTICE HOLMES AND THE SUPREME COURT 58 (1938).

106. See Mutual Film Corp. v. Industrial Comm'n, 236 U.S. 230 (1915).

107. Joseph Burstyn, Inc. v. Wilson, 343 U.S. 494 (1952).

108. See Smith v. Allwright, 321 U.S. 649 (1944).

109. See Quinn v. United States, 349 U.S. 155 (1955).

110. See Baker v. Carr, 369 U.S. 186, 270 and authorities cited in n.1 (1962) (Frankfurter, J., dissenting).

This general factor cannot, of course, account for the variations in that drift; for the pattern of starts and stops, of slowing down and acceleration that has been described. To fathom this pattern we must resort to another category of possible influence: external events. Again a word of caution is appropriate. There is no intention to suggest that the Court is merely the creature of Learned Hand's "prevailing winds"[111] or Mr. Dooley's "iliction returns." But it would be nonsense to pretend that justices are unaware of the tides of politics and opinion, that they can altogether disengage themselves from the climate they live in. The Court is part of America, and it is therefore worthwhile to look at what was happening to America during the time in question and particularly during the years when the Warren Court was achieving its modern position of almost unexampled governmental importance.

Again some of the inferences that can be drawn from such a look have already been intimated. The nation was facing novel and unsettling circumstances throughout the 1940–1952 period—the war, the new problem of world leadership, the rise of Russia as a dangerous rival, the threat of Communism elsewhere in the world, the fear of domestic subversion. In the late 1940's it seemed likely that conservatism would recapture political power after the long Roosevelt drought, and the temporary setback of 1948 seemed to augment conservative leanings toward McCarthyism and to increase the probability that the conservative victory, when it came, would be vengeful and retrogressive.[112] In the midst of these uncharted problems and prospects, at a time when America itself was bewildered and unpredictable, the Court was trying to work out a course in a field that was equally uncharted: civil rights. The wonder is not that the justices hesitated and lagged at certain critical points, but that they went as far as they did toward developing a new jurisprudence in that area.

In the 1950's the climate began to change. America was recovering from its first angry chagrin over the fact that winning the war had not resolved all problems; the nation was learning to live,

111. HAND, THE SPIRIT OF LIBERTY 165 (1960).
112. I am indebted, for this point and some of the analysis that follows, to a study by Earl Latham [THE COMMUNIST CONTROVERSY IN WASHINGTON (1966)].

albeit reluctantly, with the new problems the postwar world had brought into being. Suspicion and anxiety had begun to diminish. The Korean War had been brought to a close, not a very satisfactory one to be sure, but at least there were now no casualty lists. The anticipated victory of the conservatives had come; it turned out, however, not to be the savagely reactionary movement some had feared, but an innocuous continuation of recent history. McCarthyism had not only failed to take over the country, it had receded toward the background of the American mind. In a short time its protagonist would, symbolically, die himself.

All of this meant that the confusions and apprehensions which had sapped judicial resolution in recent years were, if not eliminated, considerably reduced. The historical importance of the Eisenhower Administration was the reassurance it gave that the clock would not be turned back either on New Deal liberalism or on Roosevelt-Truman internationalism. Thereafter it was tolerably clear that the nation would neither revert to the domestic principles of the Harding era nor retreat to a concept of "fortress America." The brief revival of such hopes or fears in 1964 was really a delusory anachronism. The decisive moment had passed twelve years before.

In this new climate the judicial impulse to expand civil rights could be given freer rein; confidence in the Court's capacity to play an active governmental part could find room for growth. The course was not all straight or smooth. In the first place there were still justices, like Frankfurter, who doubted that the Court should play such a part even if it could—for whom considerations of propriety as well as expediency argued for a modest judicial role. And in the second place, the uncertainties about how much judicial intervention the market would bear had been only diminished, not dispelled. The bold attack on racial segregation in 1954–55 gave rise to declarations of defiance and measures of resistance. The tentative venture into the issue of subversion in 1956–57 produced an alliance of southern and northern opinion that led to the congressional counterattack of 1958;[113] in the face of this, judicial

113. See MURPHY, CONGRESS AND THE COURT 127–183 (1962); PRITCHETT, CONGRESS VERSUS THE SUPREME COURT (1961).

self-confidence seemed to ebb once more. But though hostility to the racial desegregation policy persisted, it became increasingly clear as time went by that the current was running in favor of the Court's stand; though "H.R. 3"[114] came perilously close to passing in 1958, it did *not* pass, and neither did any other significant anti-Court legislation. It was not perhaps inevitable to interpret these outcomes as vindications of the Court's increasingly activist role, but it was possible so to regard them; and after a brief hesitation, judicial confidence seemed to revive and to flourish even more than before. The Court continued indeed to treat the subversion issue with kid gloves, but in other fields it never really lost the self-assurance that had begun to develop in 1953 when the "conservative revolt" turned out to be a harmless changing of the guard.

There is still another sense in which the nature of the Eisenhower years—and even the Kennedy years—may help account for the growth of judicial intervention in public policy. This was a time in which the other branches of government were peculiarly inactive, at least in domestic affairs. President Eisenhower seemed disinclined on principle to lead America any faster than it was already inclined to go, which was not very fast. President Kennedy's aspirations were more dynamic, but for all the talk about "getting America moving" he was, for various reasons, unable to move it much during his three years. Meanwhile Congress was, as usual, incapable of acting independently as a source of initiative. It is possible that the Court can be thought of as filling a vacuum left by the other branches of government, or that the judiciary has a tendency to enlarge its own role in public affairs when the normal machinery is inert or deadlocked?[115] This need not be put forward as a universal rule. The behavior of the Court is "motivated by

114. H.R. 3, 84th Cong., 1st Sess. (1955); reintroduced as H.R. 3, 85th Cong., 1st Sess. (1957); passed by House as H.R. 3, 86th Cong., 1st Sess. (1958).

115. This suggestion is perhaps related to, though I believe not identical to, the one made by Roche that the Court's power "to invade the decision-making arena" is a consequence of the fragmentation of political power, and that judicial self-restraint can be expected when there are monolithic political majorities. ROCHE, SHADOW AND SUBSTANCE 202 (1964). Compare Mendelson, *Judicial Review and Party Politics,* 12 VAND. L. REV. 447 (1959).

many factors, some often contradictory,"[116] and no doubt there can be times when all three branches of government will stall at dead center. But it may be worth noting that in the 1920's, another time when presidential and legislative initiative were almost non-existent, the Court also took on a larger share of the responsibility for governing the nation.

The remaining question is the most conjectural of all. Assuming that the Warren Court has, for some of the reasons suggested, claimed an authority to govern that differs both in degree and kind from anything essayed in the past, what are its prospects for maintaining that claim successfully? This is not, be it noted, the question whether the Court has the *right* so to command America—that is, whether constitutional text and tradition can warrant such regality. Nor is it the somewhat different question whether in terms of democratic theory the judiciary *ought* to be entrusted with such an important part in the moulding of public policy. The issue is a narrower one. Whatever the constitutional text does or does not say, whatever normative philosophy may or may not prescribe, we know that the allocation of governmental function depends to an important extent on the distribution of political power. Does the Supreme Court have enough such power to play its modern self-assigned role as a major initiative-supplying agency of modern government?

The question is almost as difficult to pose precisely as it is to answer confidently.[117] When we say that the Court lacks the power to deal with a certain subject, we are usually thinking of two often associated but distinguished points: that the policy result ordained by the Court cannot be brought about; or that the price of bringing it about (or perhaps even trying to do so) will be to impair judicial power to accomplish other tasks. The classic, well-worn example is *Dred Scott*.[118] Not only was the Court unable to "settle" the issue of slavery in the territories on the terms espoused by the majority in that decision, but the attempt to impose such a settle-

116. ROCHE, *supra*, note 115, at 203.
117. See pp. 304–305, above.
118. Scott v. Sandford, 60 U.S. (19 How.) 393 (1857).

ment damaged judicial prestige and undermined for some time the Court's capacity to play its normal part in the governmental process. But the matter is not always so clear. In a sense the Court demonstrably had the power to prohibit a federal income tax for eighteen years: no such tax was collectible from 1895[119] until ratification of the Sixteenth Amendment in 1913. But it is arguable that the cost of achieving this result was a loss of public confidence in the Court's impartiality and a decline in respect for the rule of law.[120] A definition of judicial power that failed to take account of such costs would be plainly inadequate; yet there is no known calculus for making the accounting precise. We can only accept the reminders that the Court possesses "neither the purse nor the sword" and that its power "ultimately rests on sustained public confidence in its moral sanction"[121] and assess the situation as well as possible in the light of those truisms.

Has the Warren Court bitten off more than it can chew? Does its present activist, initiating role in the governmental process overtax its powers? It is tempting to ask history for the answer, but then we meet the problem that so often confounds those who solicit guidance from the past: that the current situation is in some respects unique. Not only is the Court dealing with relatively new judicial subject matter, civil rights, and playing a new affirmative role in contrast to its traditional negativism. It is doing all this in the America of the mid-twentieth century, which is not the America of Marshall or Fuller or Hughes. And this fact of uniqueness can cut both ways. The reflection that the Court has always survived without irremediable harm the storms that have whirled around it gives no assurance that it will prove equally durable in the present novel circumstances. On the other hand, neither can we be certain that the capacities of today's Court are no greater

119. Pollock v. Farmers' Loan & Trust Co., 158 U.S. 601 (1895).

120. The income tax decision is listed by Charles Evans Hughes as one of the Court's great "self-inflicted wounds." HUGHES, THE SUPREME COURT OF THE UNITED STATES 50 (1928). It is also arguable, however, that the Court's daring innovations in the 1890's, far from diminishing its governmental influence, laid the basis for the flourishing judicial supremacy of the 1920's and early 1930's. See, in connection with both points PAUL, CONSERVATIVE CRISIS AND THE RULE OF LAW 221–237 (1960).

121. Baker v. Carr, 369 U.S. 186, 267 (1962) (Frankfurter, J., dissenting).

than those of yesterday's. Most constitutional historians would agree that the judiciary of 1935–36 was overreaching, that no court could have blocked for very long the demand for social and economic reforms that arose in the New Deal era. This does not necessarily prove that the Court of the 1960's lacks the power to accomplish different tasks under different conditions. The past may provide some clues. But the clues must be interpreted in the context of the present.

There are in the current scene some legitimate grounds for doubt about the Court's power to play the momentous part it has chosen, and there have been some danger signals. For one thing, it may be that "judicial realism" has eroded the traditional mystique that often lent support to Court authority in other days. For more than half a century scholars and judges have been repudiating the mythology that the Court is merely the impersonal voice of indisputable constitutional verities and have been emphasizing that the judicial process involves an element of free choice based on policy judgements.[122] In some notable cases the Warren Court has, with more or less frankness, created constitutional rules out of whole cloth.[123] Whether they were "good" constitutional rules is not here in question. The point is that they were patently judge-made, and that modern awareness of this fact may detract from the priestly authority that clothed the Court in the past.

It has already been noted that the modern Court is bereft of another kind of backing which historically sustained it: the active support of the business community and related elements such as commercial lawyers and the conservative press.[124] For the past twenty-five years the justices have been making it abundantly plain that the Constitution is no longer a refuge for disgruntled property holders[125] and have turned their sympathy elsewhere.

Moreover, in spite of this depletion of its historical power resources, the modern Court has gone on adding new tasks to its

122. See, *e.g.*, CAHILL, JUDICIAL LEGISLATION (1952).

123. See, *e.g.*, Reynolds v. Sims, 377 U.S. 533 (1964); Brown v. Board of Educ., 347 U.S. 483 (1954).

124. See MURPHY, *supra*, note 113, at 248; Westin, *When the Public Judges the Courts*, N.Y. Times Magazine, May 31, 1959, § 6, p. 16.

125. See McCloskey, *Economic Due Process and the Supreme Court: An Exhumation and Reburial*, 1962 SUP. CT. REV. 34.

agenda, and this progressive development poses a problem in its own right. The Court's power depends on its prestige in the eyes of the nation, which is to say on the assumption that the nation will accept its mandates and support it against retaliatory attacks. This means that the Court, like other governing bodies, must maintain a favorable balance between the forces that bolster its authority and those that oppose it—between friends and enemies, to put the matter bluntly. No doubt its capital of public support, deriving from the American tradition of respect for the judiciary, is sufficient to counterbalance the disaffection evoked by a certain number of commands that vex those who are commanded. Though the justices drew very heavily on that capital in the desegregation decisions, this alone was not too heavy a withdrawal for the Court's prestige to stand. But since then the Warren Court has gathered in a whole series of further commitments in fields like criminal procedure, school religious practices, censorship, and the rest; and it is arguable that each commitment has strained the capital a little further. Each one, that is, has augmented the accumulating mass of judicial enforcement problems, has created a new and additional body of critics and adversaries.

There is some reason to fear that the net effect of these factors has brought the Court at times during the last decade near the borderline that marks the limits of its practical jurisdiction. The success of the Court in enforcing its ordainments is often hard to appraise, but certainly the last ten years have reminded us that there may be many a slip between declaration of policy and realization of that policy in practice. Flamboyant gestures of defiance are not the problem: they tend in fact to be self-defeating, since by sharpening and dramatizing the issue they call forth the full panoply of forces disposed to defend the rule of law. The greater difficulty is presented by subtler forms of resistance—delay, evasion, and calculated inertia.[126] Desegregation has proceeded very slowly and must be described, more than ten years after *Brown,* as still in

126. See PELTASON, FIFTY-EIGHT LONELY MEN (1961); Note, *Judicial Performance in the Fifth Circuit,* 73 YALE L. J. 90 (1963). For an abstract model of various means of resistance, see MURPHY, ELEMENTS OF JUDICIAL STRATEGY 19–28 (1964).

its token phase.[127] Precise data about compliance with other judicial commands is lacking. We do not know, for example, how many school districts are still sponsoring school prayers in spite of *Engel* and *Schempp,* or how many police departments have failed to mend their ways in the light of *Mapp* and *Escobedo.* But it is perhaps not overly cynical to guess that non-compliance is considerable, that a good many people in several areas are not doing all that the Supreme Court wants them to do.

Beyond that, there have been signs of a more serious possibility: that discontent with the Court's rulings may generate retaliatory action that would impair the very structure of judicial authority. Again the more extreme and impassioned denunciations of the Court are not important except as secondary symptoms of a deeper complaint. The judiciary has often been exposed to such maledictions and has managed to survive them. But it is important to remember that the supposed supremacy of the Court is technically vulnerable. Congress has the prerogative to modify jurisdiction or otherwise neutralize judicial authority.[128] To be sure, that prerogative has seldom been invoked in our history, but this is partly because the Court has often pulled in its horns when a significant congressional reaction seemed in the making. At all events, Congress is potentially by far the most dangerous threat to judicial sovereignty. And in recent years the congressional temperature chart has been running higher than usual.[129] The Tuck Bill, which would have wiped out Court jurisdiction over state apportionment issues, easily passed the House in 1964.[130] The "Dirksen-Mansfield Rider," which would have stayed judicial enforcement of the state apportionment rulings, might well have been enacted if the statesmen had not been so eager to get back to the hustings in an election year.

Social science has here and there improved the comprehension

127. See Bickel, *The Decade of School Desegregation,* 64 COLUM. L. REV. 193 (1964).

128. See Wechsler, *The Courts and the Constitution,* 65 COLUM. L REV. 1001 (1965).

129. See MURPHY, CONGRESS AND THE COURT (1962); PRITCHETT, CONGRESS VERSUS THE SUPREME COURT (1961).

130 N.Y. Times, Aug. 20, 1964, p. 1, col. 8.

of secondary issues and processes, but answers to the big questions continue to be evasive. We do not really know why the American constitutional system has survived for a hundred seventy-five years of crowded history while most other nations have changed their organic law with bewildering frequency. We do not know why our two-party political alignment has been so persistent, nor why the American presidency, an awesomely powerful office, has never even threatened to develop into dictatorship. Explanations, some of them plausible, have been offered to account for these facts. But we cannot in the nature of the case be sure that the explanations are sufficient, that they supply a reliable basis, not only for post facto rationalizations but for confident forecast. Nor can we be sure that we fully understand why judicial review, a remarkable and far from inevitable governmental institution, has developed and endured. Considering these uncertainties, it would be thoughtlessly imprudent to shrug aside the menaces to judicial power that have just been canvassed, to be cocksure that the judiciary can perform, without setbacks and self-inflicted wounds, the extraordinary governmental tasks which the Warren Court has undertaken. The governance of men is an endless experiment, and experiment always involves some incertitude and peril. It would be a poor bargain if the cost of attempting this new role were impairment of the Court's traditional status in our polity.[131]

Yet there is an argument to be made on the other side: there are considerations lending some support to a belief that the modern Court's power is equal to its aspirations. In the first place it is of course possible that the balance between friends and adversaries has been redressed on both sides. The Court may have lost the active support of a good part of its traditional mainstay, the conservative business community; it may have offended a majority of white southerners, police chiefs, and advocates of state-enforced

---

131. "The interference of the judiciary with legislative Acts, if frequent or on dubious ground, might occasion so great a jealousy of this power and so generally a prejudice against it as to lead to measures ending in the total overthrow of the independence of the judges, and so of the best preservative of the constitution." MURPHY, CONGRESS AND THE COURT 263 (1962), quoting Chancellor Waties of South Carolina in Administrators of Byrnes v. Administrators of Stewart, 3 Des. 464, 475 (S.C. Eq. 1812).

piety. But it has also acquired some new champions. Perhaps the losses are partially compensated by an increase of amicability among those who approve recent judicial policies—that is, Negroes and northern liberals of various types. Whether the compensation is complete may be open to question. The assured support of a Daniel Webster or an Elihu Root was very comforting in the past; it remains to be seen whether their substitutes will be equally potent and dependable. But surely these new allies must be reckoned in any accounting of the modern Court's power resources.

Ironically enough, their ranks seem to have been strengthened at least temporarily by the 1964 election. Not for many years has a presidential candidate criticized the Court as sharply as Mr. Goldwater did. He chose to make the judiciary a secondary but significant campaign issue; Mr. Johnson's overwhelming victory could thus be interpreted, rightly or wrongly, as an implied vindication of the Court. Anti-judicialism was for the time being associated with one of the worst popular defeats in electoral history. More concretely, Mr. Johnson helped to carry into office an extra contingent of liberal congressmen and to decimate the array of those most likely to join an anti-Court movement. Sometimes the right enemy is as valuable as a friend.

In still another way the march of recent political events may have improved the Court's position. In the analysis above I have emphasized the scope and cumulative weight of the tasks which the Warren Court has assumed. Presumably even the most optimistic proponent of judicial activism would agree that there is a limit to the public policy burdens the judiciary can carry. At some point the camel's back would be overstrained; and while that point has apparently never been reached by the Warren Court, it may have been approached at one time or another. However, the heaviest load the Court has borne throughout most of this time is the responsibility for coping with the issue of racial discrimination. For almost ten years this arduous matter, surely the most formidable of modern domestic problems, was left virtually untouched by presidents and congresses; insofar as a national governmental policy was developing, it was being fashioned by the judiciary alone. But in very recent years, the other two branches have at length bestirred themselves to take the problem in hand, and the result has been a lightening of the Court's total burden. It is one thing for a court to guide the nation single-handed, but quite another for a court to enforce measures which Congress and the president have ordained. The new activity of the political branches in the field of racial rights may justify new confidence that the Court can successfully discharge its other modern self-assigned functions.

These considerations favoring an optimistic prognosis bring to mind another, more general speculation about the nature of current American political opinion and the relationship of the Court to American public attitudes. In reviewing the factors that might give pause to judicial activists, I have assumed *arguendo* that the Court's power to command America is in the nature of a capital fund which is diminished by each expenditure of power; and further that the potential alignment of supporters and opponents for a given judicial policy is relatively fixed. But this reckons without the possibility that the Court's political environment is more dynamic than static. It may not be true that power is automatically depleted in proportion to its exertion. Not only is it likely, as already mentioned, that a policy judgment will make friends as well as enemies in the short run. There is also the possibility that the analogy of a capital fund is faulty, that in the long run the assertion of power will to some extent augment power. Perhaps a sweeping judicial claim of authority helps generate a disposition to accept that authority; perhaps the habit of command tends to produce a habit of obedience.

Related to the last point but going beyond it, there is the further possibility that historical forces, one of which is the Court itself, can alter the pre-decision pattern of public attitudes about the specific causes the judiciary may espouse. As Myrdal argued two decades ago, American attitudes with respect to applications of "the American creed" may be more volatile than some pessimists have supposed.[132] Public discussion and education may, by focusing attention on a value-laden issue, produce a change in opinion about that

132. See MYRDAL, AN AMERICAN DILEMMA 1–25 (1944).

issue. Moreover, "stateways"—for example, legislation and legal decisions—may sometimes precipitate or hasten such alterations of the "folkways." The Supreme Court has always been in part an educative institution, but during most of our history it has used its preceptorial influence largely to maintain the folkways rather than to change them. In recent years the judicial propensity has been not merely to restrain America in certain areas but to goad it forward in others, and the effort may have been partially successful. At any rate there appears to have been an evolution of opinion about civil rights during the era of the Warren Court, and it seems plausible that the Court has shared in the process of bringing the development about, forcing the issues to public attention, and urging by word and deed a greater commitment to libertarianism.[133]

The primary example is the issue of racial discrimination. Opinion polls throughout the last twenty years suggest a gradual but steady increase in public approval of measures to outlaw discriminatory practices.[134] Another example is the apportionment area,

133. In this connection, consider these words of Abe Fortas in a public address: "Concurrently with the movement of our society, under the stimulus of developments in the law, to emancipate the Negro, there is taking place another revolution . . . [concerning the poor]. Here—as in the case of Negroes—a moral reawakening has been stimulated by the Supreme Court . . . It is probably not just chance that the Court's reaffirmation of the rights of the accused comes in the same few years as a massive re-examination of the problems of crime, and its causes and treatment . . . It is, indeed, quite possible that there is a causal relation between the two: that the waves set in motion by the Court go far beyond the courtroom and the police station: that they do in fact awaken the national conscience and act as a catalyst to cause the nation to take action to discharge neglected responsibilities." Boston Herald, May 2, 1965, p. 62, col. 3.

134. From 1942 to 1963, *e.g.*, the percentage of white adults favoring integrated education rose in the North from 45% to 75% and in the South from 2% to 30%. More significant, perhaps, is the finding that there is a direct relationship between attitudes toward integration and the degree of actual integration in the community. "Close analysis of the current findings, compared with those of the 1956 surveys, leads us to the conclusion that in those parts of the South where some measure of school integration has taken place official action has *preceded* public sentiment, and public sentiment has then attempted to accommodate itself to the new situation." Hyman & Sheatsley, *Attitudes Toward Desegregation,* Scientific American, July 1964, p. 16, at 20. In terms of sheer attitude alone, exclusive of the issue of compliance, the percentage of southerners approving the 1954 *Brown* decision has never exceeded 27%, and that high point was reached in January 1957. Northern opinion has risen from 64% favorable in July 1954 to 72% in July 1959, with a high of 74% in January 1957. A possible source of bias in the polling procedure

where it seems that the Court's decisions have not so much generated but undammed a wave of latent one-man-one-vote sentiment. Still another illustration may be the school prayer issue. For all the initial outcry against *Engel,* by the time of *Schempp* one year later it was evident that the statement of judicial policy had provoked many to second thoughts about the problem of public religious observances and had enlisted others on the Court's side.[135] Even the decisions on state criminal procedure, involving as they do public fears about skyrocketing crime rates, were recently indirectly but firmly defended by the National Association of Attorneys General, which refused to consider action deploring the Court's tendencies in this field.[136] Such an implied endorsement would have seemed improbable a few years ago.

To some extent these seeming changes in opinion can no doubt be attributed to respect for the Court and the Constitution—if the Court says that a thing must be, even though I am displeased I will support it because it is more important to me to defend the Court's authority than to have my own way about a specific issue. There is a difference between changing one's mind and acquiescing. But it is likely that for some the root attitudes have themselves been altered as a result of the "opinion catharsis"[137] which the judicial pronouncements have helped to set going. If so, the Court's policies may be bolstered, not only by the allies who are immediately and patently advantaged by a pronouncement, but as time goes on by those who can be persuaded to embrace the values which the policies proclaim. Most constitutional scholars would agree that the Supreme Court must work within the limits of public opinion

might be detected in the findings that, whereas only 15% of southern whites approved of *Brown* in November 1957, 69% of southern Negroes approved at that time. Polling data of the American Institute of Public Opinion, reported in Erskine, *The Polls: Race Relations,* 26 PUB. OPINION Q. 137, 140 (1962).

135. See BLANSHARD, RELIGION AND THE SCHOOLS: THE GREAT CONTROVERSY 50–74 (1963).

136. N.Y. Times, July 1, 1965, p. 12, col. 4. "Criticism of the Court has stopped because it turned out to be futile, Attorney General David P. Buckson of Delaware said. Others pointed out that Court critics were not prospering." All but one member interviewed approved even of Escobedo v. Illinois, 378 U.S. 478 (1964).

137. MYRDAL, *supra,* note 136, at 1033.

—if not a consensus, then something not too far from that. But the Warren Court, it might be suggested, has by its declarations sometimes assisted in bringing such a consensus into being; and conjectures about the range of judicial power are inadequate unless they take account of that self-helpful possibility.[138]

These, then, are some of the considerations that must be weighed to determine whether the Supreme Court's political power is sufficient to sustain the commanding role in which the Warren Court has cast itself. How do they all add up? What kind of net appraisal are we left with when the cons and the pros are balanced? The question and the ingredients of an answer are so complex that no easily confident conclusions are justifiable. Any conclusions can be no more than guesses, based heavily on intuitive hunches and no doubt reflecting in some measure the prejudices of the guesser.

But with those very large reservations understood, a couple of assessments can be hazarded. The first relates to the short-run outlook—to the next three or four years of judicial history. During that time at least, it seems fairly sure that the Court can continue to perform its present influential functions in the governmental process without much likelihood of provoking a damaging reaction. This surmise is based partly on the Court's comparative success in getting its way in very recent years: as with the weather, there is always some presumption that the present situation will continue tomorrow. But it also rests partly on specific political auguries. Considering the Court's identification with such an issue as Negro rights and with liberalism in the more general sense, it seems hardly probable that a president would join in or even consent to an attack on the Court in the near future. As for Congress, there may be a residue of resentment, but the legislators who are presently disposed for one reason or another to defend the Court seem potent enough to veto any meaningful rebuff to the tribunal

138. Many of the factors considered in the preceding pages may be covered by Henry Adams' offhand but characteristically acute remark: "Adams felt no moral obligation to defend Judges, who, as far as he knew, were the only class of society specially adapted to defend themselves." THE EDUCATION OF HENRY ADAMS 191 (1931).

or its policies. Something of the same sort can be said about the current state of public attitudes. The general climate of political opinion seems to have shifted quite remarkably in very recent years. Neo-New-Dealish measures of social reform which were apparently immovably stalemated a few years ago have been enacted in rapid succession with surprising ease; the political opposition that helped block them in the past seems to have lost its edge.

The long-run prospect is of course cloudier and even more suppositious. The danger signals catalogued above should not be taken lightly, nor should the encouraging factors be overrated. One has an uneasy feeling that the Court's present status is based too much on newly acquired friends who happen to agree on an ad hoc basis with current judicial policies, not enough on a spirit of long-run devotion to the rule of law as a value that transcends other policy disagreements. The more or less frank "result-orientation" of the modern Court, the widened acceptance of a "realistic" interpretation of judicial motives, may have diminished that spirit permanently. If so, and if the political winds should change, the Court might be a shorn lamb. The 1958 counter-attack on the Court, even though it failed, can still be regarded as a firebell in the night: it did come shockingly close to succeeding. Nor would it be wise to draw unlimited confidence from the suggestion that the Court can sometimes generate a consensus of approval where none seemed to exist before. This does not mean that opinion is infinitely malleable, that the Court can drag the nation to goals it is not already somewhat disposed to accept. The Court may be able to catalyze, to unlock, tendencies that are immanent in the public mind. But its recent success in performing this function is explained by the fact that it has generally guessed right about the tendencies that were immanent. If it began to guess wrong, the outlook could change drastically. Troubles of the past have come when the Court forgot that it could only reaffirm and perhaps stimulate public values; when it imagined that it could dictate them. The line between daring and rashness will have to be observed even by this most creative Court in our history. Judges will still be well-advised to husband their resources for the policy questions that really matter, rather than to squander them on trivial and reaction-charged causes. It is by no means inconceivable that a heedless miscalculation, or a series of them, could boomerang and impair not only the Court's present exalted position but its traditional status.

Barring some such catastrophe, assuming that the justices do not grow toplofty, the chances seem good that the Warren Court's version of judicial governance can be sustained for some time to come. In historical perspective, the recent developments described above can be regarded as another impressive extension of an evolution that began to gather force long ago, in the decades following the Civil War. Since then, despite cyclical ups and downs, the trend of judicial review has been broadly upward, toward a greater part in the governing process. Observers have from time to time hailed or deplored what they thought was a reversal of that trend, as when the Court seemed to abandon the *Lochner* doctrine in the early 1900's,[139] or when the spending power decisions caused Corwin to speak in 1934 of "the twilight of the Supreme Court."[140] The abandonment in 1937 of constitutional supervision in the economic field seemed, to those bred in the Field-Peckham-Sutherland tradition, almost an abdication of the judicial throne.[141] But the Court never surrendered at any of these junctures the core of its claim to share in the making of public policy; each time the claim was duly reasserted in a revised form, and the upward progress was resumed. The revisions were possible because the Court always kept escape hatches open even when its rhetoric sounded most doctrinaire. This meant that judicial review could yield to the inevitable when it became plain and thus avoid a destructive head-on clash with a relentless national impulse. The strategic importance of this flexibility should not be forgotten by the Justices of today and tomorrow. The recontinued upward movement was possible because America seems to have a so-far unsatiated appetite for government by judiciary. No doubt there are boundaries to this peculiar national taste. There have always been some specific matters not practically amenable to close judicial supervision;

139. See KELLY & HARBISON, THE AMERICAN CONSTITUTION: ITS ORIGINS AND DEVELOPMENT 527–528 (1955).
140. CORWIN, THE TWILIGHT OF THE SUPREME COURT (1934).
141. See, *e.g.*, CORWIN, CONSTITUTIONAL REVOLUTION, LTD., 113 (1941).

lately, the subversion issue may have been one of these and the power of legislative investigation another. And presumably even the general trend will find its limit at some point. But on the whole, the history of the Warren Court suggests that the limit has not yet been exceeded. The Supreme Court probably *can* play its modern, elevated governmental role in the foreseeable future. Whether it *should* is a question I have deliberately excluded here. Whether it *will* is a question for another day.

INDEX OF CASES

GENERAL INDEX

Harvard Paperbacks